SUSTAINABLE
DEVELOPMENT
AND CANADA

SUSTAINABLE DEVELOPMENT AND CANADA

::

National & International Perspectives

O.P. DWIVEDI

PATRICK KYBA

PETER J. STOETT

REBECCA TIESSEN

NATIONAL LIBRARY OF CANADA CATALOGUING IN PUBLICATION DATA

Main entry under title:

Sustainable development and Canada : national and international perspectives

Includes bibliographical references and index.
ISBN 1-55111-323-6

1. Environmental policy – Canada. 2. Sustainable development – Canada.
3. Economic development – Environmental aspects – Canada.
I. Dwivedi, O. P., 1937-.

HC120.E5S97 2001   333.7'0971   C2001-930771-3

BROADVIEW PRESS, LTD.
is an independent, international publishing house, incorporated in 1985.

North America
Post Office Box 1243, Peterborough, Ontario, Canada K9J 7H5
3576 California Road, Orchard Park, New York, USA 14127
TEL (705) 743-8990; FAX (705) 743-8353; E-MAIL 75322.44@compuserve.com

United Kingdom and Europe
Thomas Lyster, Ltd., Unit 9, Ormskirk Industrial Park
Old Boundary Way, Burscough Road, Ormskirk, Lancashire L39 2YW
TEL (01695) 575112; FAX (01695) 570120; E-MAIL books@tlyster.co.uk

Australia
St. Clair Press, Post Office Box 287, Rozelle, NSW 2039
TEL (612) 818-1942; FAX (612) 418-1923

www.broadviewpress.com

Broadview Press gratefully acknowledges the support of the Ministry of Canadian Heritage through the Book Publishing Industry Development Program.

Cover design by Liz Broes, Black Eye Design.
Typeset by Liz Broes, Black Eye Design.

Printed in Canada

10 9 8 7 6 5 4 3 2 1

CONTENTS

PART THREE: ETHICS & VALUES

PREFACE

Canadians can no longer afford to take the environment for granted. For generations the vast size of this bountiful country and its seemingly inexhaustible capacity to absorb the punishment wrought by a resource-based economy lulled Canadians into a false sense of security. We believe that this situation can no longer continue. Not a month goes by without news of an environmental disaster making the headlines—water contamination in Walkerton, killer smog, another lake acidified, another species exterminated. Although much has been accomplished in the past thirty years, many problems remain, and it is by no means clear that Canadians and their governments have the will to implement the changes in lifestyle and the strong measures necessary to move us toward sustainable development.

This book introduces the reader to the types of environmental problems that confront Canadians today, problems that arise out of the nature of the country, our economic system, our system of government, and our place in the world. *Sustainable Development and Canada: National and International Policy Perspectives* also traces the evolution of the structures and processes established to treat these problems and assesses their utility today. Our principal purpose is not to lay blame, but rather to explain. Finally, we point to possible directions which Canadians might consider to ensure the integrity of this magnificent land. Using a broad-based approach, the authors address a multitude of interconnected problems, from the state of the environment in Canada, to our role in international environmental affairs, to the ethical and spiritual challenges that underlie the current ecological crisis.

We do not discuss all problems in depth. Nor do we examine issues that have been discussed at length by other contributors to the literature. For example, the roles of the provincial and municipal governments are discussed briefly, but they do not drive the text as a whole. Our purpose is to provide the reader with an overview of environmental problems and their possible solutions from a national and international perspective. What has Canada done, what can Canada do, both inside and outside our borders, to guarantee our children's heritage?

This book reflects our experiences teaching courses in environmental policy and management. One of our team members, O.P. Dwivedi, first taught a course at the University of Guelph on this subject in the fall of 1972, when few social scientists were involved. Over the years, first Patrick Kyba, and then Peter Stoett also offered this course and added their areas of expertise to it, while Rebecca Tiessen became closely associated with it in the late 1990s. Thus, this book reflects not only our personal commitment to environmental protection, but also our experiences as public and governmental attitudes toward the environment changed since the early 1970s.

Many other people contributed in many ways to this volume. We are grateful to Michael Harrison of Broadview Press, who also provided an anonymous reviewer who made many helpful suggestions; to Charles Kless, Bernice Kozak, Emily Lawrence-Courage, Nanita Mohan, Shane Mulligan, and Laurie-Anne White, who did much of the preliminary work on the documentary literature; and, finally, to our hundreds of students over the years who shared our interest in the environment and our determination not to let it be despoiled by accident or design, to whom we dedicate this book.

O.P. Dwivedi and J.P. Kyba (Guelph),
P. Stoett (Montreal), R. Tiessen (Halifax)

PART ONE
STRUCTURE

ENVIRONMENTAL POLITICS AND POLICY

INTRODUCTION: CANADIAN ENVIRONMENTAL POLITICS

This book is designed to introduce you to the complexities of Canadian environmental policy. This is no easy task, since there are many issues to cover. Moreover, there are numerous perspectives on how best to explain the course of action taken by successive Canadian governments over the years. While concern for the environment is no longer new, and is firmly established as a necessary policy item, it remains subservient to economic interests in the Canadian setting. As such, it is difficult to ascertain where industrial or natural resource policy stops, and "pure" environmental policy begins. We make the assumption, then, that it is not productive to pursue the "pure" version, but better to accept the fact that there will always be policy and institutional overlap.

Similarly, there are perhaps as many understandings of the basic concepts of political and social science — the state, democracy, social psychology, international relations, to name just a few — as there are political and social scientists. However, we feel we can impose some order onto the confusion by splitting this book into three sections, and providing this initial chapter as a necessarily brief overview of the field of environmental policy studies. We are interested in conveying three essential factors to assist you in your pursuit of this topic: 1) the political context in which decisions are made; 2) the issue-areas which are most in need of regulation and treatment; and 3) the various perspectives on achieving sustainable development that colour the Canadian conceptual landscape. Thus we divide the book into three sections, aiming to provide an overview of the Canadian environment, political structures, and actors in the first; necessarily succinct summaries of important issue-areas and actual policies in the second; and broader philosophical and ethical/spiritual principles in the third.

At this stage we should be clear that we are not attempting to impose any particular perspective of political analysis, be it political economy or pluralism, rational choice or Marxism, on the study of Canadian environmental policy. Rather, this text is inspired by the collective eclectic intellectual orientations of the various authors, and by the need to incorporate the globalization debate into current thinking on environmental policy. It is quite clear to us that there is no single level of analysis that permits an adequate overview of the policy-making context. While government remains the key actor of our concern, others, such as non-governmental organizations (NGOs) and business lobbyists, also have a significant impact, as does the individual behaviour of citizens of both Canada and other states. However, one must begin somewhere, and though we are sympathetic to the argument that people, not abstract structures, shape history, we feel it important to present an overview of the context in which people (and governments claiming to represent them) operate.

This is done in the four remaining chapters in Part One of the book. The first outlines the current state of the Canadian and global environment. It sets the tone for the remainder of the book, because we need an awareness of the present ecological condition to understand the problems politicians, lobbyists, and citizens face. This chapter will proceed from the concluding section of the present chapter, in which we discuss the various issue-areas that warrant our concern. Chapter 3 presents an overview of the Canadian political system and of the evolution of the administrative structures most significantly involved in environmental policy formation, administration, and implementation. Canadian federalism is a complex, if intriguing, political context, and we have tried to summarize the structures and legislative functions of governments (we must always use the plural in a federal setting) so that non-political-science students can obtain a quick grasp. The fourth chapter details some of the key actors involved: political parties, business lobbies, and non-governmental organizations representing a variety of interests and positions, and the media. Finally, Chapter 5, in keeping with one of our main themes for this text, that environmental policy is made today within the broadened context of globalization, presents a summary of Canada's extensive transnational relations: the Canadian-American relationship and NAFTA; the Arctic circumpolar connection; transatlantic and Pacific ties; and multilateral engagement in international organizations such as the United Nations. Because the Canadian economy has become so heavily dependent on trade, transnational relations will always be a major factor in policy determination and outcomes, not only in terms of policies affecting Canadian soil and coasts, but also in terms of Canadian development assistance and investment abroad.

The second section of the book goes into more detail regarding particular policies that have been implemented over the last several decades. We have tended to focus on more recent developments; however, readers will note what we hope is a liberal sprinkling of historical background as well. We begin with an outline of the legal and regulatory processes employed by the Canadian state in the environmental policy realm. This is followed by a chapter focusing on risk management and, in a special section that will be of interest to many geographers and specialists, the process of environmental impact assessment (EIA). EIA is a powerful tool for determining whether the precautionary principle has been employed in new projects, and it is used in many states and international organizations today. However, it is not without its limitations, as we shall see. Our aim is to present a national overview, and not a summary of various provincial policies. Although it is clear that provincial governments are responsible for much of the environmental security of Canadians, to examine each province in detail would take us beyond the scope of this book. Part Two also includes a chapter mirroring the last chapter of Part One: a detailed summary of Canada's international commitments related to environmental protection. Despite the large number of conventions, treaties, and protocols signed by the Canadian federal government, critics charge that it does not commit sufficient resources to deal effectively with environmental problems abroad, and lacks the political will to fully implement international commitments at home. Of course, this is a difficult prospect, given the limitations inherent in a federal system in which provincial governments have most of the responsibility for implementing agreements signed by the government in Ottawa, and in a political system in which industrial and trade interests have tended to dominate the policy landscape. Finally, Chapter 9 covers recent initiatives to implement the abandoned Green Plan and the ongoing series of National Development Strategies. This will help us focus once again on the most immediate problems facing Canadians and their governments at this stage, and provides a broad overview of notable successes and failures to date.

In Part Three, we depart somewhat from the empirical and move into more conceptual discussions. It is our contention that there is only so much we can learn from studying structures, laws, regulations, and treaties. We must also take into consideration normative factors — the values and principles that give life to political culture, for better or worse. Although the section contains many concrete examples as illustrations, our main point is to present a kaleidoscope of ideas and perspectives that help shape the discourse, or dominant debates, about environmental policy today, both within Canada and on the global stage. The first chapter deals with gender issues, which for many are of paramount concern to questions of sustainable development and ecological exploitation, as well as to questions related to the distribution of resources. The next chapter discusses the new "human security" agenda that the Canadian government, in the late 1990s/early 2000s, under the leadership of former Minister of Foreign Affairs Lloyd Axworthy, proclaimed to be an integral aspect of Canadian foreign policy. This phrase may not have any real meaning, since a new and robust perspective has yet to be seen. Nevertheless, we can make some suggestions regarding its inherent weaknesses and strengths, and argue that environmental security itself is fundamental to the realization of any human right. This chapter also looks at the role of non-governmental organizations, within the context of what is often referred to as "civil society." Finally, the concluding chapter deals explicitly with environmental ethics, offering different religious and value-based perspectives that readers might find enlightening as they seek their own paths toward a sustainable lifestyle in the Canadian context.

Before examining some of the basic issue-areas that shape environmental policy today, demanding governmental response and instigating further civil society interest, we need to outline the basic pedagogical sources of such an endeavour. This book, and others like it, is ultimately the product of the marriage of two fields of inquiry: the scientific study of ecology, environmental science, and the broader theorization of human society, in particular the field of political science. We treat these fields of inquiry separately immediately below, before discussing their confluence: the study of environmental politics, what has come to be known as the subfield of *ecopolitics*.

ENVIRONMENTAL SCIENCE

Without the study of ecology as a major field of scientific work it would be virtually impossible to write this textbook. While the authors are not natural scientists, we lean heavily on scientific data to present our analyses, for without these it is difficult to gauge the levels of urgency we should attach to environmental problems. Ecology refers to the study of "the house," the biology of habitat. Moreover, it is concerned with expanding the realm of scientific understanding beyond individual organisms, to the study of the interactions between groups of organisms and the biogeochemical factors on which their lives depend. Although much of this scientific tradition is derived from Darwinian concepts of evolutionary biology, it is grounded also in a utilitarian perspective on nature which holds that nature can be used by humans to achieve increases in the quality of human life. The extent of permissible use, however, is a subject of great debate among environmental philosophers who, though they are chiefly interested in ideas, in the process are also exploring the field of ecology. The study of how political systems affect the environment, and how the environment in turn affects human society, can be broadly labelled *ecopolitics*.

We must be careful about environmental science, for several reasons. As mentioned above, it is largely a Western conception, and some of the ethical systems discussed in Chapter 12, as well as the ecofeminist approach described in Chapter 10, would reject this as destructive, rather than constructive. The Western scientific method is based largely on observation: if something cannot be established through repeated testing, its authenticity or validity as a claim is doubted. This cautious approach, some would argue, has allowed pollution to take place until it has been proven beyond doubt that it must be stopped, and by this point much damage has been sustained by the environment and affected persons alike. This being said, the international community will respond to a crisis only when there is solid evidence that it is imminent. This was seen most markedly with the evolution of the Montreal Protocol to deal with ozone-layer depletion: Once it became a widely accepted fact that CFCs were causing the damage, states were willing to move towards a solution in remarkably rapid fashion. Despite fairly widespread belief that global warming will have serious environmental consequences, such a consensus on its causes and effects has not been reached, enabling oil-exporting states to argue it is premature for such a strong response. As well, environmentalists generally support the adoption of the *precautionary principle*, which requires that the burden of proof associated with scientific testing be reversed: Any new project should not proceed until there is conclusive evidence such actions will not harm local or global ecology.

Another, closely related concern about environmental science is its claim to objectivity. One can argue that true, pure objectivity is impossible to achieve, that the analytic separation of object and subject is mythical, and that we all approach questions with some internal and often unrecognized, and therefore unreported, biases. This may be so, but we need not delve into metaphysics to understand this, especially in the field of political science. It is quite obvious that different political actors endorse different scientific findings and data that support their causes or interests. We require, at the very least, a healthy dose of skepticism when evaluating government, business, and NGO reports based on scientific inquiry. Although there is widespread consensus that certain ecosystemic and biospheric cycles, such as those circulating carbon, nitrogen, sulphur, and phosphorus, are necessary to sustain life on earth, it is a different matter to measure human encroachment on these basic providers. Similarly, we are now in the midst of what many ecologists believe is a large-scale extinction of wildlife, the result of habitat destruction, poaching, global climate change, and other factors. However, different conservationists and industrial lob-byists will either support or minimize the extent of this occurrence with contrasting data. And in the international realm, different states will often embrace different results of scientific studies. For example, at the 2000 plenary session of the Convention on International Trade in Endangered Species (attended by one of the authors), states in favour of resuming small-scale whaling and those opposed accepted different data on whale populations to support their points.

As importantly, environmental science is even less precise when it exam-ines the causes of change. While few would deny that increased populations strain natural resources, there is a spirited debate between those who see large-scale population increases in the southern hemisphere as the chief threat to planetary survival, those who see increased consumption of goods by relatively few human beings in the north as the chief threat, and those who believe human society can adapt to anything it faces, so long as science and "rationality" prevail. In fact, it is difficult to arrive at sound conclusions regarding the population issue, because it is almost impossible to produce accurate figures and statistics for most states, and there is heated contro-versy over methods of population control (family planning, contraception, etc.). Many argue that Canada has often faced an underpopulation problem, with such large expanses of virtually uninhabitable land; yet the debate over immigration policy reveals the essentially political character of this topic. Although we can learn much from the science of ecology, and would be less aware of the scope of environmental problems and their interconnectedness without it, it does not always provide obvious policy options; some would argue it can lead to misguided attempts to "manage" what is neither in our ability nor our right to manage, the natural heritage of the earth.

Nonetheless, we must heed the words of Karen Litfin, in her inter-esting analysis of the ozone protection regime: Scientists stand as author-ities, and their power "derives from their socially accepted competence as interpreters of reality" (Litfin, 1994:29). This gives them great credence not only among the general public, but among decision-makers as well. Without the ever-evolving field of environmental science, they would have little voice. Indeed, one could argue that scientific communities play an increasingly important role in the public discussion and implementa-tion of environmental policy today since they form transnational working groups and, in a broader sense, epistemic communities of like-minded professionals (see Schofer, 1999). Within these ranks, however, there is great variation: Many work for large extractive industries, while others, such as popular Canadian television personality David Suzuki, are much more pro-environmentalist.

POLITICAL SCIENCE

Few academic fields are as epistemologically divided as political science. Most political science departments offer courses on everything from Plato to electoral studies, regional development to the politics of art. The field is essentially broken into several key subfields, each of which applies in some manner to the main concern of this book. Below we summarize these subfields, and their applications will be readily recognized as you read the ensuing chapters. This continues an earlier effort by O.P. Dwivedi to explicate the links between the study of political science and environmental policy (1986).

Since we are concerned with policies, we are certainly within the realm of the broad area known as public policy and administration. Although this implies a broad array of management and administrative theories, similar to those practised and studied in the private sector, public administration is chiefly concerned with the operations of government and the relationships between bureaucrats and political institutions such as the legislature (law-making bodies), executives (those who form policy decisions and implement laws), and the judiciary (who interpret and enforce the laws of the land). There are many definitions of public administration (see Kernaghan and Siegel, 1995), but the main concern is with the formation and implementation of rules and regulations by public authorities. This is of key importance when studying environmental policy, which is formed and implemented on a number of levels in a federal political system. Furthermore, it is possible to study public administration from a comparative perspective, across states, allowing for exploration and theorization about commonalities and differences (see Heady, 1996).

Many people are engaged in the study of public administration, from students to professors in academia to bureaucrats involved in policy formation, implementation, and evaluation. As with environmental science, however, we must be careful when accepting definitive reports from government departments, since they have an inherent interest in their own survival. Furthermore, it would be a serious error to assume perfect knowledge on the part of those analysing public administration. Because we work with such imperfect information, it remains difficult either to make objective assessments or, for those developing government strategies, to make long-term commitments. For example, the Commissioner of the *Environment and Sustainable Development* report for 1998 freely admits that the Auditor General was unable to determine many key factors in an analysis of governmental achievements. For example, we do not know "the extent to which Canada is living up to its international obligations to prevent illegal traffic of hazardous waste at the border ... [or] the contribution that the set of energy efficiency initiatives now in place is making, or could make, to achieving Canada's goal for stabilization of greenhouse gas emissions ... [or] the full extent of environmental liabilities of the Government of Canada ... [or] the impact of habitat loss on the Pacific Coast salmon resource." These are just a few examples of the many gaps in knowledge that constrain policy setting. As mentioned earlier, scientific controversy will always cloud the ability to set environmental policy; however, this can be construed as a good thing, since scientific orthodoxy is often reflective of prevailing political/economic interests.

Another subfield of immediate relevance is that of Canadian government and politics. As our title suggests, we are primarily concerned with presenting a *national* perspective. Many authors have written descriptions of the Canadian political system, with varying ideological perspectives as their guide, and most political science departments offer introductory courses to students interested in learning the fundamentals of this system. When looking at a particular issue-area, such as health care, transportation, or education, it is inevitable that this complex mix of factors and actors will come into play, and in our case they do so primarily within the context of Canadian government and public administration. Chapter 3 covers some of the basics in detail, and throughout the text we will make frequent reference to the unique constellation of government agencies, political parties, public groups (see Pross, 1986), politicians, and rules and regulations that comprise the Canadian system. Importantly, all the abstract systems and functions we discuss take place within a broader normative context, in which prevalent ideas influence the policy output of institutions. Most strikingly, however, the political economy of Canada is based on the assumption that modified capitalism, as a socio-economic system of production, is essential to the success of the system (see Doern and Phidd, 1983:61-63). This implies at the very least that the so-called productive interests involved in resource extraction have had a significant impact on the overall direction of the Canadian economy and polity. But we also need to be aware of the various conservationists who actively lobby Ottawa and other decision-making centres for policy preferences, even if, as Melody Hessing and Michael Howlett point out, the public, "although an increasingly visible force in agenda-setting, remains secondary to traditional state and productive actors" (1997:134).

At the same time, experts in Canadian government can contribute to a broader subfield with direct relevance for environmental policy, called comparative politics. This involves comparing and contrasting public policies in different states and, as the authors of an authoritative text in the field suggest, there is "more to politics than authoritative and coercive activities. For example, there are political organizations such as political parties, or pressure groups [and] there are the media of communication — press, radio, television, and the like — which effect [sic] elections, legislative deliberations, and enforcement of laws and regulations" (Almond and Powell, 1996:23). Comparative politics aims to provide generalizations that hold regardless of the particular states under study, but also to distinguish between them, and the internal and external constraints faced by governments as they juggle responsibilities and debts to powerful players in the economy and society. Indeed, much of the recent work in environmental policy has assumed the character of comparative politics studies (see Jabbra and Dwivedi, 1998). At this stage we can see that all the subfields merge in an analysis of environmental policy, and that it is impossible to focus exclusively on any one.

But we must further expand our academic scope, since we live an age when international connections and obligations, threats and opportunities, define at least in part the political landscape. Indeed, many students of history would argue this has always been the case. Thus it is necessary to introduce a fourth subfield, that of international relations. Once again, there is no overwhelming consensus on what this field entails. Basically, it is concerned with the relationships formed beyond the limitations of national borders, between different states or multinational corporations or even between individuals who deal with citizens of other states on a regular basis. Within this area of study lie many others: international organizations, foreign policy, theories about world politics, international political economy, and issue-specific areas of expertise (see Sens and Stoett, 1998). An important, emergent area of sustained interest is the field of global environmental politics, which examines the international impact of conflicts over resources and international cooperation aimed at solving related problems of the global commons. Hundreds of treaties and "regimes" have been put in place (see Caldwell, 1996), with varying results, to mitigate the impact of global industrialization, and Canada has played a significant role in many cases. Of particular relevance today is a widespread concern with the process of globalization, whereby state borders become increasingly porous, and international capital (investment) is able to circumnavigate the globe, having a significant effect on the public policies of states and the actions of non-state actors alike.

Finally, no political science department would be complete without courses on political theory itself. Again, there is a broad range of historical and contemporary theory, as well as ongoing debates over what type of methodology is best employed in the pursuit of political truth (though some would argue there is no such thing as "political truth"), and over what is a just and/or equitable political order. One of the main areas of division, relevant to any study of Canadian policy, is the role of the state within society. Is the state the objective referee of pluralistic domestic politics? Does it represent the interests of the socio-economic elite, as Marxists and other critical theorists maintain? Should it stay out of people's affairs whenever possible, or should it intervene in the economy and social life of society in order to increase the quality of life or, even, to actively redistribute resources? All of these perspectives can, of course, be applied to the study of environmental politics: If one believes in a non-interventionist state, this places obvious limitations on what, if anything, governments should do to regulate pollution in the private sector. If, however, one advocates a strong state, this opens the possibility of vigorous regulation, but there will still be divisions between those advocating a central, authoritarian state capable of coercively changing patterns of pollution (often referred to as a "Green Leviathan"), and those favouring a social democratic state that would decentralize authority to enable more local control of ecological decision-making. Ecofeminists link the oppression of women with the exploitation of the environment, and deep ecologists stress the ethical primacy of biospheric egalitarianism, believing that all living forms should be viewed as inherently equal. Ecomarxists and others from the southern hemisphere often link their absolute and relative poverty to environmental problems caused by Western-style capitalism and, more specifically, by multinational corporations.

There are many divisions within political theory as it applies to ecological thinking, and these can be further subdivided according to their impact on various subfields of political science other than theory, such as international relations (see Laferriere and Stoett, 1999). The ethical and spiritual perspectives discussed in Chapter 12 add yet another layer of understanding about the relationship between humans and nature. If all of this sounds perplexing, it is. But in order to do even scant justice to the vast issue-area of Canadian environmental policy, we must keep all the subfields of political science within our conceptual and empirical reach.

CONCLUSION: THE STUDY OF ENVIRONMENTAL POLITICS

All the subfields of political science discussed above, as well as the knowledge (and controversy) generated by the study of environmental science, must be combined if we are to venture into the complexities of environmental politics, or what some, such as Dennis Pirages, call "ecopolitics." In his groundbreaking textbook for international relations students, Pirages refers to ecopolitics as the "cluster of economic, ecological, and ethical issues" that have new-found importance because of a widespread "new assessment of remaining resource-intensive growth possibilities in a finite world" (1978:30). By studying the interplay between environmental problems and societal responses, at both the national and international levels, we can advance our knowledge of Canadian ecopolitics and facilitate informed decision-making by politicians, bureaucrats, and citizens alike. One could argue that the field of ecopolitics has changed considerably in Canada, moving from an area most interested in the ownership, distribution, and extraction of natural resources to questions of quality of life. While resource-use remains a large part of the overall policy direction, as it was twenty years ago (see Dwivedi, 1980), the list of ongoing concerns has expanded considerably (Kyba and Dwivedi, 1998).

Much of this text deals with the environmental activities of the Canadian state. However, we begin the next chapter with a look at the state of the Canadian environment. It is quite impossible to provide anything but a brief summary here, and although we have tried to capture the latest trends in our overview, we are bound to have missed a few. While there have been many areas of notable improvement in terms of the environmental health of Canada, there are more problems facing us today than at any time in history. Pollution continues to be a dominant concern, from toxic waste to acid rain to our contribution to global warming. Resources, the backbone of the Canadian economy for so many years, are strained, particularly old-growth forest. The delicate Arctic environment is threatened by southern developments such as pollution and demands for increased oil and gas exploration. Canada's lakes and rivers join the coastal areas in sharing a fishery resource crisis unlike any we have seen in recorded history. The image of Canada often conveys the rushing water of the north, the stillness of the plains, and the snow-capped mountains of the Rockies. Many species of wildlife — moose, deer, bears, cougars — are represented on postcards and snapshots. However, many of Canada's species are at risk, and in some cases, are nearly extinct. Despite a profound public love of such animals, their habitat is being gradually eroded by the development of suburbs and cottage retreats; by logging, mining, and other extractive activities; and by forest fires, hazardous waste dumps, sewage disposal, and other facets of modern Canadian living. Furthermore, Canada does not exist in a vacuum; the environmental threats and concerns raised in other parts of the globe have a significant impact upon environmental policy formation in Canada.

At the same time, Canadians have much to celebrate, for they live in one of the most beautiful, varied, and inspiring natural environments on earth. How can we describe the vast space that makes up Canada? Perhaps the single most important word we can use to begin such a description is "diversity." Few countries contain the topographical differences between the west coast, mountain regions, the prairies, the Arctic, the cityscapes close to the American border, and the eastern forests. The Canadian territory is the second largest in the world, and borders on three oceans. It also borders on the most powerful economy in the world, which gives Canadians unique access to markets there. (The question of consequent political influence will be discussed later in this text.) The UN Human Development Index has named Canada as one of the best places to live over several successive years.

The question is: How can we protect this impressive heritage? As our understanding of environmental science has grown we become increasingly aware of the limits to growth. We cannot neglect the ecopolitics which will result: confrontations between business and conservationists; pressures from the international community to cap greenhouse gas emissions; new regulatory frameworks necessary for new technologies; and a host of other issue-areas unique to this epoch, yet resonant of older political debates about the role of the state and environmental ethics. Although it may be easy to argue it is in everyone's long-term best interest to protect the environment, a close examination of various stakeholders demonstrates that short-term interests are a different matter altogether.

Finally, we should reiterate the points raised above concerning the essentially contestable quality of research and argument in this field. As Donald Wells writes, environmental policy "functions in a context of uncertainty: uncertain service boundaries, an uncertain time horizon, and an uncertain production function" (1996:15). Uncertainty may be a frustrating state of affairs. Nevertheless, we intend to explore many areas in this text, and hope that the reader will emerge with an enhanced understanding of, and respect for, contemporary Canadian environmental policy, its structural context and political actors, the policies implemented by governments, and the various ecological perspectives and advocates struggling to gain the hearts and minds of Canadians.

THE STATE OF CANADA'S
ENVIRONMENT

When people around the world think of Canada they think of vast
spaces, forests, rich mineral deposits, and an unlimited supply of fresh
water. (O'Malley and Mulholland, 2000)

INTRODUCTION

Canada is consistently ranked as one of the best places in the world to live
by the United Nations Human Development Index (HDI). In fact, Canada
ranked number one out of 174 countries on this index between 1993 and
2000. Reasons for this acclaim include Canada's wealth of natural
resources, diverse ecological spaces, and pristine natural environments. The
environment is of central importance to Canadians; Canada's wealth of
natural resources and natural environments provides both economic
prospects and leisure opportunities. Canada is a large country and home to
diverse ecological landscapes characterized by an abundance of fresh water,
coastal waters, mountains, forests, wildlife, and land. All of these resources
can be found in a number of ecosystems or ecozones, of which Canada has
20 major ones: 15 terrestrial (land) ecozones and 5 marine (water) ecozones.
These ecozones provide homes for a multitude of plant and animal species.
    In an effort to preserve environmental integrity, many Canadians have
actively protested the policies of governments and industries believed to
exploit resources unsustainably. Some of these protests have resulted in
arrests, as was the case with the protests over old-growth forests in
Clayoquot Sound on Vancouver Island, British Columbia (discussed further in Chapter 10). Many Canadians have volunteered to work with environmental organizations and within their communities as activists. In
addition, as this book will demonstrate, the governments in Canada have
developed numerous policies and regulations to manage natural resources.

Despite these efforts, we are currently faced with more environment-related problems than ever before. These problems are large in scope and number, and require far more detail and attention than the limited space this chapter can provide. This chapter adopts an ecosystem approach, introduces the environmental challenges and opportunities, and provides references to additional information for further investigation. In addition, this chapter identifies some of the work that is being done to address environmental problems in local, national, and international contexts. The approach is a holistic approach to studying the environment's problems, opportunities, and responses. As such, the ecosystem approach addresses a multitude of interconnections and relationships between the various components and species that make up the ecosystem. Since humans are central to environmental decision-making and management, they have a significant impact on the ecosystem. Decisions about environmental management are informed by — and reflect — Canadian attitudes, values, and demands. We begin this examination of the state of Canada's environment with a summary of Canadian attitudes toward nature and environmental management.

CANADIANS AND THE ENVIRONMENT

Images of Canada, including tourist brochures, postcards, calendars, paintings, and other paraphernalia, portray Canada as a country of stunning landscapes and untouched natural environments. In fact, the majority of Canadians inhabit only 0.2 per cent of the country. This is perhaps not surprising when one considers that Canada is the second-largest country in the world (after Russia). Canada measures approximately 5300 km from east to west (from St. John's, Newfoundland to the Queen Charlotte Islands, British Columbia), and 4600 km south to north (from Point Pelee, Ontario, to Alert, Ellesmere Island) (Environment Canada [EC], 1997a). Many Canadians have a particular fondness for nature and outdoor recreation activities and view environmental issues as central to their health and well-being. In a study conducted in 1996, 20 million Canadians — or 85 per cent of the population — said they take part in nature-related activities (EC, 1999a).[1] More than half of all Canadians visited national or provincial parks or other protected areas for activities such as sightseeing, camping, and hiking. More than one-third of Canadians cared for birds and other wildlife around their homes, and many Canadians enjoyed wildlife viewing, recreational fishing, and hunting (EC, 1999a). However, outdoor recreation and tourism have a significant impact on the environment and can cause pollution, loss of natural landscape, and destruction of flora and fauna. For example, pollution caused by motor vehicles leads to poor air quality. Watercraft contribute to water pollution by discharging solid waste and hydrocarbons. Other forms of pollution include littering and noise pollution caused by crowds, recreational vehicles, and increased traffic. Further environmental damage is caused by forest fires and the removal of fruits, plants, and animals from their natural habitats which can lead to species loss (EC, 1997a).

The relationship between Canadians and the environment is also an economic one. The natural environment provides a great number of jobs for Canadians, one-third of whom are employed either directly or indirectly in agriculture, forestry, mining, energy, tourism, or other land-based activities. The fishing industry is also an important source of income for Canadians. As many as 145,000 Canadians rely on the coastal sector, and fishing in particular, for full-time employment (EC, 1997a). The forestry industry provides approximately one million jobs and produces an annual value of more than $20-billion worth of products (Dwivedi and Kyba, 1996). Furthermore, these natural resource-related activities account for more than one-half of all Canadian exports (EC, 1997a). Canadians are thus economically dependent on ecosystems and the resources found within these ecosystems. The following section highlights some of the ways in which people in Canada enjoy — and are dependent on — the resources they find in mountains, oceans and coastal areas, land, fresh water, forests, and wildlife.

Mountainous Resources

Within mountain regions, economic activities such as mining, forestry, resort development, and ecotourism contribute to economic growth and offer employment opportunities for Canadians. While population growth within mountainous areas is not considered a problem, the economic activities have been criticized for their ecological impact on the natural environment. One of the major criticisms is that transportation and utility corridors used to gain access to mines and forests have destroyed the habitats of a variety of species. Mountain areas are also important sources for leisure. In Canada, mountain areas are a major part of Canada's national parks system, particularly in British Columbia, Alberta, and the Yukon. A broad ecosystem approach to the management of protected areas is central to the management of mountain national parks (EC, 1997a).

Oceans and Coastal Resources

Canada has the world's largest coastline, stretching in total almost 250,000 kilometres along three of the world's five oceans (the Atlantic, Arctic, and Pacific). Canada also has the second-largest continental shelf, with an area of 3.7 million square kilometres. Currently, 6.5 million people in Canada, nearly one-quarter of the population, live in communities along the coasts. A number of Canada's large cities have coastal ports that facilitate the shipping industry, exports, imports, and trade (EC, 1997a). Canada is home to the world's largest proportion of coastal and marine resources and has one of the largest exclusive fishing zones, encompassing approximately 4.7 million square kilometres of ocean. These marine resources contribute substantially to the nation's economic growth. As noted earlier, coastal communities, fishing, and marine resources are a major source of employment for Canadians and are therefore central to the livelihoods of many. The fishing industry is constantly changing as some fish are replaced or placed under a moratorium in order to reduce the harvest of certain species (such as the short supply of cod). New markets are also being developed for different fish resources. This diversification is critical to sustaining livelihoods in coastal communities.

More than one million tonnes of fish are removed from the sea annually. In 1993, Canada exported more than $2.4-billion of fish products. Overall, "the oceans sector was estimated to be a minimum of 1.4 per cent of Canada's gross domestic product (GDP) in 1996, with contributions to the regional economy of Canada's coastal areas ranging as high as 10.9 per cent of the GDP" (EC, 1997a). The oceans and coastal areas of Canada also provide employment and economic opportunities in the oil and gas industry, shipping, ship-building, and tourism. Projections for future growth point to increased private-sector activities which are expected to continue as the main engine of growth in Canada's oceans sector (EC, 1999b). Furthermore, the oceans and coastal areas are of historical and cultural significance. Ocean-related activities represent traditional ways of life for people who fish for a living, of Canada's aboriginal people, and of Canadians' recreational interests (EC, 1997a). Moreover, the importance of oceans to Canada and other countries is greater than economic value, employment opportunities, and cultural significance, since oceans play a key role in global ecological processes that influence life and living conditions throughout the world (EC, 1997a).

Biodiversity: Wildlife and Forests

It has been estimated that Canada is home to 71,573 of the 1.5 million species in the world. In order to protect these species, Canada has made a number of commitments to biodiversity preservation. Many of these commitments have been highlighted in *Caring for Canada's Biodiversity: Canada's First National Report to the Conference of the Parties to the Convention on Biological Diversity*, written by the Biodiversity Convention Office of Environment Canada in 1995. (Canada's commitment to the Convention on Biological Diversity is discussed in further detail in Chapter 8.) Commitment to biodiversity has resulted in a 15-per-cent increase in the number of protected areas in Canada since 1990, from 690,000 square kilometres to almost 800 000 square kilometres. The total land area currently protected in Canada is more than eight per cent of the total land area of the country (EC, 1997b). Nevertheless, many environmentalists argue this is not enough, given the threats species face today. Furthermore, Canada still lacks a national endangered species act.

As noted at the beginning of this chapter, nature is an important part of Canadians' lives. Nature and wildlife are therefore culturally significant to Canadians. Protecting and preserving wildlife is a central focus of biodiversity strategies in Canada. Although Canada is not home to a very large number of species, it is working hard to protect those species that do occur naturally in the country and has been involved in the International Convention dealing with the Protection of Wildlife and Biodiversity. Within Canada, the Committee on the Status of Endangered Wildlife in Canada (COSEWIC) has been instrumental in raising awareness about wildlife endangerment. As of May 2000, COSEWIC reported that 352 wild species in Canada are at risk, threatened (likely to become endangered if changes are not made), endangered (facing imminent extinction or extirpation), extirpated (no longer existing in the wild or in their original habitat), or extinct (no longer existing). The number of species represented in each category is summarized in Table 2.1. The category with the highest rate of risk is vascular plants, with 117 of the 352 species at risk. However, fish, mammals, and birds are also at risk. The number of species at risk is up from 243 in 1995. In the May 2000 report on *Canadian Species at Risk*, COSEWIC provided a detailed list of these animals and their risk levels. Examples include the Benthic and Limnetic Stickleback fish, which have become extinct since 1999. The grizzly bear has been extirpated since the 1880s, and the American badger, swift fox, and barn owl have all joined the endangered list since 1995. Wood bison, killer whales, beluga whales, and the eastern fox snake became threatened species at the time of this report.

TABLE 2.1

CANADIAN SPECIES AT RISK

CATEGORY	STATUS EXTINCT	EXTIRPATED	ENDANGERED	THREATENED	SPECIAL CONCERN	TOTALS
Amphibians	—	—	4	1	10	15
Birds	3	2	18	7	22	52
Fish	6	2	9	13	43	73
Lepid-opterans*	—	3	1	—	2	6
Lichens	—	—	1	—	3	4
Mammals	2	4	15	12	25	58
Molluscs	1	1	5	1	—	8
Mosses	—	—	1	—	1	—
Vascular Plants	—	2	44	31	40	117
Reptiles	—	1	4	6	8	19
TOTALS	12	15	102	71	154	352

SOURCE: *Committee on the Status of Endangered Wildlife in Canada (COSEWIC) (2000) "Canadian Species at Risk," May. Online. Internet. http://cosewic.gc.ca/COSEWIC/2000_list.pdf*

Of special concern, according to the May 2000 report, are the grey fox, the polar bear, and the pacific great blue heron (COSEWIC, 2000).

Canada's wildlife is an important part of the economy as a source of tourist revenue. Canada's natural beauty and wildlife attract 1.1 million visitors annually for wildlife viewing or recreational fishing (EC, 1999a). American tourists alone spent $705.3-million in Canada in 1996. The wildlife sector earns approximately $9-billion annually, contributes $11-billion to Canada's GDP, and generates approximately $5-billion in tax revenues. Canada's wildlife also maintains approximately 200,000 jobs (EC, 1997a). However, jobs related to wildlife management and tourism are in jeopardy due to the growing threat to biodiversity and the increased number of species at risk. Threats to biodiversity include continuing, permanent alteration of ecosystems and habitats; the introduction of harmful alien species; degradation of ecosystems due to pollution and other factors; global climate change and other atmospheric change; and non-sustainable harvesting practices. There are many threats to forest-dependent species: forest harvesting; clearing for agriculture and human settlement; developments such as roads and utility corridors that fragment forests; recreational activities; and disease (EC, 1997b). Among the factors putting species at risk are changing habitat resulting from climate change; toxic contaminants in tissues of living organisms (e.g., polar bears); invasions of non-native species (e.g., the zebra mussel); polychlorinated biphenyls (PCBS); dioxin; and organochlorides used as insecticides such as DDT (dichlorodiphenyltrichloroethane). Changes in habitat can be witnessed in numerous regions of Canada. Loss of wetland habitats, in particular, has been caused by a number of factors (summarized in Table 2.2), but the most significant cause is agricultural drainage. Wetlands are excellent habitats for a number of species due to their nutrient-rich soil and vegetation. Many birds, such as herons, thrive on the vegetation and species that occur only in wetlands. However, the nutrient-rich soil is also attractive to agriculturalists who want to increase their output and expand their land under cultivation. Agricultural drainage occurs when wetlands are diverted or destroyed by farming.

Forests are also home to many of Canada's species. Of Canada's 921.5 million hectares of land area, forests cover 417.6 million hectares, or about 45 per cent of Canada's total land area (Natural Resources Canada, 1997). Canada is home to 10 per cent of the world's total forest area. A significant proportion of these forests are open forests, consisting of muskeg, marshes, and sparse tree cover. However, 57 per cent of the forests in Canada are used commercially for the production of timber and non-timber products. Of Canada's forested lands, the Canadian public owns 94 per cent; only six per cent of the forests are on private property owned by more than 425,000 landowners. Provincial governments manage about 71 per cent of Canada's forests; federal and territorial governments manage only 23 per cent. Canada's forest land base is extremely diverse, consisting of eight major forest regions, each with a different mix of predominant tree species. Overall, according to Natural Resources Canada, "more than 60 per cent of the forest cover is composed of softwoods, 15 per cent is hardwoods, and

TABLE 2.2

CAUSES & PERCENTAGES OF WETLAND LOSS IN CANADA

CAUSE OF WETLAND LOSS	PERCENTAGE OF LOSS (%)
Agricultural Drainage	85
Urban/Industrial Expansion	9
Recreational Development	2
Hydrodevelopment and lake-level management	2
Forestry and peat harvesting	2

SOURCE: *Environment Canada (1997a) "The State of Canada's Environment 1996." Online. Internet.* http://www1.ec.gc.ca/-soer/default.htm.

21 per cent is mixed woods. All told, there are 165 tree species in Canada" (1997). Native forests in Canada's west-coast rainforest consist of numerous tree species, including old-growth red cedars and hemlocks. The Canadian Shield is home to pine trees, spruce, and tamarack. Along the Great Lakes and St. Lawrence River, the trees are classified as mixed wood and hardwood. Forest structure (the layering of trees, shrubs, plants, etc.) provides habitats for two-thirds of Canada's wildlife, including mammals, birds, reptiles, amphibians, fish, insects, plants, and microorganisms. New species are continually being discovered. For example, scientists recently identified more than 60 new insect species in the canopies of coastal old-growth forests (EC, 1997b). These discoveries reinforce the need for careful management of Canada's forests.

In addition, the forest industry is an important source of income in Canada. Sales of Canadian wood and paper products totalled $59-billion in 1994. This industry is Canada's largest foreign exchange earner, exporting $32.4-billion of forest products annually (EC, 1997a). The forest industry employs approximately 900,000 workers directly and indirectly; therefore, one out of every 15 workers in the Canadian labour force is employed in the forest industry. Numerous communities rely on wood products for their livelihood (EC, 1997a). Forests are also an important source of income for the tourism sector. Old-growth forests in British Columbia attract thousands of visitors each year. Owners of small businesses such as bed and breakfasts, bakeries, and gift shops benefit from this tourism. And it is not only tourists who visit the forests: In the 1990s, old-growth forests in Clayoquot Sound, Vancouver Island, attracted more than 1000 protestors who fought to prevent massive logging plans for Clayoquot Sound and to ensure their right to employment. (This example is discussed in further detail in Chapter 10: Gender, Resources, and the Environment.)

Land and Agriculture

Most land in Canada (about 90 per cent) is either federally or provincially owned. Canada's federal government owns approximately 40 per cent of the land, most of which is located in the Yukon, Nunavut, and Northwest Territories (EC, 1997a). The other 10 per cent of the land which is privately owned is home to most of Canada's population. (The total land areas and their uses are summarized in Table 2.3.) As the table illustrates, a relatively small percentage of Canada's land is used for agricultural purposes. The management of land and land resources is increasingly impacted by urbanization, which impacts agricultural and biologically productive land by placing increased demand on the land to produce food

TABLE 2.3

LAND AND ITS USES IN CANADA		
LAND AREA IN AGRICULTURE	LAND AREA (in 1000 ha)	LAND AREA (in %)
Cultivated Farmland	33 508	3.64
Summerfallow	7 921	0.86
Grasslands, Paturelands, & Other	26 326	2.86
TOTAL ARABLE LAND	67 755	7.36
TOTAL LAND AREA OF CANADA	920 000	

SOURCE: *Environment Canada (1995) "Caring for Canada's Biodiversity: Canada's First National Report to the Conference of the Parties to the Convention on Biological Diversity," Online. Internet.* http://www.bco.ec.gc.ca/bco/ProjectsDomestCBS_e.cfm

to meet the needs of the growing population base. Growing cities require more land and more food to be produced on this land; therefore, food production needs to be sustainable. Agriculture and the agri-food industry are an important part of Canada's economy, accounting for eight percent of the GDP and 15 per cent of total employment. Over one million individuals in Canada are employed in the food-processing sector, one of Canada's largest manufacturing industries (EC, 1995b).

As Table 2.3 demonstrates, land suitable for agriculture in Canada represents only 7.36 per cent of Canada's total land mass, and only 3.64 per cent is presently cultivated. Nearly all of the land suitable for agriculture in Canada is currently in use today (EC, 1997a). A wide range of agricultural goods are grown on this land and a variety of animals graze Canada's grasslands and pastures. At present, Canada's major agricultural commodities include meat and grains. The agricultural sector is an important employer, providing jobs for approximately 400,000 Canadians who operate independent farms. In addition, more than one million people work in the various jobs provided by the agri-food sector (EC, 1997a). Also important to the economy are exports of farm products, totalling $15.2-billion in 1994 (6.8 per cent of total exports), whereas agricultural imports amounted to $11.9-billion (5.9 per cent of total imports) (EC, 1997a).

Fresh Water

Lakes and rivers cover 755,180 square kilometres in Canada (EC, 1997a). Canada's rivers discharge 9 per cent of the world's renewable water supply (EC, 1997a). However, although about 60 per cent of Canada's fresh water drains north, 90 per cent of the Canadian population lives in the south, where pollution and escalating demand for potable water are putting additional strain on freshwater resources. The demand for fresh water is compounded by increasing pressures on Canada from the United States to sell its water: "The sale of Canadian water to other countries has doubled since 1996. In 1989, 23 million litres of Canadian bottled water were sold to the United States; by 1998, this figure increased to 272 million litres. Canadian water bottlers now are the largest suppliers of bottled water to the United States" (O'Malley and Mulholland, 2000). However, Lloyd Axworthy (former foreign affairs minister) and Christine Stewart (former environment minister), announced a strategy to prevent water exports and the bulk removal of water from Canadian watersheds. The matter has been deemed a security issue, and the strategy to protect Canada's freshwater supply includes "amendments to the International Boundary Waters Treaty Act (IBWTA) to give the federal government regulatory power to prohibit bulk removals from boundary waters, principally the Great Lakes," as well as "[a] proposal to develop, in co-operation with the provinces and territories, a Canada-wide accord on bulk water removals to protect Canadian watersheds" (DFAIT, 1999b).

At present, freshwater supply for Canadians is not a problem. Most Canadians live in urban centres where clean, safe drinking water is obtainable. However, a small number of Canadians do not have access to such water. Increasing pollution in rivers, lakes, and groundwater supply poses new health risks for Canadians. For example, water pollution in Walkerton, Ontario in May 2000 resulted in several deaths and more than 1000 illnesses from bacteria that normally live in the intestines of animals or humans. In the case of Walkerton, the residents contracted E. coli 0157. Although most strains of E. coli bacteria are harmless, bacteria such as E. coli 0157 cause illness, diarrhea, and a kidney-destroying toxin that is often fatal to children and older people. This example illustrates the problems of pollution caused by some forms of agribusiness (i.e., factory farming) as well as the need for regular and timely water inspections. (Lack of access to clean, safe drinking water is discussed in further detail in the section on pollution.) One of the challenges facing Canadians in the sustainable use of fresh water is a reduction in water use. Canadians are among the highest per capita water users in the world. For example, Canadian's water use in homes averages approximately 340 litres per day (EC, 1997a). In contrast, average daily water consumption in Germany in 1998 was 129 litres per capita (Federal Statistical Office, Germany, 2000).

Other challenges facing Canadians' sources of fresh water include the reduction of untreated industrial and municipal waste water entering the environment and curbing the release and deposition of contaminants in surface and groundwater. Each day in Canada, one million cubic metres of waste water are treated. However, 17.9 per cent of Canada's urban population has no sewage treatment; 20.5 per cent of the urban population has primary treatment only; another 20.5 per cent of the urban population has secondary treatment; and 34.4 per cent of the urban population has tertiary treatment — the highest level of waste treatment (EC, 1997a).

ENVIRONMENTAL PROBLEMS

Although Canada is home to beautiful landscapes, diverse ecosystems, and numerous species, there remain many problems. Given the impact of humans on the environment, it is critical to begin by identifying the nature and extent to which population growth and population distribution are concerns for environmental management. At the turn of the century, there were approximately six billion people on earth; Canada's population of 31,006,347 represents only 0.5 per cent of the world's population (EC, 1997a). Canada's population growth rate, at 1.06 per cent per year, is fairly low. Population density in Canada is three persons per square kilometre. The reason for the relatively low population density is the disproportionate representation of Canadians in urban areas and the rate at which Canadians are moving to urban areas (EC, 1997a). Most Canadians (80 per cent) live in urban areas (EC, 1997a), the majority of which cover only 0.2 per cent of the country (EC, 1997a). More than half of all Canadians (60 per cent) live in centres with more than 500,000 people (EC, 1997a). Thirteen of Canada's twenty-five major metropolitan areas are in the Windsor-Quebec City corridor, the most heavily urbanized region in Canada (EC, 1997a). Population trends point to a growth in the number of people moving to intermediate urban areas (populations greater than 100,000 people), particularly cities surrounding Toronto and Montreal. The vast majority of Canadians (90 per cent) live in close proximity (within 160 kilometres) to the US/Canada border.

However, urban living has not diminished Canadians' love for the natural environment. Evidence of Canadians' ongoing interest in the natural environment is the number of Canadians that visit natural parks and engage in outdoor recreation. Canadians also enjoy a diversity of green spaces within urban centres, including wooded and grassland areas. Efforts are being made to increase the number of green spaces in urban centres and to protect the existing green spaces from environmental threats such as pollution and overuse. Toronto, for example, has a total of 71,994 hectares of green space. When compared to the total urban area of 160,338 hectares, this represents nearly half of the total urban space. Similar examples can be found in other Canadian cities (see Table 2.4).

TABLE 2.4

GREEN SPACE IN SELECTED URBAN AREAS		
URBAN AREA	TOTAL GREEN SPACE (ha)	TOTAL URBAN (ha)
Toronto	71 994	160 338
Montreal	68 830	157 196
Vancouver	54 169	113 058
Ottawa-Hull	28 737	55 773
Quebec City	35 471	54 246
Victoria	14 500	25 605
Halifax	12 375	23 923
London	9 588	22 523
Saskatoon	6 481	15 366

SOURCE: *Environment Canada (1997a) "The State of Canada's Environment 1996." Online. Internet.* *http://www1.ec.gc.ca/-soer/default.htm*

Urban living poses a number of environmental problems including climate change, air and water pollution caused by automobile exhaust, industrial development and manufacturing, high and unsustainable rates of energy consumption, and inadequate waste management and disposal facilities to cope with the population's demands. We address each of these environmental problems in greater detail in the following section. Clearly, these environmental problems are complex and interrelated, making it difficult to separate the numerous environmental concerns facing Canadians today. Furthermore, environmental problems have been the source of great controversy. Environmental scientists and policy-makers debate the causes and consequences of these environmental issues. The following sections introduce some of the environmental problems, and provide the context for the national and international strategies that have been adopted to remedy these problems.

Air Pollution

The link between air pollution and human health is increasingly being documented as research findings support the relationship between air pollution and respiratory problems such as asthma and bronchitis. All Canadians, no matter where they live in Canada, are susceptible to the health impacts of air pollution, since toxic substances and heavy metals that comprise air pollution can be transported long distances in the atmosphere. People living in urban areas and regions in close proximity to large urban centres are particularly vulnerable to ground-level ozone. In northern Canada, the environmental risks are also serious since toxic substances and heavy metals have accumulated over time in ecosystems, affecting food sources. However, air quality in Canada varies from region to region. Canadian cities often experience unacceptable air quality, especially in the summer months. There are many causes of poor air quality, including ground-level ozone and airborne particles, which, combined with other air pollutants, produce a condition commonly known as smog. Urban air may also contain trace amounts of toxic chemicals including volatile hydrocarbons such as benzene (EC, 1999c). Five major pollutants are assessed to determine local air quality: sulphur dioxide, nitrogen dioxide, carbon monoxide, suspended particles, and ground-level ozone. These pollutants originate in the by-products of industrial activities and the burning of fossil fuels. For the most part, they cause respiratory problems and eye irritations. Carbon monoxide impedes the absorption of oxygen into the bloodstream. But, while harmful to humans, these pollutants also have an impact upon the natural environment. For example, sulphur dioxide, nitrogen dioxide, and ozone are harmful to trees and other plants and can damage rubber, plastic, and other materials by reacting with — and weakening — them.

Ground-level ozone is particularly dangerous since it affects human health, damages vegetation, and decreases the productivity of some crops. It has also been linked to flower and shrub damage and is believed to contribute to forest decline in some parts of Canada. Safe limits of ground-level ozone are frequently exceeded in Canada, particularly during hot summers when concentrations of ozone may be double the air-quality objective. Ozone formation depends on strong sunlight and is accelerated by heat. Therefore, ozone concentrations tend to peak during the day when it is hottest. A recent study, the *Canadian 1996 NOx/VOC Science Assessment*, concluded that there is no safe level of human exposure to ground-level ozone (EC, 1999d). Ground-level ozone, along with other pollutants, makes up what is known as photochemical smog. While some of these other pollutants, such as peroxyacetylnitrate (PAN), are

TABLE 2.5

PERCENTAGES OF CANADIAN PASSENGER TRAVEL

YEAR	CAR	AIR	RAIL	BUS
1950	85	1	5	9
1970	86	9	1	4
1990	81	16	‹1	3
1994	82	14	‹1	3

SOURCE: Environment Canada (1997a) "The State of Canada's Environment 1996." Online. Internet. http://www1.ec.gc.ca/-soer/default.htm

35

also hazardous to human health and vegetation, ground-level ozone is the most abundant. One of the major contributors to air pollution and ground-level ozone is the automobile. Canada, which has one of the highest ratios of car ownership in the world, is home to more than 12 million cars (EC, 1993). As Table 2.5 illustrates, between 1950 and 1994, the percentage of people using rail and bus has steadily declined, while automobile use has stayed about the same and air travel has increased substantially.

Ground-level ozone is an urban problem, since heavy traffic and the concentration of industrial facilities increase ozone levels within confined spaces. However, air masses can carry ground-level ozone hundreds of kilometres from its site of origin to rural areas where ozone concentrations

TABLE 2.6

ANNUAL AVERAGE CONCENTRATION OF FIVE COMMON AIR POLLUTANTS

IN CANADA, PARTS PER BILLION (PPB)

YEAR	CO	NO_2	O_3	SO_2	TSP
1979	1626.19	25.21	15.62	9.52	65.89
1980	1495.35	24.74	15.83	9.02	66.79
1981	1505.56	22.78	14.97	8.25	58.64
1982	1280.00	23.00	16.17	7.53	51.88
1983	1185.37	22.13	16.58	6.29	47.75
1984	1044.90	23.18	16.78	6.60	46.45
1985	975.56	21.44	16.74	5.71	42.91
1986	930.77	22.33	16.51	5.73	42.64
1987	942.86	22.69	16.51	4.88	46.80
1988	902.27	20.89	18.76	6.13	43.75
1989	939.53	22.38	18.51	6.19	43.82
1990	804.26	20.95	17.36	6.28	38.88
1991	750.00	20.16	19.75	4.62	38.12
1992	720.83	18.38	17.58	4.95	35.10
1993	722.04	18.17	20.14	5.16	40.78
1994	643.87	17.71	20.82	4.75	41.33
1995	582.07	17.11	20.65	4.14	40.61
1996	594.69	17.43	20.99	4.80	39.28

SOURCE: Environment Canada (1997a) "The State of Canada's Environment 1996." Online. Internet. http://www1.ec.gc.ca/-soer/default.htm

can be even higher than in the cities themselves. The impact that this travelling ground-level ozone has can be observed in agricultural output, since crops such as wheat, corn, soybeans, tobacco, tomatoes, and beans are sensitive to ozone (EC, 1997a). Table 2.6 shows the trends in increasing and decreasing average levels of the five common air pollutants for Canada: carbon monoxide (CO), nitrogen dioxide (NO_2), ground-level ozone (O_3), sulphur dioxide (SO_2), and total suspended particulates (TSP). Although the average concentrations of TSP and SO_2 have decreased between 1979 and 1996, the levels of CO, NO_2, and O_3 have all steadily increased in this 20-year period.

To monitor these pollutants, National Ambient Air Quality Objectives (NAAQOS) have been established in Canada. In the process of monitoring air quality, the NAAQOS indicator defines a series of objectives to be reached and establishes limits for air quality defined as "desirable," "acceptable," and "tolerable" ranges of air quality. When a pollutant concentration reaches the maximum tolerable level, immediate action is required in order to protect the health of the general population (EC, 1997a).

Stratospheric ozone — unlike ground-level ozone — is a protective shield occurring approximately 10-50 kilometres above the earth's surface. Stratospheric ozone is important for protecting humans and the natural environment from ultraviolet radiation emitted by the sun. One of the largest factors contributing to stratospheric ozone depletion is the release of halocarbons, namely chlorofluorocarbons (CFCs), bromofluorocarbons (halons), methyl chloroform, carbon tetrachloride, methyl bromide, and hydrochlorofluorocarbons (HCFCs). These stratospheric ozone-depleting substances have been used in air conditioning and refrigeration equipment, foams, aerosols, and fire extinguishers, and as solvents and pesticides. These substances also have long atmospheric lifetimes which allow them to penetrate the stratosphere, where they react to intense UV-B radiation, releasing chlorine and bromine atoms which then react with the stratospheric ozone and break it down. The impact of depleted stratospheric ozone has been linked to a number of environmental changes such as climate change.

Climate Change

Climate change and global warming have received increasing attention in the past decade as global mean temperatures continue to rise each year. Climate change is caused by greenhouse gas emissions. Greenhouse gases can occur naturally or they can originate from industrial developments. Greenhouse gases include water vapour which can cause the earth's surface temperature to rise. Carbon dioxide (CO_2) originates from the decay of materials and the respiration of plant and animal life as well as from material and fuel combustion caused by human activity. Methane (CH_4) is a heat-trapping gas which causes the decay of matter without the presence of oxygen. The sources of methane include wetlands, rice paddies, animal digestive processes, fossil fuel extraction, and decaying garbage. Soils and oceans produce nitrous oxide (N_2O). Increases in nitrous oxide levels can be attributed to soil cultivation, the use of nitrogen fertilizers, nylon production, and the burning of organic material and fossil fuels. Additional effective heat-trapping greenhouse gases are halocarbons, which are produced by a number of industrial and home activities such as the use of CFCs. Halons can be found in some fire extinguishers, while CFCs can be found in older refrigerators, freezers, and air conditioners. CFCs damage the protective ozone layer, which filters out the sun's harmful UV rays (EC, 1999g). In the above examples, the common theme is the retention of heat in the atmosphere which, in turn, has an effect on the earth's climate. Human activities through industrial development have caused an increase in atmospheric concentrations of some of these gases (e.g., CFCs). The most significant greenhouse gas associated with human activity is carbon dioxide; atmospheric carbon dioxide eventually could cause the planet's average surface temperature to increase by 1.5–4.5°C from pre-industrial times. The average temperature during summertime is expected to increase by 2–4°C and wintertime temperatures may increase by 4–10°C. These potential increases could lead to major alterations in global and regional climates.

The potential impacts of global warming include rising sea levels, shifts in arable land, increased tropical pests, changes in forest growth, species extinction, and increased ultraviolet radiation. The impact on urban centres could require new construction to protect against extreme heat and cold as well as floods and changes in land stability (e.g., landslides and permafrost melting) (EC, 1998c). The health implications of climate change on humans include increased exposure to changes in thermal stress; changes in extreme events; increases in some air pollutants, pollens, and mould spores; malnutrition; increases in the potential transmission of vector-borne and water-borne diseases; and stresses on the general public-health infrastructure (EC, 1998c). Climate change is also expected to alter the amount and distribution of rain and snowfall, and contribute to longer growing seasons and reduced home heating expenses. However, hotter summers will likely result in greater demand for air conditioning and therefore increased energy use. Other environmental changes predicted include droughts, severe storms, and longer and more frequent hot spells (EC, 1997a). Canada's commitment to addressing climate change includes the Montreal Protocol, which seeks to limit and/or phase out the number of ozone-depleting substances produced and used in Canada (EC, 1999e), and the Kyoto Protocol, which calls for reductions in greenhouse gas emissions. However, Canada is facing difficulties meeting these targets. We discuss these commitments and their challenges in further detail in Chapter 8.

Acid Rain/Acidic Deposition

Acidic deposition, most commonly referred to as acid rain, gained media attention in the 1970s and 1980s. Research pointed to the impact of sulphur dioxide on the natural environment and urban centres. The process of acidic deposition begins when emissions of sulphur dioxide and nitrogen oxides are released into the atmosphere. These emissions are caused mostly by smelting of sulphur-bearing metal ores and the burning of fossil fuels. Smelting of metal concentrates contributed 50 per cent of the total eastern Canadian sulphur dioxide emissions in 1994 (EC, 1997c). These substances can return to the surface directly as gases or as sulphates or nitrates associated with particles. This is known as dry deposition. The substances can also combine with water to form sulphuric and nitric acids that fall as precipitation (wet deposition). Acidic deposition is not limited to the locations where these sulphur dioxide and nitrogen oxide emissions are released. They can be carried hundreds of kilometres by atmospheric currents and can settle in remote environments far from the sources of pollution. Acidic deposition is linked to damage in both natural and urban spaces. For example, acid rain has been linked to forest decline, since acid rain entering the soil affects the growth of trees. Acid rain is also linked to the decline of fish stocks and animal species, since the acid is known to kill the sources of food in rivers that these fish and animals depend on for survival. The acidification of lakes and rivers has reduced their capacity to support aquatic life. Concerns about acidification and nutrient loss in the lower Great Lakes date back to the August 1970 International Joint Commission (IJC) findings. In the IJC report, the lower Great Lakes were declared to be in a state of crisis due to acidification (IJC, 1970). More than 14,000 lakes in Canada are believed to be acidic today.

The effects of acid rain are clearly visible in many of Canada's lakes and rivers. For example, in Ontario, four per cent of 4000 lakes tested for their pH levels have been affected by acid rain. Acidification of lakes is greatest during the spring months when "sudden and intense acid doses are released into the environment. The 'acid shock,' which occurs during spring thaw, has been measured to be as high as 100 times greater acidity than normal" (Dwivedi and Kyba, 1996:214). This is particularly detrimental to the fish populations, since this is the time of year when most fish species spawn.

The acid shock can affect reproduction "by destroying the eggs or by causing birth defects which leave fish unable to reproduce" (Dwivedi and Kyba, 1996:214). The fish most sensitive to acidification are salmon and trout. Humans are also impacted by the acidification of lakes since many Canadians rely on fish for food and a decline in fish stocks reduces food availability. In addition to the detrimental effects of acid rain on lakes and rivers, the inhalation of high concentrations of sulphur dioxides and nitrogen oxides is linked to respiratory problems. Concern is growing for the quality of drinking water, since toxic chemicals are increasingly leaching into watersheds. Acidic deposition has also caused damage to urban centres and the human-made environment. Examples include the erosion of statues and the decay of marble, limestone, and other building materials.

Some progress was made during the last 10 to 15 years of the twentieth century, reducing sulphur dioxide emissions by half. For example, in 1997, emissions in eastern Canada were less than half of their 1980 levels, and 24 per cent below the 2.3-million-tonne sulphur dioxide cap in the Eastern Canada Acid Rain Program (EC, 1998c). Sulphur dioxide emissions have been reduced to some extent by switching to lower sulphur-emitting fuels, changing from leaded to non-leaded fuels which reduces nitrogen emissions, and by the widespread use of catalytic converters in automobiles in Canada. Despite this progress, many lakes and forests in eastern Canada are still being damaged, and the recovery process for natural ecosystems has been slower than anticipated (EC, 1999f). Federal and provincial governments have developed a number of policies and programs to address acid rain and its impacts. Through the Clean Air Act, Environment Canada has developed industrial standards for sulphur dioxide and nitrogen oxide emissions. One of the ongoing challenges is the limited capacity of governments to enforce environmental standards and regulations. (These challenges are discussed in greater detail in Chapter 6.) An additional challenge faced by Canadians is the impact of environmental pollution and acid rain that originate in the United States. There have been difficulties in reaching transnational agreements on pollution prevention, although a recent agreement to reduce transborder smog is promising.

Energy Consumption and Energy-Related Pollution

Canada has a wide range of energy sources including hydro-electric, wind, fossil fuels, and nuclear. Energy resources are also an important part of the Canadian economy. In 1994, "nearly 8 per cent of Canada's GDP (excluding gasoline service stations, wholesale petroleum products, and propane), 17 per cent of gross investment, and 10 per cent of gross export income were attributable to energy production" (EC, 1997a). While Canada produces a great deal of energy, Canadians use more energy per capita than people in most other countries. Canada ranks as the world's sixth-largest user of primary energy (EC, 1997d). The rate at which Canadians have been using energy has been steadily rising since 1961, as Table 2.7 illustrates. There are numerous reasons for the high rate of energy consumption in Canada. These reasons include the seasonal cold climate; hot summers requiring air conditioning; an energy-intensive industrial sector (i.e., mining, pulp and paper, iron and steel production); high demand for transportation services; a large land area and low population density, which create a high demand for transportation services; and relatively low energy prices. Since Canadians, on average, enjoy a high standard of living compared to other parts of the world, they use a number of appliances and energy-consuming products (EC, 1997a). Energy use in Canada is broken down as follows: 27 per cent for transportation, 39 per cent for industry, and 34 per cent for agriculture, residences, schools, hospitals, offices, and businesses (EC, 1996b).

But energy use contributes to pollution. For example, fossil fuels (i.e., petroleum, natural gas, and coal) contribute to air pollution, climate change, acidic deposition, and urban smog. Additional environmental problems include the emissions of toxic air pollutants, such as benzene, "released during the handling, storage, and combustion of fossil fuels, and mercury and other heavy metals which are emitted during the combustion of heavy oil and coal" (EC, 1997a). Hydroelectric power, however, supplies 12 per cent of Canadian energy requirements and is a much cleaner source of energy that does not contribute to air pollution like fossil fuels. But hydroelectric power has different environmental impacts. The use of dams and reservoirs to generate hydro power can seriously alter aquatic ecosystems. Nuclear power also contributes 12 per cent of the primary energy produced in Canada. Like hydroelectric power, nuclear power does not produce atmospheric emissions and therefore does not contribute to air pollution, climate change, acid rain, or smog. However, two-thirds of the heat produced in nuclear reactors is wasted, and only one-third is converted to electricity. Also, disposal of nuclear waste is problematic since there are limited disposal facilities and options available. Radionuclides produced during nuclear power generation require a minimum of 250,000

TABLE 2.7
CANADIAN CONSUMPTION OF ENERGY (1961-97)

YEAR	TOTAL ENERGY CONSUMED IN EXAJOULES (EJ)
1961	3.24
1970	5.63
1980	7.88
1990	9.16
1997	10.16

SOURCE: *Environment Canada (2000a) "Canadian Consumption of Energy (1961–97)" December 1997. Online. Internet. www3.ec.gc.ca/ind/English/energy/Tables/ectb01_e.cfm*

years of isolation from soil, water, and air. Additional energy sources include renewable energy such as wood, solar, and wind power. Wood, for example, supplies Canadians with 6 per cent of their energy requirements. However, wood, like fossil fuels, can contribute to local air pollution. Alternative energy technologies, such as active solar and wind power, cause less environmental stress and are likely to be used increasingly in the coming years (EC, 1997a).

Waste Production and Pollution

Canadians, as high energy consumers, are also among the highest per capita producers of household waste in the world. The waste produced in households across Canada includes packaging waste, garbage, and even hazardous waste. It is difficult to accurately determine the extent to which Canadians produce — and dispose of — hazardous waste. However, some estimates indicate that a typical household produces about 6.8 kilograms of hazardous household waste each year (EC, 1997a). Some of the common hazardous wastes produced in Canadian households include paint, household cleaning materials, pharmaceuticals, pesticides, motor oil, batteries, and broken electrical and/or battery-operated appliances. For example, approximately 250 million batteries are used annually and leak heavy metals and other toxic materials. When hazardous materials such as household cleaning materials are dumped into sewers, they eventually make their way into the rivers and lakes that supply drinking water, since sewage plants do not remove these toxic substances. As for pesticide use, it is interesting to note that hectare for hectare, up to fifteen times more pesticides are sprayed on city lawns and gardens than on country farms and fields (The Ontario Waste Management Corporation, 1993 as cited in EC, 1997a). Approximately six million tonnes of hazardous waste are generated in Canada's homes and industries annually. More than half of these materials are recycled. However, Canada also imports hazardous waste for disposal. A great deal of controversy has arisen in Canada over the import of uranium. One of the biggest problems with the storage of hazardous wastes is the lack of safe disposal facilities; therefore, the risks these materials pose for human health and the environment are great. Between 1998 and 1999, hazardous waste imports increased significantly, from 545,000 tonnes in 1998 to 663,000 tonnes in 1999 (EC, 2000b). Canada has made a number of commitments such as the United Nations Basel Convention to control the transboundary movements of hazardous waste. This commitment and some of the additional challenges and opportunities for Canadians in the production, storage, and recycling of hazardous waste are dealt with in greater detail in Chapter 7.

Canadians have attempted to control the amount of waste produced in their homes through recycling programs. In addition, more than one million home composting units have been distributed to Canadian households since 1988. These composters divert organics from landfills. Approximately 23 per cent of Canadian households composted in 1994 through home composting, or by having their organics collected by municipal governments or others for composting. Nationally, Canada has witnessed a 51-per-cent reduction in packaging between 1988 and 1996, including 1.17 million metric tonnes less aluminium, glass, paper, plastic, steel, and wood going for disposal. The amount of packaging going for disposal fell from 5.41 million tonnes in 1988 to 2.64 million tonnes in 1996, representing a 56-per-cent reduction on a per capita basis. Waste management responsibilities are shared among the three levels of government. Waste collection and disposal operations come under municipal jurisdiction, whereas the provinces are responsible for approval, disposal, and treatment facilities. Waste management issues only become a matter of federal responsibility when federal lands or resources are affected, interprovincial or international transport is involved, or federal assistance is provided. Hazardous waste management services in Canada are worth $2-billion annually, and employ 4000 to 5000 people providing services in consulting, chemical analysis, and operation of hazardous waste management facilities. One of the most hazardous of wastes is uranium; Canada has one of the largest uranium mining industries in the world (EC, 1997a).

CONCLUSION

Canadians have become increasingly aware of some of the environmental problems that they currently face. In a poll conducted by POLLARA (1999), 85 per cent of Canadians expressed concern for the state of the environment. Pollution is one of the most important concerns for Canadians. In fact, nearly half of all Canadians polled considered pollution to be the greatest environmental concern and an important risk factor in the overall state of health (Environics, 1999). Most Canadians consider the role of the federal government and provincial governments as central to addressing environmental problems, and 96 per cent of Canadians indicated that they think the federal government should maintain or increase involvement in the environment in the future (Ekos, 1998).

At the national level, the federal government has demonstrated its commitment to addressing these environmental problems through a variety of national, federal-provincial, and international environmental policies and plans of action. Some of these commitments have been mentioned in this chapter but are addressed in greater detail in the chapters that follow. Many environmental solutions are also found at the municipal and community level, where communities have taken responsibility for cleaning up or preserving their immediate natural environment, participating in environmental recycling programs, and initiating clean-up programs.

Much of the environmental work currently being done in Canada is part of a broader sustainable development vision for the country (a theme on which we expand in Chapter 9). Many of the environmental issues and problems summarized in this chapter are being addressed by governments in Canada, environmental organizations, aboriginal peoples, and concerned Canadians. Solving Canada's environmental problems and striving for sustainable development are everyone's responsibility and require a multi-stakeholder approach that ensures that all groups and individuals are able to participate in the decision-making, planning, and problem-solving processes. Subsequent chapters identify the political actors and structures involved in Canadian ecopolitics, the environmental issues faced by Canadians, the policies put in place in an effort to curb environmental problems, the strategies that have been developed to prevent environmental pollution, and the perspectives of different interest groups and people who strive to maintain the environmental integrity of the spectacular landscapes to which Canada is home.

NOTE

1   The information summarized here was taken from the Internet. Please note that throughout this book, when the Internet has been used as a source, parentheses will not indicate a page number.

THREE

THE CANADIAN POLITICAL SYSTEM
AND THE ENVIRONMENT

INTRODUCTION

Solutions to all the major problems referred to in the previous chapter ultimately lie in the realm of politics. Despite the fact that some of these problems may be largely scientific in nature, others "economic," and others still "philosophic" or "moral," in the end all require political decisions to deal with them and to specify the type and timing of the solutions attempted. Thus, the environment must compete for attention and resources with other issues of public concern, and environmentalists must confront several political realities in attempting to achieve their goals. To understand this fully, it is necessary to know something about the basic structure and operation of the Canadian political system, and the main national agency charged with environmental protection, Environment Canada. This chapter provides brief overviews of both, and outlines in some detail the historical evolution of environmental policy-making at the federal level.

CANADIAN POLITICAL STRUCTURE: A BRIEF OVERVIEW

According to its Constitution, Canada is a representative parliamentary democracy which operates in a federal state. The Canada Act, 1982, establishes the major institutions of government in Canada, divides powers and responsibilities between the federal and provincial levels of government and, largely through the Charter of Rights, determines the democratic nature of the system. Figure 3.1 outlines the most relevant aspects of the system.

Sections 9 to 90 divide the governments of Canada and the provinces into executive and legislative branches, establish the House of Commons and Senate and the provincial legislatures, and create an electoral system by which our legislators are chosen. Sections 91 to 95 establish Canada as a federal state with two separate levels of government, national and provincial, divide the powers and jurisdictions between these governments, and make municipal governments subordinate to the provincial governments which have the power to create them. Sections 96 to 101 create a system of courts for Canada, including both civil and criminal courts to which disputes can be taken for final settlement. Finally, the Charter of Rights and Freedoms, added to the Constitution in 1982, specifies the democratic rights and fundamental freedoms under which the entire system will operate. In addition, Canada relies on both British and Canadian customs and traditions as they have evolved over the years to make the system function more fairly and effectively in the modern era. All of this provides a context in which to understand why and how environmental policy is determined in Canada.

It is also important to understand how the policies which govern us come to be legislated and enforced. In theory, when the public becomes concerned over issues (environmental issues, for example) and expresses its desire to have them dealt with by government, the political parties take up these issues and provide possible solutions to them in their electoral platforms. After an election, the party with the most elected representatives in the House of Commons forms the government and, if these issues are high on that party's list of legislative priorities, then party Members or the government itself will propose legislation to deal with them. If this legislation

FIGURE 3.1

THE CONSTITUTION (CANADA ACT, 1982)	
SECTIONS 9-90	» divide government of Canada into executive and legislative branches » establish the House of Commons, Senate, and provincial legislatures » create an electoral system
SECTIONS 91-95	» establish Canada as a federal state » divide powers and responsibilities between national and provincial levels of government » make municipal governments subordinate to the provinces
SECTIONS 96-101	» establish a court system for Canada, including civil and criminal courts
CHARTER OF RIGHTS AND FREEDOMS	» lists fundamental freedoms of Canadians such as conscience, thought, belief, opinion, and expression; freedom of peaceful assembly and association; freedom of the press and other media of communication » lists democratic rights of Canadians such as the right to vote and run for election; elections to be held every five years; Parliament and legislatures to meet at least once a year

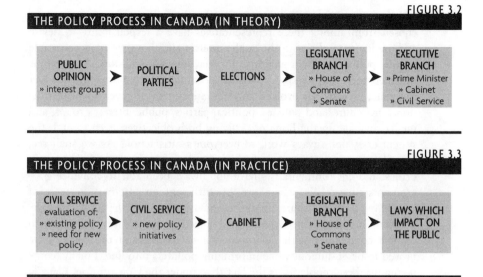

FIGURE 3.2

THE POLICY PROCESS IN CANADA (IN THEORY)

FIGURE 3.3

THE POLICY PROCESS IN CANADA (IN PRACTICE)

secures a majority in the House and Senate, it becomes law and is given to the executive branch — the Cabinet and civil service — to implement (see Figure 3.2). The success or failure of these policies is then evaluated by the public, and the issues are either deemed settled or demands for further action appear and the process begins again.

In practice, of course, the system does not operate so simply. The flow of communication between citizens and political parties is not perfect. Some public demands do not rate high on the list of priorities of either parties or governments. Of greatest importance in our context, quite often new policies emerge from the civil service's own research and evaluation procedures which point to new areas of concern and produce new initiatives never considered by the public. In fact, in the modern era governments have come to dominate the legislative process. As a result, most new legislation comes to Parliament from the Cabinet, and most of this has been produced by the civil servants who work in the several departments and agencies of government. Civil servants today are policy initiators as well as policy implementers and policy evaluators, and their contributions to the process are no less important than those of the other actors in the political system. Figure 3.3 provides a more realistic view of the policy process. This figure illustrates why, in the context of national environmental policy, attention must be paid to the Department of the Environment (Environment Canada).[1]

Nevertheless, despite the gap between theory and practice, the fact that Canada is a parliamentary democracy means that Canadians choose representatives to address their concerns in the House of Commons, provincial legislatures, and municipal councils. It also means that governments chosen from among these representatives have a responsibility to devise and implement policies in the public interest and that they are accountable to the public for their actions. In fact, the entire political system is intended to be both responsible and accountable to public opinion. Over the years, Canada has evolved an elaborate system of government institutions, procedures and policies, political parties, public interest groups, and media coverage in the hope of realizing both objectives, even though the system does not always work to everyone's satisfaction. As we shall see, Canadians have not always ranked the "environment" among their top priorities, and environmentalists have not always been able to convince governments that their issues are of sufficient importance to warrant legislation or a fair share of the national budget. Furthermore, governments do not always meet their stated objectives and are not always able to enforce compliance with environmental standards, and the courts have proved to be of dubious value in bringing polluters into line. Finally, compounding these problems, is the fact that, under the Constitution, Canada is a federal state in which both national and provincial governments share responsibility for the environment. This has led to many interjurisdictional disputes and occasionally to attempts by governments at both levels to shift the blame for their inaction onto the other jurisdiction.

With this brief summary of the main features of the Canadian political system as background, the remainder of this chapter discusses the evolution of Environment Canada, the major federal department which deals with environmental issues, and then outlines the attempts of both national and provincial governments to solve the manifold problems caused by the constitutional division of responsibility for the environment.

ENVIRONMENTAL POLITICS AND INSTITUTIONS — THE RESPONSE OF THE FEDERAL GOVERNMENT

Although resources policy had been the subject of considerable debate for years, pollution of the air and water did not emerge as a major public policy issue in Canada until the late 1960s. Media coverage of dramatic environmental crises and the activities of many new environmental groups raised public concern about the declining quality of our natural environment. Polls taken throughout the period show that beginning with the "Pollution and Our Environment" conference in 1966, and especially after the sinking of the ship *Arrow* off the coast of Nova Scotia in 1970, the problem of pollution focused public attention and assumed priority status on the national political agenda. As a result, there was considerable pressure on Canadian governments to act quickly to control pollution and to protect the environment from further degradation. The creation of the Department of the Environment (known now as Environment Canada) on June 11, 1971, was the federal government's response to the issue.

There is no doubt that the Trudeau government had a constitutional right to take this action. Although the environment as such was not mentioned in the British North America Act of 1867 (now the Canada Act, 1982), several clauses have been interpreted as justifying the exercise of federal power in this area. For example, through the sweeping "peace, order and good government" power of Section 91, Ottawa can legislate in any area deemed of national importance. As well, its unlimited power to tax gives it some measure of control over both provincial governments and private interests within the country. More specifically, via the enumerated clauses of Section 91, the federal government can legislate with regard to fisheries as a resource through its power over "seacoast and inland fisheries," regulate the use of Canadian waterways and seacoasts through its control over "navigation and shipping," control development of reserve lands through its responsibility for "Indians and lands reserved for Indians," and it can control interprovincial trade and the export of resources through its power over "trade and commerce." While provincial governments can claim more comprehensive jurisdiction over resources and the environment (as shall be detailed later in this chapter), the legislative authority of the federal government in the environmental area must not be discounted. In fact, there was no constitutional challenge to the creation of the new Department of the Environment.

The newly established department brought together within a single administrative unit most of the federal government's environmental responsibilities and activities which had previously been dispersed among several other departments and agencies. In the beginning, the Department of the Environment contained the former Department of Fisheries and Forestry, as well as the Department of Transport's Canadian Meteorology Service, the Canadian Land Inventory from the Department of Regional Economic Expansion, the Water Sector from the Department of Energy, Mines and Resources, the Air Pollution Control and Public Health Engineering Divisions from the Department of National Health and Welfare, and the Canadian Wildlife Service from the Department of Indian Affairs and Northern Development. The Canadian Meteorology Service was renamed the Atmospheric Environment Service (AES), and a major organizational innovation, the Environmental Protection Service (EPS), was created to provide a focus for pollution control and abatement. In all, Environment Canada consisted of five service branches: the AES, the EPS, the Fisheries Service, the Lands, Forests and Wildlife Service, and the Water Management Service (see Figure 3.4). By bringing all these activities together under the control of a single department, the federal government sought to enhance the status of the environment in the decision-making process and to enable the development of better integrated and coordinated environmental policies and programs.

At the outset, Environment Canada seemed to be well positioned to tackle the various environmental problems confronting the nation, especially pollution problems. The scope of the Department's activities was certainly impressive, covering the entire spectrum of renewable resources. Furthermore, Environment Canada was given the responsibility of administering several new pieces of legislation designed specifically to bolster environmental initiatives. The 1971 Canada Water Act contained a special provision for water quality management, the Clean Air Act was designed to be a "cutting edge in the fight against pollution" (Brown 1986:218), and amendments to the Fisheries Act in 1970 provided for improved means of

FIGURE 3.4

CREATION OF THE DEPARTMENT OF THE ENVIRONMENT, JUNE 11, 1971

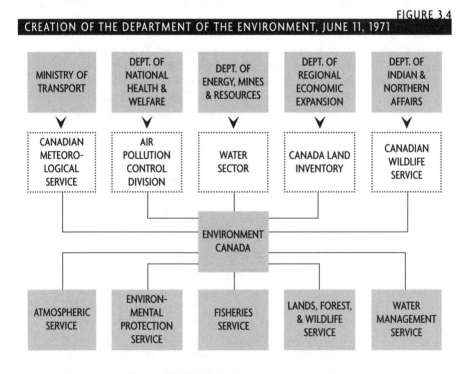

NOTE: *Administrative units shown by broken line boxes were transferred from their original departments to the newly established Department of the Environment.*

controlling industrial effluents which are harmful to fish. While the wide range of its activities and the scope of its authority left the impression that Environment Canada was to be a "super department" (Aucoin 1979:233), responsible for all environmental matters, it was in fact a renewable resource agency playing a coordinating role. Moreover, it was basically a scientific and technical research department. According to Peter Higgins, "it was brought together to generate the scientific and technical information necessary for the proper planning and implementation of a national environmental management program" (1973:6).

Despite the hopes and excitement surrounding Environment Canada in 1971, there were major obstacles in the Department's path which limited significantly its ability to fulfil its environmental mission. First, there was the limited nature of the federal role in environmental matters in Canada. According to the Constitution, the provinces have the primary responsibility for most aspects of environmental affairs. Thus, Environment Canada was limited in terms of the policies and programs it could formulate and implement. In most areas, Environment Canada had to develop cooperative relations with the provinces which, in the early 1970s, was a difficult task, due to considerable political tension between Ottawa and the provincial governments. Second, and of major importance, was the need to integrate the various units which now comprised the Department into a single cohesive unit with a unified outlook. This task posed significant problems for senior department officials since the various units had well-developed programs of their own with specific mandates and their own particular approaches to delivering services. For example, the Canadian Forestry Service had a history dating back to 1899, and its officers were reluctant to alter past practices. Similarly, the Atmospheric Environment Service (formerly the Canadian Meteorology Service) dated back even further, to 1871, and was affiliated through the World Meteorology Organization with an international network of meteorological services. The two services had relatively little in common; each had its own established traditions and a strong sense of autonomy that was well ingrained and difficult to relinquish. Thus, there were problems in overcoming the inherent differences and tensions within the Department and forging a unified organizational philosophy. Third, Environment Canada also faced the task of establishing itself within the large bureaucratic structure of the federal government. As a newcomer, Environment Canada had to be careful to forge effective relations with the older departments and agencies, especially the longer-established resource departments with which there would be competition and friction.

The manner in which Environment Canada responded to these organizational challenges and the changing nature of environmental problems confronting the nation are demonstrated in the evolution of the

Department's policies and programs. These policies and programs have evolved over the past three decades amidst many structural changes and adaptations and searches for a coherent environmental philosophy. The evolution of Environment Canada is detailed below in five distinct stages.

Phase I — The Focus on Pollution Control — 1971-1973

The initial thrust of Environment Canada's activities focused primarily on pollution control and abatement. Essentially, Environment Canada began its operations by adopting a curative stance aimed at cleaning up major pollution problems such as the Great Lakes. The curative position was intended to be a short-term strategy which would enable the Department to initiate some pollution clean-up activities while it developed more comprehensive long-term solutions. This is clearly evident in the original goals established by Environment Canada in 1971. These goals were to:

1. carry on established renewable resource programs and services
2. clean up and control pollution
3. assess and control the environmental impact of major developments
4. initiate long-term environmental programs
5. promote and support international environmental initiatives
6. develop an environmental information and education program
   (Environment Canada [EC], 1971:3)

In order to achieve these goals, the members of Environment Canada's senior management faced the immediate task of selecting an appropriate strategy to guide policy formulation and program implementation. In the simplest terms, they chose a mixed strategy to manage some problem areas and regulate others. This choice was made primarily because its main predecessor legislation, the Canada Water Act 1970, called for a managerial strategy, while pollution control required a regulatory approach.

During its first two years of operation, Environment Canada continued to provide the many renewable resource programs and services it had inherited from other departments. The Atmospheric Environment Service (AES) continued to offer weather services and to perform research and development activities. The AES also played an important role in the International Field Year on the Great Lakes (a multifaceted research and fact-finding enterprise), and was also involved in the establishment of the Global Atmospheric Research Program (GARP). Similarly, many of the Department's other services performed their tasks and responsibilities as they had in the past. The Canadian Wildlife Service maintained its primary focus on migratory birds, and the Canadian Forest Service conducted research on forestry problems such as the spruce budworm.

Another major focus of Departmental activities was the Environmental Protection Service (EPS), which was responsible for dealing with environmental problems that fell within Environment Canada's terms of reference. The EPS launched several major programs aimed at pollution control and abatement. For example, in response to water pollution, the Water Pollution Control Program was created under the authority of the Fisheries Act and the Canada Water Act. Although the intent of this program was to control water pollution generally, it focused initially on the establishment of regulations and guidelines for pulp and paper mills, fish processing plants, and effluent control regulations for toxic chemicals such as mercury. Similarly, an Air Pollution Program was established by the EPS "to preserve, restore or enhance the quality of ambient air" (EC, 1971:3). The main features of the Air Pollution Control Program included research and development studies and publications and the promulgation of national air quality standards. National standards for sulphur dioxide, suspended particles, carbon monoxide, and lead controls for gasoline were among the initial priorities for air quality objectives. A third program, the Ecological Protection Program, was created in order to establish and implement ecological protection regulations. The Ecological Protection Program had a broad cross-mission purpose that included environmental impact analyses of the proposed Lorneville thermal generating power plant in New Brunswick and the MacKenzie Valley Pipeline-Highway Project. The EPS also started an Environmental Emergency Program to provide immediate federal relief and aid to victims of unexpected ecological disasters. The EPS, with approximately 600 staff, quickly became Environment Canada's main instrument to combat pollution problems in Canada.

A third important area of Environment Canada's early activities was related to the functions of the Department's Water Management Service. As implied by its name, the Water Management Service utilized a managerial perspective in designing and implementing its programs. The Service's Inland Waters Branch was responsible for improving the quality, management, and wise use of Canada's water resources. To accomplish this task, the Canadian Centre for Inland Waters was established as the primary research facility for the development of an extensive inventory of the country's water supply. Most importantly, the Water Management Service was instrumental in negotiating parts of the Canada-United States Great Lakes Water Quality Agreement signed on April 15, 1972. As Munton notes: "The essence of the agreement, such as originally proposed by Canada at meetings two years earlier, was a set of common water quality objectives, compatible standards, commitments on implementing programs to achieve these objectives and procedures for monitoring sub-sequent progress" (1980:163).

During this first stage in the evolution of Environment Canada, the Department's policies and programs were designed primarily to respond to pollution problems. The curative stance adopted by Environment Canada sought to control pollution after the fact rather than at the source. In fairness to the senior managers of Environment Canada who adopted this stop-gap approach, the Department required an initial period of time to settle into the bureaucratic milieu of the federal government and to develop more effective long-term solutions to deal with national environmental problems. Toward the end of 1972, however, Environment Canada undertook an extensive evaluation of its activities, which led to a major reorganization of the Department in early 1973. This reorganization ushered in the second phase of the Department's evolution, which was characterized by the adoption of conservation-oriented, managerial solutions to the nation's environmental problems.

Phase II — Organizational Change toward Enhanced Environmental and Resource Management — 1973-1976

The second phase of the evolution of Environment Canada showed a much greater awareness and appreciation of the limitations of the environment. During this period, policy development within Environment Canada began to emphasize the need to conserve the nation's natural resources. Thus, resource management policies were designed with conservation in mind. Perhaps the single most significant event which contributed to this change in policy orientation was the "oil shock" of 1973. Following the OPEC decision to increase the price of oil dramatically, the unprecedented escalation in energy costs caused the public to realize that Canada's natural resources were not unlimited. Moreover, the ensuing energy crisis instilled in the public the notion that, in order to ensure a continuous and dependable supply of vital natural resources, it was necessary to manage and use natural resources more efficiently and wisely. As a result, Environment Canada began to focus and integrate its environmental policies and programs in order to enhance the management and wise use of natural resources. One of the consequences of this new managerial strategy was a shift from the curative stance to a preventative and anticipatory posture that aimed at dealing with environmental problems at their point of origin rather than after the fact. Thus, during the second phase in the evolution of policy development in Environment Canada, the

Department adopted a broader-based, holistic approach to dealing with environmental problems.

At the beginning of 1973, Environment Canada underwent a major reorganization designed to facilitate policy coordination and to expand and enhance the quality of its services. The former Fisheries Service was elevated in status to become one of two major service sectors. The goals of the new Fisheries and Marine Service were to maintain healthy fish stocks and to maximize economic returns derived from the fishing industry. The reorganization of the Fisheries Service was a prelude to further changes that were to occur as the fisheries component grew in importance within the government's economic development framework and in light of the regional nature of fisheries in Canada. As well, a new Resource Management Branch was created which reflected Environment Canada's efforts to improve its resource management function.

Environment Canada's new emphasis on environmental and resource management was also reflected in the creation of the Environmental Management Service on January 1, 1973. The EMS grouped together the Canadian Forestry Service, the Inland Waters Branch, the Canadian Wildlife Service, and the Lands Directorate in a single service organization. The intent underlying the creation of the EMS was to develop closer relations among these somewhat disparate units. For example, under the direction of the EMS, the Canadian Forestry Service continued to conduct research into the spruce budworm problem, but also began to develop a forest fire management program to assist various control agencies in fighting forest fires and expanded its reforestation program and forest product development activities.

The 1973 reorganization also produced a new Planning and Finance Service which provided Environment Canada with a mechanism to develop a cohesive central capacity for long-term policy development with respect to planning, finances, personnel, and coordination. The Planning and Finance Service's focus on long-term environmental management was made evident in two publications: *Environment Canada, A Ten Year Plan — 1975-1985* (1974) and *Fourth Quarter Century Trends in Canada* (1975). These two documents provided a general framework which outlined the nature and scope of Environment Canada's concerns and projected future endeavours.

Toward the end of 1973, a second major organizational innovation took place with the creation of the Federal Environmental Assessment and Review Office (FEARO). FEARO was created to develop and administer the Department's emerging Environmental Assessment Review Process (EARP). In line with Environment Canada's efforts to instill a stronger environmental awareness in resource development policies, it began to develop an assessment and review process to provide the government with better information to assess the environmental effects of major development projects. The EARP was based on a Cabinet directive, issued in December 1973, which authorized the Minister of the Environment to establish a review process to ensure that:

» environmental effects are taken into account in the planning of new federal projects, programs, and activities
» an environmental assessment is carried out for all projects that may have an adverse effect on the environment, before commitments or irrevocable decisions are made
» projects with potentially significant environmental effects are submitted to the Department of the Environment
» the results of these assessments are used in planning, decision-making, and implementation. (Estrin and Swaigen, 1978:53)

The government also extended the EARP to include any new project that involved federal property and funds: "This latter aspect ensured that the federal approach would come into contact with the provinces through many jointly funded projects and lead to joint federal-provincial studies in addition to those conducted by the federal government itself" (Mitchell, 1980:55).

In 1974, the growing importance of the Fisheries and Marine Service was deemed to merit the appointment of a Minister of State for Fisheries. The new minister, Romeo Leblanc, was to assist the Minister of the Environment by taking control of the Department's responsibilities for the fisheries of Canada. Although the appointment of the Minister of State for Fisheries lessened the burden on the Minister of the Environment, it also began a tense five-year period in which the fisheries portfolio and the environment portfolio were juxtaposed within a single departmental structure. As the importance of fisheries activities continued to grow, especially after the 1975 Law of the Sea Conference at which Canada was a strong advocate for the extension of the 12-mile territorial limit to 100 miles, the federal government decided to raise the status of the Ministry of State for Fisheries to the departmental level. Thus, in 1976, Environment Canada became part of the new Department of Fisheries and the Environment.

Phase III — The Conserver Society — 1976-1979

The third phase in the evolution of policy development in Environment Canada was based on the emergence of a new environmental philosophy which focused on the fundamental reasons underlying environmental problems such as pollution. The new approach began with the premise that human existence depends upon harmonious relations with the environment. In order to achieve this harmonious relationship it was necessary to transform the "consumer-society" into a "conserver" society. Obviously, a change of this magnitude would have to be brought about over a long period of time. Thus, Environment Canada launched some long-term planning initiatives to nurture the development of a conserver-oriented society. The Ten Year Plan for 1975-1985 was revised, and the new Planning Guideline for Environment Canada detailed major "perspectives" related to energy, food, population, resources, transportation, the economy, and health education.

In the latter part of 1976, Environment Canada was at the peak of its influence in the federal bureaucracy. When the Department was officially transformed into the Ministry of State for the Environment in the fall of 1977, the Minister was given broad ranging horizontal responsibilities. The new tasks of the Minister of State for the Environment, as laid down in the Department's mission statement, were to "promote and encourage the institution of practices of conduct leading to the preservation and enhancement of environmental quality, and cooperate with provincial governments or agencies thereof, or any bodies, agencies or persons in any programs having similar objectives" (EC, 1982:15). The Minister was also authorized to advise the heads of other departments, boards, and agencies of the federal government on all matters pertaining to the preservation and enhancement of the quality of the natural environment. Furthermore, the Minister could issue, with Cabinet approval, environmental standards and guidelines to be used by other federal departments, agencies, and Crown corporations. This process was intended to bring forth a cohesive environmental outlook to instil the conservation-oriented environmental policies and practices developing in Environment Canada in every decision-making body involved in any aspect of environmental concern. Thus, in 1977, Environment Canada had the potential to influence the entire government of Canada. However, as part of the Department of Fisheries and the Environment, it had neither the power nor the capability in terms of personnel or financial resources to achieve these lofty ideals.

In April 1978, the AES was transformed into the Canadian Climate Centre in order to provide more integrated climate-related services for the resource development sectors, particularly energy, agriculture, fisheries, and land-use management. In November of the same year, the Great Lakes Water Quality Agreement between Canada and the United States was amended to introduce new provisions for the elimination of toxic waste, the revision of water quality objectives and deadlines, and to deal with land use and air pollution effects on water quality. As well, during this time, the EPS began to focus its research activities on the emerging issue of acid rain and, in conjunction with the Canadian Climate Centre, to expand the Long Range Transport of Airborne Pollutants Study Program.

By 1978, however, the nation was in the midst of an economic recession, and the environment began to decline in importance in the Trudeau government's priorities. The federal government began to emphasize industrial growth and development, resulting in the emergence of a sectoral-based industrial strategy in the late 1970s. Thus, the conservation-oriented policies and programs of the third phase of Environment Canada's evolution which attempted to achieve more harmonious relationships between people and the environment gave way to greater flexibility and adaptability in environmental policy formation.

THE RISE AND FALL OF THE REGIONAL BOARDS

It is necessary at this juncture to mention the Regional Boards, an organizational tactic adopted early in the Department's existence to deal with issues which arose simply because of Canada's sheer size and diversity. During the 1970s, Environment Canada was one of the most decentralized departments in the federal bureaucracy. For example, the Fisheries and Marine Service had more than 90 per cent of its personnel in the field. Several factors explain the unusually high dispersal of Environment Canada's personnel throughout the different regions of the country. First, the nature of Environment Canada's activities required that most of its personnel be located in the field where they could provide the multiplicity of services offered by the Department. Second, in order to deal effectively with various environmental problems and issues which differed greatly from region to region, it was necessary for Environment Canada to develop a strong regional identity and to maintain a large regional representation. In response to this regional imperative, Environment Canada required a special mechanism which would enable both internal policy coordination and a departmental voice in the regions. That special mechanism was the Regional Board.

In the midst of the dramatic organizational changes that occurred between 1973 and 1979, the internal dynamics of the Department's activities were meant to be held together by the Regional Boards: "The Regional Boards were the coordinating linchpins in Environment Canada's early efforts to meet its holistic environmental mission in the regions" (Brown, 1986:8). Five Regional Boards representing the Atlantic, Quebec, Ontario, Prairie, and Pacific regions were created by Environment Canada. The Boards' membership consisted of the senior members of all the services and directorates operating in the region, which in some cases totalled 16 members. Basically, the Regional Boards were responsible for communications, coordination, and innovation. In terms of communications, the

Boards were to formulate quick regional responses to Ottawa's initiatives, provide information to the Department's Senior Management Committee, and act as the focal point in negotiations with outside agencies, particularly at the provincial level. The Boards' primary coordination functions centred on implementing the EARP in the regions, but also included other operational and research activities. The Regional Boards were also responsible for identifying opportunities for the development of integrated regional approaches to deal with environmental problems and issues. This task was based on the assumption that the development of integrated responses was beyond the scope of any single service. The Regional Boards' innovative activities extended also to personnel management, including recruitment, training, and retirement.

Although the Regional Boards were intended to provide a strong focus for the various departmental services operating in the regions, such as the coordination and administration of the EARP, the actual record of the Boards during the 1970s is one of unrelenting decline. The Boards simply lacked the authority to coordinate effectively because of their exclusion from the Department's Senior Management Committee. As such, on their annual treks to Ottawa, the Regional Board Chairmen were able only to present the regional viewpoint, which was easily discarded or ignored by the Senior Committee. In addition, within the regions, the large size of the Boards prevented them from becoming effective management structures. As a result, they became more forums for discussion and the exchange of information among the Board members than policy initiators. The decline of the Regional Boards also mirrored the fading political importance of Environment Canada in the latter part of the 1970s. Thus, as the environment declined in status in the government's priorities, it became increasingly difficult for the Boards to have an impact on the decision-making process in Ottawa. Once the shift from holistic environmental management to sectoral resource management occurred, the Regional Boards were unable to exert influence over the various resource sectors. In fact, by 1979, the Regional Boards were no longer capable of performing their responsibilities and were replaced by the Regional Directors General.

Phase IV — Canada's Second Environmental Decade and the Role of Environment Canada in the 1980s

In 1979, the federal government underwent another major reorganization which resulted in the creation of several new departments designed to meet the challenges of the 1980s. The former Department of Fisheries and the Environment was divided into two separate departments — the new Department of Fisheries and Oceans, and a revamped Department of the Environment. Because of this change, Environment Canada lost one of its largest services from its original structure — the Fisheries and Marine Service — although the Parks Canada Service was added to the Department. Thus, Environment Canada became the custodian of the nation's natural and historical heritage. Given the fiscal constraints of the time, the Department now had to develop new goals and objectives in order to accomplish "more with less."

One of the most significant features of the restructured Department was its new mandate which authorized the Minister to "foster harmony between society and the environment for the economic, social and cultural benefit of present and future generations of Canadians" (Brown, 1986:3). In contrast to the Department's original direction in 1971, which focused activities primarily on pollution in the context of renewable resources policy, the new mandate was significantly broader in scope, providing it with a more comprehensive outlook to deal with the full range of environmental problems and issues in Canada. In order to fulfil its mandate, the senior officials of Environment Canada formulated a new set of organizational goals to guide the development and implementation of environmental policies and programs. This process was interrupted by the brief Conservative interlude in Ottawa when Joe Clark came to power. However, following the resurgence of Pierre Trudeau and the Liberals, Environment Canada finally released the four principal objectives that were to guide departmental policy for the next decade:

1. To ensure that human activities are conducted in a way that will achieve and maintain a state of the environment necessary for the health and well-being of man, the health and diversity of species and of ecosystems, and the sustained use of natural resources for social and economic benefit.
2. To conserve and enhance Canada's renewable resources of water, land, forests and wildlife in their related ecosystems and promote their wise use in a sustainable manner for economic and social benefit.
3. To facilitate the adaptation of human activities to the environment.
4. To protect for all time those places which are significant examples of Canada's natural and cultural heritage. (Brown, 1986:3)

Environment Canada was restructured into six service components plus the Federal Environmental Assessment and Review Office. The six service components were the Atmospheric Environment Service, the Environmental Conservation and Protection Service (formerly the Environment Management Service), Communication Service (including scientific and legal advisors), Planning, Parks (the newest addition to the Department), and the Finance and Administration Service.

Whereas in the past Environment Canada had relied on regulatory and managerial approaches as its primary strategies for environmental policy development, the Department during its second decade began to downgrade the regulatory approach and to focus more on education and public information. The underlying assumption was that a better informed public, with a greater appreciation and awareness of environmental problems and issues, would be more effective than regulatory measures which dealt with problems after the fact. According to the then Minister of the Environment, John Roberts, the Department's new approach sought "to relate environmental considerations to social, economic and cultural development from the start. This strategy attempts to create harmony between society and its environment by preventing costly conflicts from developing in the first place" (Roberts, 1982).

As revealed in the Department's Strategic Plan of August, 1982, Environment Canada established some priority tasks to guide the activities of its program services. Eight issues dominated the list:

1. toxic substances
2. acid rain
3. forests
4. water management
5. environmental considerations in energy development
6. the North
7. maintenance of the land resource base
8. climate change. (EC, 1982)

The list of priorities would be revised in accordance with changing public and political priorities and in response to Environment Canada's effectiveness in resolving particular problems. In 1985, the Department published a document titled *Environmental Issues in Canada: A Status Report*, which provided a brief summary of Canada's priority environmental problems, recent information relating to research on the issues, and a brief description of some of the corrective measures which had been taken to deal with the situation. By this time, the eight priority areas had expanded to twelve with the addition of marine pollution, eutrophication, agricultural land loss, and wildlife conservation, and acid rain was now placed at the top of the list.

In the context of a broad social-purpose definition, Environment Canada was involved in the conservation, promotion, and development of physical resources. Although conservation was generally considered to be antagonistic to the objectives of promotion and development, by the end of the decade Environment Canada began to espouse the idea that these activities are in fact complementary. In its 1987-88 Annual Report, for example, the Department promoted the concept of sustainable development, which had emerged as a key recommendation of the World Commission on Environment and Development (see Chapter 9). Environment Canada supported the main recommendation of the Commission that "every nation must integrate environmental considerations into economic decisions, and growth must be achieved through sustainable development" (EC, 1989:1). Thus, in its 1989-1990 Expenditure Plan, the Department included a section outlining its intention to incorporate the concept of sustainable development into all its future programs and policies.

THE ROLE OF THE REGIONAL DIRECTORS GENERAL

Once again, it is necessary to interrupt the chronological narrative in order to discuss the impact of the regions. Throughout the 1980s, Environment Canada remained one of the most decentralized federal departments. As mentioned earlier, the position of Regional Director General (RDG) was established in each of the Department's five regions in April 1979, to replace the Regional Boards. The RDG concept was intended to improve the effectiveness of the Department's regional management structure and to provide a corporate presence for matters which extended beyond the scope of any one of its particular services. Regional Directors General were given four main areas of responsibility:

1. the general conduct of Environment Canada's relations with the provincial governments
2. the coordination of all departmental responsibilities in the region
3. the management of designated integrated programs
4. support services, including personnel, public information, capital acquisitions for operational laboratories, and aspects of finance and administration. (Brown, 1986:16)

In effect, the Directors were intended to be the Department's principal representatives and spokespersons in the regions. They were to be the Department's senior contacts with provincial governments, other federal departments, and non-governmental organizations. Internally, the Directors were expected to perform a major role in planning, coordinating, and evaluating regional priorities and programs. In order to overcome the problems which brought about the demise of the Regional Boards, the Directors were to report directly to the Deputy Minister, to be included in the Department's Senior Management Committee, and to be given control of the Land Directorates in their regions with an operational budget of $2.5-million.

Despite the augmented status and authority of the Regional Directors General, they too fell victim to many of the same problems which had plagued the Regional Boards. They were subjected to similar organizational and managerial pressures which had limited the effectiveness and initiatives of the Regional Boards. Following some early successes, the Directors encountered hostility from provincial governments who were averse to any formal planning functions by the federal government that touched on their areas of jurisdiction. In addition, the Directors met with great difficulty in coordinating regional programs. When the federal government adopted the Policy and Expenditure Management System (PEMS) in 1980, it led to a more stringent top-down managerial approach. Thus, the Directors were able to effect only rudimentary control over program management and coordination in their regions. As well, by the end of the decade, the Regional Directors General had lost control of the Land Directorates, and they were excluded from the Executive Committee which had replaced the Department's Senior Management Committee. In sum, the experiment cannot be considered a success.

THE CANADIAN ENVIRONMENTAL PROTECTION ACT (CEPA)

It is also necessary at this point to draw attention to an important legislative initiative concerning the environment which occurred late in the decade. In May 1988, the House of Commons passed the Canadian Environmental Protection Act (CEPA), which gave the federal government the power to protect human health and the environment from the risks associated with the use of toxic substances. The legislation adopted a comprehensive regulatory approach to controlling toxic contamination of the air, waterways, oceans, and soils and empowered the government to take action against polluters and polluting activities.

The Act also created a list of priority substances to be assessed for their health and environmental impacts. These assessments would identify the need for regulatory controls. These sections authorized the development of regulations, in particular with regard to waste handling and disposal practices, and effluents and emissions. Activities such as the handling and disposal of wastes were also regulated under CEPA (EC, 1988). Existing regulations aimed at protecting various sectors of the environment were subsumed under regulations of the Canadian Environmental Protection Act.

In addition, Environment Canada developed an Enforcement and Compliance Policy that spelled out responses to violations of the Act. In cases of non-compliance, resulting action could take the form of massive fines of up to $1-million per day, as well as jail sentences for industry and government officials who permitted or allowed pollution contrary to the regulations. In this way, CEPA re-emphasized the Department's focus on the prevention of environmental degradation. However, as so often has happened with environmental initiatives in Canada, CEPA did not live up to its promise. Very few prosecutions for violations of CEPA regulations took place during the following decade and, in fact, the Act would undergo substantial revisions in 1999 (see Chapters 6 and 7).

Phase V — Towards Sustainable Development — 1990-2000

The publication of *Our Common Future* by the Brundtland Commission in 1987 had a major impact on Environment Canada, leading to what might be called the fifth phase in its evolution. The changes were neither sudden nor dramatic since, as will be shown in Chapter 9, the concept of sustainable development had been the subject of much discussion in the Department for several years. Nevertheless, the Report reinforced a process which had been ongoing for some time and which led eventually to significant changes in the Department's emphasis, objectives, and procedures. Perhaps the most obvious results of the process were the Round Tables on the Environment and the Economy, Canada's Green Plan, and the Environmental Assessment Act.

The National Round Table was created in 1988 with a sweeping mandate to:

» evaluate the environmental implications of government policies and measures, such as fiscal policy, taxation, royalties, subsidies, and regulations
» evaluate decision-making processes in the public and private sectors and report on how they might be changed to better reflect the principles of sustainable development
» investigate sustainable development practices in waste management
» look at how external trade, foreign policy, international agreements, and aid can be used to encourage and support sustainable development internationally
» develop means to communicate the principles of sustainable development to the public to encourage the development of more environmentally responsible values and actions. (Government of Canada [GC], 1991)

The National Round Table is composed of representatives from both the public and private sectors, which includes business, non-governmental organizations, academics, and private citizens. Round Tables have now been established in all provinces and territories and in some municipalities. All provide their respective governments and the public in general with considered advice about how best to ensure that economic development is indeed sustainable environmentally. As such, they have the potential to be valuable additions to the environmental decision-making process in Canada, although their performance to date has varied greatly.

The Green Plan, introduced by the Mulroney government late in 1990, built on the work of the National Task Force on Environment and Economy established in 1986 to recommend steps to move Canada toward sustainable development. It also reflected the views of several thousand Canadian citizens and groups who, in the spring and summer months of 1990, responded to the government's call for guidance in this area. The plan which resulted from this consultative process had as its major goal "to secure for current and future generations a safe and healthy environment and a sound and prosperous economy" (GC, 1990b:9). To achieve this objective, the Plan set out the following "priority-areas":

1. clean air, water, and land
2. sustainable use of renewable resources
3. protection of our special spaces and species
4. preservation of the integrity of our North
5. global environmental security
6. environmentally responsible decision-making at all levels of society
7. minimizing the impacts of environmental emergencies.

Over and above this, the Plan established targets, many of which included specific timeframes, within which these objectives would be reached. By way of example, the Plan committed the government to the virtual "elimination of the discharge of persistent toxic substances into the environment"; "shifting of forest management from sustained yield to sustainable development"; completion of the national parks system by the year 2000; "preservation and enhancement of the integrity, health, biodiversity and productivity of Canada's Arctic ecosystems"; "stabilization of carbon dioxide and other greenhouse gas emissions at 1990 levels by the year 2000"; and "provision of timely, accurate and accessible information to enable Canadians to make environmentally sensitive decisions" (GC, 1990b:13-14). In addition, the government pledged to spend $3-billion over the ensuing five years to meet the Plan's targets and also to publish "state of the environment" reports regularly so that Canadians would be able to evaluate the progress that had been made. Other noteworthy initiatives outlined in the Green Plan included the Code of Environmental Stewardship (eventually implemented in June 1992), which committed the government to act "in an environmentally responsible manner by integrating environmental considerations into all aspects of its operations" (GC, 1990b:160); the Office of Environmental Stewardship, which was created within Environment Canada to facilitate the implementation of the Code; expansion of the Environmental Choice Program (begun in 1988) to encourage both producers and consumers to consider sustainable development in the manufacture and purchase of goods; and the establishment of a new Cabinet Committee on the Environment with the responsibility "to manage the Government's environmental agenda and ensure that policies, programs and other initiatives requiring federal support are fully compatible with the Government's environmental goals" (GC, 1990b:160). As well, the Minister of the Environment would continue to be a member of the key Cabinet Committee on Priorities and Planning. Finally, the Green Plan noted that the government had introduced the Canadian Environmental Assessment Act (CEAA) earlier in 1990, which was intended to "entrench in law the federal government's obligation to integrate environmental considerations into its project planning and implementation processes" (GC, 1990b:19). (The CEAA will be discussed in more detail in Chapter 7.)

The Round Tables, the Green Plan, and the Environmental Assessment Act marked the transition between Phase IV and Phase V of Environment Canada's evolution. The link between the environment and the economy became paramount in the Department's thinking and "sustainable development" became the driving force behind most of the Department's multifarious activities. Sustainable development provided Environment Canada with a new sense of direction, and the Department's specific objectives and procedures changed to meet this challenge. The long-time goals of environmental protection, conservation, and rehabilitation remained, but they were no longer regarded as ends in themselves. Rather, they were now viewed as means toward the greater goal of sustainable development. Furthermore, as laid down in the Green Plan, additional objectives were added to Environment Canada's list of priorities, including global environmental security and environmentally responsible decision-making. In the past, the Department had tended to rely for advice on its own experts and those in business and the universities. In the future, according to the Green Plan, "effective public participation [is needed] to help integrate environmental considerations into decision-making processes within government and industry. Decision-makers recognize that we can no longer rely solely on experts for the solutions to environmental problems. Instead, we need input from a wider cross-section of the population ... public consultation providing that input is therefore an essential part of the environmental policy-making process. ... the Round Tables and the opportunities open to citizen intervention included in the Environmental Assessment Act are intended to foster this process" (GC, 1990a:18).

It must be repeated that Phase V of Environment Canada's evolution did not begin overnight. Rather, it was the product of many years of development. Nevertheless, Environment Canada embarked on the 1990s with a focus for its activities never before seen in its history. Its mission throughout the decade was to "make sustainable development a reality in Canada by helping Canadians live and prosper in an environment that needs to be protected, respected and conserved" (EC, 1990; 1995; 1998), and much of value has been accomplished under its auspices. For example, all departments and agencies of the federal government are now required to produce plans for their implementation of sustainable development and to report yearly on their progress toward that end. In addition, the position of Commissioner of Sustainable Development was created in 1995 to assess the federal government's efforts to achieve sustainable development,[2] and, in 1999, the Chrétien government amended the Canadian Environmental Protection Act to give it greater power to protect human health and the environment. Under the terms of the Act, new measures will be implemented to assess and control toxic substances and Environment Canada will have new powers to prosecute polluters (for further details see Chapter 6). Furthermore, the Department's priorities continue to sharpen with the shift of Parks Canada to the new Department of Canadian Heritage, and the new House of Commons Standing Committee on the Environment and Sustainable Development has demonstrated surprising independence in its criticisms of government action and/or inaction. Finally, the need to respond to international initiatives over issues such as climate change has enhanced the status of Environment Canada in the Ottawa hierarchy, as it has come to be realized that it is the only department whose principal responsibility is to find "better ways of integrating economic, social and environmental goals within the framework of sustainable development" (GC, 1998b).

Nevertheless, Environment Canada's acceptance of the concept of sustainable development did not mean that the Department suddenly possessed all the means necessary to fulfil its mandate. In fact, and as always, it remained subject to the priorities of its political masters, and the records of both the Mulroney and Chrétien governments show a remarkable inconsistency in the realm of environmental policy and practice. Indeed, every step forward seems to have been followed by a step backward. In the first place, the Green Plan, which had created such high hopes, could not withstand the pressures of Ministers of Finance determined to reduce budget deficits. Between its high point in the budgetary year 1992-93 and its low point in 1998-99, the budget of Environment Canada declined by more than 70 per cent. While much of this decrease can be attributed to the transfer of Parks Canada to the Department of Canadian Heritage, it is still a fact that the monies granted to the Department to fulfil its mission declined by approximately 30 per cent during the 1990s with a predictable impact on its ability to perform its many tasks. The Mulroney Cabinet spent less than 30 per cent of the funds allocated to the Plan's various programs, and the Plan itself was quickly shelved by the Chrétien Liberals after they came to power in 1993. In addition, the Liberals decided to de-emphasize the regulatory approach to pollution prevention, which further undercut the philosophy behind the Canadian Environmental Protection Act. Even Liberal back-benchers attacked the 1999 amendments to the Act as a sell-out to the petroleum, chemical, and pulp and paper companies which would delay the phasing out of dangerous products that endanger the health of Canadians, and environmentalists dismissed the proposed Species at Risk Act as offering only limited protection for endangered plants and animals.

It also seems clear that lack of government action will force Canada to renege on its commitment to reduce greenhouse gas emissions under the Kyoto Protocol, and the list of such failures could continue indefinitely. In fact, ever since its creation, Environment Canada has suffered from a lack of political will and public support that might have enabled it to meet its responsibilities in full. The institutional structures and motivating principles to do so, for the most part, are in place. What is needed now is the determination to proceed. Past experience indicates that this may well be lacking, especially at the Cabinet level, although, in fairness, it must be admitted that the federal government's ability to act on environmental issues is limited somewhat by the constitutional requirement to share responsibility with the provinces as well as the national government's willingness during the past decade to leave the enforcement of environmental policies to the provinces (see, especially, Harrison, 1996).

FEDERAL-PROVINCIAL ENVIRONMENTAL RELATIONS

In 1867, when the original division of powers occurred in the new federation, there was no mention made of the "environment" in the British North America Act. Consequently, over the years, both federal and provincial governments have acquired the authority to respond to what we now call "environmental" issues. As mentioned earlier in this chapter, the federal power is limited by the Constitution to a few specific areas, although it can on rare occasions fall back on its general right to make laws for the "peace, order, and good government" of Canada. The provinces, however, received several specific grants of power in areas which relate directly to the environment. In fact, it is correct to claim that today they bear principal responsibility for domestic environmental matters within their borders. For example, Section 92: sub-sections 5, 13, and 16 give the provinces jurisdiction over the management and sale of public lands belonging to the province and the timber and wood on these lands, property and civil rights in the province, and all matters of a merely local or private nature in the province. Section 106 gives them control of natural resources, a power confirmed and expanded in the Canada Act of 1982. In addition, the provinces were given the right to establish and control municipal institutions in Section 92:8, which gives them the power to intervene in all environmental issues faced by local governments within their borders. Although the federal government was the first to create a department of the environment in 1971, all provincial governments followed its lead over the next few years, either creating their own new or transforming existing agencies into environment ministries.

This division of powers between the federal and provincial governments has resulted in a variety of political and jurisdictional problems in the environmental area. In many instances, for example, problems such as air and water pollution do not fall within the exclusive jurisdiction of either level of government, and there have been difficulties determining which level has the power to deal with them. As a result, the environment has given rise to several significant political and administrative challenges for Canada in terms of designing and implementing effective policies and programs: "The general rule is that where overlapping jurisdictions exist, both levels of government are free to deal with the matter" (Estrin and Swaigen, 1978:14). However, in cases when federal and provincial laws conflict, federal law has priority. Since most environmental problems in Canada involve both levels of government, a good deal of effort has been spent trying to avoid such conflicts. In fact, federal-provincial coordination has become a vital and necessary part of the governmental response to environmental problems and, for the most part, there has been a high degree of cooperation between Ottawa and the provinces in devising solutions to these problems. The basic premise underlying the formulation of intergovernmental environmental policies and programs is that most environmental problems extend beyond territorial borders, and hence, the management and protection of the environment must involve a cooperative and coordinated effort between the federal and provincial governments in order to achieve environmental objectives. In most policy fields, federal-provincial relations have been fraught with political tensions, but the environment has been a fortunate —

if partial — exception: there has been a much greater tendency for the federal and provincial governments to cooperate and work together. Evidence of this can be found in the proliferation of joint federal-provincial environmental policies and programs over the years. The remainder of this chapter examines some of the problems encountered and the various intergovernmental environmental coordinating mechanisms as well as the several types of environmental policies and programs which have been implemented during the past three decades.

Intergovernmental Coordinating Mechanisms: The Role of the Canadian Council of Ministers of the Environment

The actual history of joint federal-provincial environmental programs begins with arrangements with certain provinces in the forestry and fisheries sectors. Over the course of the first half of the twentieth century, similar types of federal-provincial arrangements related primarily to resource development continued to be made on an ad hoc basis. However, at the beginning of the 1960s both levels of government began to establish more formal mechanisms to coordinate their activities in resource and environmental management. Perhaps the most important of all intergovernmental coordinating mechanisms has been the Canadian Council of Resource and Environmental Ministers (CCREM).

The CCREM was born out of the "Resources for Tomorrow Conference" held in Montreal in 1961. The Council was established as a result of recommendations from the conference to act as a forum for federal-provincial exchange of information relevant to the field of renewable resources. The CCREM was officially incorporated as a permanent advisory body in 1964, and was served by an on-going secretariat composed of personnel who were members of neither the federal nor the provincial civil services. The CCREM was made up of eleven ministers from the resource or environmental sectors of their respective governments. All members of the Council were equal in status and the presidency rotated annually. The CCREM generally met once a year; however, the Council's activities were maintained on a continuing basis of interaction by a coordinating committee consisting of eleven senior bureaucrats, usually deputy ministers, who oversaw the Council's programs. In 1988, the Council's name was changed to the Canadian Council of Ministers of the Environment (CCME) to better reflect its principal concerns. Today the Council includes representatives from Yukon, Nunavut, and the Northwest Territories.

Most of the Council's principal activities are performed by a variety of committees, composed of experts in particular fields and provided administrative assistance by the Council's secretariat. The committees are involved in a wide range of projects such as studies concerning environmental problems of relevance to all governments. As well, the various committees act as intergovernmental advisory bodies and as steering committees for conferences and seminars. In essence the committees are a clearing house for information from all member governments of the Council. Another important aspect of the Council's activities is its involvement in active programs to promote greater public awareness of environmental problems through the provision of information to interested citizens or groups. In sum, the Council provides for a relatively flexible institutional framework for the continuous exchange of information and views among governments.

Following its creation in 1964, one of the first activities undertaken by the CCREM was the compilation of a list of federal-provincial and interprovincial environmental programs. On March 31, 1964, the CCREM published "An Inventory of Joint Programs and Agreements Affecting Canada's Renewable Resources" which listed 64 federal-provincial and 5 interprovincial programs. The various programs dealt with basic resources such as air, land, water, and wildlife or with the use of these resources for recreation, agriculture, fisheries, and forestry. The programs involved a variety of arrangements between the federal government and the provinces ranging from conditional grants to shared-cost programs. The majority of these programs were bilateral agreements between the federal and individual provincial governments. The federal government's role in these agreements emanated from four basic programs which were established at different intervals from the end of World War II to the first years of the 1960s. The federal programs were statutory programs established primarily under the Maritime Marshland Rehabilitation Act, the Prairie Farm Rehabilitation Act, and the Agricultural Rehabilitation and Development Act.

During the latter part of the 1960s, the CCREM began to focus its activities on generating information about specific resource and environmental problems. The Council began to play an important role in investigating the increasingly serious pollution problems affecting the nation. In 1966, the CCREM was instrumental in organizing the "Pollution and Our Environment" Conference referred to earlier in this chapter. The Conference provided a national forum for all interested groups and organizations to present their views and concerns about rising pollution problems and how they might be treated. The Conference was of major significance because of the information it generated and because it enabled the federal and provincial governments to exchange information and interact with a wide variety of concerned individuals and organizations. Following the

Pollution and Our Environment Conference, the Council's activities were oriented to developing an enhanced data bank of the nation's natural resources. Publications such as *The Administration of Water Resources in Canada* and the *Administration of Outdoor Recreation in Canada* in 1968, and the *Forestry Reader* in 1970, provided the federal and provincial governments with some of the most comprehensive lists of the nation's natural resources.

In September 1971, as public pressure on both levels of government to respond to pollution problems became stronger, the Council was reorganized with an expanded mandate to meet the greater needs of the ministers through the exchange of information and viewpoints. Since 1971, the CCREM has been a significant influence on the design and implementation of environmental policy-making. Federal and provincial governments have incorporated much of the expert work and information produced by the Council's various committees in the formulation of their policies. For example, the CCREM had a significant impact on the formulation of a national forestry policy in 1979. The Council's proposed *National Forestry Policy* formed the basis for negotiations between the federal and provincial governments on the substantive aspects of this vital policy field for Canada. In the 1980s, the CCREM continued its active role by releasing a number of reports, including *Proceedings of a Seminar on Herbicides and Forest Renewal* held in 1984. In 1985, the CCREM released two reports, *Canadian Water Quality Issues* and an *Inventory of Water Quality Guidelines and Objectives*. In 1986, the CCREM published *Controlling PCBs — the Nature of the Problem*.

The Canadian Council of Resource and Environment Ministers also established the National Task Force on Environment and Economy in October 1986 to promote dialogue on environment-economy integration. The Task Force drew upon the experience and expertise of a wide variety of people: Canada's environment ministers, business leaders, representatives from the environmental organizations, and the academic community. This Canadian initiative was linked to others at the international level. The World Commission on Environment and Development, headed by Norwegian Prime Minister Gro Harlem Brundtland, was constituted in 1984 under United Nations sponsorship. The World Commission visited Canada in 1986 and met with CCREM ministers. The World Commission Report (the Brundtland Report), completed in April 1987, was debated in the United Nations General Assembly in October 1987. It advocated major institutional reforms to promote sustainable development in both developed and developing countries.

The (Canadian) National Task Force on Environment and Economy presented its report to the CCREM in September of 1987. The report's main objective was to promote environmentally sound economic growth through private- and public-sector cooperation. The report pointed out that conservation and economic development are invariably linked and should not be pursued in isolation. The Task Force stressed the importance of sustainable economic development and agreed on measures to achieve this. The report recommended a number of measures to ensure informed decision-making; a stronger demonstration of leadership by governments and business leaders; continued Canadian leadership in the international arena; the development of conservation strategies at the national, provincial, and territorial levels; and a major communications and public participation program on environment and economy. In September 1987, Environment Ministers agreed to develop action plans to implement the recommendations falling under their areas of responsibility (CCREM, 1990:46).

In October 1988, the Task Force prepared a progress report on the implementation of the recommendations of the Task Force on Environment and Economy. Three key areas were examined: the creation of multisectoral Round Tables on Environment and Economy, the preparation of government Action Plans, and the development of Conservation Strategies. The members of the Task Force stated that, although progress was being made in different ways in different provinces and territories across the country, it was still slower than necessary. To maintain the momentum toward achieving sustainable development, the federal government published its *Green Plan* in 1990 in which it committed itself to "a cooperative approach to national environmental action" (GC, 1990b:22).

As stated earlier, the Council underwent a name change in 1988, becoming the Canadian Council of Ministers of the Environment (CCREM). In recognition of the need for more effective and efficient cooperation between the levels of government, the Council adopted a "Statement on Interjurisdictional Co-operation on Environmental Matters" which committed the governments to work together to:

1. harmonize environmental legislation, policies, and programs across jurisdictions
2. develop national environmental objectives and standards in order to ensure that a consistent level of environmental quality is maintained across the country
3. ensure that consistent strategies are developed to address emerging environmental issues of national, international, and global importance
4. improve the linkages between domestic and international policies and programs on environmental matters, and
5. harmonize environmental assessment and review procedures. (GC, 1990b:132)

During the following decade, the Council developed a classification scheme for contaminated sites, a policy on toxic substances management, a phase-out plan for PCBs and CFCs, and guidelines with respect to water quality and the efficient use of municipal water supplies. It has completed a study on packaging, developed a pollution prevention strategy, and helped prepare Canada's position for the United Nations Conference on Environment and Development. It also played an instrumental role in the negotiations which led to the signing in January 1998 of the Canada-wide Accord on Harmonization by the federal and all provincial governments in the country except Quebec. Under the terms of the Accord, each level of government will retain its existing constitutional powers, but all agree to coordinate their activities and publicize their work in their defined areas of responsibility. Sub-agreements were also signed at that time which dealt with environmental assessments, inspections, and the development of national standards in the areas of air, water, and soil quality. The ministers also approved a work-plan to create national standards on particulate matter, ground-level ozone, benzene, mercury, dioxins, and furons, and ordered the preparation of other sub-agreements under the Accord on enforcement monitoring and reporting, research and development, and environmental emergencies. The Accord will be reviewed periodically to ensure it is achieving its intended goals.

When it was announced, the Harmonization Accord received a mixed reception. Many applauded it as an example of the type of cooperation necessary in a federal state such as Canada. Others, however, were not so laudatory. For example, the Environmental Harmonization Working Group of the Canadian Environmental Network, representing more than 50 health, labour, aboriginal, and environmental organizations, opposed the Accord on the grounds that it would hand over to the provinces federal responsibilities in key areas such as the setting of national standards, environmental assessment, and enforcement. The House of Commons Standing Committee on the Environment and Sustainable Development, after public hearings, recommended that the minister defer the agreement, and the Environment Commissioner at the time concluded that:

> there are weaknesses in the design. There [are] no audit provisions to verify information, no accounting of federal funds transferred, no requirements to report on evaluation results, and limited guidelines for annual reporting. [Furthermore] The Federal-Provincial Committees designed to manage the agreements were never established ... (Emmett, 1999)

Thus, given the determination of most provinces to guard their jurisdictions jealously, it seems that the Canadian Council of Ministers of the Environment will not have an easy task ensuring that national standards to protect the environment are put in place and upheld. The apparent tendency of the Chrétien government to vacate the environmental field as much as possible will make the task even more difficult.

Federal-Provincial Ministerial Conferences and Consultative Committees

Another important mechanism for the formulation and coordination of federal-provincial environmental policies and programs has been the federal-provincial ministerial conference. Since 1971, the ministerial level conference has become the most publicized forum for interaction between the two levels of government on environmental matters. As might be expected, however, these conferences have tended to be political showcases rather than effective policy-making meetings. In 1971, the first federal-provincial environmental ministerial conference was held to present and familiarize provincial ministers with the federal government's new Department of the Environment and its various environmental policies and programs. From 1971 to 1975, annual ministerial conferences were held at which the ministers discussed a variety of matters, from setting national effluent standards to improving financial formulae for pollution abatement. By the middle of the decade, the ministerial conference began to lose its pre-eminent status, and the CCREM (later the CCME) emerged as the most important mechanism for federal-provincial interaction and coordination on environmental matters.

While the ministerial conferences have dominated the public limelight, much of the actual work in terms of designing and coordinating federal-provincial environmental programs has been performed by a variety of consultative committees. At the management level, committees of senior bureaucrats, primarily of deputy ministerial status, act as administrative liaisons to the ministers and oversee the implementation of joint programs. The senior bureaucratic committees tend to be more concerned with efficiency and effectiveness than with the establishment of policy priorities and consequently are oriented toward organizational functions such as finding solutions to common problems. At the technical and operational level, there are a host of specialized committees. These committees are made up of experts drawn from the federal and provincial public service who are less concerned with jurisdictional and political issues. The various committee members share a common technical and professional commitment to protect and maintain the quality of the natural environment. For this reason, the consultative committee system has become the backbone of federal-provincial relations on environmental matters.

In the early 1970s, when the federal government began to withdraw from its view of concurrent responsibility in favour of letting the provinces assume a larger share of the responsibility for environmental and resource management, a series of "Master Accords" were signed between the federal and provincial governments. The many consultative committees were instrumental in negotiating the specific details of the Master Accords. Essentially, the Master Accords were bilateral agreements between the federal government and individual provinces which outlined the guidelines to be followed in federal-provincial relations pertaining to the environment. The Master Accords delineated the respective roles and responsibilities of the two levels of government. They also established specific environmental quality objectives and standards, and provided for the necessary financial arrangements and timetables, but left the actual implementation largely to the provincial governments. Thus, the Master Accords were of paramount importance in creating a cooperative working relationship between the federal and provincial governments in environmental matters when most other areas of federal-provincial relations were troubled by political tension and disagreement. Following the signing of these agreements, there was a proliferation of joint federal-provincial programs. The Harmonization Accord discussed in the previous section may be considered one of these Master Accords.

Federal-Provincial Environmental Programs — 1975-2000

During this period, numerous joint programs and projects between the federal and provincial governments were implemented to address a wide variety of environmental problems and issues in Canada. The ever-increasing number of these intergovernmental programs reflected the continuing need for close cooperation and coordination of federal-provincial environmental activities in order to be effective in dealing with the problems. The joint programs vary in size and scope, ranging from short-term study and research projects to long-term conservation and management programs involving millions of dollars and thousands of hours of labour. They cover the entire environmental spectrum, from land, air, and water to wildlife, recreation, fisheries, and forestry. Over the years, certain noticeable trends have emerged in the design and implementation of this type of intergovernmental program. First, between 1975 and 1980, there was a major emphasis on water management; however, since 1980, this focus has diminished in favour of more programs related to land-use management, wildlife, and air pollution, especially acid rain. Second, there has been a trend for the federal government to play the role of financier and supplier of equipment, information, and technical expertise, whereas the role of the provincial governments has been program implementation. Third, there has been a noticeable increase in the number of joint environmental programs over the period.

The negotiation and coordination of the federal government's role in intergovernmental environmental programs and projects are the responsibility of Environment Canada. Within the Department, the various services, such as the Atmospheric Environment Service and the Environmental Management Service, among others, are responsible for the design and implementation of specific intergovernmental programs and projects in their area. In fact, each service is and has been involved in several joint efforts with its counterparts in the provinces and with the implementation of specific intergovernmental programs and projects in its area. By way of example, one can point to the National Air Pollution Surveillance Network of the 1970s in response to the problems of acid rain, the 1988 Canada-Quebec Convention designed to address the major environmental problems of the St. Lawrence River Basin, and the 1994 Canada-Ontario Agreement on the Great Lakes Basin. Under the terms of this agreement, both levels of government agreed to a strategy to eliminate persistent toxins, upgrade sewage treatment plants, improve storm water quality, audit commercial pesticides, rehabilitate several species, and conserve and protect human and ecosystem health. At present, more than 100 major federal-provincial environmental programs and agreements are in effect and the number continues to grow. The proliferation of joint environmental programs illustrates the necessity of cooperative interaction and coordination of activities in order for the governmental response to be effective in dealing with these problems. There is still a considerable amount of effort needed by both levels of government before we can feel assured of the long-term safety and protection of the environment in Canada. The current level of federal-provincial environmental relations seems to be progressing in that direction, albeit slowly, given the cutbacks in environmental expenditures at both levels in recent years and the general attitude that governments should do less rather than more, even in such an important area.

CONCLUSION

Beyond a brief outline of the Canadian political system (a vital part of the policy context under discussion in the rest of this book), this chapter has illustrated how environmental thinking within Environment Canada has evolved from its initial concern with pollution control and abatement to its current approach of fostering harmony between people and the environment and the concept of sustainable development. It is clear that Canada's future, in terms of economic, social, and cultural growth, is dependent on maintaining and preserving a high level of environmental quality. As the nature of Canada's most urgent environmental problems changes over time, we must continue to look to Environment Canada and its evolving mission to maintain and protect the environment for our use and enjoyment.

At the same time, it must be recognized that solutions to Canada's major environmental problems require the action of both federal and provincial levels of government, and that fragmentation and ambiguity of jurisdictional responsibility hinder the development of effective responses to these problems. Sections of the Canada Act give conflicting signals concerning the proper role of different governments in environmental management.

Furthermore, it is essential to understand that provincial needs and aspirations vary. Provincial goals may conflict with national objectives, and acceptance of this fact should caution against attempts to fashion "blanket" solutions for the entire country. Nevertheless, we must acknowledge that only the federal government can set minimum standards to ensure that no province becomes a haven for polluting industries. Hence the need for federal-provincial cooperation and the attention paid over the years to designing structures and procedures to foster this cooperation. Although problems continue to exist (many caused by the recent focus on deficit reduction), a strong foundation has been laid on which to build future cooperation between the federal and provincial governments. It is up to the environmental community to do what it can to ensure that cooperation for environmental purposes remains high on the priority list of all governments in Canada. Our next chapter explores in more detail the various actors, or stakeholders, within that community.

NOTES

1   For a more complete description of the Canadian political system, see R. Jackson and D. Jackson, *Politics in Canada* (Scarborough: Prentice Hall, 1990).

2   The Commissioner is part of the office of the Auditor-General of Canada and thus shares the independence and powers of that office.

FOUR
ACTORS: FROM PARTIES TO PROTESTORS

INTRODUCTION: ACTORS IN POLITICS

The previous chapter introduced the structures involved in environmental policy-making, and detailed the evolution of Environment Canada as the principal national governmental organization. This chapter will focus more explicitly on the many other actors, often referred to as "agents," involved in environmental policy decision-making, including the state, political parties, non-state actors, and the media. However, given the large number of individuals involved in environmental policy formation, implementation, and debate, we have limited the discussion to the principal collective agents; in other words, we deal here with groups of people who converge in their political activity out of concern for the environment. There can be no doubt that certain individuals, such as Maurice Strong, Canada's head delegate to the United Nations Conference on Environment and Development in 1992, or the various environment ministers and Prime Ministers throughout the preceding three decades, have had an inordinate influence on agenda-setting and decision-making. We will return briefly to this theme later. Ideally, however, the political process in a liberal democracy is based on interaction between and among various groups struggling to have their own agenda and interests represented by government officials, and (again ideally), to have their interests enshrined in actual legislation, so we must examine the groups involved.

After a preliminary discussion of the state itself, we move to a brief examination of what some consider the heart of liberal democracy, the political parties on the Canadian scene. With one notable exception, the environment has not been the central issue-area for the political parties of Canada. However, over time, each has had to respond to the public's oscillating interest and concern with related issues, and political parties remain the main means of organizing and articulating formal political activity.

Other agents play vital roles as well, including First Nations representatives, lobby and interest groups, non-governmental organizations, and the media. Although some authors, such as Donald Wells, refer to scientists as important actors in their own right, we refrain from doing so, not only because the importance of environmental science is self-evident, but because scientists work for and with all of the organizations named below, including academic institutions (see Wells, 1996:40-42).

The State

Before we examine specific groups, a few words are needed on what is arguably the most important actor of all, the state itself. Although we stress the role of individual responsibility and that of civil society throughout this text (and especially in Chapter 11), it may be argued that the various levels of government outlined in the preceding chapter — federal, provincial, and municipal — are the main players in environmental protection, since only government can enforce effective laws and codes of conduct. Ultimately, it is the government that makes policy, and government officials enforce that policy with fines, public criticism, or even jail sentences. Government does all this, however, within a framework for discussion that generally favours continuity over change, one in which large industries are given more than their fair share of input, but public discussion also plays a formative, if not defining, role. In addition, if it does not maintain the support of various constituencies — voters, campaign contributors, bureaucrats, and others — the government of the day will lose legitimacy and be replaced. The state, however, usually survives the vicissitudes of political struggles.

Every political scientist probably has a unique conception of what, exactly, the state is, and what it does. Marxists argue that the state represents the interests of a ruling elite, and government is simply an instrument for maintaining the present socio-economic status quo. This is but a rough caricature of Marxism, which often takes into account the "relative autonomy" of the state, and the role of social institutions in forging the acceptance of a hegemonic elite. In other words, the state has interests of its own, over and above those of both society and the groups within it, and the rulers of the state have a special responsibility to ensure that these "state" interests prevail over all others within its borders. The institutions that form what Marxists term the "superstructure" of society — law, education, religion, and others — socialize the population to accept this hierarchy.

Others believe the state is the place where various social agents, including interest groups and lobbyists, can argue for their own representative interests, and the government policy which emerges is based on some sort of pluralist accommodation, or even compromise, among these interests. This is the standard liberal democratic interpretation of the state which suggests the state can maintain its legitimacy by allowing citizens a direct say in the process of governance, usually through voting rights. Others argue that states should play a major role in the economy, redistributing the wealth of the land to lessen social inequity. Still others argue that the state should play a minimal role, with little interference in matters of the economy, providing only the basics for a functioning capitalist society, such as the protection of private property, education, and national defence.

All these interpretations of what the state does and should do have validity, and it is not our task to define the "right" version here. This task is best left to the reader. We will see, however, that environmental protection policy is often determined by the government's willingness to force change upon actors who would, all else being equal, prefer continuity. The difficulty of implementing forceful environmental policy becomes evident when we look at the array of forces aligned against it. Although many citizens and interest groups, particularly non-governmental organizations, have been active in pushing for enhanced environmental protection measures, Canadian federal and provincial governments have generally been more concerned about other issues, such as job creation, unemployment, and health care; large industries hold considerable sway in Ottawa and the provincial capitals; and that the relevant administrative mechanisms, such as the Department of Environment Canada, are not viewed as exceptionally important branches of government. Furthermore, as environmental issues appear increasingly before the courts for settlement, many essential decisions will be based on court orders that are, in theory, beyond immediate political influence.

Another important factor we must keep in mind in any discussion of the contemporary state is the close linkage between the state and the outside world. It is difficult today to distinguish clearly between domestic and foreign policy. While the principle of sovereignty (the legal right of a government to make decisions within its own borders) remains paramount in the United Nations and other international institutions, governments must cope with the ups and downs of the world economy as well as political problems that emerge in other areas. Environmental protection is especially relevant here, since it is impossible to protect the environment on a purely national level. In Canada's case, officials must cope with the environmental policies of the largest industrial state on earth, the United States, which borders Canada on the south and, with Alaska, on the north as well. Furthermore, the long-term implications of problems such as global warming and ozone-layer depletion demand a global approach, involving states in Europe, Asia, Africa, and Latin America. There is no way to avoid the global nature of environmental problems today, and we must keep in mind the wide array of actors, state and non-state in orientation, that exist outside of Canada, yet maintain an influence within it.

At present, however, we are concerned principally with Canadian stakeholders. As the term implies, these are people who form groups with a "stake" in the process of policy formation. They may play a direct role, as politicians running for office and belonging to political parties, or they may be active in a more specific context, such as members of conservation groups protesting the destruction of old-growth forests in British Columbia. Kathryn Harrison and George Hoberg, among others, refer to the latter as "policy entrepreneurs," found in government agencies or interest groups (1991:24). They may be representatives of industries, extractive and manufacturing, that rely to varying extents on the exploitation of natural resources. They may be native Canadians dependent on hunting or fishing for subsistence. In all cases they meet on the stage of ecopolitics, but the level of their personal stake varies with their position in society.

This chapter aims to introduce the reader to four categories of stakeholders in the environmental policy debate. While it is clear that we are being arbitrary in selecting these four groups, we stress also the importance of a broader understanding of the stakeholder process. Individuals and informal groups are stakeholders too. In fact, one could argue that Canadian citizens in general qualify as the main actors, and, since Canada's actions have a global impact on some issue-areas (such as global warming), even non-Canadians have a stake in Canadian environmental policy. However, we focus on what are arguably the four most visible groups in the Canadian context: political parties, First Nations, industrial lobby groups, and non-governmental organizations or environmental interest groups, and end with a brief discussion of a common link, the national media. Since we have discussed bureaucracy in the preceding chapter, we do not include the various departments involved as stakeholder groups here, but they do have a career-oriented stake and great influence at the higher levels of hierarchy as well.

It is true that political parties have much broader concerns than "the environment" as it is traditionally understood. However, since environmental policy cannot be ignored by any major political party contending for power, and since if they do obtain power they are immediately immersed in the complexities of related decision-making, they qualify as relevant actors. Similarly, interest and lobby groups usually represent industrial interests with wider concerns related to trade and other aspects of regulatory policy. Nevertheless, it is clear that large industries, particularly those engaged in substantial resource extraction activities (such as mining, oil, and coal), must formulate sustainable development policies themselves, and are constantly interacting with Ottawa in order to present their own voice. Some argue that these groups wield disproportionate power and have a greater influence than is popularly believed. We include First Nations as a separate group because of their immediate, traditional reliance on the ecosystems which sustain them, although many other groups, such as farmers, have a similar dependency, and many native Canadians live in urban settings. However, First Nations have become political actors on the environment in a number of interesting ways.

Non-governmental organizations (NGOS) dedicated to environmental issues have a direct interest in the environment in at least two ways. They seek to influence governmental policy and consumer activity to mitigate harm to the environment according to their own conception of sustainable development. But they are also dependent, to varying degrees, on public acceptance of environmental problems as serious issues worthy of sustained attention. NGOS are under severe financial pressure, relying primarily on donations from the public to fund their activities, which makes their activities even more challenging. They are also dependent, to some extent, on the availability of the last group of actors we discuss in this chapter, the media. For both public consumption and persuasion, the media are an undeniably significant factor in environmental politics today. All of these groups compete for attention and favour with the central governing institution, the modern state.

Canadian Political Parties

When most people think of politics, they think first of political parties, competing against one another for the right to govern the state. Political parties "are organizations that seek to get their members elected to political office and to gain and maintain control of the government. They pursue this objective both inside and outside government" (Kernaghan and Siegel, 1995:488). The established political parties in Canada — the Liberals, Progressive Conservatives, the New Democratic Party, the Bloc Québécois, and the newly formed Canadian Alliance — have extensive networks of communication and self-promotion. Politicians make their mark in political parties, and depend on their parties for recognition and support. Within Parliament, parties attempt to maintain strict discipline, so that all members vote alike on most issues, and the concept of cabinet responsibility holds generally that ministers must toe the line (which means the Prime Minister's position) or resign. Opposition parties are engaged constantly in an effort to embarrass or disrupt the party holding power. Outside of Parliament, parties continuously gauge public opinion for possible electoral advantage, and they are often immersed in the arduous process of selecting leaders and official platforms, as well as campaigning for potential voters. And, in a federal state such as Canada, parties run on both provincial and national stages.

In terms of liberal democratic theory, political parties are often seen as crucial to what is termed "brokerage politics": They compete amongst themselves to gain power, and in the process help broker the concerns of different segments of Canadian society. They serve as a conduit between public opinion and the government, or the state itself. Of course, not everyone agrees with this benevolent depiction. For example, this perspective suggests that ideology, or strongly-set political predispositions, do not factor to a great extent into the life of political parties. Some analysts, such as William Christian and Colin Campbell, dispute this assumption, arguing that business liberalism and welfare liberalism form the two main ideological perspectives in the Canadian polity (Christian and Campbell, 1990). Both forms of liberalism are committed to private property and liberty, but business liberals minimize the role of the state, while welfare liberals see the state as a tool for achieving greater social justice and equality. The New Democrats, on the political left, strongly support welfare liberalism or, in some cases, limited socialism. Others argue that political parties have a virtual stranglehold on the political process in Canada and should be superseded by other institutions less prone to intrapolitics (see Lyon, 1992).

One of the most difficult dilemmas caused by the dominance of political parties in Parliament is that party discipline demands that members of Parliament (MPs) vote in agreement with the elite leaders of their party. As one observer notes, the individual MP "is caught between a rhetoric telling him to be independent and to think for himself, a power structure which leaves him with little to do except work on constituency matters and worry about re-election ... and policies with widespread appeal, but with which he has little connection, and which link government directly with citizens, bypassing MPs and parliament" (Franks, 1987:31). While it is true that in the United States members of Congress typically vote according to the immediate interests of their home constituency, this has generally not been the case in Canada. Because the Prime Minister and his/her key advisors have so much power concentrated at the top, the suggestion often is made that individual MPs have little impact on the formation of government policy, except when they play a critical role as members of the opposition. At the same time, however, it is clear that the ability to form political parties is viewed as one of the main features of democracy, and it is difficult to conceive of Parliament without them.

The environment has never been a central issue for any of Canada's major political parties. The Green Party, which has not yet achieved significant electoral success, is the only party that consistently puts ecological concerns at the centre of its platform, calling for a highly interventionist state that supports research and development into "green" technologies. The Green Party is unique in that it has an international following. Individual parties have gained electoral success in Germany, and consumer advocate Ralph Nader ran as the Green Party presidential candidate in the recent American election. In Canada, the Green Party has solicited political donations (which serve as tax breaks for contributors) to fund court cases for environmental protesters, and has helped to publicize the work of environmental NGOs. But it has rarely been considered a serious candidate for office, perhaps because it appears to be fixated on one issue — albeit a very interlinked and broad-based one — rather than the myriad of issues that other parties contend with when developing their electoral platforms. Furthermore, the Green Party insists that fundamental change is necessary in order to deal effectively with the environmental problems currently faced by Canadians. As one observer notes, they "would undoubtedly do far better electorally if they were to telescope the evolution experienced by the CCF/NDP and adopt a conventional organizational style and a platform which stressed cleaning up the environment rather than fundamentally changing the system that creates the ecological degradation" (Lyon, 1992:133).

For the Liberals, Progressive Conservatives, Alliance, and Bloc Québécois, with a few notable exceptions during certain campaign years, the environment has been a side issue at best. The New Democratic Party has probably put more energy into environmental concerns than the others, but it has had limited electoral success in recent years. As a party that represents the left of the political spectrum, the NDP (formerly known as the Cooperative Commonwealth Federation, or CCF) is the largest party to be openly critical of the socio-economic status quo, and often engages in pointed public debate over military spending and strategy and environmental concerns. Many NDP voters list the environment as one of their principal concerns. However, the NDP traditionally has relied heavily on labour unions, which are often split on environmental issues. On the one hand, it is clear that unions and social advocacy groups support the general concept of sustainable development and would like to see tougher penalties imposed against large-scale polluters. On the other hand, many unionists work in industries that are to some extent engaged in activities that result in pollution or the extraction of natural resources, such as forestry, and are at least as concerned about keeping their jobs.

The NDP's situation is typical: Political parties must be seen to support the policies favoured by their own supporters, and this considerably complicates any attempt to arrive at a clear position on many issues, including ecological matters. The ruling parties of Canada, with few exceptions (and even then mostly at the provincial level), have been the Liberals and the Progressive Conservatives. Both have been supported by business interests, and although there is considerable variation in their policies, they often have been similar in intent, if not delivery. Presently the Liberals are in power, and have appointed a federal Environment Commissioner who reports directly to Parliament, with powers of investigation similar to those of the financial Auditor General. (We will discuss the Auditor General's report in greater detail in a later chapter.) In general, however, the environmental record has been sporadic at best. As often happens, there is a gap between promises and policies. Previous to the current Liberal leadership, the Progressive Conservatives under Brian Mulroney formed the government. Though this was by any definition a pro-business party, the PCs did introduce several environmental initiatives, especially at the national level, including the federal Green Plan process, the establishment of the National Round Table on the Environment and Economy, the International Institute for Sustainable Development, and, perhaps most importantly, the Canadian Environmental Protection Act (CEPA) and the Canadian Environmental Assessment Act (CEAA). (These are discussed in later chapters of this volume.) Michael Howlett refers to these as "largely housekeeping matters occasioned by difficulties encountered by federal officials in the implementation of earlier legislation and Cabinet guidelines in the areas of toxic regulation and environmental assessments" (1997:105). He also points out that the Mulroney government was in power during a time when international attention was fixed on the environment, thus influencing domestic policies in the process (1997:113). Nevertheless, it is clear that parties with ideological biases against "big government" still may find themselves implementing fairly extensive policies.

The Bloc Québécois and the Canadian Alliance do not put the environment high on their agenda either, and this is significant since one or the other has formed the official opposition in recent years. The BQ is largely seen as a single-issue party: It is preoccupied with protecting the rights of Quebec and pushing for the eventual separation of that province from the rest of the country. However, certain ecological issues, such as the fate of the St. Lawrence River, are of obvious interest to the Bloc. The Bloc is also concerned with the continued promotion of hydropower, which it claims should exempt Canada from more stringent greenhouse gas emissions reduction requirements. However, these are largely regional issues, which any Quebec government would have to deal with, more than they are ideological ones affected by a party's evolved positions. The Alliance, however, is generally perceived as a far-right wing party more concerned with limiting governmental interference than with promoting environmental protection. The rights of landowners in Alberta and other agricultural areas are a major issue for the Alliance, which predisposes it to oppose intrusive species protection acts. The Alliance has declined to develop provincial parties, and the environment is often a more lively issue-area in provincial elections than in national ones. For example, the next election in Ontario, where Mike Harris' Progressive Conservatives have been in power for several years, will question that government's privatization of water-testing operations in the wake of the tainted water disaster in Walkerton. Provincial political parties must deal with questions related to their leader's relations with Ottawa, especially regarding health care and equalization payments. Although it is not as well publicized, initiatives such as the environmental "harmonization accord" by their very nature are also electoral.

Besides facilitating the competition for power, parties are often valued for other roles they play, such as fostering the career development of individual politicians who may make substantial differences on their own. Parties play an important role in shaping the perspectives of their individual members, but we should not lose sight of the role played by individuals within the broader context of policy-making. Although most politicians have not viewed the environment as a major cause, some have made it their chief focus during their time in the legislature, and in their active work on committees and international organizations. One such politician is Charles Caccia, who was born in Italy in 1930 and graduated in Forestry Economics at the University of Vienna in 1954. Mr. Caccia settled in Toronto shortly thereafter, where he taught courses and managed a publishing firm. He entered politics in 1964, when he was elected to the City of Toronto and Metro Council; in 1968, he was elected to the House of Commons as the Liberal MP for Davenport. Although he has served on many House of Commons Standing Committees, Caccia is best known for his work on environmental matters. Appointed Minister of the Environment in 1983, his tenure there saw the implementation of the international 30 per cent Club for Acid Rain Reduction, the establishment of the Water Commission for Canada, the reduction of lead in gasoline, the establishment of Environmental Impact Assessment Guidelines, and the creation of Wildlife Habitat Canada. In 1989, he established the Parliamentary Centre for Environmentally Sustainable Development, and in 1985, the UNEP awarded him the coveted Global 500 award. He has served as Chair of the Standing Committee on Environmental and

Sustainable Development and is also a Commissioner for the World Commission on Forests and Sustainable Development.

As Caccia's career suggests, there are individual MPs who have escaped the narrow confines of party membership and pushed for the environment as a major issue-area for Canadian governments. But when it comes to an executive-dominated political system such as we find in Canada, the will to accomplish serious change must come from political parties, which continue to dominate the political process.

First Nations

Many argue that, as people traditionally dependent on the land for subsistence, the First Nations of Canada have a natural affinity with the environment, as well as a profound stake in its preservation. But it is also the case that First Nations groups have become politically adroit and active on the environmental front, from adding ecological concerns to land claims, to protecting their rights to hunt and fish, to participating in international events. For example, during an important conference on forestry issues in Geneva in 1993 to negotiate a successor to the International Tropical Timber Agreement, one of the more significant events was a statement by the Nuu-Chah-Nulth Tribal Council of British Columbia, informing international delegates that the Council had participated in logging blockades over concern with rapid deforestation. According to one observer, such an intervention was a "source of irritation for the Canadian delegation" but served to remind delegates that "forest dwellers live not just in tropical forests but also in temperate forests..." (Humphreys, 1996:120). In fact, the Tla-o-qui-aht First Nations, who declared Meares Island a Tribal Park in 1984, were one of the first groups to blockade old-growth forestry in Clayoquot Sound.

In July 1995 the UNEP commended the Haudenosaunee Six Nations Confederacy for their work and dedication to protecting the environment. Many programs exist to integrate traditional environmental knowledge with policy-making, particularly in the north. Examples include the Dene Cultural Institute Pilot Project in the Northwest Territories (and Nunavut), and the establishment in 1993 of a Chair of Traditional Knowledge at the Canadian Museum of Nature. In 1995, the Friends of the United Nations group commissioned an international panel to choose 50 model communities that had demonstrated "an outstanding collective approach to environmental issues and the social development of their inhabitants." Three of the winners were from Canada: the Sanikiluaq Inuit community in the Northwest Territories, the Walpole Island First Nation in Ontario, and the Ouje-Bougoumou Cree community in Quebec (Canada, 1996:16). Nevertheless, one is more likely to encounter descriptions in the popular media of conflict between native and non-native Canadians. Current disputes over salmon fishing on the west coast, lobster fishing in the Atlantic region, coastal fishing rights on Lake Huron, and others, indicate the explosive nature of resource scarcity and treaty claims.

Politically, aboriginals in Canada have not been close to the centre of power. They are barely represented in Parliament, and their various attempts to achieve self-government have failed. However, "recently settled aboriginal land claims and management agreements also specify rights and obligations relating to resource management in affected lands.... By their application they have created a third tier of government." The James Bay and Northern Quebec Agreement of 1975 is an example, although it has been ridden with controversy in the recent decade (Vanderzwaag and Duncan, 1992:19). Aboriginals have also been involved in managing forestry in British Columbia and fisheries throughout the country. In northern Canada, the Inuit have a strong presence in the newly formed Nunavut government, and ecological concerns are often front and centre at the international Arctic Council (see Chapter 5), in which the Inuit Circumpolar Conference and other aboriginal groups have a permanent observer's seat. But the historical inequity consequent to European settlement has taken its toll on Canada's aboriginals, most of whom live below the poverty line in unfit housing. Many have drifted to large cities where they live in urban poverty, with little connection to the land that once formed the centre of their culture.

Two considerations are important when viewing the First Nations of Canada from an ecological standpoint. First, it is clear they have much accumulated knowledge that we forsake and deny at our collective peril; this traditional knowledge (or "tk") is valuable to governments and industries alike. Secondly, they too live in the increasingly global economy that drives resource extraction today. It is essential to avoid fitting First Nations people into a common caricature. There are wide differences among them, and they are positioned differently vis-à-vis Ottawa and the international community. As Wallace and Shields note in their interesting essay on Canadian values and the environment, "Native people, for whom the forests and coastal regions are a home and resource, not an aestheticized 'wilderness,' have proved no more certain to promote an externally scripted environmentalist agenda than to advance one written by multinational forest or fish-canning companies" (Wallace and Shields, 1997:388). We can be certain, however, that First Nations people will be involved in the process of environmental policy formation in Canada, either as part of decision-making or as protestors.

Industrial Lobby Groups

Many argue that it is inappropriate to focus solely on political parties and government departments in order to understand the process of environmental policy formation. They are correct. Indeed, the Canadian economy was based on resource extraction and trade for many years, and to some extent still is. The industries that drive the economy are powerful vested interests, and one need not be a Marxist to believe these companies will exercise inordinate influence in Ottawa and the various provincial capitals. On the formal level, this is done by professionals whose job it is to lobby politicians and, increasingly, the public. Consultants or professional lobbyists are individuals who, for payment and on behalf of a client, communicate with public office-holders in an attempt to influence government decisions. Consultant lobbyists may include government relations consultants, lawyers, accountants, or other professional advisors. They are required to register when they arrange a meeting between their client and a federal public office-holder, and for each undertaking for a client when they lobby for the awarding of contracts, grants, or legislative proposals.[1] Of course, there are many informal ties between corporate interests and politicians that are not well publicized.

A more coordinated form of lobbying, however, is accomplished through "industry associations," organizations which represent different corporations engaged in similar activities, or across an industrial sector. Several of these organizations predominate when it comes to environmental policies in Canada. To get a sense of their importance we might begin, ironically, by turning to a public sector department: Industry Canada attempts to increase the knowledge and awareness of sustainable development practices in the private sector as part of its Sustainable Development Strategy; one can find a review of 17 companies on its website (strategis.ic.gc.ca/ssg/sd0012ie.html. 2000-03-31), including Air Canada, Alcan Aluminum, Chrysler Canada, Dow Chemical, International Business Machines (IBM) Canada, Northern Telecom, Shell Cannonade, and Suncor Energy. In addition, nine industry associations are reviewed:

Air Transport Association of Canada
Automotive Industries Association of Canada
Canadian Association of Petroleum Producers
Canada Chemical Producers Association
Canadian Electricity Association
Canadian Gas Association
Canadian Pulp and Paper Association
Canadian Steel Producers Association
Information Technologies Association of Canada

Of these, only the Air Transport Association and Information Technologies Association do not participate in extensive environmental documentation, the Voluntary Challenge and Registry Program for Climate Change, the adoption of environmental management systems, and the adoption of eco-efficiency elements. Critics charge that these measures are too little too late. Nevertheless, the industries make a concerted effort through their associations to demonstrate their willingness to take steps toward sustainable development policies (we must keep in mind the difficulty of defining that term, however).

There are no strict ground rules when it comes to the positions advanced by these associations; in fact, they differ according to their own interests and future prospects. For example, the Canadian Association of Petroleum Producers is concerned with the Kyoto Protocol on global warming (see Chapter 5); predictably, it argues the Protocol is unrealistic for implementation at this point in Canada, since restraining carbon dioxide and other greenhouse gas emissions would harm the economy (the coal industry in Alberta has expressed similar concerns). However, the Canadian Gas Association, which represents marketers of natural gas, supports the Kyoto Protocol, since natural gas emits fewer greenhouse gases than coal or oil and may become the fossil fuel of choice should Kyoto's targets ever be met. While some associations accept limited governmental intervention in managing their sectors, others are concerned primarily with limiting it. For example, the Crop Protection Institute is concerned about the regulation of pesticides, while the Canadian Chemical Producers Association lobbies to reduce legislative control and increase the visibility of voluntary programs.

One commonality surfaces, however: All these associations prefer a voluntary approach to changing current environmental practices. This position follows a liberal/business/neo-conservative ideology which suggests that the marketplace be the ultimate decision-maker: in order to be competitive, firms will move toward sustainable policies to maintain the confidence of domestic and international investors and buyers. Some of the industry associations are concerned with trade questions. The Canadian Steel Producers Association, for example, argues that whatever compromises are reached between the issues of trade and the environment should not put Canadian industry at a disadvantage relative to international competitors. The Industry Canada website (referred to above) similarly emphasizes the gradual success of companies' and associations' voluntary sustainable development initiatives, especially in the chemical industry, and the widespread participation noted in the Canadian Industry Program for Energy Conservation (CIPEC). Furthermore, on a transnational level, many companies and associations are developing environmental management systems consistent with the International Organization for Standardization (IOS) 14000 series. Some also have signed Memoranda of Understanding (MOU) with Natural Resources Canada, which outline their commitment to reducing greenhouse gas emissions.

A public-private joint venture related to this activity is the Canadian Business Environmental Performance Office (BEPO), which is associated with more than 20 business organizations (virtualoffice.ic.gc.ca/BEPO). BEPO is concerned mainly with providing information "to support the growth and development of all Canadian industries," but is also a helpful source of information regarding what steps corporations are taking to limit the environmental problems resulting from their activities. Beyond this, the corporate sector receives assistance from various governmental departments and ministers themselves. The point of the famous "Team Canada" missions, for example, is to facilitate trade between Canadian companies and developing states such as China and Brazil. These high-profile events usually involve the Prime Minister and the provincial Premiers. The Canadian Forestry Service, a department of Natural Resources Canada, manages the International Forestry Partnerships Program on behalf of the Canadian Council of Forest Ministers; it "endeavors to keep foreign audiences well informed about Canada's sustainable forest practices and to prevent misinformation from causing problems for Canadian forestry exports" (Natural Resources Canada, 1997). Obviously, this involves arguing against the claims of some the NGOs mentioned below. As described in our section on the state in this chapter, some Marxists suggest that governments often play the role of lobbyist for industrialists.

It is reasonable to be circumspect about the claims made by the industrial associations concerning the rate of progress Canadian corporations are making, voluntarily, to deal with environmental problems caused by their industries. Indeed, with such success on paper, one might expect most of the environmental problems caused by large-scale industry in Canada to simply disappear. However, many environmentalists are critical of the voluntary approach, arguing it demands too little from corporations that use the label to justify continuing with business as usual. The Accelerated Reduction/Elimination of Toxics (ARET) program, begun in 1994, is the longest running multisectoral voluntary program in Canada, covering 117 toxic substances and involving over 275 companies across 8 major industrial sectors. But the program lacks standardized reporting methods, and "there are no consequences or fall back actions when participants fail to meet targets" (Gallon, 1997). Companies can also include reductions based on government regulations, such as INCO's $600-million rebuilding of its smelter at Copper Cliff, Ontario, which resulted in a 90-per-cent containment of sulphur dioxide (Gallon, 1997). Others argue that, in the case of the Harris government in Ontario (which has put the Canadian Industry Packaging Stewardship Initiative [CIPSI] on the back burner), "when a government is intent on deregulation, the policy instrument of voluntarism is inherently incapable of achieving its objectives" (Chang, Macdonald, and Wolfson, 1998:21). Authors of a recent article detailing the death of the CIPSI argue that voluntarism "must be seen for what it is — a smoke-screen, intended to mislead the public and to hide the fact that what is taking place is a significant reduction in levels of environmental protection" (Chang, Macdonald, and Wolfson, 1998:24). Indeed, the attempt to influence public opinion is taken very seriously by the industrial associations mentioned above. We will return to this theme in our discussion of the media.

Although the rate of change is slow, Canada is a leading state when it comes to the development of environmental technology. In fact, we should add one more industrial lobby group, The Canadian Environmental Industries Association, established in May 1989 (see Brown, 1992). Industry, Science and Technology Canada defines the environmental industry as "one which provides products and services which have as their effect the conservation, protection, and enhancement of the environment." The Mulroney government announced a \$4-million Environmental Industries Sector Initiative in 1989 to foster this area of activity (Brown, 1992:166). The development of this industry not only strengthens Canada's technological reputation abroad, but challenges the conventional wisdom that a harsh choice must be made between jobs and environmental protection. Clearly, in some cases, environmental protection can generate jobs. However, it would be premature to conclude that such industries will have much influence in Ottawa and provincial capitals in the near future.

Non-Governmental Organizations: Environmental Interest Groups[2]

Corporations are not the only organizations lobbying governments. Non-governmental organizations (NGOS) are also lobbyists, though they often are more occupied with generating public support than with directly affecting decision-makers.[3] There are many different types of NGOS active in politics: the standard feature distinguishing them from the lobbyists discussed above is that they do not operate for profit, but generate funds in order to promote a cause. Some NGOS accept funding from governments, while others do not. Some are very large and highly organized, dealing with a multitude of issues, and with international counterparts with similar goals; others are quite small, intensely focused on one issue-area only, and limited to a regional concern. While some engage in high-risk, publicity-grabbing acts (and some even engage in sabotage), others participate in the formal governmental consultation process. Many observers feel NGOs are representative of civil society, but others are critical of this assumption, noting that NGO leaders are not elected by the general population and therefore do not share the political legitimacy of politicians.

The number of environmental non-governmental organizations (ENGOs) in Canada is truly remarkable. Their number has grown steadily since the end of World War II. However, it is one thing to say that many ENGOs are involved, and quite another to suggest that they wield sufficient power to have a sustained impact. What follows are short descriptions of various ENGOs active in Canada, and a survey of their different structures and goals.

Friends of the Earth Canada (FOE) is a national organization, with affiliates in other countries, involved in a broad range of environmental protection programs. Like other ENGOs, FOE advocates change through research, advocacy, education, and cooperation. FOE originated as a selective coalition/confederation of stronger regional and provincial ENGOs, each of which focuses on issues unique to their regions. FOE attempts to work in collaboration with other organizations, government agencies, industry, and other stakeholders, and is currently involved in campaigns for ozone protection, promoting global-warming education, and the organizing of a "Rainforest Rescue League" and a "Water Conservation for Canada" project. FOE is primarily concerned with pollution and ozone protection, and releases an annual report on Canada's ozone protection policy (in which Canada received a D+ in 1999).

Greenpeace is one of the most famous environmental agencies with offices worldwide, and international headquarters in Amsterdam. Greenpeace uses non-violent, direct interventions that raise awareness and allow public opinion to have a greater effect on decision-makers. Critics of the organization suggest that these direct actions are unsafe, unproductive, and may erode the credibility of other environmentalist actions. Greenpeace is unique in that it does not accept any government funding and remains independent of governments, political parties, and industry (though the international office does receive funding from the Dutch government). It is probably the world's most readily recognized NGO, and employs public relations experts as well as scientists. Greenpeace has three broad ongoing campaigns: climate and energy (especially nuclear energy), biodiversity of the forests of Canada, and toxins and health. To achieve its goals, Greenpeace uses direct action as well as research programs, lobbying, and education. It has considerable resources at its disposal, and has become a household name through its campaigns to stop commercial whaling and its opposition to nuclear testing. Internationally, it focuses on the issue of Genetically Modified Organisms, a major concern in Europe and in parts of Canada.

The International Fund for Animal Welfare (IFAW) was established to fight against the killing of harp and hood seals for commercial use. It has since expanded to include a wide range of animals. Like many ENGOS, IFAW is an organization that fights against commercial exploitation and illegal trade and the destruction of wilderness habitat, and participates in rescuing animals in distress. IFAW, however, also focuses on other types of animal welfare including the prevention of animal cruelty (through cosmetic testing and pet abuse) and the creation of an emergency relief team to rescue animals after natural and man-made disasters. The organization focuses on a partnership structure to implement its policies. IFAW works closely with government departments, other ENGOS, and the public. In the area of endangered species protection, IFAW is currently focusing its efforts, with other groups, on global campaigns to stop the expansion of the worldwide whaling industry, the illegal trade of African elephant parts, and Canadian and Russian spring bear hunts. To initiate change, the IFAW concentrates largely on research projects, including a research vessel used to study and protect marine mammals. Founder Brian Davies began a campaign against the slaughter of baby harp seals in 1965, and continues to protest the seal hunt through efforts to tarnish Canada's image abroad. The seal industry claims such groups sensationalize the issue, using the "photogenic qualities of newborn harp seals to shift the focus of the debate from an issue of rational utilization of a natural resource to an emotional appeal" (Mulrennan, 1998:67).

The Sierra Club of Canada, part of the international Sierra Club community, focuses on loss of animal and plant species, deterioration of the planet's oceans and atmosphere, the ever-growing presence of toxic chemicals, overpopulation and overconsumption. In Canada, the organization's mission is to promote energy efficiency, to protect forests from clear-cutting, to conserve biodiversity, to expose the risks of pesticide use, to follow up global commitments made at Rio in 1992, to expose economic causes of global environmental decline, and to advocate a nuclear phase-out and challenge the government's sale of CANDU reactors abroad. This broad mandate is achieved by eight regional Canadian Sierra Clubs. At the chapter level, the Sierra Club wages campaigns unique to each region. In the area of endangered species protection, the Sierra Club helped to form the Canadian Coalition of Biodiversity and the Canadian Endangered Species Coalition with other national conservation organizations. In 1997, the Sierra Club waged a petition campaign to the Ministry of Environment on Endangered Species Bill-65 (which eventually died). As well, it releases annual "Rio Report Cards" on federal and provincial government action taken to meet commitments made at Rio in 1992, and is part of a coalition pushing for reform of multilateral lending institutions, such as the World Bank and International Monetary Fund.

Some ENGOs function on a regional basis and are concerned with specific habitat areas or provincial jurisdictions. For example, the Manitoba Wildlife Federation is the oldest conservation group in that province. Like other federations, it has local affiliate clubs of hunters, anglers, and naturalists throughout the province. The Federation is a charitable organization, and founded the MWF Habitat Foundation Inc. to collect cash and land donations to help preserve natural areas. Landowners can contribute toward preserving wildlife while retaining their land title. The Federation runs a number of projects, both through the organization proper and by encouraging local initiatives. Conservation programs run by the MWF include the development of fisheries habitat restoration projects and the supporting of research on various diseases in fish and wildlife. The MWF, more so than other regional wildlife federations, focuses heavily on hunting and angling issues. The Federation monitors and responds to federal and provincial proposals on hunting and firearms issues and runs training and education programs. Many of the conservation programs appear to be administered to allow for hunting and angling opportunities rather than for conservation itself.

Environment Probe is an Ontario environmental organization created from its larger parent body, Energy Probe Foundation. The Foundation, now consisting of Energy Probe, Pollution Probe, Environment Probe, Consumer Policy Institute, and the Margaret Laurence Fund, has also partially funded several independent organizations such as Friends of the Earth (with other ENGOs), the World Rainforest Movement, and the International Rivers Network. Environment Probe is a well-respected group, with University of Toronto professors and CBC Radio staff sitting on its board of directors. It does not run hands-on, grassroots-level conservation programs, but focuses on the publicizing of environmental issues and property rights through periodic reports, newspaper editorials, research studies, and interaction with various levels of government. Environment Probe is more an academic advocacy group than a nature organization. Each year, the organization chooses several new campaign issues. In 1999, it campaigned for endangered species legislation. Environment Probe's campaigns consist both of letter-writing campaigns directed at members of the government, factual summaries of the issue to raise awareness, and research studies, articles, or books to determine the next appropriate course of action. Previous campaigns include Forestry (1996), Property Rights: The Key to Environmental Protection (1995), and Turning Free Trade to the Environment's Advantage (1989).

OceanNet is an action-oriented grass roots group founded in Newfoundland. Its primary mandate is to help reverse the polluting of oceans and the destruction of marine wildlife by lost "ghost" fishing nets.

By partnering with diving clubs, schools, fishermen, community organizations, NGOs, and government agencies, OceanNet implements many projects, some of which are innovative and quite successful. OceanNet's projects include the locating and retrieval of "ghost" fishing nets, beach clean-up programs, designation and development of marine conservation areas, development of educational materials, organizing workshops, and research into marine issues such as the impact of oil spills, contamination, and debris on Newfoundland's beaches and its species. In 1997, OceanNet participated in the Summit of the Seas, at which time the organization announced its desire to expand and develop chapters of OceanNet worldwide. The project Clean-up Committee, which couples ocean divers with environmental organizations to improve the quality of polluted water, has been exported to other provinces and to the United States.

One of Canada's defining landscapes is the great North, and the Canadian Arctic Resources Committee (CARC) is a citizens' organization with members across the country. CARC staff are based in Ottawa as well as at the Northern Frontiers Visitors Centre in Yellowknife. The organization does not run conservation programs typical of southern areas, but does run research projects and is at the forefront as an advocate for responsible resource use in the North. The Committee has published numerous articles, books, guides, and handbooks on issues such as responsible tourism and resource management of the North. CARC's activities include participation in environmental reviews of the BHP diamond mines. As part of the Northern Environmental Coalition (with Ecology North, CNF, and WWF), CARC brought forth independent expert witnesses to the public hearings. As well, the Committee was involved in presentations and questioning at the Water Board Hearings. CARC was also involved in discussions on the environmental agreement and protected areas strategy for the Northwest Territories and the Arctic Environmental Protection Strategy. To participate in these events, CARC set up the Arctic Futures Fund to provide funds for research, advocacy, publishing, and public awareness.

In addition to single NGOs that work on their own, many NGOs have formed coalition groups in order to amplify their voice and spread their educational programs. One of the more robust of these coalitions is the Canadian Coalition on Biodiversity (CCB), an alliance of eight non-profit conservation groups: the Canadian Biodiversity Institute, Ocean Voice International, Canadian Nature Federation, Rare Breeds Canada, Fall Brooks Centre, Sierra Club of Canada, Friends of the Earth, and Western Canada Wilderness Committee. Another is the Canadian Endangered Species Coalition (CESC), established by the Canadian Nature Federation (CNF), the Canadian Parks and Wilderness Society (CPAWS), WWF, and the Sierra Legal Defence Fund (part of the Sierra Club) in the early 1990s.

The coalition's goal is the passage of effective federal legislation to protect and recover endangered species and their habitats. The coalition is supported by over 150 smaller organizations. We should also mention Public Research Interest Groups (PIRGS) launched originally by Ralph Nader (recent Presidential candidate for the Green Party in the United States) in the US, with 200 chapters in the US and 18 in Canada. In the early 1980s, various PIRGS organized a cross-border "Acid Rain Caravan" (see Farbridge and Cameron, 1998), putting additional pressure on the Reagan and Trudeau governments to deal with the acid rain issue. PIRGS have a strong presence on university campuses, where environmental issues are usually quite popular concerns.

Yet another form of ENGO with wide connections to others, and to the corporate and public sector, is the legal advocacy group. Perhaps the most prominent Canadian example is the Canadian Environmental Law Association (CELA), established in 1970 by a group of law students and community activists. Although environmental law was embryonic in the early 1970s (see Chapter 6), CELA addressed issues such as waste sites in Ontario, urban lead pollution and noise complaints, mercury pollution in the English-Wabigoon river system, the loss of wetlands, and other threats to Ontario's natural heritage, particularly on the Niagara Escarpment. As part of Ontario's community-led legal clinic system, the Ontario Legal Aid Plan provided core funding for CELA in 1977. Some of its objectives are

» to provide equitable access to justice to those otherwise unable to afford representation for their environmental problems
» to advocate for comprehensive laws, standards, and policies that will protect and enhance environmental quality in Ontario and throughout Canada
» to provide the public with information, research, advice, and educational materials to assist them in addressing environmental problems
» to work with communities, neighbourhoods, individuals, and public interest groups to foster long-term sustainable solutions to environmental concerns and resource use
» to mitigate the recent erosions of the environmental protection framework from degradation, budget cuts, harmonization of standards, and corporate self-regulation.

CELA is very involved in the Canadian ENGO community. Since its birth, the demands placed upon the organization have led to the founding of issue- or regionally-based ENGOS such as Great Lakes United, the Canadian Environmental Defense Fund, Forests for Tomorrow, and the Its Not Garbage Coalition. CELA staff are also involved in the Ontario

Environmental Network and the Canadian Environmental Network. Producing and sharing background materials and campaigns with the members of these networks allows CELA to carry out its law reform campaigns. As CELA's staff have legal expertise, the Association often works with issue-centred, smaller NGOs to provide them with an understanding of the complexities of environmental law. Recently, CELA participated on the Steering Committee of "Common Frontiers," a project which connects Canadian, Mexican, and US organizations on issues of trade and the environment, while developing further links to like-minded organizations in Latin America. Common Frontiers monitors the impacts of NAFTA implementation as well as the negotiations toward bilateral and multilateral trade agreements with Latin American countries such as Chile (CELA website, 2000). CELA is also among the founders of the Campaign for Nuclear Phase-Out, a national coalition advocating the phase-out of all nuclear power generators and uranium mines.

Several persistent questions arise regarding the future of ENGOs. Chief among them are concerns over whether they should maintain their general status as enemies of large industry, or seek a more conciliatory approach. For example, the high-profile World Wildlife Fund is "among a small number of groups that have aggressively sought to tap into corporate sources" (Wilson, 1992:115). Many environmentalists are critical of this cooperation, suggesting it amounts to the co-optation of critical voices. Similar questions arise as to how involved ENGOs should become with governments. Fund-raising is difficult at the best of times, yet accepting government assistance may tarnish an image of autonomy. There remains a longstanding fear that accepting government funding might lead to an exploitable dependence. Regardless, it is clear that both ENGOs and industry associations rely heavily on the presence of yet another important political actor to get their point across to the public: the media.

THE MEDIA

One of the most memorable images related to environmental awareness occurred in the early 1990s, preceding the UNCED summit, when the global media disseminated photographic and video images of forest destruction; satellite imagery of the Brazilian Amazon showed images of over 7000 simultaneous fires (Humphreys, 1996:18). More recently, widespread coverage of the tainted water tragedy in Walkerton, Ontario, led to nationwide concern over the hazards of unsafe drinking water. The power of the media to shape public opinion is a factor any political scientist must remember, but this seems especially salient when it comes to the environment as an issue-area. Since most ecological concerns are not in people's "backyards," they need to be informed of what is happening elsewhere. However, the media is also an instrument used by all the actors discussed above in order to generate public opinion on various issues.

"As even a quick perusal of news coverage will attest, environmental groups are usually able to attract the attention of the media. And the media's treatment of the movement is generally quite sympathetic — and also usually quite superficial" (Wilson, 1992:122). They tend "to degrade things by adopting an adversarial focus, which simplifies things into a good guy/bad guy dichotomy" (Roberge, 2000:4). Sometimes journalists give equal weight to a widely accepted scientific opinion and the beliefs of a few dissidents (global warming). Nonetheless, it is hard to overestimate the impact of the news media on the thinking of the average Canadian. For many, the media are the only source of information concerning environmental problems. As one observer notes, much of the public policy debate over the environment "is not fought directly in the legislative arena, but in the court of public opinion" (Switzer, 1997:130). This is a factor not lost on the NGO sector, which runs ads in both newsprint and television and makes extensive use of the Internet. Large corporations respond with well-crafted publicity campaigns extolling the environmental virtues of their work. The two sectors engage in different tactics, however:

> A pro-environmental group that wants to pay for an advertising campaign must spend the same amount of money as any company to gain access to the media. Since environmental groups cannot buy as much broadcast time, they seek to maximize the impact of the message so as to reach their goals; consequently, they often bank on the originality that a sensationalist approach can very easily provide. (Duval, 1995:57)

Companies use public relations campaigns since "to many in business, environmental groups have captured the media, which are no longer capable of reporting their activities objectively" (Switzer, 1997:131). The media survive because of advertising, and there is no doubt that few ENGOs can compete with large corporations when it comes to paying for prime-time television spots. However, some argue the Internet is eroding this commercial advantage, because it is relatively easy and affordable to present web-based information and advocacy. All of the major ENGOs have constructed web sites that are easily accessed in today's information economy. Similarly, political parties have adopted the Internet as a means of communicating election platforms, and the government uses it extensively to publish its documentation. Moreover, as always in the Canadian context, we must keep the influence of non-Canadian factors in mind, in particular the influence of the American media, which saturate the television channels of most Canadians.

As in our discussion of political parties, we can discern many perspectives on the role of the media in a liberal democracy. Ideally, the media play a "critical role as two-way channels of communication between the governors and the governed. Newspapers, magazines, television, and radio carry information from the public to politicians and bureaucrats and from these officials to the public. The media serve as 'filters' for this information; they aim also to influence the attitudes and behavior of both government officials and members of the public. Thus, the media both reflect and influence public opinion" (Kernaghan and Siegel, 1995:503). It is important, therefore, to monitor the media closely and to see how certain stories are cast. No doubt the larger questions about sustainable development and society are lost in news media coverage of sporadic events, since it "tends to focus on short-term concerns regarding public health and safety, a focus reflected in public opinion surveys" (Fletcher and Stahlbrand, 1992:179). This frustrates some environmentalists, who feel that long-term questions, such as global warming and species reduction, should preoccupy us at the present time.

CONCLUSION

We have dealt mainly with various politically active groups in this chapter. We should not, however, forget the contributions of active and well-connected individuals such as Maurice Strong, mentioned in our introduction. Strong was born in Manitoba in 1929, and worked with the energy and financial sectors. He resigned as president of Power Corporation in 1966 to head Canada's External Aid Office, later reorganized as the Canadian International Development Agency. He was the Secretary General of the groundbreaking UN Conference on the Human Environment from 1970-1972, then became the first Executive Director of the UN Environment Programme (UNEP). After a brief return to the energy sector, he emerged as an Under-Secretary-General at the UN, and was the Secretary-General of UNCED in 1992. It is hard to overstate the extent of his involvement in environmental policy and the promotion of environmental education, though his ties to the energy industry have led some critics to suggest he has had, in effect, the best of both worlds. Others, such as Elizabeth May, who leads the Sierra Club and was once a (disgruntled) policy advisor to the federal Minister of the Environment, have cut across both the non-state and governmental spheres of engagement.

However, as this chapter has demonstrated, Canadian ecopolitics is fundamentally about the interaction between various groups competing for power or policy preference. This competition occurs against the backdrop of Canadian federalism. As one popular textbook on Canadian politics concludes, "the practise of executive federalism, the absence of synchronicity between the federal and provincial elections, and the difficulties inherent in mediating the differences across the diverse Canadian regions all point to the importance of federalism in fragmenting the Canadian party system" (Archer, et al., 1995:412). Further, with the notable exception of the Green Party, the environment is not a dominating issue-area when it comes to party platforms and elections. NGOs and interest groups also compete for their share of the market of public ideas and policy preferences, and First Nations groups continue their fight for land rights and access to natural resources. The media are instrumental in covering the issues raised and in relaying the messages put forth by the various actors, but given the limitations they face they can only present cursory overviews of complex problems.

We make no claim to have covered all of the relevant groups involved in environmental policy formation here. For example, we should not overlook the influence of advisory bodies, such as the Standing Committee on Environment, the National Round Table on Environment and Economy, and the Science Council of Canada, which play a role in advising ministers regarding policy formation, though it would be unwise to overestimate their overall impact (see Filyk and Cote, 1992; federal advisory systems are also mirrored at the provincial level). Outside of government, spontaneous consumer boycotts, messages from the entertainment world, and the occurrence of natural or human-induced disasters all spark increased interest and controversy in environmental politics. The confines of political analysis suggest we focus on key actors, but we should keep in mind the colourful collage of political agents that exists.

However, none of these agents, as groups or as individuals, operates in a neat, hermetically sealed container named Canada; they all interact with the outside world as well. In the next chapter, we will look at the increasingly important international context of environmental policy-making.

NOTES

1   See Industry Canada's "Consultant Lobbyists Registration Requirements" at the webpage http://strategis.ic.gc.ca/SSG/lr00028e.htm

2   Thanks to Emily Lawrence Courage for research compiled for this section.

3   We acknowledge the fact that corporations are, in essence, NGOs. However, we are using the term here to refer to non-profit-seeking groups with varying degrees of national and international organizational structure.

THE TRANSNATIONAL CONTEXT

INTRODUCTION

On December 20, 2000, John Manley, Canada's Minister of Foreign Affairs, announced the appointment of long-time parliamentarian Gilbert Parent to the post of Canada's "Ambassador for the Environment." His responsibilities will be to represent the ministers of Foreign Affairs and the Environment at international environmental negotiations and meetings. Such a post would have been unthinkable a mere 20 years ago; but with the 2002 World Summit on Sustainable Development fast approaching, it now seems quite essential.

There are at least two ways international factors play an increasingly significant role in environmental policy questions. As mentioned in the previous chapter, the political actors we have described so far act in a transnational context. Their decisions, and the strategies they adopt to achieve their goals, whether they are politicians, bureaucrats, managers of multinational corporations, or members of NGOs, are taken and formulated with the impact of the non-Canadian world at least partially in mind. Secondly, it is increasingly common that environmental issues play an important role in the formation of foreign policy, since internal decisions have an impact abroad and external decisions affect the Canadian government's decision-making abilities as well. Furthermore, other areas of concern, such as trade and development aid policy, have to include some consideration of the environmental consequences of both short and long-term goal-making. The growth of the world economy and the process vaguely referred to as globalization have had a profound impact on public policy-making, especially regarding concerns over issues that span borders.

This chapter has two essential purposes. The first is to situate Canada in world politics: to describe the political relations Canada has with the rest of the world, and the possibilities and constraints this presents to decision-makers in Ottawa and other international actors, such as Canadian firms engaged in trade, or members of non-governmental organizations with transnational linkages. The second purpose is to present a rough survey of global ecopolitics, which is a burgeoning academic field in its own right, encompassing geopolitics, political economy, human rights, ecology, and other issue-areas. We aim, therefore, to present a brief overview of the transnational context in which Canada operates, complementing previous discussions of the environmental, administrative, and political contexts. In Chapter 8 we will return to the theme with an empirical survey of Canadian environmental diplomacy.

CANADA AND THE WORLD

All states in the international system possess certain common characteristics. They all have governments with sovereign jurisdiction within their borders, though the strength of this jurisdiction may vary greatly. They have a geographically defined space, marked by territorial borders, and a permanent population residing within it. And they have been recognized by other states as independent, legal entities. Of course, there are exceptions, or anomalies, to this general rule. Some states have more stable and effective governments than others; some have ongoing border disputes with their neighbours; some are not members of the United Nations and thus lack official recognition, although, as in the case of Taiwan, they are considered states by many. But, by and large, these are the basic attributes we normally apply to a state: sovereignty, population, borders, and external recognition. Canada long ago achieved all of these prerequisites, despite its past as a British colony and political tensions between its founding nations.

Another common attribute is that states operate in what international relations theorists like to call an "anarchic environment." This does not mean there is no sense of order to things. On the contrary, many would argue that dominant powers, or ideas, or international institutions, help create a fairly ordered world. It means there is no formal, central source of authority that can dictate policies to states. Certainly, international institutions, such as the UN, the North Atlantic Treaty Organization, and the World Trade Organization, have the ability to influence states, and some of the more powerful states might be considered centres of authority, or even "hegemons." But there is no central government which can order a state's affairs, or completely manage the highly competitive global economy, or enforce international law, the way a national government can within its own borders. This is highly relevant for environmental policy, since this decentralized decision-making environment, in the context of a competitive economy, often makes cooperation difficult.

But we should not confuse decentralization with equality. While all states are technically equal under international law and the Charter of the United Nations, it is clear that some states have much more power and capacity than others. The Security Council of the United Nations, the central decision-making body of the organization, is composed of five permanent members (United States, Russia, China, the United Kingdom, and France) who have the right to veto anything substantive the Council considers doing. Some states, such as China and India, have such large populations that their influence on environmental matters is strong indeed. Others have more money to spend on assistance projects, or more military power to employ, on their own or through alliances. And it can be argued that, because of the influence of the transnational media sources such as television and the Internet, some states have more impact on the spread of ideas as well.

Canada is not one of the most powerful states on earth in either military or economic terms, though it is a member of the often cherished "G8" club. It has come a long way since achieving independence from British colonialism, and has a definite presence on the world stage, with active participation in United Nations peacekeeping operations and in most of the major multilateral institutions dealing with economic and social issues. It is a member of NATO and has a close military relationship with the United States. Canada is highly dependent on trade to maintain its standard of living, and Ottawa has long been an advocate of a fairly open, or liberal, international trading regime. Though it is a federal state, the British North America (BNA) Act of 1867 gives authority to the national government in Ottawa in matters related to foreign affairs; the principal bureaucracy there is the Department of Foreign Affairs and International Trade (DFAIT), which is headed by separate ministers for both foreign and trade policy. However, provincial governments do participate in foreign affairs, whether by pursuing trade contracts abroad or by implementing international policies at home.

After World War II, the United Nations was created in order to avoid another conflict of that magnitude. However, the international system soon bifurcated into the Cold War, with the United States leading the capitalist camp, and the USSR, now known (again) as Russia, leading the communist side. It was always quite clear which side Canada was on, since the United States soon supplanted the United Kingdom as Canada's closest and most influential ally, and Canadian membership in NATO was rarely questioned in Ottawa (except by the NDP and other left-of-centre parties). When the USSR dissolved and the Cold War ended, the bipolar system went with it, leaving an even more complex system with various regions competing for economic supremacy. Though many would characterize the current system as unipolar — meaning there is really only one superpower, the United States — others would consider it a multipolar one in which several states, such as China and India, have increased power, and certain regions, such as the Middle East and central Africa, maintain the volatility displayed in the past. Some theorists contend that the dangerous stability of the Cold War was preferable to the current order (see Mearsheimer, 1990, for a famous example). Canada is most often characterized as a middle power state, and like any other middle power it faces an uncertain international climate and a rapidly changing global economy.

There can be little doubt that Ottawa plays the game of world politics within Washington's shadow. Many argue that this invariate should be viewed in a positive light, since the American economy has a tremendous influence on that of Canada. Canadian exports have doubled since the late 1980s, largely due to the strength of American demand for products. No other bilateral trade relationship is as powerful, and few are as secure. The economies of Canada and the United States have become inextricably tied with the advent of the Canada-US (and subsequently, North American) Free Trade Agreements. At the same time, however, many Canadians are unhappy with this situation, arguing American dominance exacts a high cost in terms of the autonomy of Canada's political sovereignty and cultural industries. In fact, many fear that a distinct Canadian political culture is gradually eroding, and that the Canadian relationship with the United States limits the scope of environmental policy decision-making on important resource questions.

It is difficult to overstate the influence of the proximity of the United States in the Canadian environmental policy setting context. Not only is the US responsible for the majority of Canadian imports and exports, but it also exports ideas about environmental policy and regulations (see Hoberg, 1991; Munton and Castle, 1992). Canada is in a unique position, located next to what is, by most accounts, the most powerful state in the history of civilization, as well as the greatest polluter and consumer of resources. The world economy, for better or worse, is largely dependent on the American economy; its military prowess is unmatched; its international commitments are broad and often intrusive, though an isolationist sentiment in Washington limits them. Over three-quarters of Canadian trade is across the American border, and thousands of Canadians live and work in the United States. People in both countries share television programs and many household brand names, as well as cultural icons. As the two economies and polities become increasingly enmeshed, we can identify a process of integration with far-reaching consequences for the weaker power.

Nonetheless, a distinct Canadian identity prevails, often based on the fundamental fact that Canadians are not American. This is especially evident in Quebec, where the French language separates much of American from Québécois culture. But one can also see evidence of a desire to avoid the total integration of Canadian and American society. This surfaces during debates about increased free trade, cultural autonomy, differing approaches to health care, national defence issues, and, to a limited extent, environmental policy. Not only is the United States the world's most powerful economy, it is the world's biggest polluter. No other state has made such an enormous contribution to global warming (though several others, including China, threaten to do so); long-standing diplomatic negotiations over the transborder acid-rain problem have unsettled relations throughout the last three decades; American military installations in the north have left toxic waste; and the increase in trade between the two states has increased the environmental problems associated with vehicle emissions and other stages of the production process.

In fact it was a Canada-US transborder dispute that set the tone for much of the international public law on the environment that followed. In 1941 a triparty board of arbitration, including the US, Canada, and Belgium, ruled that a Canadian smelter located seven miles from the state of Washington was emitting extraordinary levels of sulphur dioxide and harming American territory in the process. This has become known as the Trail Smelter Arbitration. It made explicit the presumption that states have an obligation not to allow activities (be they publicly or privately funded) which incur harm or loss for their neighbours. On another note, the International Joint Commission (see Chapter 8) serves as a model of bilateral cooperation between states sharing a border. The border between Canada and the US extends for approximately 8900 kilometres and includes some 3800 kilometres of fresh water and oceanic territory. Cooperation is not always possible, however, as the Pacific Coast dispute over salmon stocks suggests. Indeed, this dispute has resulted in the anger of many stakeholders, from First Nations and Alaskan fishers, to sports fisheries operators, to politicians in both the US and Canada.

Although Canada and the US have had to deal with many environmental and resource-related issues over the past century, they did not occupy an important place on the diplomatic agenda until the 1960s, when public awareness of ecological issues increased. Since then, two distinct approaches have evolved: When the goals of the two states appear harmonious, the disputed subject matter is referred to established bodies such as the IJC or to newer structures such as the International Saint John Water Quality Committee. This is part of a broader pattern. Joseph Jockel argues that most bilateral issues are dealt with through a "management culture" that has evolved at the level of the state executives and diplomatic personnel (Jockel, 1990:3-8). When interests are opposed, the issue is left to a lengthy and often frustrating system of diplomatic negotiations for resolution, as in the current dispute over salmon quotas (Kyba and Dwivedi, 1998:35-36).

Indeed, many fishing disputes, on the east and west coasts, have involved the United States. This is hardly surprising, given the proximity and appetite of Canada's superpower neighbour to the south. What may be more surprising, perhaps, is the aggressiveness with which Canada pursues its claims in these matters, whether it be overfishing off the coast of Maine, or claiming jurisdiction over straddling stocks of crustaceans, or imposing obstacles to salmon fishing in the west. For example, Canada was quite aggressive with its transit licence measure in 1994, according to which American salmon vessels from Washington and Oregon heading to and from Alaska were required to purchase a licence. This was certainly an aggressive measure in the eyes of the Americans involved, but it did not contravene international law. At the time, vice-president Al Gore intervened, promising to renegotiate a new pacific salmon treaty and to refrain from overfishing, and Canada then withdrew the transit licence measure. Canada also threatened to seize American vessels fishing for sedentary species of scallops; this was consistent with the UNCLOS and the 1958 Geneva Convention on the Continental Shelf.[1] Though the US and Canada entered a short dispute over whether the Icelandic scallops in question were in fact sedentary species, the US eventually accepted this categorization. Of much more serious nature is the dispute over the Pacific Salmon Treaty of 1985, which has been roundly condemned as inadequate for managing the shared resource of west-coast salmon.

There has also been a steady concern with the acid rain question in Ottawa, since the Ohio steel valley exports much of its sulphur dioxide across the Canadian border. As one author suggests, the Americans "preferred to keep acid rain off the bilateral agenda, but Canadian determination kept it there" (Cataldo, 1992:397). The Air Quality Agreement was finally signed in Ottawa on March 13, 1991. Two experts on the US-Canadian Air Quality Agreement add that, ironically, "the Reagan Administration moved extremely quickly in late 1986 and early 1987 to conclude an ... agreement with Mexico. Why the contrast? The fundamental difference between the Canada-US and Mexico-US cases is that in the latter it is the United States who is the major recipient of transboundary pollution. The major air pollution problem along the Mexican-American border is a new, very large, Mexican smelter ... thus a problem on which the Reagan Administration found little research was needed and on which action was taken immediately" (Munton and Castle, 1992:222). We should note that, in late 2000, an "Ozone Annex" under the Air Quality

Agreement was negotiated; it is intended to reduce transborder smog, particularly in the eastern provinces.

Another sticking point has been the location of the Distant Early Warning (DEW) system, set up in the 1950s to detect incoming Soviet bombers. Half of the 42 stations were decommissioned in the 1970s, and the rest in the 1980s. But the sites contain PCBs and other wastes, and the American government did not commit itself to aiding in the cleanup until the mid-1990s, and then only in an agreement covering half the sites (see Moon, 1997). After receiving a pledge for $100-million from the US over the next ten years, Canada agreed to pay for the clean-up with equipment purchased from the Pentagon. While Canadian critics argue the US could do much more, American critics argue that the DEW-line was set up to protect Canadian, as well as American, cities from Soviet attack during the Cold War. This is a familiar theme in the history of defence policy in Canada: How much of a contribution should Canada be obligated to make to NATO and NORAD (the North American Air Defense Command, founded in 1957)? This has become a particularly touchy issue as the United States prepares to embark on a mission to complete a satellite-based missile protection system which many Canadians feel is counter-productive to the process of nuclear disarmament. Unfortunately, as often occurs with defence issues, environmental security is sacrificed in the pursuit of national security.

Free trade is another issue of great historic importance in the Canada-US relationship. As early as 1854 a Reciprocity Treaty between Britain and the US was signed, though it was terminated in 1866 at the request of the US. Following Confederation and the eventual independence of Canada, the question of open borders with the rapidly growing southern neighbour's economy has been a persistent electoral issue. Shortly after the election of Brian Mulroney as Prime Minister in 1984, the Canadian government became determined to enter into a formal agreement. The 1988 CAFTA (Canada-US Free Trade Agreement) "reflected a sense of resignation among policymakers that it is not possible to utilize state actions to diversify Canada's trade relations to any substantial degree from the pattern imposed by the international marketplace" (Hessing and Howlett, 1997:66). It was a clear commitment to the larger idea of a continental economy. Critics argue that job loss inevitably accompanies free trade agreements (Hertig, 1991) since they favour some sectors over others and lead to the migration of capital to areas where there is cheaper labour or low environmental standards. Nevertheless, many Canadians attribute their high quality of life to relatively open access to the American market, by far the world's largest.

Although the US-Canadian axis is more significant overall, the signing and implementation in 1994 of NAFTA also brings Mexico into the picture. Mexico is a burgeoning state, heavily overpopulated in its urban areas, with serious environmental regulation problems of its own. Although NAFTA came with a side agreement on environmental questions (the North American Agreement on Environmental Cooperation), much of the treaty was negotiated in private and, "for many, NAFTA signifies an erosion of the democratic process that is the foundation for resource and environmental policy" (Hessing and Howlett, 1997:242). NAFTA, critics charge, increases pollution by increasing trade, and intensifies the process of urbanization in Mexico as agriculture becomes increasingly commercialized and industrialization is increased by foreign investors anxious to produce goods cheaply and then to export them to the American market.

The environmental side agreement for NAFTA established the Commission on Environmental Co-operation (CEC), which hears complaints about environmental problems in any of the three states (see Chapter 8). It is currently working to establish a North American Clearinghouse on Pollution Prevention Techniques and Environmental Technologies to supplement the work of the North American Pollution Prevention Information Network. This is intended to "eliminate the differences in access, quality, promotion, and dissemination of information that currently exist between the NAFTA partners" (CEC, 1996:15). The CEC is also mandated to develop recommendations on environmental management, encourage effective enforcement of environmental laws and regulations in each country, and to help settle disputes between the parties and among their citizens. (We will return to the question of this institution's effectiveness in Chapter 8.) We should keep a basic fact in mind: It is only when one of the countries persistently fails to enforce its existing environmental laws that trade sanctions can occur. This has led critics to point out that a country could avoid sanctions by limiting its environmental policies in the first place. Furthermore, private companies have new rights to sue governments if they lose market potential due to new policies, and this may be even more constraining (see Johnson and Beaulieu, 1996).

Beyond the Canada-US and NAFTA context, an important connection lies in the north: Canada is an Arctic state, and belongs to the Arctic Council, a multilateral forum involving the circumpolar states of Canada, the United States, Russia, Denmark (Greenland), Iceland, Finland, Norway, and Sweden (see Young, 1996). Canada has even appointed an Arctic Ambassador, Mary Simon, an Inuit and former head of the Inuit Circumpolar Conference. These states have pledged to administer the Arctic Environmental Protection Strategy, referred to in Chapter 8 (see Stoett, 2000; Huebert, 1998). As the polar ice caps threaten to melt away,

Canada will face new sovereignty issues in the north: previously inaccessible waters will be open to new shipping routes (Griffiths, 1997). The radioactive waste in Russia's north is a serious concern (see Feshbach and Friendly, 1992), as are the toxins, such as DDT, which find their way from the south and into the food chain, including mother's milk, affecting native peoples (Dewailly, et al., 1989). Canadians, the vast majority of whom live in the south of the country, close to the American border, often forget that they are living in a circumpolar state, and that the Arctic is vital to both the country and to global geophysical systems.

Beyond these regional relationships, however, it is worth remembering that Canada has many other relations requiring diplomatic attention. Although trade and relations with Asian states have improved over the past several decades, especially with the advent of APEC (Asia-Pacific Economic Cooperation), Canada has always had even stronger ties to Europe: political affiliations with the United Kingdom and France, and an ongoing relationship with the European Union. The latter was strained by the dispute over offshore fishing in 1995, when Canada seized a Spanish trawler for overfishing turbot, but that dispute has been resolved through international negotiations. Canada is a member of the Commonwealth, an association of states associated with the once-mighty British Empire, and of La Francophonie, a group of French-speaking states. In both cases this ties Canada to countries in the southern hemisphere. Beyond this, Canada has been populated by a wide variety of ethnic groups over the years, beginning with the First Nations groups who themselves have transnational links with other indigenous peoples in South America, Russia, and elsewhere. In addition, there has been a vast influx of Ukrainians, Italians, Germans, Dutch, and other Eurasian groups; Haitians, Americans, and Asians have also come in great numbers, ensuring a cosmopolitan demography for Canada and the need for attentive governments to be aware of developments in the various home states.

Many describe Canada's foreign policy as a liberal internationalist one, since Canada is quick to join multilateral organizations and to contribute to them. Canada has been host to many important international conferences on issues ranging from global warming to the reduction of landmines, and is host to international conventions, such as the Convention on Biological Diversity Secretariat in Montreal. Unlike the United States and Russia, Canada pays its United Nations due in full and, usually, on time. Although the Department of Foreign Affairs and International Trade (DFAIT) has undergone budget cuts and decreased its workforce abroad, one can still safely argue that Canada is fairly well represented on most continents, and within most countries. It has contributed to development assistance programs over the years, chiefly through the Canadian

International Development Agency (CIDA). Although funding levels have dropped in recent years, and most of the "aid" Canada sends abroad has been tied to the promotion of Canadian exports, it maintains a fairly positive relationship amongst southern hemispheric states.

As we can see, then, there are many channels of communication and influence reaching into the Canadian political landscape. Although Canada has a strong multilateral tradition, it is often considered highly dependent upon, even dominated by, the United States. Canadian foreign policy must be formulated in an evolving context in which many trade barriers have fallen, capital has unprecedented range, military conflict is fuelled by arms sales from the north to the south, and, most importantly for our purposes, many environmental problems have been recognized as global in scope. Currently the transnational context is most often associated with the process of globalization, a word used so often by politicians, business leaders, and non-governmental organizations that it may be becoming meaningless. Globalization is generally taken to refer to the lowering of trade barriers, and the increasing flow of capital across borders. A more profound definition suggests that a process of technological and cultural convergence is taking place as the free market either entices or forces non-Western people into a Western lifestyle, complete with a reliance on Western markets.

Critical theorists equate modern globalization with old-fashioned imperialism, while neo-liberals argue that it represents the cumulative impact of rational choices, and that it promotes cooperation and the establishment of international institutions. Others argue the enhanced ability of international investors to pick and choose where they put their money means governments have less autonomy over their own affairs (Ross and Trachte, 1990), and are forced to offer inducements, such as lax environmental standards and poor working wages, to attract investment. Optimists suggest that globalization will facilitate both the communicative capacity (especially through the Internet) and the technological ability to deal with environmental problems. Perhaps ecological matters will be better addressed as states gradually cede some of their sovereign prerogatives to international institutions such as the World Trade Organization or the UN's Commission on Sustainable Development. The prospects are interesting, but far from obvious; while these organizations may be able to overcome divisions between states (and that in itself is problematic), critical observers suggest that such institutions are developed to facilitate the spread of industrialization, not to curtail it unless absolutely necessary, by which time it may be too late. One thing is certain: Canada is, and will remain, an international player on this stage. Heavy dependence on trade, a strong multilateral tradition of engagement in UN affairs, close proximity to the United States, and other factors make this a safe assumption. Therefore, it is vital that we have an idea of the international context in which Canadian environmental policy is made.

GLOBAL ECOPOLITICS

We discussed ecopolitics, as the political space where controversy, conflict, and cooperation over environmental issues takes place, in Chapter 1. While it is obvious that this occurs at the national level (and, in a federal state such as Canada, at the provincial level also), it has become increasingly apparent that some of the major confrontations over resources and the environment have been, and will be, at the international level. Many of these, in turn, are clearly global matters, involving many states and non-state actors alike.

As outlined in Chapter 2, Canadians face a plethora of environmental problems, most of which have international implications. At the level of the micro-environment, humanity continues to struggle with infectious diseases. For example, the AIDS virus is proving to be the most pernicious and deadly plague of our time. This is clearly an international issue, since the resources needed to deal with the threat are tremendous and cannot be supplied in whole by those states, mostly in sub-Saharan Africa and Asia, which are most immediately affected. AIDS hurts not only those with the disease, but those who must care for them or who are left behind, often as orphans, when the victim dies. The United Nations has organized confer-ences and created an institution, UNAIDS, to coordinate international efforts to prevent and treat the disease, but there has been only limited suc-cess. Recently, after a well-publicized conference in South Africa, the United States agreed to lend African states $1-billion per year to assist in the effort. Critics charge this is too little, too late, and only puts these states further into debt.

Most of the problems discussed in the context of global ecopolitics, however, are macro in nature. They centre on questions of the commons, areas where many states have access, but no single state has jurisdiction. This includes the oceans, space, the atmosphere, and Antarctica. The commons are viewed as areas of obvious concern because everyone has an incentive to exploit them at an unsustainable rate, even though all involved will eventually suffer the consequences. This is true for many resources found within the territorial jurisdiction of states, such as forests and endangered species, but it also true in the long-term for the oceans and the atmosphere. We have multilateral agreements in place to deal with many of the ensuing issues, but they are not universal and there are still problems with how the various costs involved are to be distributed, and how compliance with such agreements can be effectively enforced. While some states play leading roles, others are clearly lagging behind in the domestic implementation required to adhere to such treaties. (As we will see in Chapters 8 and 9, Canada has a rather mixed record in this regard.)

The major international rift, not surprisingly, is between industrialized states in the north and "less-developed" states in the south. Although it is clear that the north traditionally has been the greater polluter, contributing to global warming and ozone-layer depletion, the south's expanding economies are producing more greenhouse gas emissions than ever before. This worries northern states, which see a global threat in this growth. But leaders in southern states argue they have every right to develop along the industrial lines of the north, and that attempts to impose stricter environmental controls now represent a colonialist attitude on the part of the developed nations. At the very least, southern states want compensation for limiting their pollution. Although some progress was made toward establishing international regimes capable of dealing with this division at the Earth Summit in 1992, it has been insufficient to deal effectively with the demands of either the north or the south. Similar debates colour the attempt to preserve biodiversity in species-rich areas in Latin America and Asia; southern states argue they have no inherent obligation to preserve what those in the north refer to as the "common heritage of mankind."

Even if we had more adequate means of compensation, one could argue that, due to the anarchical nature of the international system described in the preceding section, it would be very difficult to enforce international agreements, especially if they limited economic prospects. It is important to understand that international law does not function at the level of a national legal system; there is no central authority that can charge people with infractions, haul them into court, and incarcerate them if necessary. This is especially true of international environmental law, which consists of a series of agreements signed by states and a small number of international institutions, such as the United Nations Environmental Programme (UNEP), which are authorized to help implement those agreements. Before delving into environmental diplomacy in the age of globalization, however, a few words on treaties and conventions are necessary.

A treaty has the binding force of international law, and becomes part of the national legal code once it is ratified by a state. In the Canadian case, ratification involves a positive vote in Parliament. More common in the environmental law area are conventions, which have many of the same attributes of treaties, but are generally aimed more specifically at particular issue-areas, such as global warming or ozone-layer depletion. A protocol is an even more detailed device: it is the official record of a diplomatic conference that shows actual commitments. For example, the Kyoto Protocol outlined steps signatories would take to achieve the goals of the framework convention on climate change, though critics charged the Canadian commitment "will prove just as hollow" as the one made in 1992 (Macdonald and Smith, 1999:108). Finally — and this is an important distinction — declarations are statements of intent, but are not legally binding.

We should point out also that most treaties and conventions have convenient "opt-out" clauses, and are in that sense less than binding themselves. But declarations and resolutions passed by international organizations do have symbolic value. For example, in October 1996, the World Conservation Union, a global alliance of 880 agencies and governments from 133 countries, unanimously endorsed a resolution supporting designation of Clayoquot Sound as a United Nations Biosphere Reserve (UNESCO finally officially declared it as such in February of 2000). No doubt, this adds to extant pressure on the British Columbia government to preserve as much of the area as possible. Similarly, the work of the Intergovernmental Panel on Climate Change (see IPCC, 1995) has helped convince (some) politicians and businesses that global warming is a serious long-term threat to humanity. However, there are also concerns that large efforts at "summit diplomacy" serve as little more than photo-opportunities for politicians, generating promises they often have little concrete ability (or, worse, genuine intent) of keeping.

Indeed, environmental diplomacy has become a growth industry during the last three decades. Canadian diplomats and policy officials have been particularly busy, signing agreements on everything from the 1968 Agreement on the Rescue of Astronauts, the Return of Astronauts and the Return of Objects Launched into Space, to the comprehensive "Agenda 21" at the Earth Summit in 1992. Other treaties signed include the International Convention for the Regulation of Whaling, from which Canada withdrew in 1982, the Convention on Long-Range Transboundary Air Pollution of 1979, and the 1989 Basel Convention on the Control of Transboundary Movements of Hazardous Wastes and Their Disposal. While major events such as the 1992 Earth Summit capture public attention, most forms of environmental management take place at a more bureaucratic level, as officials and conferences of the parties to major conventions meet and hammer out final clauses in agreements, push to have them ratified at home, and begin the arduous task of actually implementing new commitments.

In the Canadian case, most interaction with other governments involves the United States. Although continental relations will always be a primary concern in Ottawa, it is undeniable that we live in an increasingly interdependent global political system. Many decisions taken in Ottawa on issues, such as global warming and ozone layer depletion, require a nuanced understanding of the international context. Indeed, global sources of pressure may exert a greater force than domestic constituencies in many issue-areas. This is obvious from an ecological perspective, since the Canadian land mass and sea zones do not exist in a sealed container. Canadians are to some extent at the mercy of what other states do; environmental policy in China, India, and Africa will affect the climate and products imported into the country. At the same time, Canada's domestic behaviour influences other states, since Canadian greenhouse gas emissions and import policies have an impact on questions of the commons and on the export policies of many states looking to the Canadian market.

Of all the complex issues before the Canadian government at the present, global warming is the most difficult yet most visible indication of this essential interdependence. As the global climate warms, Canadians must be concerned with the impact in several areas. For example, the Arctic ice mass is melting at what appears to be an unprecedented rate, and the Northwest passage could soon become navigable throughout the year. Many analysts believe this would threaten Canadian sovereignty, since ships would avoid the longer route between Asia and Europe. (In the previous chapter we detailed a related conflict with the United States over the use of American ice-breakers in the area.) Some argue that Russian dams have forced salt water into the Arctic, causing the ice to melt, rather than global warming. Nevertheless, there is widespread consensus that global warming is occurring and that sea levels will slowly rise as a result, affecting coastal communities. Beyond this, there are concerns over the impact of global warming on Canadian resources, in particular agriculture and forestry, as various species migrate northward to escape the heat.

But there's more: If global warming makes others areas less hospitable, there will be increased pressure for immigration to cooler regions such as the northern hemisphere. Erratic weather patterns will disrupt economic activity, and the struggle for scarce resources may lead to increased conflict. All of this points to the need to establish means of global and human security to protect individuals from a variety of security threats, from landmines to unsafe drinking water, and to enhance Canada's own security. (We will return to this theme in Chapter 11.) It is essential to remember that individual diplomatic commitments, such as those discussed in the present chapter, are made within the broader context of an evolving foreign policy perspective which emanates from Ottawa. Regardless of the long-term dangers of global warming and other global issues, Canadian foreign policy remains fixated on trade; indeed, the Canadian economy is heavily dependent on trade with the United States, and the government actively seeks trade opportunities around the world. We would be mistaken to conclude, even with the large and complex environmental diplomatic architecture that has surfaced in recent decades, that the global environment is a priority in Ottawa.

It is also important to realize that governments are not the only actors in global environmental politics. Multinational corporations have a tremendous impact, since they devise strategies for either dealing with environmental quality issues (for example, the International Standards Organization) or for ignoring them. The industrial lobbyists discussed in Chapter 4 are also at work abroad, in foreign capitals and international organizations. They are well equipped and often expansion-oriented, always on the lookout for new markets and sources of natural resources. They often have Canadian subsidiaries and therefore seek to influence Canadian domestic policy as well. Canadian companies themselves are now major investors abroad, in everything from mining concerns in Latin America to production facilities in Asia. Their conduct reflects on the international community's view of Canada as a whole, for better or worse. We will return to this theme in Chapter 11 when we discuss oil drilling in south Sudan, zinc mining in south Spain, and gold mining in Kyrgystan.

However, corporations are also taking positive steps to coordinate their environmental standards. The logic here is simple: One of the main reasons corporations might invest in projects with dubious environmental controls is to benefit from a competitive advantage. However, if all companies adhere to similar standards, this is not possible. The International Organization for Standardization published the ISO 14001 in 1996. It establishes a coordinated framework of controls to manage environmental protection. The series covers a wide range of related environmental management topics, including environmental performance evaluation, life cycle assessment, and environmental auditing, based on what is termed the cyclical process of "plan, implement, check and review."[2] In theory, the ISO 14001 aims to support environmental protection and prevention of pollution in balance with socio-economic needs, and demands that corporations make policy commitments to legal compliance, pollution prevention, and continual improvement. Critics argue this type of self-regulation by industry does not capture many subsidiary operations around the globe, and it allows standards to be set too low for actual improvement. The current (1996) edition of the standard requires public availability of a company's environmental policy only. A significant step forward would be to require external reporting of environmental performance; this may be done when the ISO 14001 is revised in 2001. Many NGOs would be more satisfied if this were to lead to increased public scrutiny of large corporations that claim they are "going green."

NGOs play an important role on the world stage as well. One can identify a growing list of issue-areas — forestry, sealing, trapping, global
warming, hazardous waste disposal, and others — in which non-state
actors have contributed to policy formation at a variety of levels. One
author refers to this as "catalytic diplomacy," in which there are "sym-
bioses between the activities of ... state and non-state actors" (Hocking,
1996:450). The clear-cutting controversy in British Columbia was interna-
tionalized by Greenpeace and the Friends of Clayoquot Sound. Similarly,
anti-trapping groups promoted a damaging boycott of Canadian furs in
Europe. Perhaps the most visible presence of an NGO, however, was in the
anti-sealing movement, in which the International Federation for Animal
Welfare (IFAW) harshly condemned the commercial seal hunt off the east
coast. This campaign began as early as 1965 and continues today, as the
IFAW runs newspaper ads in North America and Europe and publicizes
illegal sealing activities. One video portrayed "seals being pulled from the
water with large hooks, struggling after being shot non-fatally, and lying
in bloody piles after being skinned" (Mulrennan, 1998:67). Needless to
say, there is considerable animosity between the sealing industry and such
groups, but their transnational impact is of great interest. Indeed, one can
identify a more general divide between members of NGOs, who carry their
largely urban-centred pro-environmentalist bias with them, and local
hunting and trapping groups, who resent the impact on their livelihoods
of NGO campaigning.

Fairly extensive consultation with NGOs occurred in the preparation for
UNCED as well (see Cooper, 1992), although many NGOs declined to participate in the official meetings, opting instead to hold a simultaneous conference near Rio de Janeiro. The politics within the larger groups is a story
in itself. For example, there is internal dissent within Greenpeace over that
organization's blanket refusal to consider the possible merits of genetically
modified foods. Some critics charge the organization is relying on its anti-
GMO campaign to fulfil its budgetary needs, overlooking the scientific realities of the situation.[3] Heavy NGO presence can be witnessed at the
Conferences of Parties for major international agreements, such as the
Convention on International Trade in Endangered Species.

When it comes to environmental diplomacy, Canada has been relatively
active on the international stage (see Chapter 8). Nevertheless, critics
charge Canada has not matched its rhetoric with domestic commitment.
For example, Canada was the first state to sign the historic Convention on
Biological Diversity, but has yet to pass a comprehensive federal endangered species protection act. Similarly, little concrete action — beyond
some of the "voluntary" measures described in Chapter 4 — has been taken
to allow Canada to reach the goals put forth at the Kyoto conference on

global warming. And, although Canada has for many decades been respected as a donor state interested in the welfare of the southern hemisphere, this concern has also reflected self-interest, and aid levels have been dropping steadily for many years.

These problems are not, by any means, unique to Canada. In general, though it is no longer a nascent field, environmental diplomacy continues to experience complications similar to other areas of world politics. Although there have been hundreds of multilateral and bilateral treaties and conventions signed by hundreds of states, we still face central problems related to cooperation between sovereign governments and the competitive world economy in which they operate. As globalization proceeds, many groups struggle against its immediate and long-term impacts, including economic dislocation and unemployment, cultural homogenization, and the intensified exploitation of natural resources.

Canada has attempted to balance its hungry trade policies with a "human security" approach extolled in Ottawa. It is obvious, however, that the former are more dominant. But it is also clear that government officials in Ottawa, and even in provincial capitals, cannot ignore the transnational context in which they operate. There has been much literature emerging from the field of international studies suggesting that the older concept of national security may be supplanted by environmental security, a more encompassing term which recognizes threats to the environment caused by economic processes as well as by enemy attacks.[4] This concern certainly applies to Canada in the case of protection of the coasts and, of course, the Arctic (see Gizewski, 1993-94; and Huebert, 1999). Other literature points to the possibility that conflicts over resources are, themselves, causes of violent conflict (see Homer-Dixon, 1994), though little has been done concerning the Canadian context.

CONCLUSION

This chapter has presented a short description of Canada's main foreign policy concerns and actors, and has delved into the complexities of global ecopolitics. Canada must constantly struggle between the intense pull of its southern neighbour and a commitment to multilateralism. Canada has strong ties to several European states, in particular France and the United Kingdom; it has connections with the Arctic states; and ties have grown with Asia. NAFTA has shaped the political economy of Canada in recent years, but Ottawa maintains a distinct foreign policy based on United Nations participation and a strong pro-globalization stance. Meanwhile, it is fair to say that environmental problems have become increasingly global in scope, and that international law and institutions so far have not been up to the task of solving them. The main problems that have evolved are the reluctance of states to sacrifice sovereignty for environmental issues (and their readiness to do so for investment purposes), and the north-south split, which continues to dominate discussions on global warming and other large-scale issues.

We turn now to the second section of this text, which covers the actual policies and regulations that shape Canadian environmental policy today.

NOTES

1   Article 77 of the UNCLOS gives coastal states the right to manage straddling stocks of so-called "creepy crawlies."

2   The structure of ISO 14001 also provides a common basis for integration with elements of occupational safety and health management, and quality management systems such as ISO 9000.

3   See http://www.foodsecurity.net/news/newsitem.php3?nid=249&tnews=news

4   This is part of a broader reconceptualization of security, which has met both positive and negative responses. See Walt (1991) and Stoett (1999) for discussions.

PART TWO
POLICY

SIX

ENVIRONMENTAL LAWS AND REGULATION

INTRODUCTION: UNDERSTANDING THE ENVIRONMENTAL REGULATORY SYSTEM

In Chapters 3 and 4, the basic structures and processes of the Canadian political system were outlined. Chapter 7 will discuss specific policy responses to challenges posed by environmental hazards, such as toxic wastes, and the need to evaluate the potential environmental impact of development projects. However, in order to understand in a meaningful way the formulation and implementation of environmental laws and regulatory policy in Canada, it is necessary to briefly examine the regulatory process as well.

Regulations are designed to modify human behaviour. In other words, governments regulate in order to make people behave in a prescribed manner which will lead to the realization of desired objectives aimed at achieving standards through the implementation of guidelines. However, regulations are not the same as standards and guidelines. Standards imply strict and rigid rules of behaviour in which the concepts of equality of law and fair treatment are applied. Guidelines are associated with flexibility applied to unique or unusual circumstances. Regulation is one of the more coercive governing instruments used by the state to achieve desired objectives. Regulations involve direct sanctions and penalties; it is assumed people will modify their behaviour to comply with regulations rather than incur the penalties. Ideally, "[r]egulations, standards and guidelines (and therefore implementation and enforcement) embrace both reliable, predictable behaviour and unreliable, unpredictable, unique circumstances" (Doern, Prince, and McNaughton, 1982:1).

In the environmental policy field, the enactment of laws and the formulation of regulations, standards, and guidelines rely significantly on scientific and technological knowledge. As we suggested in Chapter 1, science is of major importance in establishing causality which, in many cases, becomes the basis for regulatory decisions. For example, natural science may determine that specific types of activities, such as the emission of sulphur dioxide fumes into the atmosphere, cause environmental problems such as acid rain. The social sciences also play an important role in the regulatory process by predicting the best ways of changing behaviour to encourage people to avoid producing additional environmental hazards. There tends to be a false perception in modern society that science and technology provide precise answers and means to deal with environmental problems. Unfortunately, this is not the case. There is a considerable amount of imprecision and uncertainty in both natural and social scientific data. To illustrate this point, we can focus on the growing public concern over the health hazards and environmental effects of toxic substances. Although scientists have demonstrated causal linkages between certain toxic substances and cancer, the exact nature of the relationship is unknown. Consequently, efforts to develop regulations for the use of toxic substances produce much controversy. Scientific arguments can be used and exploited by all interested parties in the regulatory process.

Regardless of all the debate, disagreement, controversy, and uncertainty, legislation and incentives within and outside of legislation are primary components in approaching environmental regulation. Legislation typically encourages ecologically appropriate behaviour through sanctions and incentives by means of economic or social rewards or benefits. Incentives in general are seen as outside of typical regulatory practices. At times economic instruments are used as policy tools to provide incentives and financial aid in pursuit of environmental goals (CCME, 1996). Interestingly, the first well-defined exercise incorporating environmental considerations into a budget-making process in Canada was the 1994 Federal Task Force on Economic Instruments and Disincentives to Sound Environmental Practices (Canada, 1996).

Environmental regulations have been in existence in Canada since the nineteenth century. Many of these regulations predate the creation of environmental departments and agencies. However, most environmental regulations are more recent, the product of the past thirty years. Beginning in the early 1970s, when public concern about the increasing menace of visible pollution problems pressured the federal and provincial governments to take effective action to deal with pollution problems, environmental regulations have become a major factor in Canadian society, directly or indirectly affecting all Canadians.

From the initial concern with pollution problems, the focus of environmental regulatory policy has evolved to encompass a broader-based environmental management philosophy to deal with a variety of problems and issues such as toxic chemicals, acid rain, waste management, and many others. During this period, greater knowledge and experience has been gained, and new and improved legislation has been put in place. Consequently, environmental regulation in the early 2000s is much different from that of the early 1970s. "Early environmental regulation was the product of relative economic prosperity" (Doern, Price, and McNaughton, 1982:2), whereas current environmental regulation is viewed by many as a barrier to economic growth. It is important to appreciate that current environmental regulatory policy and practices have evolved over time and must therefore be examined in the historical context of their development. In other words, the past provides the key to understanding the present.

FEDERAL ENVIRONMENTAL LAWS AND REGULATIONS

In Canada, federal environmental regulatory policy is based on several statutes, including the Canadian Environmental Protection Act, the Fisheries Act, the Canadian Environmental Assessment Act, the Canada Water Act, the Pest Control Products Act, and several more (see the appendix for a complete list of federal and provincial environmental statutes). Unlike the Government of Ontario regulatory philosophy which deals with air regulation issues at the point of impingement, federal environmental regulatory policy is based on the philosophy of preventing pollution, rather than contending with environmental damage after the fact. This may be illustrated by examining some federal statutes.

The Clean Air Act, law from 1970 to 1988, empowered the Department of the Environment to conduct a national program of air pollution surveillance in Canada; to set national air-quality objectives; to set national emission standards applied at the source of air pollution; and to set emission guidelines containing emission limits, as well as to regulate the composition of fuels produced or imported into Canada. Under the authority of the Clean Air Act, the Minister of the Environment could conduct research on air pollution and publish information obtained by the Department of the Environment. In 1988, the Clean Air Act was repealed and its provisions incorporated into Part V of the Canadian Environmental Protection Act (CEPA). Under section 113 of CEPA, environmental offenders are subject to fines as high as $300,000 on summary conviction, for contravening a national emission standard, importing prohibited fuels, or contravening other regulations set out in the Act. An indictable offence can result in fines as high as $1-million (Canada, 1985b, Section 13). As well, contravention of any provision of CEPA can result in fines of up to $200,000 under section 116 of the Act.

TABLE 6.1

COMPARING CEPA 1988 AND CEPA 1999

SUBJECT	CEPA 1999	CEPA 1988
Pollution Prevention	» Cornerstone of the new act, requires pollution prevention planning for toxic substances	» Pollution control was priority, with no authority to require pollution prevention planning
Toxic Substances	» Virtual elimination of most toxic substances, emergency plans for toxic substances, 2 years to formulate action and 18 months to finalize action	» Virtual elimination not in the act, no deadlines for taking action to prevent pollution, and 5 years to assess "priority" substances
Intergovernmental Cooperation	» National Advisory Committee (NAC) established with representatives from federal, provincial, and aboriginal governments. Thus CEPA 1999 recognizes for the first time the increasing role of aboriginal people in environmental protection. The NAC is to provide both policy and technical advice.	» Role of aboriginal people not defined.
Meeting International Obligations	» Specific authority granted to regulate Canadian sources of international air and water pollution when another level of Canadian government is unwilling or unable to deal with the pollution course, to implement the international Convention on Prior Informed Consent for hazardous chemicals and pesticides in international trade, and a more stringent regime for ocean disposal.	» The authority to regulate Canadian sources of international air pollution, but not water pollution. Ocean dumping and hazardous chemicals and pesticides in international trade not mentioned.

CONT'D

Until 1999, the 1988 Canadian Environmental Protection Act was composed of seven key parts. Part I allowed the minister to establish objectives, guidelines, and codes of practice to enhance and protect environmental quality. Part II provided for the regulation of toxic substances, including the compilation of a Priority Substances List of toxic or potentially toxic substances. Part III regulated the manufacture and use of "nutrients" which contribute to algae growth in products such as various cleaning agents. Part VI concerned the activities of federal government departments and activi-

TABLE 6.1 (CONT'D)

COMPARING CEPA 1988 AND CEPA 1999 (CONT'D)

SUBJECT	CEPA 1999	CEPA 1988
Hormone-Disrupting Substances	» Government is required to conduct research on hormone-disrupting substances	» No such requirement mentioned
Public Participation	» Public is given a new *right-to-sue* if government fails to enforce CEPA 1999 due to a significant harm to the environment; requirement to establish a National Pollutants Release Inventory so that Canadians can get information about pollution in their communities, and a new CEPA Environmental Registry which gives access to public regarding administration of the act, regulations, ministerial notices, and various administrative agreements.	» No CEPA Environmental Registry and no right to sue; instead, a right to "request an investigation." A National Pollutants Release Inventory established under the discretion of Minister.
Enforcement	» CEPA enforcement officers authorized to issue on-the-spot orders to stop violations and prevent pollution, and a provision for alternative dispute resolution to avoid costly court procedures.	» Can issue warning letters and lay charges, but no authority to stop violations, and no alternative dispute settlement system

SOURCE: Canada, *Department of Environment, A Guide to the New Canadian Environmental Act, Ottawa: Minister of Public Works and Government services, March 2000.*

ties on Crown lands. Part v regulated "International Air Pollution." Part vi regulated ocean dumping. Part vii provided general rules on regulations, inspections, agreements with the provinces, investigation of offences, and punishment.

However, a need was felt to strengthen CEPA for the new millennium, especially to emphasize pollution prevention planning rather than pollution control as the basic philosophy. After a series of committee hearings in the House of Commons, a new Canadian Environmental Protection Act was approved which received Royal Assent on September 14, 1999. The basic differences between the old and new versions are outlined in Table 6.1. In addition to the above-listed changes, the new CEPA 1999 enshrines in its preamble the following guiding principles: sustainable development, pollution prevention, the precautionary principle, the polluter pays principle, and removing threats to biological diversity. The "precautionary principle" is to be applied where there are threats of serious or irreversible damage. In addition, the Act requires that the federal government avoid duplication with other federal regulations; defines broadly terms such as ecosystem, biological diversity, pollution prevention, and sustainable development; reinforces the importance of intergovernmental cooperation in protecting the environment and requires that the federal minister consult with provinces and territories; establishes for the first time an equal right of the three aboriginal (territorial) governments in Canada; and establishes an assessment process for new animate products of biotechnology (such as living organisms). Finally, the new Act removes a provision by which the federal facilities (departments, agencies, federal Crown corporations, federal parks, buildings, banks, airlines, broadcasting, aboriginal lands, etc.) were exempted from provincial environmental regulations; now the Minister is authorized to establish guidelines and codes of practice akin to provincial regulations. The 1999 CEPA is much improved legislation. Since it was implemented only in 2000, it is too early to provide an assessment of its effectiveness.

The former Clean Air Act enabled Environment Canada to establish emission guidelines which were basically suggestions to industry as to the levels of pollutants which should not be exceeded in Canada, a role now absorbed by the CEPA. The guidelines are set by the government in conjunction with members of industry. The federal government utilizes the "best practicable technology" approach as the basic criterion for determining emission guidelines. Thus far, guidelines have been established for a number of industrial activities, including arctic mining, asphalt paving plants, cement plants, and coke ovens. By working closely with industry, the guidelines tend to reflect the minimum emission levels which industry is prepared to accept. However, in most cases, unless they are adopted as provincial standards, the federal guidelines are not legally enforceable. The first national emission standard was put into effect on August 1, 1976, to regulate secondary lead smelters. The standard specifies the maximum amount of lead in each cubic metre of air which may be emitted by a plant which produces refined lead, lead alloys, or lead oxide. Since 1976, emission standards for asbestos mining and milling and for mercury emissions in chlor-alkali plants have been established. The CEPA also enables the federal government to establish "specific emission standards" on works, undertakings, and businesses that fall within exclusive federal jurisdiction.

The former Clean Air Act, as administered by the Department of the Environment, was designed to enable the federal government to regulate the emission of pollutants into the air. The government's establishment of air quality objectives for desirable, acceptable, and tolerable levels of atmospheric pollutants was intended to protect public health by setting limits on the concentration of contaminants in the air. The replacement of the Clean Air Act by the CEPA in 1988 provided the first step in comprehensive environmental regulatory legislation. CEPA continued the government's commitment to regulate the emission of air pollutants as well as to provide a regulatory framework for toxic substances, nutrients that encourage algae growth, undertakings by federal departments and undertakings on federal lands, and ocean dumping. Ministry guidelines in conjunction with legally enforceable standards have become the cornerstone of Canadian environmental policy and the government's commitment to sustainable development.

The federal government also plays an important role in protecting and maintaining water quality in Canada. In this regard, the most important statute is the Fisheries Act. "It is the federal government's major tool for enunciating and enforcing its water quality objectives, and the federal Department of the Environment hopes it will act as the basis for achieving a nation-wide uniformity of water quality" (Estrin and Swaigen, 1978:144). The standards for water quality established under the Fisheries Act are intended to be minimum national standards. The provinces can set and enforce more stringent regulations under their own legislation. Similar to many other environmental statutes, the Fisheries Act contains a general prohibition against pollution:

> No person shall deposit or permit the deposit of a deleterious substance of any type in waters frequented by fish or in any place under any conditions where such deleterious substance or any other deleterious substance that results from the deposit of such deleterious substance may enter any such water. (Canada, 1985a, Section 33-2)

The Act defines a deleterious substance as any substance that alters or contributes to the degradation of water quality so that it endangers aquatic life. Regulations established under the Fisheries Act specify the amounts of a deleterious substance that may be deposited in the water without contravening the Act. Thus far, regulations have been established for a variety of industrial activities. For example, the Fisheries Act contains regulations for mining activities, specifying the amount of arsenic, lead, copper, nickel, zinc, total suspended matter, and radium 226 which may be deposited in the water. Similar regulations have been set for oil and gas, the wood industry, including pulp and paper mills and logging, agriculture, and thermal and nuclear power plants. Anyone or any plant or factory caught breaking the law is liable to pay fines of up to $100,000 in a summary conviction, and up to $500,000 for an indictable offence. The Fisheries Act also enables the Minister of the Environment to review the plans and specifications of any proposed new operation, or information on any aspect of an ongoing oper-ation, to determine if it poses a water pollution threat. If the minister finds fault, he or she can request or order changes and modifications.

While the Fisheries Act is the primary statute used by the federal gov-ernment to regulate water quality, the government can also use the Canada Shipping Act and the Canada Water Act to control particular aspects of water pollution. The Canada Shipping Act enables the Cabinet to make regulations for nearly every aspect of marine activity that could give rise to pollution. The Canada Water Act has three parts, of which only the third part has a measurable effect on Canadian waters. Part III of the Canada Water Act contains specific regulations to control the amount of phos-phorus in cleaning agents. Under the Act, regulations for phosphate levels in laundry detergents have been prescribed. The various statutes described above enable the federal government to play a significant role in control-ling water pollution through the use of regulatory policies.

The federal government also makes use of environmental regulations to control and prevent pollution in several other areas. For example, the Federal Pest Control Products Act is used to regulate pesticide products manufactured, sold, or imported into Canada. This Act is administered by the Department of Agriculture and governs the classification, registra-tion, and labelling of all pesticides used in Canada. However, provincial governments may exempt particular pesticide products from the regula-tions of the Act. The aim of the Pest Control Products Act is to regulate potentially hazardous chemical products at the source or point of origin. Consequently, no pesticide product can be imported or sold in Canada unless it has been registered and conforms to the Act's standards. Standards are set out by the Plant Product Division of the Department of Agriculture. Regulations created under the Act name and classify pesti-cide products and provide precise instructions for the registering, pack-aging, and labelling of the products. Persons or companies found contravening the regulations of the Pest Control Products Act are liable to stiff penalties and fines and, in some cases, a two-year jail sentence. Under certain circumstances, some products, such as those which are used specifically for research purposes or other non-market applications, may be exempted. However, these products then fall under the operation of the Food and Drugs Act, another important federal statute used to regu-late potentially hazardous chemicals.

Unlike economic regulation, which is premised on the need for government intervention to correct imperfections in the marketplace, social regulation is a more recent by-product of the 1960s and the early 1970s, concerned with ensuring health, safety, and fairness. It is important to note that the development of most social regulation in Canada occurred during a period of economic prosperity. The first wave of social regulation forced many industrial activities to invest large amounts of capital to upgrade plant facilities to make them safer and more environmentally sound. These changes produced some marked improvements in environmental quality. However, as economic conditions began to deteriorate, and since further large-scale capital investment would only produce marginal improvement in safety and environmental quality, there was an outcry against over-regulation and the need for more cost-effective regulations. Many industries argued that major changes in Canadian society, especially in the area of economic activity, created the need for regulatory reform. The need to adjust social and environmental regulations to suit the changing conditions of Canadian society indicates how the guiding principles and values underlying the formulation of regulations must be constantly realigned and balanced in response to changes over time. Similar regulatory reform processes have also been instituted by several provincial governments.

More recently there has been a federal initiative to revise regulatory implementation and enforcement policy within the CEPA. Now, under CEPA, formal court processes such as prosecution are an option to achieve compliance, although they are rather expensive and slow (Canada, CEPA, 1997). Other more efficient and economical enforcement tools exist, one of which is the Environmental Protection Alternative Measures Program (EPAM). This program permits violators to negotiate with the federal government to correct the violation, thereby avoiding a lengthy court process, but excludes those who have caused serious and irreversible harm to the environment, and or who are repeat offenders. Beyond this, the EPAM provides enforcement tools that include environmental protection compliance orders, maximum penalties of $1-million per day or up to five years in prison, assurance that violators cannot benefit from the proceeds of their crime, court-sentenced mandatory educational programs at the expense of offenders, charges to restore damage done to the environment, and payment for ecological research caused by the offence. Thus, we can conclude that the regulatory process in Canada is a dynamic one in which the formulation and implementation of regulations are continuously changing and evolving to meet the needs of dominant sectors of Canadian society. However, it is clear that, given the federal nature of the Canadian political system, provincial standards and guidelines are often or equally more important.

PROVINCIAL ENVIRONMENTAL LAWS AND REGULATIONS: SELECTED JURISDICTIONS

In this section, we focus our attention on provincial environmental laws and regulatory policies, by selecting (due to space constraints) four jurisdictions: British Columbia, Ontario, Quebec, and Nova Scotia. We believe these four jurisdictions can provide us with a general perspective on the role of provincial governments in facing environmental challenges. Unfortunately, there is a dearth of policy literature regarding the northern territories and prairie provinces.

British Columbia

The appendix includes all the relevant legislative acts which the Provincial of British Columbia has enacted, totalling nineteen. Among these, we have selected four laws: (a) Environmental Management Act, (b) Environmental Assessment Act, (c) Ministry of Environment Act, and (d) Waste Management Act. The scope and jurisdiction of these four laws are examined below.

(a) *Environmental Management Act:* Environmental issues in British Columbia are managed under the Environmental Management Act, which defines the term "environment" to mean the air, land, water, and all other external conditions or influences under which humans, animals, and plants live or are developed (Article 1.1). Another term exclusively defined is "environmental emergency," which means an occurrence or natural disaster that affects the environment, and which includes a flood, a landslide, and a spill or leakage of oil, or of a poisonous or dangerous substance (Article 1.1). Under this Act, a detrimental environmental impact occurs when a change in the quality of air, land, or water substantially reduces the usefulness of the environment or its capacity to support life (Article 1.2). Furthermore, the legislation authorizes the minister to manage, protect, and enhance the environment, including:

» planning, research, and investigation with respect to the environment;
» development of policies for the management, protection, and use of the environment;
» planning, design, construction, operation, and maintenance of works and undertakings for the management, protection, or enhancement of the environment;
» provision of information to the public about the quality and use of the environment;

» preparation and publication of policies, strategies, objectives, and standards for the protection and management of the environment; and

» preparation and publication of environmental management plans for specific areas of British Columbia which may include, but need not be limited to, measures with respect to the following: flood control, drainage, soil conservation, water resource management, fisheries and aquatic life management, wildlife management, and air management. (Article 2)

These provisions can be enforced by a conservation officer of the British Columbia government, and the minister may designate a person employed in the Ministry of Environment as a conservation officer. With respect to appeals against the decision of the ministry officials, there exists an Environmental Appeal Board which has the powers of protection and privileges of a commissioner under the British Columbia Inquiry Act.

(b) *Environmental Assessment Act:* The Environmental Assessment Act is intended to promote sustainability by protecting the environment and fostering a sound economy and social well-being; to provide for the thorough, timely, and integrated assessment of the environmental, economic, social, cultural, heritage, and health effects of reviewable projects; to prevent or mitigate adverse effects of reviewable projects; to provide an open, accountable, and neutrally administered process for the assessment of reviewable projects, and of activities that pertain to the environment or to land use; and to provide for participation, in an assessment under this Act by the public, proponents, First Nations, municipalities and regional districts, the government and its agencies, the government of Canada and its agencies, and British Columbia's neighbouring jurisdictions (Article 1). BC is the first jurisdiction in which there is legal binding on the provincial government to seek participation not only from the environmental NGOs, but also from the First Nations, and municipal and regional councils.

(c) *Ministry of Environment Act:* The British Columbia government has enacted a separate law pertaining to the provincial Ministry of Environment which is established with the power and authority

» to encourage and maintain an optimum quality environment through specific objectives for the management and protection of land, water, air, and living resources of British Columbia;

» to undertake inventories and to plan for and assist in planning, as required, for the effective management, protection, and conservation of all water, land, air, plant life, and animal life;

» to manage, protect, and conserve all water, land, air, plant life, and animal life, having regard to the economic and social benefits they may confer on British Columbia;

» to set standards for, collect, store, retrieve, analyze, and make available environmental data;

» to monitor environmental conditions of specific developments and to assess and report to the minister on general environmental conditions in British Columbia;

» to undertake, commission, and coordinate environmental studies;

» to develop and sustain public information and education programs to enhance public appreciation of the environment;

» to plan for, design, construct, operate, and maintain structures necessary for the administration of this Act or for another purpose or function assigned by the Lieutenant Governor in Council; and

» to plan for, coordinate, implement, and manage a program to protect the welfare of the public in the event of an environmental emergency or disaster. (Article 4)

These powers are substantive, enabling the officials of the Ministry of Environment to seek compliance and monitoring as well as to set standards for environmental quality control and assurance.

(d) *Waste Management Act:* The fourth act included in this brief survey deals with waste management. Under the Waste Management Act, the British Columbia government is authorized to control effluents, which means any substance that is discharged into water or onto land and which

» injures or is capable of injuring the health or safety of a person,

» injures or is capable of injuring property or any life form,

» interferes or is capable of interfering with visibility,

» interferes or is capable of interfering with the normal conduct of business,

» causes or is capable of causing material physical discomfort to a person, or

» damages or is capable of damaging the environment. (Article 1)

The Waste Management Act requires that recycling be used for any disposal of a product or substance; and that remediation measures be undertaken to eliminate, correct, or mitigate the negative effects of any waste on the environment or human health (Article 1). Finally, there is provision of an appeal to the Environmental Appeal Board. Through these four and other environmentally related laws (see appendix) and regulations, the Government of BC exercises control of environmental pollution.

Ontario

Beyond a largely declaratory "Environmental Bill of Rights" introduced by the New Democratic Party administration in the early 1990s, environmental regulation in Ontario is based on four principal statutes: The Environmental Protection Act, the Water Resources Act, the Pesticides Act, and the Environmental Assessment Act. These acts are administered by the Ontario Ministry of the Environment (OME), the government's principal environmental department. Of the four statutes mentioned above, the Environmental Protection Act and the Water Resources Act are most frequently used to regulate the environment in Ontario.

(a) The *Environmental Protection Act* is designed to provide for the protection and conservation of the natural environment. However, the Act is used primarily to protect and conserve the natural environment against pollution. The Act contains a general prohibition, "that no person shall deposit in, add to, enter discharge into the natural environment any contaminant ... in an amount, concentration or level in excess of that prescribed by regulations" (Ontario, 1971, Article 5). Under the authority of the Environmental Protection Act, the Minister of the Environment has the power to investigate pollution problems, conduct research, commission studies, convene conferences, organize seminars, and publish information relating to contaminants. Article 83 of the Act permits designated provincial officers to enter a site or plant at any reasonable time to conduct surveys, examinations, investigations, tests, and inquiries.

A variety of regulations intended to control pollution have been established under the Environmental Protection Act. In most cases, the regulations have set specific guidelines and standards for the emission of contaminants into the environment. In Ontario, the standard-setting function is concentrated in the Environmental Assessment and Planning Division, while implementation occurs primarily through the field offices which operate under the regional operations and laboratories division. The Environmental Assessment and Planning Division consists of several branches such as the Air Resources Branch, the Pollution Control Branch, and the Water Resources Branch, among others, which provide the scientific and technical information for regulations.

Before examining some of the specific regulations established under the Environmental Protection Act (which we will limit to the area of air pollution due to space constraints), it is necessary to understand the basis for standard-setting adopted by Ontario. The Ontario government has adopted an "effects" approach for the development of regulatory standards to control air pollution. It is described by OME officials as follows:

Ontario has followed a purely effects philosophy in its air standards-setting procedure. In order to have a uniform standard throughout the province for each contaminant, and to have that standard contain some rational relationship to ambient air quality objectives, the Ontario emission standards are stated in terms of time concentrations at the point of impingement (on a receptor) of the effluent stream, rather than as a conventional source emission number. This choice was made in recognition of the fact that ambient air quality is a function of both emissions and transport. The point of emission is related to the point of impingement by codified use of plume rise and diffusion equations. Thus, this type of emission standard takes some reasonable cognizance of emission conditions, micrometeorology, and usage and topography. (Martin and Kupa, 1977:5)

As is demonstrated below, the Ontario government's "effects" approach is different from the federal government's "best practicable technology" approach. The latter concept requires the immediate removal of contaminants to the lowest practicable limit. In many cases, the best practicable technology approach imposes lower levels of emissions than does the effects approach.

Regulatory standards and guidelines intended to control air pollution are contained in section 14 of the Environmental Protection Act. The OME has established extensive restrictions upon the maximum amounts of specific contaminants that may be emitted into the air under a General Air Pollution Regulation. The General Regulation states that

No person shall cause or permit to be caused the emission of any air contaminant to such extent or degree as may
   a) cause discomfort to persons;
   b) cause loss of enjoyment of normal use of property;
   c) interfere with normal conduct of business; or
   d) cause damage to property. (Ontario, 1970a, Regulations 15)

The General Air Pollution Regulation consists of three distinct types of standard: the traditional nuisance standard, the black smoke standard, and scientific standards based on sophisticated measurement techniques. The nuisance standard prohibits the kind of air pollution which would be considered a nuisance under common law. Section 6 of the Regulation is a nuisance standard because it prohibits the emission of any air contaminant to an extent or degree that may cause discomfort to persons, loss of enjoyment of normal use of property, interference with normal conduct of business, or damage to property. There is no need to use scientific analyses to prove nuisance. Often, complaints by individuals showing substantial irritation is all that is required for action. The nuisance standard has been extremely useful in controlling certain specific types of pollution such as noise pollution, demolition, blasting, drilling, and sandblasting. The nuisance standard has drawn the ire of many polluters who claim that it is too vague to be legally enforceable. Thus far, the courts have upheld the validity of the regulation, which undoubtedly pleases government officials who otherwise would have to draft numerous standards and regulations to protect the public.

The black smoke standard is used to control contaminant emissions beyond a certain density by comparing their degree of greyness or blackness with shades of grey on a standardized chart. The standard is used to regulate the emission of smoke, dust, ash, soot, and fumes, and other solids or gases which are visible to the naked eye. Sections 7 and 8 of the Regulation prohibit the emission of any visible contaminant that has shades of grey darker than number 1 on the Visible Emission Chart. The OME has encountered several difficulties in implementing the black smoke standard. First, it has been extremely difficult to develop a workable Visible Emission Chart. Prior to 1974, OME inspectors measured smoke by using a smoke density chart comprised of five shades of grey. However, this chart was of limited value because many industries emitted smoke which was red, yellow, or white. Second, only provincial inspectors are able to present evidence based on this regulation.

The OME General Air Pollution Regulation also uses modern scientific standards to control pollution. However, the standards are based on measurements at the point of impingement, where the pollutant actually comes into contact with humans, animals, vegetation, or property. Standards are prescribed in Schedule 1 of the Regulation. Maximum allowable concentration levels have been established for 84 contaminants, including mercury, arsenic, and lead. The enforcement of these standards requires sophisticated measurement techniques which are generally beyond the capabilities of the average citizen. It therefore places additional burdens on the OME to conduct the appropriate measurements on a regular basis. Despite some of the administrative problems, the General Air Pollution Regulation provides an excellent illustration of the regulatory measures used to control air pollution under the Environmental Protection Act.

(b) The *Ontario Water Resources Act* is the second major piece of legislation used to control and regulate pollution in the province. The Act contains a general prohibition against the discharge of pollutants that cause harm. The General Prohibition provides that

> Every municipality or person that discharges or deposits or causes or permits the discharge or deposit of any material of any kind into or in any well, lake, river, pond, spring, stream, reservoir or other watercourse or on any shore or bank or into any place that may impair the quality of the water is guilty of an offence. (Ontario, 1970b, Article 32.1)

Under the authority of the Act, the Minister of the Environment has broad powers to supervise all surface and ground waters; examine any waters in the province to determine what, if any, pollution exists, and its causes; control and regulate the collection, production, treatment, storage, transmission, distribution, and use of water for public purposes. Certificates of approval are required for the discharge of sewage into a body of water. The minister can levy stiff fines against any municipality or person found contravening these regulations. The Ontario Water Resources Act does not contain environmental standards to regulate specific substances. It simply provides an overall definition of what may constitute pollution of the aquatic environment. In 1978, the OME published the "Water Management, Goals, Policies, Objectives and Implementation Procedures" (Ontario, 1978). This document (although referred to here in its 1978 vintage) still provides goals, policies, and in some areas, specific objectives as to what it considers to be acceptable water quality. In this area, the Province of Ontario makes use of regulatory standards and guidelines established by the federal government to control water pollution.

(c) The *Ontario Pesticides Act* is used to control and regulate the use of all pesticide products sold in Ontario. The potential health hazards and environmental damage associated with the use of pesticides have resulted in the development of one of the most comprehensive regulatory systems in Canada. The Pesticides Act contains a prohibition similar to the Environmental Protection Act forbidding any person to dispose of any pesticide product which is likely to cause environmental damage. The resolutions of the Act make necessary the acquisition of licences and permits and, in some cases both, in order to use certain pesticide products. The Act is administered by the OME's Pesticides Control Section. Under the authority of the Pesticides Act, the OME has the authority to issue control orders and injunctions to regulate the use of pesticides. The OME relies on the Act's regulatory provision to ensure proper use and control of pesticide products in the province. Specific regulations have been established for all pesticide products which are classified and listed in six schedules, according to a descending order of toxicity and level of expertise required for use. No pesticide can be sold in the Province of Ontario unless it is listed in one of the six schedules.

(d) In July 1975, the Government of Ontario passed the *Environmental Assessment Act*, intended to prevent environmental damage before it occurs and to enable some public participation in the environmental decision-making process. Under the Act, any provincial undertaking, which is broadly defined to include policies and programs as well as projects, must undergo an environmental assessment to determine the potential environmental and socio-economic impact. All interested parties and intervenors are provided an opportunity to examine the environmental assessment document and to request a public hearing by the Environmental Assessment Board established under the Act (Jeffery and Dwivedi, 1988). When no hearing is held by the Assessment Board, project approval must be granted by Cabinet.

The Environmental Assessment Act has drawn some criticism because many projects or undertakings have been exempted from its regulations. For example, the Act does not apply to the private sector, except for major private undertakings that are designated by regulations. However, the meaning of the term "major" is unclear, and as such many private projects have escaped the assessment process. Similarly, the government can also restrict the application of the Act by issuing exemption orders. The Environmental Assessment Act is broad enough in scope to cover a wide range of public and private sector undertakings.

Quebec

The Province of Quebec has enacted seven pieces of legislation which impinge on the environment (see appendix). Among these, we have selected three pieces for this survey.

(a) *Environmental Quality Act*: This legislation defines the environment as the water, atmosphere, and soil, or a combination of any of them, or more generally, the ambient milieu with which living species have dynamic relations. In addition, the law empowers the Ministry

» to coordinate resources devoted by government departments and bodies to the problems of quality of the environment;
» to prepare plans and programs for the conservation, protection, and management for the environment and emergency plans to fight any form of contamination or destruction of the environment;
» to grant, on the conditions determined by regulation of the

Government, loans or subsidies to bodies or individuals to promote the training of experts in the fields contemplated by this Act; and

» to obtain from the departments of the Government, any body under their jurisdiction, municipalities, and school boards, any information necessary for the application of the Act. (Article 2)

In addition, the legislation has a provision for a Bureau d'audiences publiques sur l'environnement which enables the public to appeal governmental decisions. The Act also includes regulations for waste management and the use and disposal of hazardous materials.

(b) *Ministry of the Environment Act:* In order to operationalize the Environmental Quality Act, the Quebec government has enacted the Ministry of the Environment legislation establishing such an institution. The Ministry Act empowers the minister to propose policies and programs for the protection of ecosystems and biodiversity; the prevention, abatement, or elimination of water, air, and soil contamination; the establishment and management of ecological reserves; the protection of threatened or vulnerable plant species; and the development and carrying out of activities related to observation and knowledge of nature (Article 11).

In addition, the minister is responsible for the implementation, and for the purpose of performing his functions, the minister is authorized to enter into an agreement, according to law, with a government other than that of Quebec, a department of such a government, an international organization or an agency of such a government or organization; enter into agreements with any person, municipality, group, or body; carry out or commission research, inventories, studies, and analyses; obtain from government departments and public bodies the information required to elaborate and implement his policies, plans, and programs; compile, analyse, and publish available information; and advise the government on any matter within his competence (Article 12). Further, the minister is responsible for the management of the water in the domain of the state and for the management of water as a natural resource (Article 13). We can see shades of the Quebec government's tendency to develop its own foreign policy agenda here, in contrast to other provincial governments which, generally, leave foreign policy matters to the federal government.

(c) *Pesticides Act:* The other important legislation is concerned with pesticides. The Pesticides Act authorizes the Quebec Minister of the Environment to coordinate research carried out by government departments and agencies on environmental problems related to the use of pesticides; carry out or commission research, studies, inquiries, or analyses pertaining to the effects of the use of pesticides on the quality of the environment and on human health, and generally, on any topic relating to pesticides and alternatives to their use; devise, foster, and ensure the implementation of plans and programs to train specialists, educate and inform the public, and promote awareness in the field of pesticides; and compile, analyse, and publish available statistical data relating to pesticides (Article 9).

Nova Scotia

For the province of Nova Scotia, we have selected its major environmental legislation, the *Environment Act*, which has the following objectives: to support and promote the protection, enhancement, and prudent use of the environment while recognizing the following goals: maintaining environmental protection as essential to the integrity of ecosystems, human health, and the socio-economic well-being of society; maintaining the principles of sustainable development, including:

» the principle of ecological value, ensuring the maintenance and restoration of essential ecological processes and the preservation and prevention of loss of biological diversity;

» the precautionary principle to be used in decision-making so that where there are threats of serious or irreversible damage, the lack of full scientific certainty shall not be used as a reason for postponing measures to prevent environmental degradation;

» the principle of pollution prevention and waste reduction as the foundation for long-term environmental protection, including the conservation and efficient use of resources, the promotion of the development and use of sustainable, scientific, and technological innovations and management systems, and the importance of reducing, reusing, recycling, and recovering the products of our society;

» the principle of shared responsibility of all Nova Scotians to sustain the environment and the economy, both locally and globally, through individual and government actions;

» the stewardship principle, which recognizes the responsibility of a producer for a product from the point of manufacturing to the point of final disposal;

» the linkage between economic and environmental issues, recognizing that long-term economic prosperity depends upon sound environmental management and that effective environmental protection depends on a strong economy; and

» the comprehensive integration of sustainable development principles in public policy-making in the province. (Article 2)

Nova Scotia appears to be the only province in which the stewardship principle and the principle of shared responsibility have been used in its objectives. It also includes a provision for a "polluter pay principle." The legislation includes provisions for the following: the polluter pay principle confirming the responsibility of anyone who creates an adverse effect on the environment to take remedial action and pay for the costs of that action; taking remedial action and providing for rehabilitation to restore an adversely affected area to a beneficial use; the government to act as a catalyst in the areas of environmental education, environmental emergencies, environmental research, and the development of policies, standards, objectives, and guidelines and other measures to protect the environment; encouraging the development and use of environmental technologies, innovations, and industries; providing access to information and facilitating effective public participation in the formulation of decisions affecting the environment, including opportunities to participate in the review of legislation, regulations, and policies and the provision of access to information affecting the environment; and providing a responsive, effective, fair, timely, and efficient administrative and regulatory system (Article 2).

The legislation also defines the term "environmental effect" which means in respect of an undertaking, any change that the undertaking may cause in the environment, including any effect on socio-economic conditions, on the environmental health, physical and cultural heritage; and any change to the undertaking that may be caused by the environment (Article 3). The Province of Nova Scotia may appear to have a smaller number of environmental laws than British Columbia, Ontario, and Quebec. However, its flagship legislation is comprehensive enough to give the Minister of Environment ample authority to check on-going pollution and to secure environmental health.

Even in this brief survey, the sheer scope of the environmental laws and regulations of these four Canadian provinces demonstrates that, despite differences in their scope and jurisdictions, each province has enough authority vested through its legislative power to promote a healthy and sustainable environment — providing, of course, that the political will to do so is there. It may be argued that this will, or lack of will, is reflected in the extent to which regulations are enforced and, more specifically, what type of punishment is visited upon transgressors. We turn now to a brief discussion of the role of the national criminal code in this process.

THE CRIMINAL CODE

The Law Reform Commission of Canada published five tests or signposts which could be used to determine whether a particular offence should be classified as a crime or reduced to the status of a regulatory offence: offences are seriously harmful; they are committed with the required mental element (meaning that the offence was done intentionally, recklessly, or as a result of criminal negligence); the needed enforcement measures would not themselves contravene fundamental values; and treating them as crimes would make a significant contribution to dealing with the harms and risks they create.

The application of these tests to instances of pollution provides a safeguard against the danger of transforming all pollution offences into Criminal Code crimes. It is clear that most pollution offences are best treated as regulatory offences, controlled by federal and provincial legislation. Many pollution offences occur as a result of negligent acts or omissions done in the course of otherwise legitimate activities, without causing serious harm. The Criminal Code as it exists today prohibits only those offences against persons and property. It does not, in any direct manner, prohibit offences against the natural environment. A working paper published by the Law Reform Commission of Canada supports the proposition that the natural environment should now become an interest directly protectable, in some cases, by the Criminal Code. Some acts which seriously harm or endanger the environment, provided they meet the tests of a real crime, should be prohibited as a crime against the environment. This approach ensures that the environment will be adequately protected by the Criminal Code while maintaining the belief that most pollution offences should be treated as regulatory offences (Law Reform Commission, 1985:2).

REGULATORY RESULTS AND ACTION PLANS

The environmental regulatory policy in Canada has proven fruitful in a variety of ways, by producing direct results and by creating more focused policy and increased public participation in policy-making. An example of a direct result of environmental regulatory policy in Canada is the case of the Pulp and Paper Effluent Chlorinated Dioxins and Furans Regulations (under CEPA). This particular regulation has resulted in a reduction of more than 98 per cent in the release of chlorinated dioxins and furans from their source (Environment Canada, 1996a). The case of the federal Toxic Substances Management policy exemplifies the development of more focused policy. This policy was created in 1995, in response to a call for the virtual elimination from the environment of all toxic, persistent, and bio-accumulative substances that result from human activity; also included in the call was a complete life-cycle management system for all other substances of concern that are released to the environment (Environment Canada, 1996a). An illustration of increased public participation in policy-making is the National Enforcement Workshop held in 1998. This workshop brought together people from the community and Environment Canada staff and managers, and resulted in the development of an Enforcement Action Plan for the enforcement of CEPA and the pollution prevention provisions of the Fisheries Act (Environment Canada, 1998b).

Action plans in Canadian environmental regulatory policy are significantly aided by the Canadian Environmental Industry Strategy (CEIS) and the government's "Green Industry" initiatives, which are expected to help the environmental industry grow annually by 10 per cent between 1996-2001. In particular, the Canadian Environmental Industry Association is an example of an organization that represents and helps to develop the environmental industry (Canada, 1996, p. 28).

CONCLUSIONS

At the outset of this chapter, we delved briefly into the regulatory process in Canada. We have demonstrated by taking examples from federal and four selected provincial jurisdictions that, although the number of environmental laws may differ, each jurisdiction has ample power to protect its environment if proper policies are formulated, and the regulatory regime is properly managed and is transparent (open to public scrutiny). We also showed that regulations are intended to modify or change human behaviour in order to achieve desirable goals and objectives. In the area of environmental regulations, the obvious objectives are to preserve and protect the environment from unnecessary damage. Underlying the formulation of regulations is a constantly shifting set of basic values, principles, and criteria which are a vital part of the foundation of Canadian society. Therefore, since Canadians place a high value on maintaining the high quality of the natural environment, it is not surprising that there has been a proliferation of environmental regulations over the past twenty-plus years to achieve this desirable goal. Although governments prefer to use less coercive means to achieve policy objectives, both the federal and provincial governments have relied to a considerable extent on regulations in order to modify and change our behaviour in terms of how we treat the environment. Although some groups argue this has produced a climate of costly over-regulation, other groups argue for the need for more stringent regulations. Inevitably, the regulatory process produces winners and losers, and neither group is generally satisfied. Ultimately, we must hope that all Canadians will benefit from environmental regulatory policy.

APPENDIX
A LIST OF MAIN FEDERAL AND PROVINCIAL
ENVIRONMENTAL LEGISLATION

JURISDICTION	NAME OF LEGISLATION
FEDERAL	Arctic Waters Pollution Prevention Act
	Atomic Energy Control Act
	Canada Shipping Act
	Canada Water Act
	Canada Wildlife Act
	Canadian Environmental Protection Act (1999)
	Department of the Environment Act
	National Round Table on the Environment and the Economy Act
	Canadian Environmental Assessment Act
	Fisheries Act
	Forestry Act
	Wild Animal and Plant Protection and Regulation of International and Interprovincial Trade Act
	Hazardous Materials Information Review Act
	International Rivers Improvement Act
	Migratory Birds Convention Act (1994)
	National Energy Board Act
	Navigable Waters Protection Act
	Northwest Territories Waters Act
	Nuclear Liability Act
	Pest Control Products Act
	Territorial Lands Act
	Transportation of Dangerous Goods Act
	Weather Modification Information Act
BRITISH COLUMBIA	Ecological Reserve Act
	Environmental and Land Use Act
	Environmental Management Act
	Environmental Assessment Act

JURISDICTION	NAME OF LEGISLATION
BRITISH COLUMBIA (CONT'D)	Health Act
	Land Act
	Litter Act
	Ministry of Environment Act
	Motor Vehicle Act
	Pesticides Control Act
	Pollution and Control Objectives for the Chemical and Petroleum Industries
	Pollution Control Objectives for the Forest Products Industry
	Pollution Control Objectives for the Mining, Smelting and Related Industries of British Columbia
	Sustainable Environment Fund Act
	Transport of Dangerous Goods Act
	Utilities Commission Act
	Waste Management Act
	Weather Modification Act
	Environmental Assessment Act
ALBERTA	Alberta Environmental Research Trust Act
	Dangerous Goods Transportation and Handling Act
	Department of the Environment Act
	Energy Resources Conservation Act
	Environmental Council Act
	Environmental Protection and Enhancement Act
	Land Surface Conservation and Reclamation Act
	Natural Resources Conservation Board Act
	Oil and Gas Conservation Act
	Public Health Act
	Public Lands Act
	Special Waste Management Corporation Act
	Transportation of Dangerous Goods Control Act
	Water, Gas and Electric Companies Act
	Waters Resources Commission Act
	Wilderness Areas, Ecological Reserves and Natural Areas Act
SASKATCHEWAN	Clean Air Act
	Conservation Easements Act
	Dangerous Goods Transportation Act

JURISDICTION	NAME OF LEGISLATION
SASKATCHEWAN (CONT'D)	Ecological Reserves Act
	Environmental Assessment Act
	Environmental Management and Protection Act
	Litter Control Act
	Ozone-Depleting Substances Control Act
	Pest Control Act
	Pest Control Products (Saskatchewan) Act
	Pollution (by Livestock) Control Act
	Pollution (by Livestock) Control Regulations
	State of the Environment Report Act
	Wildlife Habitat Protection Act
MANITOBA	Contaminated Sites Remediation Act
	Dangerous Goods Handling and Transportation Act
	Endangered Species Act
	Environment Act
	Environmental Assessment and Review Process for Proposed Provincial Projects
	High Level Radioactive Waste Act
	Manitoba Hazardous Waste Management Corporation Act
	Mining and Metallurgy Compensation Act
	Ozone Depleting Substances Act
	Pesticides and Fertilizers Control Act
	Public Health Act
	North American Environmental and Labour Cooperation Agreements Implementation Act
	Rivers and Streams Act
	Sustainable Development Act
	Waste Reduction and Prevention Act
	Conservation Agreements Act
ONTARIO	Conservation Authorities Act
	Consolidated Hearings Act
	Dangerous Goods Transportation Act
	Endangered Species Act
	Environmental Assessment Act
	Environmental Bill of Rights
	Environmental Protection Act

JURISDICTION	NAME OF LEGISLATION
ONTARIO (CONT'D)	Lakes and Rivers Improvement Act
	Ontario Waste Management Corporation Act
	Ontario Water Resources Act
	Pesticides Act
	Public Utilities Act
	Transboundary Pollution Reciprocal Access Act
	Waste Management Act
QUEBEC	Conservation and Development of Wildlife Act
	Ecological Reserves Act
	Environment Quality Act
	Ministry of the Environment Act
	Pesticides Act
	Tree Protection Act
	An Act respecting the establishment and enlargement of certain waste elimination sites
PRINCE EDWARD ISLAND	Dangerous Goods (Transportation) Act
	Environmental Tax Act
	Environmental Protection Act
	Natural Areas Protection
	Pesticides Control Act
	Public Health Act
	Transboundary Pollution (Reciprocal Access) Act
	Water and Sewerage Act
NEW BRUNSWICK	Clean Air Act
	Clean Environment Act
	Clean Water Act
	Conservation Easement Act
	Ecological Reserves Act
	Endangered Species Act
	Environmental Impact Assessment Guidelines
	Environmental Trust Fund Act
	Health Act
	Pesticides Control Act
	Transportation of Dangerous Goods Act
NOVA SCOTIA	Clean Nova Scotia Foundation Act
	Conservation Easements Act

JURISDICTION	NAME OF LEGISLATION
NOVA SCOTIA (CONT'D)	Dangerous Goods Transportation Act
	Environmental Act
	Health Act
	Special Places Protection Act
	Water Act
	Wildlife Act
NEWFOUNDLAND	Dangerous Goods Transportation Act
	Environmental Act
	Health and Community Services Act
	Environmental Assessment Act
	Pesticides Control Act
	Waste Material Disposal Act
	Waters Protection Act
	Wilderness and Ecological Reserves Act
	Waste Management Act

SEVEN

ENVIRONMENTAL RISK ASSESSMENT AND MANAGEMENT

INTRODUCTION — THE MEANING OF RISK

Driving along the Trans-Canada highway near Kenora, Ontario, on April 13, 1985, four members of the Eyjolfson family came up behind a flatbed transport truck carrying four hydro-electric transformers. For nearly 25 kilometres their car trailed the truck as they headed westward. As the truck manouevred around corners, a black oily substance splashed from one of the transformers, covering the Toyota's windshield and air vents, and leaving a black trail along the road. At a Kenora gas station, Mr. Eyjolfson asked the truck driver if he should be concerned about the spill, but the driver responded, "No problem, it's just mineral oil," and the Eyjolfsons continued on their way (Janigan, 1985:14). Nevertheless, the truck driver did contact the head office of Kinetic Ecological Resource Group in Nisku, Alberta, the company transporting the transformers from Quebec to Alberta. After receiving the call, Kinetic alerted the Ontario Environment Ministry's office in Thunder Bay that a toxic spill had just occurred. Within half an hour, the provincial government began to close almost 70 kilometres of highway, and the next day in Winnipeg, the Eyjolfsons learned to their horror that the so-called "mineral oil" was in fact transformer coolant laced with highly toxic polychlorinated biphenyls, the infamous PCBs. Over the next few days, the Eyjolfsons were examined by doctors but were found to have suffered no immediate damage to their health. At the same time, the province kept the highway closed as work crews tried to remove as much of the 100-gallon spillage as possible and resealed portions of the highway with new asphalt at a cost of approximately $1-million. This incident and others, such as the E-coli outbreak in Walkerton in 2000 and the long-standing health hazards of the Sydney Tar Ponds, serve as important reminders to all Canadians that we do not live in a risk-free environment.

In fact, life on earth today is fraught with risk. Not only do we live with the threat of a possible nuclear Armageddon, we must also contend with political turmoil, wars, economic upheavals, crime, natural disasters, and a growing number of serious environmental problems. These and many other types of risk are an ever-present factor in our lives as well as the society in which we live. Whether as individuals caught up in the mundane decisions of daily routine or as politicians, public servants, business executives, or judges involved in the broader political, economic, or legal decisions that affect society, we all spend some time considering the nature of the risks that we encounter. In this regard, we are all concerned with how to identify risks, cope with them, minimize them, and how to determine if and when the risks are acceptable. Thus, risk assessment and management have emerged as one of the most important, yet highly controversial, aspects of the public policy process in recent years.

For our purposes in this chapter, we associate risks with particular events or actions. The events or actions may be relatively insignificant, such as using a can of insect repellent, or they may be large, as in the use of airplanes to spray hundreds of hectares of crops with pesticides. Nevertheless, for every event or action, whether small or large, there is some element of risk. The word "risk" is used in many different ways by various academic disciplines and, as a result, there tends to be some confusion as to what it means. For example, in one context "risk" is used to mean a hazard or a danger — that is, an exposure to peril. In another, "risk" is used to mean the probability or chance of suffering an adverse consequence. In order to encompass the several different types of environmental problems and issues and make them relevant in a discussion of risk assessment and management, a broad definition of what is meant by "risk" is required. Therefore, for the purposes of this chapter, "risk" is defined as *the likelihood of undesirable effects on humans and/or the environment from exposure to any harmful source.*

Of course, in our ever-changing and increasingly complex modern industrial society, there are many different types of risk. Some years ago, the Science Council of Canada classified risks broadly according to the following categories:

1. voluntary risks
2. risks that can be modified by the risk-taker's behaviour
3. risks that are taken involuntarily
4. risks in which there can be no direct awareness of the existence of hazard — e.g., low-level radiation exposure
5. short-term hazards, as opposed to long-term risks, in which the consequences of exposure may only be seen years after the exposure has ended

6. a special category of risks in which the individual may not be in a position to assess the benefits or damage of a procedure — e.g., the use of drugs. (Science Council, 1977:26)

In this chapter, we are concerned with a particular area of risks related to environmental problems and issues. Environmental risks arise in, or are transmitted through, the air, water, soil, or the biological food chains, to humans. Environmental risks are harmful or hazardous to people who have not chosen voluntarily to incur their consequences. The causes and characteristics of environmental risks are extremely diverse. Some environmental risks, such as air and water pollution, are the by-product of human activities such as technological and economic development, while others, such as floods, hurricanes, and earthquakes, are the result of natural processes. In some cases, the environmental risks can be reasonably well anticipated, such as flooding in the spring or air pollution from smoke stacks, whereas in other cases, the environmental risks may be totally unsuspected at the time a product is used, such as with the use of pesticides which years later were found to be highly toxic to humans. Moreover, the effects of environmental risks on human health vary significantly between different segments of the population and different regions. In addition, ecosystems themselves are also at risk, which may have an indirect impact on humans.

Public concern about the health effects associated with environmental risks has increased dramatically since the early 1970s. For example, as the nature and scope of risks to human health from air and water pollution became better understood, there was increasing public pressure on governments to develop more effective means of controlling pollution in order to reduce risks. However, reducing or managing environmental risks is a complicated and difficult endeavour involving crucial public policy decisions. Part of the difficulty is that many of the activities which produce environmental risks such as air and water pollution also provide many benefits to society. Consequently, public officials are forced to search for an optimal balance between socio-economic benefit and environmental risk when formulating environmental risk management policies. Not only must policy-makers consider questions such as whether particular types of activities are safe enough and whether "safe" is truly safe, but also how to distribute risks among the population. In order to make decisions about risks, policy-makers must assess the risks and weigh them against the socio-economic benefits of particular types of events or actions. A formal process for assessing and evaluating risks has emerged over the past three decades and risk assessment and management has become a powerful decision-making tool.[1]

THE PROCESS OF RISK ASSESSMENT

Risk assessment in our context is a formal process to determine whether the risks associated with particular events or actions are acceptable or should be avoided. It involves a formal and systematic process that requires that the environmental impacts of a proposed action and its alternatives be identified, evaluated, and considered by decision-makers before policies are adopted. Thus, the process involves three distinct but closely related activities: risk identification, risk estimation, and risk evaluation.

Risk identification involves recognizing the existence of a particular hazard and the definition of its characteristics. The identification of risks is not as obvious as it might seem, especially with regard to environmental risks that affect large segments of the population. Many factors contribute to the recognition of the existence of hazards, and public perceptions of risk can vary significantly. Quite often, basic values and emotions will influence perceptions of risk, causing some individuals and groups to perceive risks that do not exist or to disregard real risks. Furthermore, the gap between risk perception and reality can distort the allocation of resources in the environment field. For example, in the classic case of acid rain, the Reagan administration's disregard of the environmental hazards posed by this pollutant detracted from efforts to reduce its attendant risks.

The second stage in the risk assessment process, risk estimation, involves the use of scientific, technical, and medical research and analyses to quantify the nature and characteristics of the hazard under investigation in measurable terms. This includes attempts to estimate the magnitude, duration, and intensity of adverse consequences and their associated probabilities, as well as a description of the cause-and-effect linkages. The scientific, technical, and medical research and analysis used in the estimation of environmental risks generally provide the basis from which policy-makers reach decisions about the acceptability of risks and the types of policies and instruments which are to be employed in reducing the risks. In fact, the scientific and medical information and data have a major bearing on the establishment of health and environmental standards and guidelines. In specific terms, the scientific and medical aspects of risk estimation are concerned with collecting information and data on such factors as the conditions of exposure to a particular hazard, the adverse effects, and the relationship between exposure and effects. Due to the extensive amount of time and resources required to perform scientific and medical research, risk estimation tends to be very expensive. As well, a variety of research methods and techniques is needed in order to produce reliable data. Some of the basic research methods and analytical techniques used in estimating environmental risks are monitoring and health surveillance, testing and screening procedures, and modelling.

Environmental monitoring is a process of repetitive observation of particular events or actions in order to collect information and data. The primary purpose of environmental monitoring is to detect the presence of harmful substances and to provide early warnings of environmental threats. The monitoring process involves gathering samples for analysis and comparison. Sophisticated monitoring techniques based on the use of advanced measuring instruments are currently employed in many environmental monitoring programs. The repetitiveness of the monitoring process, combined with the cost of equipment and personnel, makes environmental monitoring an expensive endeavour; however, it is necessary in order to provide reliable and accurate data for analysis. In Canada, both the federal and provincial governments have established elaborate environmental monitoring programs in a variety of areas. For example, the National Air Pollution Surveillance Network (NAPS) is a long-term program designed to gather information about the emission of pollutants and their toxicity and effects on the environment. Under Environment Canada's Environmental Protection Service, highly advanced monitoring instruments are spread throughout the country to gather pertinent information which is analysed and used to combat air pollution. As well, specific types of testing and screening procedures have been developed to identify sources of environmental risk. Testing is also of major importance in quantifying much of the data collected about harmful environmental substances into comparative terms. In recent years, scientific testing has progressed significantly, producing more precise and accurate measurements that enable a better approximation of the risks. For example, we have become familiar with the measurement of air and water pollutants in parts per million. Although most people find it difficult to conceptualize pollutants expressed in such minute terms, testing conducted in such precise detail has been of great value in revealing sources of environmental risk which were previously unknown. In Canada, federal and provincial agencies conduct elaborate tests and monitor chemicals and drugs before they can be sold in the marketplace.

The third and most important stage in the risk assessment process is risk evaluation, whereby judgments about the significance and acceptability of risks are made. During this stage, various evaluation techniques are used to compare the risks against the benefits in order to determine their acceptability. Perhaps the most common evaluation technique used is "cost-benefit" analysis. However, cost-benefit analysis is of limited value because of the difficulty encountered in estimating the aesthetic value of forests or clean lakes. The formal risk assessment process has been viewed as an effort by technically qualified persons to determine the effects, degree of risk, and probability of occurrence of particular events or actions. Until recently, the risk assessment process has been regarded from a narrow perspective as being primarily a scientific and technical endeavour. Although scientists do play an important role in risk assessment, the process must be viewed in a much broader social and political context in which the final judgments and decisions on the acceptability of risks are made by public officials.

From a historical perspective, risk assessment has evolved from an initial focus on impact assessment to a broad-based systemic or holistic approach to evaluating and assessing the nature of risks. Initially, impact assessments dealt primarily with evaluating specific effects of particular events or actions. These impact assessments were used to describe the known impacts of various events based on straightforward quantitative research methods. However, as the problems confronting society became more complex, partly due to more sophisticated scientific means of examining them, greater emphasis came to be placed on understanding the true nature of their impacts and the possibilities of occurrence. In addition to the use of more sophisticated and precise scientific research techniques, theories of probability and modelling techniques were developed and applied on a broader systemic basis. As well, today more attention is being paid to societal values and the role they should play in the process. Thus, the systemic, or holistic, approach used in risk assessment is more valuable because it attempts to improve the means of managing or reducing risks before adverse consequences are suffered. However, with a broader-based approach to risk assessment, there has been a significant increase in information and data about risks, and these have not simplified but rather have made making decisions about risks more difficult and complicated.

THE GOVERNMENTAL FRAMEWORK FOR RISK ASSESSMENT

Since the late 1960s, the governmental response to the public's concern about the health risks associated with a growing number of environmental problems in Canada has been the passage of several acts designed to protect society from unnecessary hazard and harm. For example, the Clean Air Act was passed to improve and maintain the quality of the air that all Canadians breathe, and the Canada Water Act and the amended Fisheries Act were designed to protect and preserve the quality of the nation's water. Under the statutory authority of these and other types of legislation, formal risk assessments have been conducted and utilized to develop appropriate standards, guidelines, and regulations to protect the public from health, safety, and environmental hazards. In addition, despite the initial skepticism of business leaders that governmental regulation might have an adverse effect on the Canadian economy, the detrimental effects of environmental degradation and their long-term consequences convinced governments to take another major step toward the maintenance and improvement of environmental quality. This innovation was the introduction of environmental risk assessment procedures known as Environmental Impact Assessments (EIAs).

An environmental impact assessment is a study of the effects that a program, project, or other undertaking might have on the natural and/or human environment. It is a planning aid which tries to measure the direct and indirect costs of an action in terms of environmental degradation, use of energy and resources, and social disruption, among other probable effects, and weighs the costs against the benefits to be derived from the project. Its purpose is to discover the problems an undertaking might cause before a final decision is made to go ahead with it. The use of environmental impact assessments represented an important shift in governmental thinking since the various costs of projects could be estimated prior to their inception. Furthermore once approved, the costs associated with projects could now be charged to those who caused the damage. In the years since 1973, the federal and most provincial governments passed significant environmental risk assessment legislation, although in recent years some of these governments have decided to follow a practice of "deregulation" which has dramatically weakened the assessment process in some provinces.

THE FEDERAL RESPONSE – THE ENVIRONMENTAL ASSESSMENT AND REVIEW PROCESS

In June, 1971, when the Department of the Environment came into being, its first minister, Jack Davis, asked his civil servants to explore the idea of an environmental assessment plan. Subsequently, on December 20, 1973, the Cabinet approved a recommendation for an Environmental Assessment and Review Process (EARP) for all federal departments and agencies, with the exception of certain Crown corporations and independent regulatory commissions. EARP's principal purpose was "to ensure that the environmental consequences of all federal proposals are assessed for potential adverse effects early in the planning process before irrevocable decisions are taken" (Government of Canada [GC], 1988b:13). EARP was to apply to all federal development proposals, including industrial, commercial, construction, resource management and extraction, and transportation plans. This responsibility of the Minister of the Environment was reaffirmed in the Government Organization Act of 1979 and an Order-in-

Council proclaimed in 1984 set out and clarified various EARP roles, responsibilities, and procedures. Until the implementation of the Canadian Environmental Assessment Act in January 1995, that Order-in-Council provided the legal authority for Environment Canada to apply EARP to all initiatives proposed by federal departments, including any public-sector endeavour in which the federal government had a major stake.

Under the EARP operating guidelines, each department was expected to conduct its own initial assessment of its proposed projects. If it was found that there were likely to be significant environmental effects because of the undertaking, the project was referred to the Minister of the Environment who would request that the Federal Environmental Assessment and Review Office do an independent assessment. FEARO would conduct its review by appointing an Environmental Assessment Panel consisting of from three to seven persons selected from a list of experts approved by the Minister of the Environment. Members were chosen for their knowledge, credibility, and objectivity, and each panel was responsible for establishing its own detailed operating procedures. The panel would receive from the proponent — that is, the department which proposed the project — an Environmental Impact Statement. The panel would hold public hearings on the statement and prepare a report containing its recommendations which would be submitted to the Minister of the Environment as well as to the minister of the initiating department. The recommendations would also be made public. Although these recommendations were not binding, the minister whose department proposed the project had to respond to them, and it was expected that the department would pay close attention to them. In this fashion, federal projects would proceed with or without modification or would be postponed or abandoned altogether.

Over time FEARO became the focal point within the federal government for providing information on the EARP to the public, other federal departments, other levels of government within Canada, and to foreign governments and international organizations. In this task it was aided for a decade by the Canadian Environmental Assessment Research Council (CEARC), created in 1984. CEARC was composed of 12 members appointed by the Minister of the Environment from the public and private sectors to promote research to improve the scientific, technical, and procedural foundations of the environmental impact assessment process. In the last year of its existence, FEARO had a budget of over $8-million to administer its programs. Nevertheless, throughout their years of operation, FEARO and the EARP came under increasing criticism for several reasons. In the first place, FEARO did not have the legal authority to compel federal departments to comply with its recommendations. Second, it did not have the ability to reject out-of-hand inadequate impact assessments submitted by the initiating departments. Third, both those responsible for the EARP and those affected by it became convinced that public opinion, which until then had no formal role in the process, should have input at the very beginning of the environmental impact assessment process. Fourth, there was no requirement that federal departments keep an on-going record in a public registry of all documents related to a particular assessment. Fifth, there was no obligation on the part of the government to follow up once the panels' reports were published to ensure that their recommendations were carried out by the initiating departments. Finally, although the concept of sustainable development was accepted by the Mulroney Cabinet in its *Green Plan*, it had not spread to all corners of the federal government. These and other concerns were addressed in the Canadian Environmental Assessment Act of 1995.

The Canadian Environmental Assessment Act — 1995

The Canadian Environmental Assessment Act (CEAA) is today the cornerstone of the reforms introduced by the federal government in the field of environmental assessment. Tabled in the House of Commons as far back as 1990, the Act was designed to reduce various ambiguities in the procedures used by FEARO. In fact, FEARO was replaced by the Canadian Environmental Assessment Agency. The new act established in law, for the first time, the responsibilities and procedures to be used in the environmental assessment of projects involving the federal government. It applies to all projects for which the federal government possesses decision-making jurisdiction in its capacity as proponent, land manager, financial contributor (even in conjunction with the private sector or in joint management with other levels of government), or as regulator of the Canadian economy. There are four main purposes of the legislation:

1. to ensure that the environmental effects of projects receive careful consideration before federal departments and agencies take action
2. to encourage federal departments and agencies to consider taking actions which promote sustainable development, a healthy environment, and a healthy economy
3. to ensure that all projects being undertaken by the federal government do not cause significant damage to the environment, even outside the federal jurisdiction
4. to ensure that there is an opportunity for public participation in the environmental assessment process. (GC, Estimates 1994:115)

These purposes are to be guided by four basic principles:

1. the process is to be implemented as early as practicable in the project's planning stage
2. self-assessment remains a basic element of the process directing federal departments and agencies
3. public participation and accountability are to be fundamental to the assessment process
4. the level of effort required to mount an environmental assessment for a project should equal the scale of the likely environmental effects from the project. (GC, Estimates 1994:115)

The Canadian Environmental Assessment Agency created by the Act was authorized to undertake research and studies in matters of environmental assessment and to encourage the development of assessment techniques, practices, and regulations. In addition, the Act established a registry to encourage and facilitate the participation of the public in the assessment process and to foster federal-provincial cooperation in the harmonization of environmental assessment procedures. Further examples of the new agency's scope include the assessment of projects on native land, and of previously exempted crown corporations and projects outside Canada's borders in which the federal government has an interest. The Agency was also to represent the government of Canada in relevant international activities such as the UN Economic Commission for Europe Convention on Environmental Impact Assessment in a Transboundary Context and other similar international and Canada-US organizations.

In its review of the Act published in December of 1999, the Agency referred to its successes as follows:

» The Act has helped achieve sustainable development through the promotion of sound economic development while reducing adverse effects on our environment
» The Act has helped provide concerned individuals and organizations with opportunities to influence decisions on projects that will affect them
» The Act has promoted the concept of "one project-one assessment" by encouraging cooperation among departments and other jurisdictions to reduce unproductive overlap and duplication
» Under the principle of self-assessment, the environment has become the responsibility of every department in the federal government. (CEAA, Review 1999:3)

At the same time, it noted that the Act, as it stands, appears to be unnecessarily complex. A less ambiguous, more straightforward process could go a long way toward promoting public confidence in the process, providing a greater measure of certainty and predictability to the private sector, and ensuring a more appropriate use of scarce resources by the public sector (CEAA, Review 1999:3). Thus it would appear that the federal government still has some way to go toward making Canada a global leader in environmental risk assessment and management. At the moment, it is not clear that the present federal government possesses the will to take these necessary steps.

ENVIRONMENTAL ASSESSMENT IN THE PROVINCES

Because the Constitution divides responsibility for the environment between the two major levels of government in Canada, the provinces have also been active in the area of environmental assessment. In fact, EA legislation and procedures are present today in all provinces, although, as might be expected in a country as diverse as Canada, there are wide variations between them. Space limitations make it impossible to discuss all of the provinces in detail. Therefore, we have decided to focus on Ontario alone because it was the first province to enact environmental legislation of this type, and because it provides a longer time frame through which to judge the success or failure of the assessment process.[2] Ontario passed its Environmental Assessment Act and created its Environmental Assessment Board in 1975. The remainder of this section discusses the Act under which the Board exercises its authority as well as the Board's role in the environmental assessment process.

Ontario Environmental Assessment Act (EAA)

The Environmental Assessment Act was the result of a protracted consultation process by the Ontario government which considered and compared the various assessment models in existence at that time. The purpose of the legislation, as set out in Section 2, "is the betterment of the people of the whole or any part of Ontario by providing for the protection, conservation and wise management in Ontario of the environment through comprehensive assessment at the earliest possible stage in the planning process" (Ontario, Debates 1973).

Under the provisions of the EAA, a proponent to whom the Act applies must prepare an environmental assessment and submit it to the Minister of the Environment for review. The Act then proceeds to set out, at least in general terms, the requirements of the assessment document (Environmental Impact Statement) and, in addition, defines "environment" in the widest possible terms. The public, after notification of both the assessment and completion of a government review coordinated by the Ministry of the Environment, then has a minimum of thirty days to examine and comment on both documents in writing to the minister and, more importantly, to request a hearing by the EAB (Environmental Assessment Board) on the application. When a hearing has been requested, the minister is obligated to refer the matter to the EAB unless, in his or her absolute discretion, the request is considered to be frivolous or vexatious, or a hearing is unnecessary or may cause undue delay (Ontario, 1980a, Section 12-2-6). In cases in which a hearing is held by the EAB, the decision concerning both the acceptance of the assessment and the approval to proceed with the undertaking are within the exclusive jurisdiction of the EAB, subject only to the minister's power. However, the Cabinet has 28 days after receipt of the Board's decision to vary or rescind any decision made by the EAB. In the event that a hearing is not required by the minister or any member of the public, the minister may, with the approval of Cabinet, approve or reject the proposed undertaking and impose conditions of approval. Today, the scope of the Act includes all public sector proposals for undertakings, unless excluded by a ministerial exemption order in accordance with Section 29, or regulation pursuant to Section 40(f). Private-sector proposals are, by and large, not subject to the Act at the present time, unless specifically designated for inclusion by regulation.

The Environmental Assessment Board (EAB)

The Environmental Assessment Board in Ontario exercises its authority pursuant to three principal statutes: the Environmental Assessment Act (discussed above), the Environmental Protection Act, and the Ontario Water Resources Act. In addition, members of the EAB may sit from time to time with members of the Ontario Municipal Board to hear applications brought under the Consolidated Hearing Act and constitute, in effect, a separate board called the Joint Board. Although the EAB and the Joint Board are empowered to hold public hearings under the above-mentioned legislation, only in the case of applications brought under the Environmental Assessment Act or pursuant to the Consolidated Hearings Act does the EAB or the Joint Board have the decision-making power to approve or reject proposed undertakings. Under the provisions of the Environmental Protection Act and the Ontario Water Resources Act, the

EAB (after a public hearing has been held) submits a report to a Ministry of the Environment official (the Director of Approvals), who makes the actual decision after taking into account the Board's recommendations (Ontario, Statutes 1981:361). Thus, the key steps in the environmental assessment process in Ontario are as follows:

1. the proponent consults with the Environmental Assessment Branch on the Act's requirements
2. the proponent consults with interested government ministries, agencies, and public groups and deals with their concerns
3. the proponent prepares the environmental assessment document
4. the proponent submits it to the Minister of the Environment
5. the Environmental Assessment Branch conducts a review of the document by consulting with those ministries, agencies, and groups which have an interest in the proposed project
6. a review is published and the public is invited to make submissions on the project. A hearing before the Environmental Assessment Board can be requested at this stage
7. the minister accepts the environmental assessment document or calls for further research or revisions
8. the Minister of the Environment or the Environmental Assessment Board decides whether or not to approve the project. Within 28 days of the Board's decision, parties can ask the minister to alter the decision. Also, within the 28 day period, the minister, with the approval of Cabinet, may alter the Board's decision or require a new hearing
9. if approval is granted the proponent can proceed with the project. Terms and conditions may apply. (OMOE, 1978:2-3)

The Board functions as a quasi-judicial statutory tribunal and, as such, operates independently of the Ministry of the Environment or any other government ministry or agency. When it exercises a decision-making authority, as is the case with respect to applications under the Environmental Assessment Act, the Board is also subject to the rules of natural justice which, for the most part, are codified under the Statutory Powers Procedure Act of 1971. These rules in effect provide a procedural framework for the conduct of hearings by statutory tribunals having decision-making power.

In sum, the Environmental Assessment Act requires that all proposals, plans, or projects of Ontario departments and agencies undergo a two-stage environmental assessment. The first stage, organized and conducted by the Ministry of the Environment, involves the preparation and submission of an impact assessment to the Environmental Assessment Board. This statement is normally made available to the public for examination. Interested individuals can request that the Minister of the Environment arrange public hearings; however, the minister can deny this if he/she believes the request is frivolous or of no public benefit. The EAB can accept or reject the assessment statement and make recommendations about the project. The second stage involves the approval of the project by Cabinet. Unless altered by the minister or Cabinet within a period of twenty-eight days, the recommendations of the Environmental Assessment Board are final.

The environmental impact assessment process was slow to be implemented in Ontario due to the difficulties encountered in establishing guidelines and regulations that identified projects requiring assessments. Although the government indicated initially that assessment guidelines would include major construction, hydro projects, sewage and water treatment plants, and highways, among other types of projects, hundreds were allowed to escape the process because the Cabinet was convinced that environmental assessments would cause undue delay and expense or because of the political controversy such assessments could incite. Industrialists claimed that environmental assessments would bring economic development to a grinding halt, while some environmentalists sought these as a "cure-all" for both major and minor environmental problems. Thus, Ontario governments tended to avoid opposition by not applying the Environmental Assessment Act in the early years. Nevertheless, the environmental impact assessment process as established in Ontario did offer the promise of a systematic, comprehensive public review of all the factors that go into making a decision that may have adverse environmental consequences. This hope was heightened with the passage of the Ontario Environmental Bill of Rights in 1993. This Act recognized the "inherent" right of the people of the province to a healthy environment and had as its principal purposes the protection, conservation, and, where reasonable, the restoration of the integrity of the environment (Ontario, Bill 26, 1993). It also established an Environmental Registry to provide the public with information about proposals, decisions, and events that could affect the environment; required the Minister of the Environment to give public notice of such proposals; invited the public to comment on such matters; confirmed the public funding of these interventions; and created the post of Environmental Commissioner to ensure that Ontario ministries and agencies acted in accordance with all relevant environmental legislation. Furthermore, it granted leave to any two persons resident in the province to apply to the Environmental Commissioner to review any policy or regulation which they deemed harmful to the environment; permission to citizens to sue any person who contravened any act designed to protect the environment; and provided employees with protection from reprisal by their employers should they inform the minister of any contravention of provincial environmental legislation. The Act was by no means perfect, but it did strengthen the environmental assessment process in Ontario.

These positive steps came to an abrupt end with the election of the Harris Conservatives in 1995. Within a year the new government passed the Environmental Assessment and Consultation Act which it declared would make the process quicker and more efficient. The Act gave the Minister of the Environment wide discretion to control every aspect of the process, with the result that EAB hearings dwindled to almost none. Furthermore, Cabinet retained the power to overrule the Board for whatever reason it chose and did away with the provision of funding for public participation in the assessment process. Together with draconian cuts to the budget of the Ministry of the Environment, all this meant that environmental assessment in Ontario became considerably less effective[3] and will have to be restored if it is to fulfil its original purposes.

In conclusion to this section, it can be said that environmental impact assessments were a welcome addition to federal and provincial environmental policies. However, the effectiveness of these assessments has been limited by several factors. One of the major problems has been the difficulty of establishing pertinent regulations and guidelines. As a result, many new projects have gone forward without assessment. A second problem is that many assessments have focused on development projects in which economic considerations have overshadowed environmental consequences. Another major problem is that of related scale. Most provinces do not require environmental assessments of small-scale projects, and it is clear that several small projects may combine to cause significant environmental damage. As well, the discretionary nature of most environmental assessment procedures has diminished their effectiveness. In most jurisdictions, elected representatives are given considerable leeway in deciding which proposals will be included or excluded from the assessment process, what information will be made available, and what role the public will play. While discretion does permit flexibility, it must not be abused to the detriment of the environment. Despite these problems, however, environmental impact assessments can be of vital importance in raising concerns and alerting both public and governments to the environmental costs of projects before they begin. When one considers the risks to both humans and the environment extant today (two of which are discussed below), it is clear that environmental assessment should have an important role to play in the process. Whether it will be allowed to do so in light of the ideological dislike of such regulation found in some governments today remains to be seen.

ENVIRONMENTAL RISK ASSESSMENT AND MANAGEMENT — CASE STUDIES

There are many hazards that one could point to to prove the utility of risk assessment and management: nuclear radiation, lead poisoning, food additives, and biotechnology, to name a few. However, in this chapter we have chosen to focus on two — toxic chemicals and hazardous wastes — because of their intrinsic importance and the regimes created to regulate them.

CASE STUDY I — TOXIC CHEMICALS

Although many labels have been used to describe the society in which we live, perhaps none is more fitting than the "chemical society." Whether we are aware of the phenomenon or not, we are surrounded by a constant deluge of chemicals. It is estimated that well over 63,000 chemicals are in regular use in North America, and that, on average, 700 new chemicals are added every year (Jackson and Weiler, 1982:19). These chemicals have provided our society with many benefits. We are all familiar with the various "wonder drugs" that have virtually eliminated many dreaded diseases. We enjoy fresh produce that is available year round in unprecedented quantities. No longer do we marvel at the wide variety of food products at the supermarket which seem to have unlimited shelf life. For these benefits, we must pay homage to sciences such as chemistry and biochemistry which have created the multitude of chemicals without which our lives would be vastly different. Since the end of World War II, science has contributed a great deal to increasing our health and comfort. Indeed, its motto could be: "better living through chemistry." However, along with the many benefits, there has also been an ominous burden placed on society. The many chemicals which have contributed so much to improving our society also pose serious threats to human health and the environment.

Clearly, we face dangers from toxic chemicals. Toxic chemicals are poisonous substances which are harmful to plants and animals. The term "toxicity" refers to the degree to which a substance is injurious to a plant or animal. Toxic chemicals can be classified into two broad categories, organic and inorganic. Certain natural chemical substances, such as inorganic metals, salts, acids, and bases, are highly toxic. The second category is composed of synthetic organic chemicals. Some of the better known of these which are highly toxic are PCBS, DDT, and dioxin. One of the more prevalent uses for synthetic organic chemicals has been in the agricultural industry in the form of pesticides, herbicides, and fungicides. However, synthetic organic chemicals are also used widely in many other industries.

The effects of toxic chemicals on human health and the environment are many and varied, depending on the level of exposure, the dosage, and the type of contaminant. Although science has been unable to determine with precision the effects of toxic chemicals on human health, it has been demonstrated that these effects manifest themselves in subtle ways. They can diminish reproductive capacity, cause birth defects and mental aberrations, and in many cases they are highly carcinogenic. For example, chlorine, which is widely used to purify water, is now suspected of reacting with other elements to form carcinogens in the very water it is supposed to be cleansing. Toxic chemicals also cause respiratory ailments and contribute to many other types of disease and health problems. Indeed, we face a serious and steadily increasing threat from toxic chemicals.

For many years, scientists and public officials concentrated on finding effective solutions to combat bacterial diseases which plagued society. Consequently, they were ill-prepared to deal with the problems caused by toxic chemicals which are infinitely more difficult to combat. As well, several factors have made it difficult for society to come to terms with the dangers and harmful effects of toxic chemicals. Part of the problem is the lack of precise and accurate scientific knowledge. Thus far, there is too little knowledge about the medical effects of toxic chemicals. For example, the causes of cancer remain a mystery to scientists. Hence, while toxic chemicals are suspected of causing cancer, there is little concrete evidence about the nature of the relationship between toxic chemicals and cancer. Moreover, the effects of toxic chemicals are not easily discernible. In some cases, toxic chemicals act slowly and the harmful effects might not be evident for as long as 20 years. As a result of limited scientific knowledge, it is extremely difficult to set standards or develop regulations for the use of toxic chemicals.

A second factor which has worked against our willingness to confront the problems caused by toxic chemicals is that they do provide many benefits to society. We are confronted with a major dilemma in determining whether the benefits are outweighed by the disadvantages. This dilemma is clearly illustrated in the case of the chemical compound DDT. DDT was created by a German scientist in 1874; however, its value as an insecticide did not become known until World War II. During the War, DDT was used as a delousing agent. Following the War, DDT was hailed as a means of stamping out insect-borne disease and "winning the farmers' war against crop destroyers overnight" (Carson, 1962:29). In the post-war era, DDT was quickly put into worldwide use as one of the most effective insecticides. In many Third World countries, DDT became highly effective in controlling the mosquitoes responsible for the spread of malaria. However, as early as 1950, scientists in the United States began to suggest that the potential hazards of DDT had been underestimated. By the early 1970s, DDT was banned in Canada and the United States. However, many nations did not follow this lead. For example, at the 23rd World Health Assembly in 1970, the World Health Organization stated that "the withdrawal of DDT would be a major tragedy in the chapter of human health" (Green, 1976:102). The withdrawal of DDT in Sri Lanka due to government pressure resulted in a major increase in the number of deaths caused by malaria in 1968-69. Though it is highly toxic, DDT can provide many benefits to millions of people. Consequently, the dilemma as to whether the benefits of toxic chemicals such as DDT outweigh the disadvantages remains a major part of the difficulty we face in dealing effectively with toxic chemicals.

Another factor which has added to the difficulty of dealing with toxic chemicals is the prohibitively high cost of implementing effective solutions. Even when problems are clearly identified and solutions designed, the costs of implementing them are often very high, if not prohibitive. In times of financial restraint, governments are unlikely to contribute large amounts of money to deal with toxic chemicals. Furthermore, the private sector, concerned with increasing profits, is also unlikely to make willingly the large expenditures necessary to deal with toxic chemical problems. Consequently, the financial aspect of dealing with toxic chemicals is a major obstacle which significantly affects society's ability to confront the problems caused by toxic chemicals. Thus, considering science's ability to create new chemicals and alter existing chemical compounds, it seems inevitable that the toxic chemical problem will become more serious before we are forced to deal with it. Nevertheless, some measures have already been put in place.

The Governmental Response to Toxic Chemicals

As the growing public concern over toxic chemicals became more pronounced during the 1970s, Canadian governments began to respond to the problem by developing guidelines and regulations for the monitoring, testing, and surveillance of chemicals. For example, in 1976 the passage of the Environmental Contaminants Act by the federal government was viewed as a major advance toward improving the control of chemical contamination of the environment. Prior to the passage of this act, most chemicals were manufactured and sold without any testing regarding their toxic implications. The Environmental Contaminants Act empowered the Department of National Health and Welfare and the Department of the Environment to ban or restrict the use, manufacture, or importation of any chemical in Canada. In order to fulfil this responsibility, the Department of National Health and Welfare established an Environmental Contaminants Review Board to collect and assess pertinent information about the hazardous effects of chemicals. The Department of the Environment delegated its responsibilities in this matter to its Environmental Protection Service. However, the capabilities of both departments to gather sufficient information to make decisions related to banning or restricting the use, manufacture, or importation of chemicals in Canada were severely limited.

To determine the potential hazards and toxic implications of a single chemical requires extensive testing conducted by highly trained professionals working in modern research laboratories. Aside from the costs involved in training and recruiting qualified personnel and building research facilities, there is also a considerable time factor required for performing adequate tests. In many instances, testing can take several years to generate information which can be used to make regulatory decisions. Thus, when we consider that more than 700 new chemicals are created each year, the possibility of monitoring and testing even a small percentage of these chemicals is daunting. Confronted with these limitations, and even with shared knowledge from the United States, public officials in Canada are handicapped in their ability to make effective regulatory decisions. Nevertheless, we have little choice but to look increasingly to our governments to devise better means of protecting society and the environment from the problems caused by toxic chemicals.

The Constitutional, Legal, and Managerial Framework

JURISDICTIONAL ISSUES

As is the case in most policy fields in Canada, both the federal and provincial governments have jurisdiction over various aspects of the use and regulation of chemicals. The nature of this divided jurisdiction emanates from the constitutional division of powers between the federal and provincial governments and from the many factors involved in the manufacture and use of chemicals in Canada. In regard to the constitutional division of powers, concurrent jurisdiction was given to both levels of government in the area of agriculture. Since the agricultural sector is one of the main users of chemicals in the form of pesticides, herbicides, and fungicides, both levels of government have the power and authority to regulate chemical usage. Aside from the concurrent jurisdiction in the area of agriculture, the various types of activity associated with the manufacture and use of chemicals also involves the jurisdictions of both levels of government. By way of illustration, the provincial governments have the authority to regulate industrial activities within the province, including the use of chemicals in industrial processes. The federal government, with its broad-based residual powers and authority over matters which are of national or international concern, can regulate the use, manufacture, and importation of chemicals from an environmental, transportation, and health and welfare perspective. Consequently, we encounter a situation in which there is no clear-cut jurisdiction over the use of chemicals in Canada, and thus conflict and tension between the two levels of government is not unusual. Fortunately, however, the federal and provincial governments have been able to cooperate and work together in providing the nation with some (though not completely adequate) means of regulating the use of chemicals in Canada.

FEDERAL AND PROVINCIAL LAWS

The federal government's role in responding to the various problems caused by toxic chemicals has focused on regulating the manufacture, importation, and registration of chemicals. The federal government has passed several pieces of legislation which enable it to perform these regulatory functions. The Pest Control Products Act, administered by Agriculture Canada, is designed to control the classification, registration, and labelling of all pesticides that may be used in Canada. According to the Act, "no controlled product can be imported into or sold in Canada unless it has been registered, conforms to the Act's standards, and is packaged and labelled as prescribed" (GC, Statutes 1970). The Act provides precise instructions as to how a product is to be registered, packaged, and labelled. Under the Act, chemical control products are classified into three categories: domestic, commercial, or restricted. The domestic category consists of relatively safe products which are used in homes and gardens. The products found in the commercial category can be used safely by commercial operators in a variety of settings, including farms, hospitals, and commercial establishments such as restaurants and hotels. Restricted products require more detailed labels specifying precise means of usage and qualifications for persons who may use the product. The Pest Control Products Acts provides the federal government with two important means of controlling toxic chemicals. First, the government has the authority to accept or refuse an application for registration, and secondly, the government has the power to stipulate what should appear on the labels of all pesticide products. Therefore, all pesticides, which are one of the major sources of toxic chemicals, must undergo the regulatory procedures established by the Pest Control Products Act.

Pesticides are only one of the many sources of toxic chemicals which enter the environment. Another important source is the numerous chemicals used in foods and drugs. The federal government's Food and Drugs Act is the primary piece of legislation used to regulate this source of potential danger. Administered by the Department of National Health and Welfare, the Food and Drugs Act is designed to protect the consumer against health hazards and fraud in the consumption and sale of food, drugs, cosmetics, and medical devices. According to the Act, no person shall sell any food that has in or upon it any poisonous or harmful substance. The Act provides inspectors with the power to examine any such article that may contravene approved standards. The regulation of chemicals in food and drug products is specified in Schedules A to H of the Food and Drugs Act. The Act and its regulations are constantly being amended as new information about chemicals used in food and drugs is made available to the Department. Thus, the Food and Drugs Act is another important means by which the federal government controls toxic chemicals.

Similarly, the Environmental Contaminants Act, passed in 1974, was designed to protect human health and the environment from toxic substances before they can cause harm by controlling them at source, either at the point of manufacture or at the point of importation. The Act was intended to enable the federal government to regulate toxic chemicals in Canada. It gave power to the federal government to collect information on substances which might contaminate the environment. The information-gathering aspect of the Act was comprehensive; no one was exempt from the operation of the Act, and it attempted to cover all means of entry of the substance into the environment. The Act specified that any company that manufactures or imports a chemical compound for the first time into Canada must notify the government. The company has to provide all pertinent information about the product to the government, including the name of the chemical compound, the quantity produced or imported, and any information regarding chemical hazard. If not satisfied, the government could ask the company to carry out tests to discover if the chemical is hazardous. A Schedule to the Act listed substances and classes of substances that the government believes pose a significant danger to human health and the environment and for which regulations have been prescribed under the Act. The Environmental Contaminants Act became part of the Canadian Environmental Protection Act in 1988. As well, the federal government can make use of other legislation, such as the Hazardous Products Act and the Clean Air Act, among others, to regulate particular types of activities associated with the manufacture, sale, and importation of toxic chemicals in Canada. Finally, amendments to the Canadian Environmental Protection Act passed in June of 1999 direct the federal government to catalogue 23,000 toxic substances in use in Canada, commit the government to the "virtual elimination" of most dangerous toxics, and also require Ottawa to conduct research on the health effects associated with the use of toxic chemicals. In sum, the various federal laws establish minimum standards and regulations which must be enforced throughout the nation. The provincial governments can enact more stringent standards and regulations within their areas of jurisdiction if they so wish.

Whereas the federal government's role is primarily concerned with regulating the manufacture, sale, and importation of chemicals, the role of the provincial governments is concerned with regulating the use of chemicals. In this regard, the provincial governments have sought to control the manner in which chemicals are used by creating legislation specifying by whom, how, and where chemicals may be used. For example, in 1973 the government of Ontario passed one of the most comprehensive pieces of environmental legislation regulating the use of pesticides. The Pesticides Act brought forth a complex system of licences, permits, and requirements for record-keeping, storage, selling, display, and transportation which sought to ensure that only properly registered pesticides are sold and used in proper ways by the right people. The Act specifies that only pesticides registered and approved by the federal Pest Control Products Act may be sold and used in Ontario. These pesticides are classified into six categories listed in the Schedules of the Pesticides Act, according to their descending order of toxicity and level of expertise required for use. According to the Act,

> No person, whether acting or not acting under the authority of a license or permit under this Act or an exemption under the regulations, shall deposit, add, emit, or discharge or cause or permit the deposit, addition, emission or discharge of a pesticide or of any substance or thing containing a pesticide into the environment that causes or is likely to cause impairment of the quality of the environment. (Ontario, Statutes 1982)

The Pesticide Act imposes two major prohibitions in addition to the federal Pest Control Products Act. First, there is a prohibition forbidding the use of any pesticide which may contaminate any body of water. Second, there is a prohibition stipulating that pesticides may not be stored in the same area as food or drink. Thus, the Pesticide Act provides a comprehensive regulatory system which enables the government to control the use of pesticides in Ontario, should it desire to do so. Similar types of regulations have been adopted by most other provinces as part of their pesticide policies.

The Ontario government also relies on several other types of legislation to control the use of chemicals in the province. For example, the Environmental Protection Act enables the Minister of the Environment to conduct research related to contaminants. Accordingly, if pesticides are deemed to be contaminants, the government can use this act to control their use. Similarly, the government can make use of other legislation to control the use of chemicals in other types of activities. Combined with federal legislation, provincial laws such as those in Ontario provide for a complex regulatory regime to control toxic chemicals in Canada, should the government wish to use it. Unfortunately, this has not always been the case. Fifteen years ago, one commentator on the situation in Ontario concluded that reforms were needed to:

» facilitate greater cooperation among members of society, organizations, and governments
» encourage mediation and other non-adversarial forms of decision-making
» facilitate greater public involvement in the decision-making process
» improve political and corporate accountability for decisions affecting the environment
» provide a better information base on which environmental decisions may be made
» encourage diversity and experimentation among governments and other institutions with regard to enforcement and compliance mechanisms
» adopt a "polluter pay" principle that requires that all victims of environmental degradation by fully compensated. (Emond, 1985:148)

Today, most of these changes are still needed, but, given the determination of the Harris government to free industry from government regulation, it is unlikely they will be made.

FEDERAL AND PROVINCIAL DEPARTMENTS AND AGENCIES

Despite the good intentions underlying the creation of federal and provincial laws to regulate toxic chemicals, their effectiveness depends on how well they are managed and enforced. The management of the numerous regulations is the responsibility of several departments and agencies at both levels of government, and the division of responsibility between several departments and agencies is a reflection of the complexity of the process required to regulate toxic chemicals. The various departments and agencies have had to develop close relations in order to provide for the effective regulation of toxic chemicals. At the federal level, the major departments involved are the Department of Agriculture, the Department of National Health and Welfare, and the Department of the Environment.

The Department of Agriculture's mandate is to promote the development of the agricultural sector in Canada. The Department's position with regard to the use of pesticides is that they are essential for the production of food at affordable prices. Although the Department considers pesticides essential for food production, it also recognizes the need to regulate these chemical products in order to safeguard the public and the environment. Thus, the Department is responsible for the administration of the Pest Control Products Act. More specifically, this responsibility has been delegated to the Department's Plant Products Directorate. The directorate has a Pesticide Division which regulates pest control products by evaluating data on usefulness and safety, registering acceptable products for marketing, and inspecting products in the marketplace. The Pesticide Division oversees the regulation and application of pesticide products. As well, it has inspectors with broad-based powers to enforce all aspects of the Pest Control Products Act. The inspectors tend to work closely with their provincial counterparts to regulate the use of chemical products in the agricultural industry in Canada.

Prior to 1973, the responsibility for testing the chemicals used in food and drugs was performed by the Food and Drug Directorate of the Department of National Health and Welfare. In 1973, this directorate was amalgamated into the new Environmental Health Directorate. This directorate consists of three bureaus and three scientific divisions. Of particular concern to the regulation of toxic chemicals is the Bureau of Chemical Hazards. This bureau is concerned with the health effects of chemical and microbiological agents in the environment. The bureau also contains the Monitoring and Criteria Division which is responsible for determining the nature and quality of chemicals to which we are exposed in the environment and the workplace. It analyses environmental samples and studies how chemicals are transported, altered, and concentrated in the environment in order to predict the risk of human exposure. The Environmental and Occupational Toxicology division investigates the relationship between exposure to chemicals and the response such exposure will likely elicit in humans. The Pesticides Division of the Bureau, mentioned earlier, assesses the potential hazards of new and existing pesticides. All three divisions make recommendations for regulating chemicals, including the establishment of standards for their use. The information and recommendations generated by the Bureau of Chemical Hazards are instrumental in the decision-making process for the registration and application of pesticide products and chemicals for use in food and drugs.

The Department of the Environment's Environmental Protection Service (EPS) is responsible for the administration of the environmental contaminants sections of the Canadian Environmental Protection Act. When toxic chemicals are determined to be contaminants, the EPS has the authority to regulate them. The Department's strategy is to prevent or minimize the release of toxic chemicals into the environment. The EPS has played an important role in establishing national standards to control the emission of toxic chemicals into the environment. Toxic chemicals were one of the Department's top priorities during the 1980s and remain so today. Thus, Environment Canada continues to promote greater public awareness and concern about the health and environmental hazards posed by toxic chemicals.

The three federal departments mentioned above are the principal departments involved in regulating toxic chemicals. Other departments, such as Consumer and Corporate Affairs, Transport, Labour and Foreign Affairs and International Trade (DFAIT), are peripherally involved in other areas of toxic chemical regulation. For example, at the time of writing, officers from DFAIT are participating in an international conference to draft a treaty aimed at protecting the planet from Persistant Organic Pollutants (POPs), some of the most toxic chemicals ever produced by humans. Aside from the involvement of federal departments, provincial departments and agencies have also become very active in managing and regulating the use of toxic chemicals in their provinces. For example, in the province of Ontario, the Ministry of the Environment is responsible for administering the Pesticides Act.

The Pesticides Act is actually administered by the Hazardous Contaminants and Standards Branch of the Ministry, and a Pesticides Appeal Board has been created to oversee the licensing process. The Board's functions are to hear appeals and make decisions pertaining to the issue, renewal, or refusal of licences. As well, it can suspend or revoke licences or issue control orders. The Act also created a Pesticides Advisory Committee consisting of fourteen members. The Advisory Committee is responsible for reviewing the content and operation of the Pesticides Act and for making recommendations to improve it. The Committee undertakes an annual research program with three basic objectives:

1. to find alternative pesticides for those which are deemed to be environmentally hazardous
2. to determine potential environmental hazards caused by pesticides currently in use
3. to reduce pesticide inputs into the environment. (Ontario, Statutes 1982)

Since the majority of pesticides in Ontario are used for agricultural production, the Ontario Ministry of Agriculture and Food plays a role in regulating the use of toxic chemicals. The Agricultural Ministry's activities are coordinated with those of the Ministry of the Environment. The Ministry of Agriculture issues annual spray calendars to assist farmers in their use of pesticides. Another important part of the provincial government's role in controlling the use of toxic chemicals is the generation of data and information about the toxic effects of chemicals on the environment. The government of Ontario has established a Provincial Pesticide Residue Test Laboratory at the University of Guelph. This laboratory conducts about 15 per cent of the government's research into pesticide residues and provides analytical services to other government departments and agencies. The close cooperation between these two ministries has given the province of Ontario one of the most effective systems for administering a complex regulatory regime to control toxic chemicals, although Alberta imposes much stricter regulations for users of pesticides listed in the schedules of its Pesticides Act. The difference between the provinces in their approach to regulating the use of pesticides illustrates important jurisdictional issues with regard to toxic chemical regulation in Canada.

Jurisdictional issues pertaining to the type and enforcement of environmental standards for the regulation of toxic chemicals persist throughout the nation. Although the federal government has established minimum national standards, the provinces have the authority to exempt certain chemicals from regulation. As well, the provinces are responsible for enforcing the regulations. Whether for economic or other reasons, when a province exempts some chemicals from regulation or does not enforce regulation, the issue of protecting human health and environmental quality surfaces. Should there be the same type of regulation throughout the nation when the nature of the problem varies in different regions? These issues are a most controversial part of the politics of regulation, in which the different levels of government seek to satisfy their constituents and safeguard the public from the hazards of toxic chemicals.

The Politics of Regulation

The regulation of toxic chemicals in Canada is a complex and intricate process. It has also become the source of much tension and dispute between the various groups and organizations involved in the process. Because the scientific basis for the regulation of toxic chemicals is imprecise in terms of furnishing the requisite knowledge needed to make effective regulatory decisions, public officials have been placed in a somewhat difficult position. Although there is a consensus recognizing the need for toxic chemical regulation, public officials face the task of designing regulations which maximize the benefits derived from the use of chemicals and minimize the disadvantages. Thus far, regulatory policies have satisfied neither the chemical manufacturers, who claim they are over-regulated, nor the environmental public interest groups who want stricter regulations.

The chemical industry agrees that there is a need for regulation; however, the manufacturers argue that current regulatory procedures are burdensome and that they stifle the development of newer and safer chemical products. They claim that the regulatory process which all new chemical products must undergo has become overly complicated, time consuming, and costly. In order for new chemical products to become registered, they must undergo rigorous testing which may take several years to complete. The costs and time delay involved are of serious concern to the industry. They too are concerned with the safety and the health of their clients and conduct considerable testing before they introduce new products. The time delays and costs of the regulatory process significantly diminish the manufacturers' incentive to invest in the development of new, safer, and more effective pesticides.

In contrast to the position of the chemical industry, a variety of environmental and public interest groups advocate more stringent regulation of toxic chemicals. The environmentalists argue that the primary objective of chemical manufacturers is profit. They contend that in the highly competitive chemical industry, the drive for profits supplants the manufacturers' concerns about the safety of their products. In other words, the environmentalists do not trust the chemical manufacturers and, therefore, call upon the government to impose stricter regulations in order to protect public health and the environment. These fears are not without foundation. There are numerous examples of chemical products that have been introduced in the marketplace which have had detrimental effects on human health and the environment. For example, there are many pesticides that do not provide complete details for use and storage, nor contain enough information on their potential health hazards or what to do in case of an emergency. Moreover, there is a lot of controversy related to the type and quality of testing of chemical products performed by the industry. Does the chemical industry use the same standards and testing procedures as those employed by government agencies? In light of these concerns, environmentalists prefer to be safe rather than sorry, and therefore advocate more stringent policies for toxic chemicals.

Both the chemical industry and environmentalists exert considerable political pressure on public officials in their effort to design effective regulatory policies. There are also numerous market forces which affect the regulatory process. For example, one of the paramount goals of modern society is to achieve a level of food production to satisfy the needs of a growing population. Without doubt, the use of pesticides has greatly increased food production and kept food prices at reasonable levels. Both Canada and, to a larger extent the United States, have developed large-scale agricultural industries which produce enormous quantities of food products which are sold throughout the world. Without the use of pesticides and the continual search for newer and better pesticides, food production could decrease significantly and there likely would be a major increase in food prices. Canadian and American farmers would be hard-pressed to compete in the world market, and many nations dependent on North American food production would suffer. Accordingly, the market is a major force which must be taken into account by public officials.

At the same time, there is much inefficiency and waste associated with the implementation of toxic chemical regulations. For example, if only a few workers in a modern industrial plant are exposed to hazardous chemicals, and if adequate protective equipment is available, doesn't it make more sense to have them use personal protective equipment rather than require the entire plant to undergo costly engineering changes? Quite clearly, the high cost of regulation is a major factor to be considered in developing toxic chemical regulations. After all, consumers desire reasonably affordable products that are safe to use. Thus, the interplay of political and market forces creates a difficult situation for public officials who seek to develop regulatory policies to satisfy all concerned. Regulatory policies will continue to evolve as new information becomes available and as more and more chemical products are created. However, we must be increasingly wary of the health hazards and environmental effects which toxic chemicals pose for our society. It is imperative that we recognize the scope and magnitude of the toxic chemical problem and continue to search for better means of controlling this menace. We must also strive to elect governments committed to this goal.

In sum, we live in a chemical society, surrounded by thousands of chemicals that provide many benefits which make our lives easier, safer, and more comfortable. However, these same chemicals also pose a serious threat to society in terms of health hazards and the environmental damage which they cause. There is little doubt that toxic chemicals are a serious threat; however, there is much controversy about the precise nature of this threat. Thus far, our scientific knowledge and understanding of the hazards are limited. Without precise data and information, it is difficult to determine whether the advantages outweigh the disadvantages. Nevertheless, as was demonstrated earlier, public officials have sought to maximize the benefits and minimize the costs of chemical use by designing and implementing regulatory policies to control the use of toxic substances. Because of the numerous types of chemicals and the multiplicity of their uses, regulatory policies in Canada are complex and intricate. Thus far, they have satisfied neither the chemical industry nor the environmentalists. Due to the many forces and factors which are intertwined in the use of chemicals, public officials face a considerable challenge in formulating effective regulatory policies to control toxic chemicals. Where there is a lot of scientific knowledge about health hazards, such as in the case of asbestos or mercury, there has been more effective regulation. In many other cases, where there is little knowledge or understanding, regulations seem inadequate and the consequences are dramatic. The effectiveness of public policy in dealing with the toxic chemical problem is affected by many factors. One of the most important of these is the degree of public concern with developing effective solutions. As the public becomes increasingly aware of and interested in the toxic chemical problem, and governments face greater public demand for effective regulation, public policy should evolve to provide more effective standards and better protection for individuals against the hazards of toxic chemicals.

CASE STUDY II — HAZARDOUS WASTES

Closely related to the problem of toxic chemicals are the difficulties involved in the handling and disposal of hazardous wastes. In order to understand the gravity and magnitude of the hazardous waste problem, it is necessary to clarify what hazardous wastes are. According to the Task Force on Hazardous Waste Definition, hazardous wastes are those discarded materials or substances in solid, semi-solid, liquid, or gaseous form which, due to their nature and quantity, require specialized waste management techniques for handling, transport, storage, treatment, and disposal because they may cause or contribute to adverse, acute, or chronic effects on human health or the environment when not properly controlled. Although it has been difficult to determine whether a waste substance is damaging to human health or the environment, it is classified as hazardous if it has one of the following characteristics:

» ignitability at relatively low temperatures
» corrosivity — highly acidic or alkaline
» reactivity — explodes or generates gas
» toxicity — produces acute or chronic health effects on people or animals or affects the growth of plants
» radioactivity
» infectiousness
» carcinogenicity — causes cancer
» mutagenicity — damages the genes, thus affecting future generations of humans, animals, or plants
» teratogenicity — causes birth defects. (Jackson and Weiler, 1982:21)

In order to determine if a waste substance possesses one of the above characteristics, rigorous scientific testing must be conducted which generally takes a considerable period of time. Indeed, as recently as 1999, Brian Emmett, first Commissioner of the Environment and Sustainable Development,[4] criticized the federal government because out of the thousands of potentially hazardous substances in use in Canada only 70 would be assessed by the year 2000 (Emmett, 1999). In most cases, until there is concrete evidence that a product is hazardous, it is not classified as such.

Hazardous wastes are a by-product of the modern industrial age. In our desire to implement more and better ways of producing goods, scientists have used their knowledge and talents to create a plethora of chemicals. As mentioned earlier, more than 700 new chemicals are created each year and there are more than 63,000 different chemicals in industrial use in North America. While these chemicals have been created to serve specific functions which produce positive results, quite often they also have negative effects which are hazardous to human health and the environment. Once created, these chemicals are difficult to destroy or dispose of when their usefulness has run out or when they are classified as hazardous. According to Dr. Samuel Epstein, a noted expert on chemical pollutants, "these chemicals are not just familiar ones, but exotic ones which have never previously existed on earth and to which no living thing has previously had to adapt" (1979:27). Thus, society faces a critical problem in determining how to handle and dispose of hazardous wastes. The highly toxic chemical compounds known as PCBs provide an important illustration of the nature of the hazardous waste problem which confronts us.

During the 1930s and 1940s, PCBs were heralded as one of the new wonder chemicals which would solve many industrial problems. The particular chlorine, hydrogen, and carbon compounds which make up polychlorinated biphenyls in their liquid form are chemically inert. Thus, PCBs became the ideal material for a variety of uses, as a coolant and insulator for electric transformers, a dust suppressant sprayed on gravel roads, and a plasticizer in paints, rubbers, and waxes. PCBs were widely used without restriction throughout the world until it was found that the same properties which made them useful to industry also made them a lethal toxin that threatened human health and the environment: "In 1968, a human disaster focused international attention on the chemical when the use of PCB contaminated cooking oil resulted in skin cysts, nausea, numbness, and an above average incidence of malignant tumors, still births and birth defects among 1300 victims" (Finlayson, 1985:20). Further studies during the early 1970s linked PCBs with cancer, skin disorders, and hair loss, and other health effects. The United States banned the use of PCBs in 1972. However, it took Canada seven years longer to ban the use of PCBs. In 1979, when PCBs were banned in Canada, Environment Canada estimated there were about 16,000 tons of the chemical in use throughout the nation. The majority of PCBs were placed in storage throughout the country because no province possessed the specialized treatment facilities to destroy PCBs by burning them at a temperature of 1600 degrees Celsius. Until such time as Canada's complete stock of PCBs can be destroyed, they will remain a serious threat to public health and the environment.

PCBs are but one example of the nightmare. The magnitude of our hazardous waste problem is much greater when we consider that there are hundreds of chemicals now classified as hazardous. Moreover, each year approximately three million pounds of hazardous wastes are generated by industry. Although we may never be able to eliminate the production and use of chemicals for industrial development completely, it is imperative that we develop more effective means of identifying potential hazards before their introduction and of disposing of hazardous wastes before we suffer major environmental and health disasters.

Hazardous Wastes — A Problem that Cannot Be Buried

One reason hazardous wastes have become such a high-profile environmental issue in recent years is that they have been handled so poorly in the past. Until relatively recently, highly toxic wastes were often dumped in insecure landfills, and decommissioned industrial sites were routinely abandoned without being properly cleaned up. As a result, unrecorded amounts of hazardous wastes have been deposited in landfills, waste dumps, rivers, and lakes throughout North America. In the United States, there are estimated to be more than 50,000 chemical dumps. The Office of Technology Assessment, one of the main research organizations of the United States Congress, contends that there may be at least 10,000 hazardous waste sites that pose a serious threat to public health in the United States. In the province of Ontario, a survey conducted in 1979 revealed almost 800 previously unknown dump sites. The research team which conducted this survey estimated that as many as 3000 more such sites may exist in southern Ontario alone (O'Hara, 1981:26). This legacy of chemical graveyards is the result of years of uncontrolled dumping. In many cases, the disposal of hazardous wastes was quite often performed by unknowing, inexperienced, or unconcerned individuals and companies. Firms and industries have always been interested in the most cost-efficient means for disposing of their waste products, including hazardous wastes. Instead of pursuing more costly but environmentally safer disposal methods, many companies simply buried their hazardous wastes in landfill sites or dumped them into rivers and lakes. Guided by the principle of "out of sight, out of mind," hazardous wastes were disposed of in the most callous fashion.

Unfortunately, we are beginning to pay the price for years of neglect and lack of action. The thousands of hazardous waste sites which dot the landscape pose a serious threat to the environment and public health, especially to those people who live near these dump sites.

In recent years, the discovery of several major hazardous waste dump sites has alerted the public to the impending dangers they face from chemical polluters. Perhaps the most highly publicized case has been the Love Canal, which received national media attention in the United States and Canada when it was declared an emergency in 1978. In Canada, many similar horror stories also have come to light. In LaSalle, a residential section of Montreal, 16 families were forced to abandon their homes when it was discovered they were living on top of a toxic waste dump site. In St. Basile-le-Grand, near Montreal, 3500 residents were evacuated after the accidental burning of a warehouse containing PCB waste. In Hagersville, Ontario, public health was threatened by a dangerous fire at a used-tire storage facility. And in Sydney, Nova Scotia, tar ponds have long been notorious for their threat to human health. As more and more hazardous waste dump sites are discovered, and as more and more occurrences such as those just mentioned come to light, public concern about the impact of chemical pollutants on human health has increased. In some cases the health effects of living close to a waste site become evident rather quickly. However, in most instances, the health effects are not easily discernible and may take years to be felt. Jane O'Hara describes the "phantom nature" of chemical pollutants in the following way: "Odourless. Colourless. Tasteless for the most part. Often they are present only in parts per billion. Toxic in some cases. Carcinogens in others. Mixing and mingling to form new chemical cocktails" (1985:26).

A most important aspect of the hazardous waste problem is that most people are unaware of the dangers they are inhaling or consuming in their air, water, and food. Since most chemicals are fairly recent creations, there is little or no prior experience or knowledge about the danger caused by exposure to these chemical contaminants. Some effects, such as damage to genes from cancer-causing agents, might not arise for twenty years or more, and might not become evident until the next generation. In fact, the International Joint Commission reported recently that chemicals which mimic human hormones and lead to infertility are turning up in fish caught in the Great Lakes (IJC, 1999). Nevertheless, despite our uncertainty about the health effects caused by hazardous wastes, each year hundreds of new chemicals are introduced into society and millions of pounds of hazardous wastes are generated. As the health effects of improper disposal become better known, it becomes more evident that we have created a menacing waste problem that cannot be buried. The question thus becomes: What are we doing to prevent further tragedies?

Many of these problems could be averted in the future if a reduction in hazardous waste outputs could be achieved. As the State of Canada's Environment Report put it in 1991, "Some wastes can be substantially reduced or eliminated altogether by changes in manufacturing processes or the use of alternative chemicals. Other wastes can be reused, either as is or with reprocessing." A study of hazardous wastes generated in Canada in 1986 estimated that about half had high potential for recycling. Many hazardous wastes can be captured and detoxified at source through simple procedures such as filtration and the addition of neutralizing agents. Caustic liquids, for example, can be safely neutralized with acids to produce a simple salt and water solution. Some wastes, such as oils, can be degraded biologically through the action of micro-organisms. Other wastes that cannot be disposed of by these processes can be destroyed by means of controlled high-temperature incineration. This is the most effective way of disposing of persistent toxic chemicals such as PCBs and organochlorine pesticides. Such incinerators operate at very high standards of efficiency and are designed to achieve 99.9999 per cent destruction of PCB wastes (GC, 1996). Recycling has also been encouraged through hazardous waste materials exchange programs: "Industries are invited to list wastes they must dispose of with the exchanges. Others, who may be able to use such wastes as raw materials, are then provided with the opportunity to contact the disposer and receive the wastes without charge" (MacDonald, 1993:191). Matching the needs of potential users with supplies available from producers benefits both parties. However, these programs account for only a small portion of the hazardous waste management initiatives. Wastes that cannot be reduced or recycled require safe disposal to reduce the possibility of health and environmental risk. Environment Canada has estimated that at least 65 per cent of all hazardous wastes can be managed on site, or in the location where they were generated:

> Although industries have made convincing progress in reducing releases of many air and water pollutants, they have not been nearly as effective in dealing with hazardous wastes. Unlike air and water pollutants, hazardous wastes are largely an industrial problem, and the solutions to it involve important changes in industrial practices, particularly in terms of reducing the outputs of hazardous wastes and recycling more of the wastes that are produced. (GC, 1996)

The Waste Management Industry

In response to the growing problem of hazardous waste disposal, several private-sector companies have emerged to provide the specialized types of services required for the disposal of industrial hazardous wastes. Originally these companies were involved in the collection and disposal of solid wastes; however, they soon branched out into the disposal of other hazardous wastes when they realized that this provided an important source of profits. Two factors have contributed significantly to increased revenues from liquid and hazardous waste collection and disposal. First, there is a constant need for garbage to be collected. Second, and most importantly, increased government regulation of liquid and hazardous wastes makes industries more dependent on waste management companies. Unfortunately, the waste management industry's safety record and disposal methods have been fraught with violations and negligence.

The Role of Governments in Hazardous Waste Management

THE FEDERAL GOVERNMENT
The safe disposal of hazardous wastes ranks high on the list of Environment Canada's concerns. However, the role it can play is limited because most aspects of the collection and disposal of hazardous wastes fall within provincial jurisdiction. Nevertheless, within its restricted sphere, the federal government over the years has tried to play an active role in promoting safer and sound waste management practices.

The Environmental Contaminants Act (ECD) of 1975 was intended to control the manufacture of new substances and to address the problems caused by others already in existence. It gave the federal government the power to collect information on potentially harmful substances and to cooperate with the provinces to prevent their abuse. However, the Act quickly faced criticism because its reactive approach to dealing with problems, which might be seen as appropriate in relation to toxic substances, was a procrastinator's dream come true, insofar as the timely and comprehensive management of many waste substances was concerned (Castrilli, 1985:1-2). Furthermore, the Act was backed by insufficient funding and ran into difficulties when some provincial governments refused to cooperate in applying its provisions. As a result it was subsumed under the new Canadian Environmental Protection Act when it was proclaimed in 1988.

Today, the federal government, through Environment Canada, is restricted to providing assistance and guidance in the development of a comprehensive system for managing hazardous wastes and to the establishment of uniform objectives and standards of practice across the country (http://www.ec.gc.ca/fmd/fact_c.htm). A list of hazardous wastes has been incorporated in the Transportation of Dangerous Goods Act (TDGA), which enables the federal government through the Department of Transport to establish safety procedures for the handling of dangerous goods by rail, truck, air, or water, and the TDGA "manifest" system is used for interprovincial and international waste movements and complements the provincial systems in an attempt to provide a total national system. In addition, when it ratified the Basel Convention on the Transboundary Movement of Hazardous Wastes and their Disposal in 1992, the Canadian government committed itself to "reduce the generation of hazardous wastes and their hazardous recyclable materials and their transboundary movement to a minimum" (GC, 1998a). In its attempt to meet these obligations, the federal government in recent years has strengthened those sections of the CEPA which deal with hazardous wastes and has also engaged in further discussion of the problem with the provinces individually and through the Council of Ministers of the Environment.

THE PROVINCIAL GOVERNMENTS

The primary responsibility for hazardous waste management resides with provincial governments. In recent years these governments have started to treat the problem more seriously. For the most part, provincial governments have adopted two approaches for managing the collection and disposal of hazardous wastes — the "waybill" system and the monitoring of waste disposal and handling operations. In Ontario, for example, whenever liquid waste is carried away from a producer's property for disposal, a waybill must be filled out. The waybill indicates the amount and type of wastes being handled, who generated the wastes, and the destination where they are to be disposed. Two copies of each waybill are forwarded to the Ministry of the Environment, one by the producer of the waste and the other by the person disposing of the waste. Every two weeks, the Ministry checks to make sure that it has received both copies of the waybills. In this way, the Ministry of the Environment attempts to keep track of all hazardous wastes and to ensure that they are disposed of at approved sites. The use of the waybill system has been criticized because its definition of liquid industrial wastes is different from the province's waste management regulations. For example, "waste that is wholly used or recycled" is not included under waybill regulations. Furthermore, the waybill system does not have any provision covering liquid industrial wastes which are either stored or disposed of on the generator's property. Thus, a considerable amount of liquid waste goes unrecorded by the Ministry of the

Environment, which raises the fear that liquid industrial wastes may be disposed of in illegal or unsafe ways.

A second aspect of the provincial government's approach to hazardous waste management is monitoring disposal sites, although for the most part operators of waste disposal facilities have been given the primary responsibility for monitoring their own operations. The government licenses facilities to receive industrial wastes. The operators of these certified facilities conduct their own tests on particular waste disposal processes. The results of these tests are forwarded to the Ministry of the Environment. Because of the potential for abuse of this system, the Ministry also has its own monitoring program which may involve spot checks of the licensed operators and monitoring stations upwind and downwind of incinerators.

Continuing dissatisfaction with the waybill system and the monitoring of disposal facilities in Ontario resulted in the government establishing its own Ontario Waste Management Corporation (OWMC) in 1980. The OWMC was made responsible for establishing a new comprehensive waste management system for Ontario, but was disbanded by the Harris government in 1995. Also lost at this time was the Corporation's plan to build its own waste treatment and disposal facility. Today, the situation in Ontario gives no cause for complacency. Statistics show a dramatic increase in the number of waste-generating facilities, a similar increase in the transfer of hazardous wastes from site to site, and a near doubling of the amount of hazardous waste exported to Ontario by American companies taking advantage of the weak Canadian dollar and less stringent disposal regulations. According to the Canadian Institute for Environmental Law and Policy, in Ontario at present there are "major gaps in the framework of laws and regulations for controlling the handling and disposal of hazardous wastes ... A thorough overhaul and modernization of the province's laws and regulations regarding the generation, handling and disposal of hazardous wastes is needed" (1999). The Ministry of the Environment has announced plans to deal with some of these problems, but it is not clear yet whether the Harris government has changed its emphasis from granting relief to polluters to guaranteeing a healthy environment for the citizens of Ontario.

MUNICIPAL GOVERNMENTS

Although the powers and authority of municipal governments are granted by the provinces, municipalities have come to play a significant role in hazardous waste management. Due to their close proximity to particular hazardous waste problems, municipal governments are the most immediately affected level of government in attempting to address the issues posed by such wastes. Municipalities have played an important role in hazardous waste management in three ways. First, local governments generally have been provided with the authority to enact by-laws controlling nuisances, waste disposal, industrial use of sewers, and related matters. Second, the protection of public health and the abatement of nuisances traditionally have been delegated to local health boards under provincial law. Local health boards have taken a strong interest in hazardous waste problems and have initiated investigations under their authority to deal with health issues. Third, municipal governments are responsible for zoning by-laws. Such by-laws have been instrumental in determining the location of hazardous waste facilities. However, although municipalities play an important role in hazardous waste management, they have met a major stumbling-block which has hampered their success. The NIMBY (not in my backyard) syndrome has seriously affected the ability of municipal governments to find locations for new hazardous waste facilities. In fact, many municipalities have used their authority to prevent the building of hazardous waste sites in or near their communities. As the generation of more and more hazardous wastes continues, it is essential that more and better hazardous waste management facilities be built, and they have to go somewhere.

In sum, there is no doubt that hazardous wastes pose a serious threat to human health and the environment. While it seems that we must continue to use and create new products for industrial purposes, and hence to generate more hazardous wastes, it is imperative also that we develop better means of managing them. Hazardous waste management is of concern to all Canadians and therefore we must all participate in the process of developing more effective hazardous waste management systems. But this cannot be achieved until our attitude toward the problem produces sufficient will to take necessary measures. Several distinct steps could be taken to improve hazardous waste management. Industries could reduce the amount of waste generated by recycling, reusing, and substituting less dangerous chemicals in their production processes. Governments could develop more comprehensive regulations and, most importantly, they must be willing to force industries to comply. The waste management industry could adopt more stringent safety methods for collection and disposal of hazardous wastes. It could also invest in new types of technologies which improve the disposal of hazardous wastes. Individuals too can play a role by pressuring the various actors involved in hazardous waste management to perform their duties and responsibilities in the most effective manner. These measures will not eliminate hazardous wastes, but they might provide a means for managing them so that human health and the environment are less threatened than they are today.

CONCLUSION

There can be no doubt that we live in a risky world. Although we can reduce or even eliminate some risks, we also create new and sometimes more hazardous risks. As individuals, we are limited in our ability to protect ourselves and our families from many kinds of risk. Therefore, we look to governments to protect us from unnecessary and dangerous risks. As shown in the case studies, the governments' approach in Canada has been to determine what is a risk and to limit exposure to hazards to what is considered a safe level. In order to determine what is a safe or acceptable level of risk, public officials have come to rely on the formal processes of risk assessment. Thus, risk assessment has become a valuable tool for policymakers because it makes use of a variety of scientific, economic, and social methods to identify, estimate, and evaluate risk. However, risk assessments are not always able to provide precise solutions to all problems. Nevertheless, since health, safety, and environmental risks will always be a part of our society, we must continue to use and refine the risk assessment and management process in an attempt to protect individuals and to create a healthy and safe environment. The precautionary principle dictates that it is better to be safe than sorry!

NOTES

1   For further information, see Davies (1996), Callow (1998), and Jasnoff (1999).

2   For information on environmental assessment in other provinces and federal-provincial harmonization agreements on environmental assessment see, for example, http://www.gov.ab.ca/env/protenf/EPEA.eiaproce.html and http://www.ceaa.gc.ca/act/re199230_e.thm

3   For a complete analysis of the impact of the Harris government's changes, see Valiante (1999).

4   Emmett was replaced as Commissioner by Johanne Gelinas in August of 2000.

EIGHT
INTERNATIONAL COMMITMENTS

INTRODUCTION

In Chapter Five, we discussed the transnational context in which contemporary environmental policy is made. Indeed, environmental diplomacy has become a cottage industry in its own right, involving both highly visible summitry and the more mundane, day-to-day coordination that takes place between states and through international organizations. Most states have signed a number of international agreements dealing with conservation, biodiversity, atmospheric pollution, and a variety of other issues, and Canada is no exception. This chapter will examine Canada's regional agreements, both continental and Arctic, and then discuss global commitments resulting from summit diplomacy and regime-building.

There are a number of themes to keep in mind. When a government signs a formal international agreement, it is in effect sacrificing a small portion of its ability to make unilateral decisions. This is why it is probably an exaggeration to refer to the current era of globalization as the beginning of the end for the modern nation-state, which would become superfluous once enough agreements are signed and international organizations take over the task of running things. Some predict that, in the process, citizen loyalty will shift towards institutions such as the United Nations. However, this is unlikely. In fact, states rarely sign foreign policy commitments without ensuring there is a way out, usually termed "opt-out clauses." For example, Canada withdrew from the International Convention for the Regulation of Whaling in 1982, before that institution passed a global moratorium on commercial whaling. In some cases, such as the UN Law of the Sea, which Canada signed but never ratified, a commitment which is made abroad does not materialize at home.

The question of commitment is central here, because it is easier to parade through high-level conferences and make promises than it is to return home and keep them. Implementing international agreements requires policy cohesion among various government departments and, of course, provincial and municipal authorities, and there is often opposition from the various non-state actors described in Chapter Four. As the case of global warming demonstrates, it is often difficult for the federal government, which has jurisdiction over foreign affairs, to convince the provinces that helping keep Canadian commitments is in their best interest. Related to this point is the further question of whether Canada qualifies as a "leader" or a "laggard" in the field of international environmental policy. Although a surge in activity in the 1980s and early 1990s suggested Canada was ready to play a leading role, more recent developments encourage a less impressive conclusion.

We readily admit using an arbitrary approach in selecting the issues discussed in this chapter. As Figure 8.1 indicates, Canada has made many international commitments regarding the environment (Figure 8.2 represents only some of them). However, we have covered the more important issues, and have taken care to describe those which resurface again in both the next chapter and the last section of this book.

REGIONAL AGREEMENTS

Canada is signatory to a number of regional agreements on both bilateral and multilateral levels. In this section, we examine three: one dealing with the joint management of the Canada-US border (the longest undefended border in the world); another with an historic trade deal signed between Canada, the US, and Mexico; and a third involving several circumpolar states aimed at protecting the Arctic region.

The International Joint Commission

The International Joint Commission (IJC) was established under the 1909 Boundary Waters Treaty to prevent and resolve disputes between the US and Canada. It is one of the oldest bilateral institutions in existence today. The Commission is composed of six members: three are appointed by the US President (on the advice and approval of the Senate), and three by the Governor in Council of Canada, on the advice of the Prime Minister. The IJC is intended to act as an independent and objective adviser to the two governments. To fulfil this hefty mandate, the Commission considers for approval applications affecting boundary or transboundary waters, and may manage these projects as well. The Commission has created over 20 boards, made up of experts from both countries, to carry out these responsibilities.

The Great Lakes region has been the central focus of much of the IJC's work. The area had military-strategic significance during the War of 1812 and in other US-British conflicts. Today its importance is derived from the fact that it is the largest freshwater area in the world, and in several key locations (such as Detroit, Toronto, and Niagara Falls, New York), is heavily industrialized. In 1972, Canada and the US signed the Great Lakes Water Quality Agreement, agreeing to work together to control pollution in the Great Lakes and to clean up waste waters from industries and communities. In 1978, they updated the Agreement, adding a commitment to rid the region of "persistent toxic substances." Nine years later, the government amended the Agreement with a protocol to report on progress and to have the IJC review "Remedial Action Plans" in 43 areas of concern (IJC, 2000). These action plans contain strategies to clean up pollution and promote sustainable development, prepared by the governments and communities of the Great Lakes. The governments meet biennially to discuss progress and report periodically to the Commission. The Commission monitors and assesses progress under the Agreement and advises the countries. As well, the Commission aids the governments in setting up joint programs under the Agreement, including providing for two binational boards, the Great Lakes Water Quality Board and the Great Lakes Science Advisory Board (IJC, 2000; Spencer et al., 1981). Water levels in the Great Lakes are also under the jurisdiction of the IJC. Any project which might affect transboundary water levels is subject to approval by the Commission. The IJC runs the Great Lakes program through its regional offices in Windsor and Detroit.[1]

The Commission has approved the construction of hydroelectric power stations and dams in the St. Mary and St. Lawrence rivers and monitors their operation. As well, the IJC has authorized work along the Niagara River. The Commission studied and reported on the broader questions of variations in the Great Lakes-St. Lawrence River system in response to a request from the governments of Canada and the US. Boards for investigation, pollution surveillance, and control assist the Commission in their continuing responsibilities. Dams on the Kootenay, Osoyoos, and Columbia rivers, which run through BC, Washington, Idaho, and Montana, were approved and are monitored by the Commission. Rules for sharing the St. Mary and Milk rivers in Alberta, Saskatchewan, and Montana were established by the Commission. In the midwest, the Commission handles interactions between Saskatchewan, Manitoba, and North Dakota related to the Souris River. It also sets emergency water levels and helps to protect water quality in the Rainy Lake system through

Minnesota, Manitoba, and western Ontario. In the east, the Commission has participated in the regulation of dams on the St. Croix River, in New Brunswick and Maine, and the protection of its water quality (IJC, 2000).

Air pollution is an environmental issue related to water quality in North America. The IJC has a role in overseeing the implementation of the 1991 Canada-United States Air Quality Agreement, achieved after protracted intergovernmental negotiations to address the acid rain crisis. Under the Agreement, the Air Quality Committee was established to report biennially on progress, and the IJC prepares summaries of comments from individuals and groups on the Committee's reports. The 1991 Air Quality Agreement led Canada to commit to reduce sulphur dioxide emission by 40-per-cent from 1980 levels in the seven most eastern zones by 1994. A permanent national cap was set at 3.2 million tonnes (1 tonne = 1.1 ton) by 2000. The US committed to reducing its annual sulphur dioxide emission by 10 million tons by 2000, with a national cap of 8.95 million tons per year by 2010 (this is a 40 per cent reduction from 1980) (Canada-United States Air Quality Agreement, 1992:1-2, 15). This agreement builds on previous experience with the Long-Range Transboundary Air Pollution protocols signed with the European Union, which impose limits on sulphur dioxide, nitrogen dioxide, and volatile organic compounds. The responsibilities of the IJC, as outlined in Article IX of the Agreement, are to invite comments, through public hearings when appropriate, on each progress report prepared by the Air Quality Committee; to submit to the parties a synthesis of views presented at the hearings; and to release the synthesis of views to the public after it is seen by the parties (1992, 70). In addition, the parties can consider other joint references to the IJC.

In the strategic plan of the IJC, published in *Focus on IJC Activities* in 1997, the IJC outlines its desired actions in the twenty-first century. The plan targets selected transboundary impacts on water supply, floods, transboundary air pollution, threats to aquatic ecosystems, and threats to coastal zones as their most pressing areas of action. The Commission proposes the staged creation of a series of international watershed boards across the US-Canada border, including community members, local and state/provincial officials, and others with relevant knowledge. The duties of the boards are to include monitoring, studying, alerting, advising, and reporting on a range of transboundary issues. The Commission's plan includes four additional proposals. One is to undertake three priority studies: a review of water demand, supply, and quality; transboundary air quality issues; and environmental data and indicator availability and needs. Another is to clean house by reviewing more than 20 of their orders (some of which are 80 years old) to ensure that they reflect current issues. An interesting Commission proposal is to seek a reference from Canada and the US to review nuclear issues, including those associated with the impending decommission of reactors in the Great Lakes basin. The final proposal is the creation of a general report on the state of the entire transboundary environment every two years, to be made available to the governments and the public (Chamberlin and Legault, 1997).

One of the IJC's guiding principles is to include public participation as best it can when taking action. The Commission holds meetings every two years to discuss progress in cleaning up the Great Lakes. It also sponsors conferences, meetings, and roundtable discussions in which community members and organizations can have their say. The Commission's newsletter, *Focus on the IJC Activities*, is published triennially. The Commission refers to the record of the public forum in their Biennial Reports (the last was held in Milwaukee in 1999) (IJC website, 2000). The IJC has been surprisingly vocal on the question of dioxins and other pollutants, stressing the need for large-scale clean-ups and reductions in industrial uses. However, we must remember that, "even though its members pledge to perform their duties in an impartial manner, the members are political appointees. In order to carry out its mission the Commission depends heavily on the services of national officials from both countries. Hence, it is most unlikely that the IJC would take a hard-line position and risk angering either country" (Glode and Glode, 1993:34).

The North American Free Trade Agreement and the Commission on Environmental Co-operation

The objective of the Canadian government's Green Plan is "to secure for current and future generations a safe and healthy environment, and a sound and prosperous economy" (NAFTA, 1992:1). In 1990, reforms were introduced to strengthen the federal Environmental Assessment and Review process, including a non-legislated assessment process for federal policies or programs affecting the environment. The NAFTA was the first major policy initiative and the first trade agreement to undergo an environmental review as outlined in the Green Plan.

The Environmental Review of NAFTA was produced by the Government of Canada in 1992, the year the NAFTA was to go into effect. Provincial governments and representatives from industry, ENGOs, labour, and academics contributed to the debate over NAFTA, and its potential environmental effects, and, presumably, their opinions were considered in the Environmental Review. The Review examined four key areas: Environmental Provisions, Environmental Screening, Industry Migration, and Follow-up Mechanisms. The Review concluded cautiously that "the

FIGURE 8.1

ENVIRONMENTAL PROVISIONS INCLUDED IN NAFTA

CHAPTER	PROVISIONS
Preamble	» identifies sustainable development, environmental protection, and enforcement as fundamental objectives of NAFTA.
Chapter 1 (Objectives)	» examines the NAFTA's relationship to international environmental agreements on endangered species, ozone-depleting substances, and hazardous wastes. When inconsistencies occur, Canada's commitment to these international agreements takes primacy over NAFTA actions.
Chapter 7 (Sanitary and Phytosanitary Measures)	» allows the signatory states to take measures they consider appropriate to protect human, animal, and plant life or health in their own territories.
Chapter 9 (Standards-Realted Measures)	» protects the rights of the federal, provincial, or local governments of Canada to determine their own levels of environmental protection.
Chapter 11 (Investment)	» states that NAFTA countries should not lower health, safety, or environmental standards to attract investment.
Chapter 17 (Intellectual Property)	» permits the NAFTA countries to exclude from patentability plants, animals, or inventions that could harm the environment or its biodiversity.
Chapter 20 (Dispute Settlement)	» includes mechanisms for the submission of environmental concerns to dispute settlement panels to allow them to be considered in the decision-making process.

SOURCE: *NAFTA, 1992.*

environmental effects of the NAFTA will depend on the trade action and investment decisions taken as a result of the Agreement" (NAFTA, 1992).

In addition to the mention of environmental issues in the agreement itself, calls for greater environmental security and labour rights led to the adoption of two side agreements on labour and environmental issues. What concerns us most here is the establishment of the North American Agreement on Environmental Cooperation (NAAEC). The objectives of the NAAEC are many, simplified as follows:

» fostering the protection and improvement of the environment;
» promoting sustainable development;

» increasing cooperation between parties in the areas of conservation, protection, and enhancement of the environment, including wild flora and fauna;

» developing and improving environmental laws, regulations, and policies, and enhancing compliance with and enforcement of those laws, and promoting public participation in the development of those laws;

» promoting economically efficient and effective environmental measures, including pollution prevention policies and practices. (NAAEC, 1993:2)

Through the NAAEC, the Commission for Environmental Cooperation (CEC) was established. The CEC consists of a Council, a Secretariat, and a Joint Public Advisory Committee. Since the CEC is an environmental organization which grew out of expanded economic integration, its primary objectives are to advance understanding of the relationship between trade, the economy, and the environment, and to promote cooperation among the three signatory states to create an integrated approach to environmental protection. The Council of the CEC, composed of cabinet-level representatives from the three states, meets once a year, or at the request of any party. The Council serves as a forum for discussion of environmental matters that affect North America, and considers questions and differences that may arise between the parties. The Council reviews disputes between the NAAEC members, using a complex resolution process. It oversees the Secretariat and any ad hoc, standing, or working groups of the Commission. Through these groups, the Council considers and develops recommendations on a variety of environmental issues. All such decisions and recommendations of the Council are passed by consensus.

The Secretariat is headed by an Executive Director who is chosen by the Council for a three-year term, which may be renewed once. The position rotates between nationals from Canada, the US, and Mexico. The Executive Director appoints his/her staff, taking into account the lists of candidates offered by the parties. Ideally, the staff of the Secretariat is to work independently of all three governments. This is important as it is the responsibility of the Secretariat to consider submissions from any non-governmental organization or person asserting a failure of a NAAEC member to effectively enforce its environmental law. The Secretariat then decides whether the submission warrants a response from the accused country, or a factual record to further examine the submission. As well, the Secretariat of the CEC prepares the Annual Report of the Commission and Secretariat Reports on matters within the annual program.

The Joint Public Advisory Committee rounds out the CEC. The JPAC is composed of 15 citizens from Canada, the US, and Mexico. Each member country appoints five members on the basis of their relevant expertise. The

Committee provides advice to the Council on any matter within the scope of the NAAEC, and provides the Secretariat with relevant scientific, technical, or other information for the development of a factual record.

The CEC has developed a three-year action plan based on the recommendations of the Council. The action plan is divided into four areas: Environment, Economy and Trade; Conservation of Biodiversity; Pollutants and Health; and Law and Policy (CEC website, 2000). The Environment, Economy and Trade program is subdivided into two program initiatives: to understand the linkages between the areas, and to promote the use of "green goods and services." The relationship between the environment, trade, and the economy is examined through three projects: Critical and Emerging Environmental trends in North America, Assessing Environmental and Trade Relationships, and Financing and the Environment. Green goods and services are promoted through three separate projects: Facilitating Trade in Green Goods and Services (subtitled Promoting Sustainable Agricultural Production and Trade), Facilitating Conservation of Biodiversity as it Relates to Trade in Wildlife Species, and Sustainable Tourism in Natural Areas.

The CEC has identified the most promising ways, instruments, and mechanisms to protect and preserve biodiversity, particularly corridors for transboundary migratory species. The CEC goals include establishment of an ecosystem monitoring system to detect environmental trends and give early warning of environmental emergencies; creation of a network of experts to analyse threats to biodiversity; promotion of the sustainable use of the products and services afforded by biodiversity; and improvement of information, understanding, and awareness of biodiversity across the continent. To achieve these goals, the CEC has divided the program into three parts: diagnosis of the current state of the environment, development of strategies, and implementation of mechanisms, projects, and information management systems. Currently, the CEC Conservation program includes

» the North American Biodiversity Conservation Strategies: Strategic Directions for Conservation of Biodiversity and Ecosystem Monitoring Initiative (commencing in 2001);
» a Stewardship for Shared Terrestrial and Marine Ecosystems and Transboundary Species; and
» improving Information on North American Biodiversity through the North American Biodiversity Information Network.

The mission of the Pollutants and Health program is to prevent or correct the negative effects of pollution in North America by establishing regional cooperative initiatives. Four programs, and their respective projects,

196

address the issues of pollution and the protection of human and ecosystem health. The Cooperation on North American Air Quality Issues examines transboundary air quality issues with its projects for trinational coordination in air quality management, including the Trinational Air Quality Improvement Initiative: North American Trade and Transportation Corridors. It also develops technical and strategic tools for improved air quality. The Pollution Prevention program runs projects on regional pollution prevention, including the first North American Symposium on Children's Health and the Environment. The Sound Management of Chemical and the North American Pollutant Release and Transfer Register programs each manage one project.

The Law and Policy program addresses regional priorities regarding the obligations and commitments contained in the NAAEC. One of its programs, Environmental Standards and Performance, focuses on strengthening regional cooperation in the development and improvement of environmental laws and regulations. The programs provide a forum for discussion on environmental legal issues and domestic strategies for their implementation. Another program, Enforcement Cooperation, supports a regional forum of senior enforcement officials, and responds directly to the NAAEC members' obligation to effectively enforce their respective environmental laws.

The CEC also offers grants for conserving and enhancing the environment in Mexico, Canada, and the US. In 1995, the CEC created the North American Fund for Environmental Cooperation (NAFEC) to support community-based projects that address some aspect of the three-year program. The NAFEC has made 142 grants totalling $5.4-million (US) since 1996 (CEC, 2000). According to its Secretariat, the CEC plays four essential roles: convenor of agreements and discussions; catalyst "to spur on worthwhile existing initiatives, undertaken largely by others" (1999:2); research and policy analysis; and "information hub."

One of the more ambitious undertakings is the Sound Management of Chemicals project, "an ongoing intergovernmental initiative to reduce the risks of persistent toxic substances to human health and the environment" (1999:70), including the development of North American Regional Action Plans for various chemicals such as DDT, chlordane, mercury, and PCBs. These action plans are complex, involving many other international treaties and the private-sector chemical companies themselves (see CEC, 1998). The CEC undertakes regional studies in order to recommend policies, such as the Upper San Pedro River Initiative. The Upper San Pedro is a valuable transborder riparian habitat for migratory songbirds, and "the depletion of groundwater in the rapidly developing border region between the US and Mexico" threatens its very existence (CEC, 1999b:13).

The CEC may be seen as an embryonic institution which, like the IJC, can provide scientific support and encourage policy harmonization. Greater expectations, however, would be misplaced, for it is unlikely the CEC will be capable of forcing any of the three governments to adopt specific policies or avoid unsustainable development projects. It remains "without teeth." As written in a *Globe and Mail* editorial,

> It is not clear to anyone what follows from this exercise, or why environmental groups would go to all the effort of presenting a complaint to the CEC when, even if their claim were accepted and reported on — and only one has been — there would be zero consequence to any wrong doing. It looks as if, frustrated in their efforts in national venues, environmentalists are willing to accept even the hollowest of moral victories in multinational ones. (27 May 2000)

One unsettling aspect of the NAFTA is that governments now have to give consideration to potential fiscal costs before passing what might be urgently needed regulations. If a company feels it has been unfairly precluded from making a profit in another signatory country it can appeal to the dispute resolution mechanism under NAFTA and sue for compensation. The most publicized case occurred in April 1997, when the American company, Ethyl Corporation, launched a complaint against the Canadian government and, soon after, filed a $200-million lawsuit against the government of Canada for harm done to its subsidiary, Ethyl Canada, by the banning of the gasoline additive MMT. The Canadian government, following the lead of the Environmental Protection Agency in the United States, banned MMT in 1995, claiming it increased fuel emissions in automobiles. Ethyl not only disputed this claim, but argued that Canada's actions were tantamount to property expropriation and damaged the company's reputation. Eventually, the Canadian government settled with the US company by lifting the ban and paying Ethyl $13 million, revising its earlier claim that there was sufficient evidence that MMT is harmful to the environment. This case has raised great concern among environmentalists and Canadian nationalists.

The long-term impact of increases in trade, and the overall effectiveness of the CEC, are questions that cannot be answered here. We should note that there are other forms of trilateral environmental coordination among Canada, the United States, and Mexico. The North American Waterfowl Management Plan (NAWMP) is an example of trilateral cooperation on a regional level. The Plan was signed by the US and Canada in 1986, and Mexico joined in 1994. North America is home to 43 species of ducks, geese, and swans that depend on habitats in two or more countries for their survival. Six members from each state constitute the NAWMP Committee, appointed by the director of the national wildlife agency in each country. They work to coordinate policies to preserve wetlands and to review scientific and technical data on the status and dynamics of waterfowl populations (NAWMPC, 1998). However, against a backdrop of industrialization, they have met with limited success. But that such a body exists attests to the potential of trilateral relations for policy coordination in the name of conservation.

The Arctic Council

The Arctic has been ignored for many years, but public attention is being focused there now that global warming threatens to make the Northwest Passage accessible to international shipping on a year-round basis (Mitchell, 2000a). In 1969, the United States tested Canada's sovereignty over the Northwest Passage by sending the oil tanker Manhattan through the Passage, setting off an international incident resulting in Canada's unilateral decision to declare Arctic waters under Canadian jurisdiction. However, the Cold War and general ignorance of Arctic environmental problems conspired to relegate Arctic issues to the backburner until the end of the superpower military rivalry (though submarines still patrol the area), and concerns over the melting of the polar ice caps took precedence.

The Arctic Council is a forum for cooperation in the Arctic established by the eight Arctic states: Canada, Denmark, Finland, Iceland, Norway, Russia, Sweden, and the United States. In September 1996, the Arctic states established the Council by signing the Declaration on the Establishment of the Arctic Council in Ottawa. In September 1998, the Arctic Council concluded its organizational phase (chaired by Canada) and held its first ministerial-level meeting in Iqaluit. The Council is an historic achievement, the only intergovernmental forum involving the eight Arctic states. In 1991, the same states established the Arctic Council's predecessor, the Arctic Environmental Protection Strategy (AEPS). As proposed by the Finnish government, the goal of the AEPS was to address environmental issues specific to the region and to initiate multilateral responses to pollution in the Russian Arctic. The Arctic Council inherited this objective as one of its two primary goals. The second objective involves sustainable development in the Arctic, including the economic circumstances of local and indigenous residents as related to preserving the environment.

The participation of indigenous and local Arctic residents in the work of the Arctic Council is significant. Four organizations — the Inuit Circumpolar Conference, the Saami Council, the Association of the

FIGURE 8.2

CANADA'S MAJOR INTERNATIONAL ENVIRONMENTAL COMMITMENTS

YEAR	COMMITMENT
1909	» Treaty between the United States and Great Britain Relating to Boundary Waters
1916	» Convention between US and UK for the Protection of Migratory Birds in Canada and the United States
1946	» International Convention for the Regulation of Whaling (Canada withdrew in 1982)
1963	» Treaty Banning Nuclear Weapons Tests in the Atmosphere, in Outer Space, and under Water
1971	» Convention on Wetlands of International Importance
1972	» Canada-USA Great Lakes Water Quality Agreement » Stockholm Declaration on the Environment » London Convention on the Prevention of Marine Pollution by Dumping of Wastes and Other Matter » Convention Concerning the Protection of the World Cultural and Natural Heritage
1973	» Convention on International Trade in Endangered Species of Wild Fauna and Flora
1978	» Protocol on the International Convention for the Prevention of Pollution from Ships
1979	» Convention on Long-range Transboundary Air Pollution (LRTAP)
1982	» UN Convention on the Law of the Sea (signed but not ratified)
1985	» Vienna Convention on the Protection of the Ozone Layer reduction of sulphur emissions or their transboundary fluxes by at least 30 per cent » Canada-US Agreement Concerning Pacific Salmon

CONT'D

Indigenous Peoples of North, Siberia and the Far East of the Russian Federation, and the Aleut International Association — all representing indigenous peoples of the Arctic, are recognized by the Arctic Council as "Permanent Participants." They participate within the Council much like the Arctic states, but do not have voting privileges. The integration of NGOs into such a organization is interesting and impacts the structure of the Council. The Council was established as "forum," rather than an intergovernmental organization, allowing for such informal cooperation (on the downside, it has no legal personality) (Bloom, 1999).

FIGURE 8.2 (CONT'D)

CANADA'S MAJOR INTERNATIONAL ENVIRONMENTAL COMMITMENTS (CONT'D)

YEAR	COMMITMENT
1986	» Canada-US Agreement on the Transboundary Movement of Hazardous Waste
1987	» Montreal Protocol on Substances That Deplete the Ozone Layer
1989	» Basel Convention on the Control of Transboundary Movements of Hazardous Wastes and Their Disposal
1991	» Canada-US Air Quality Agreement » NOx Protocol to the 1979 LRTAP Convention » Declaration on the Protection of the Arctic Environment
1992	» UN Framework Convention on Climate Change » Convention on Biological Diversity » Agenda 21 » "Rio Declaration" » Statement of Guiding Principles on Forests
1993	» North American Agreement on Environmental Co-operation
1994	» International Tropical Timber Agreement » Protocol to LRTAP on Sulphur Emission Reductions
1995	» UN Agreement on Straddling Fish Stocks and Highly Migratory Fish Stocks (signed but not ratified)
1996	» Comprehensive Nuclear Test Ban Treaty
1997	» Kyoto Protocol on Climate Change (signed but not ratified) » Canada-Chile Agreement on Environmental Co-operation
2000	» Biosafety Protocol for Biodiversity Convention (signed but not ratified)

SOURCE: *Report of the Commissioner of the Environment and Sustainable Development (Ottawa, 1999),* 2-14.

The AEPS established four working groups. The Arctic Monitoring and Assessment Program (AMAP) monitors levels and assesses the effects of anthropogenic pollutants in the Arctic. The Conservation of Arctic Flora and Fauna (CAFF) encourages the exchange of information about, and coordinates research on, species and habitats of Arctic flora and fauna. The Emergency Prevention, Preparedness and Response (EPPR) working group provides a framework for cooperation to respond to the threat of environmental emergencies (such as oil spills or nuclear emergencies). Chief among its concerns is the establishment of an early notification system for

FIGURE 8.3

THE ARCTIC ENVIRONMENTAL PROTECTION STRATEGY (AEPS)

The Council is an outgrowth of the AEPS. Signed in 1991 in Finland, the AEPS is a political, but not legal commitment, to establish a framework for cooperation. Its primary objectives are:

» to protect the Arctic ecosystem, including humans;

» to provide for the protection, enhancement, and restoration of environmental quality and the sustainable utilization of natural resources, including their use by local and indigenous peoples in the Arctic;

» to recognize and, to the extent possible, seek to accommodate the traditions and cultural needs, values, and practices of the indigenous peoples as determined by themselves, related to the protection of the environment;

» to review regularly the state of the Arctic environment;

» to identify, reduce, and, as a final goal, eliminate pollution.

SOURCE: *The AEPS, 1991 (as quoted in Young, 1998:203).*

accidental pollution or a threat of such pollution. Finally, the Protection of the Arctic Marine Environment (PAME) group takes preventive and other measures regarding marine pollution in the Arctic. The PAME works directly with or through international organizations (see Young, 1998:210–16 for more details on each group). The actions of the four working groups make up the Arctic Council's contribution to environmental protection just as they do under the AEPS. The second objective of the Arctic Council, "to oversee and coordinate a sustainable development program," has been less successful. Since the term has many definitions, there was difficulty in creating a comprehensive sustainable development program, or even a list of priorities, on which all eight Arctic states could agree. Through negotiation, the Council members decided that the Sustainable Development Program would manage specific projects, led by the Senior Arctic Officials (SAOs) (Young, 1998). The SAOs, the representatives from the Arctic states, and the representatives from the Permanent Participants work together in the Sustainable Development Working Group, which coordinates the projects and proposes future initiatives.

Individual Arctic states provide voluntary funding for Arctic Council programs. In practice, states propose projects or choose working groups to support, and any interested government takes the lead in implementing and paying for them. There is no set contribution, and not all states give money to all projects. For example, Norway pays most of the $430,000 (US) operational cost of the AMAP secretariat. Iceland has contributed approximately 50 per cent of the $220,000 (US) annual budget for CAFF (the other half is voluntarily cost-shared among the Arctic countries), and hosts the PAME, contributing $75,000 (US). Finland contributed $30,000 (US) to the EPPR, with additional funding divided among the Arctic countries (Arctic Council, 1998). This inequitable system is not popular. However, the US claims it never agreed to fund programs other than on a non-assessed basis, making the possibility of changing the current practice unlikely (Bloom, 1999).

There are divisions among the members on a number of issues, including the utilization and export of marine mammal products, the proper approach to oil exploration, and the question of post-Soviet nuclear clean-ups. The United States has insisted on leaving military matters off the agenda, which frustrates some northern activists. Another major issue concerns the control of Persistent Organic Pollutants (POPs). The long-range transport of POPs from foreign sources is of particular concern to Canada, given the evidence of POP contamination in the Canadian Arctic and the Great Lakes. These pollutants are slow to degrade, accumulate in fatty tissue, and bioconcentrate as they move up the food chain. The first meeting toward the negotiation of a Global Convention on POPs was held in Montreal in June 1998. It is clear that the Arctic Council states need to look beyond circumpolar neighbours for lasting solutions, not just to other states, but also within their own jurisdictions.[2] Although Canada played a leading role in establishing the Council and supplied its Ambassador for Northern Affairs, Mary Simon, to be the first chairperson, there is a gap between the rhetoric and the actual commitments made by Ottawa to protect the environment in the north. Meanwhile, pressure to exploit the resources there remains common (see Stoett, 2000).

In all the cases described above, Canadian governments have accepted the importance of environmental considerations. The IJC was formed specifically to deal with what are, inherently, resource questions. The CEC was, perhaps, an afterthought, driven by perceptions in all three states that the NAFTA negotiations were excluding significant ecological issues, and that NAFTA threatened to encourage a "race to the bottom" in terms of environmental standards (whether or not this has occurred, despite the NAAEC, remains to be seen). The Arctic Council has environmental protection at the heart of its mandate, though it is certainly a diplomatic forum as well. But, in all three cases, these institutions have limited autonomous decision-making authority. For better or worse, the same can be said for the global multilateral institutions in which Canada participates (see below).

GLOBAL COMMITMENTS

As we have indicated throughout this textbook, Canada's relationship with the world is a complex one. Regional connections are obviously important, and have a tremendous impact on Canadian ecology, culture, and policy decisions. However, it is more and more common to refer to Canada within the context of a globalized economy and, as importantly, within the global biosphere. In the political realm, the work of many international organizations and special international conferences has led to the signing of several conventions of interest to Canada during the past 25 years. We offer only a sample of these here.

Climate Change

It has become obvious that climate change is a major threat to human security. While some Canadians may welcome warmer winters, the ecosystemic challenges posed by ozone depletion and global warming cannot be overestimated. Although international concerns with pollution were evident in the early 1970s, in particular at the UN Conference on the Human Environment in Stockholm, 1972, it was not until the early 1980s that the idea that the stratospheric ozone layer was being destroyed by certain chemicals became widely accepted. In 1985, spurred by accelerating ozone-layer loss[3] and increases in skin cancer, the Convention for the Protection of the Ozone Layer was signed in Vienna. Canada was the first country to ratify the Convention in 1986. In 1987, Canada hosted a UNEP-sponsored conference that led to the signing of the historic Montreal Protocol on Substances That Deplete the Ozone Layer.

Signatory states agreed to freeze and then reduce their production and consumption of chloroflurocarbons (CFCs) by 50 per cent of 1986 levels by 1998, and to freeze halon production and consumption at 1986 levels until 1993 (OECD, 1999:66). As of 1990, signatory states banned imports of CFCs and halons from non-signatory parties. In 1992, Protocol participants furthered their commitment with an agreement to phase out all CFCs and to establish recovery and recycling programs (Kyba and Dwivedi, 1998:38). The phase-out schedule for methyl bromide, added to the list of controlled substances in 1992, was discussed at the ninth meeting of the parties held in Montreal in 1997. Parties advanced the phase-out dates to 2005 for developed countries and to 2015 for developing countries (DFAIT, 2000b). An essential compromise attached to the ozone layer regime is that northern states have pledged to aid southern states in developing alternatives to CFCs and halons, widely used in refrigeration and industrial applications. This is significant, since it accepts the principle that the northern states are more able to cope with regulatory shifts in policy, and that they bear an added responsibility because they produced most of the pollution in the first place.

However, it has been difficult to realize effective and equitable responses to the even larger problem of global warming, one of the most tenacious international environmental issues. Approximately half the energy radiating from the sun to the earth penetrates the earth's atmosphere; the rest is reflected back into space by the ozone layer, clouds, and aerosols. Greenhouse gases, such as vapour, carbon dioxide, methane, and nitrous oxide, trap the heat and warm the earth's atmosphere. Many scientists believe the gradual atmospheric warming detected over the past 200 years is caused by anthropogenic emissions of greenhouse gases (McBean and Hengeveld, 1998; Halucha, 1998). The list of possible dangers associated with global warming is lengthy. It could allow "the spread of vector-borne diseases and the speedy return to the North of defeated diseases such as malaria" (Halucha, 1998:287). We have mentioned the challenges to Canadian sovereignty posed by an acceleration of the melting of Arctic ice. As certain vegetative species migrate northwards, the prairies face increasing frequency of drought, and boreal forests could be displaced by grasslands. Some predict that, globally, the flooding of coastal zones (a result of increases in sea levels), and increases in desertification in the southern hemisphere, will force more and more people to seek refuge in northern climates, such as Canada, challenging Canada's immigration policies.

It was at a conference in Toronto in 1988 that one of the first official calls for attention to this issue was made; later that year the UNEP and World Meteorological Organization established the Intergovernmental Panel on Climate Change (IPCC). In 1992, at UNCED, the Framework Convention on Climate Change (FCCC) was signed. It came into force in early 1994 with 166 signed parties. In 1997, parties to the FCCC met at Kyoto, where the Kyoto Protocol was signed; the overall approach was to try to reduce the collective emission of greenhouse gases to 5.2 per cent less than 1990 levels by 2010. In the end, different states were allowed to make different reduction commitments (without this concession it is unlikely any agreement could have been reached). Canada accepted a reductions target for greenhouse gases of 6 per cent from 1990 levels by 2008-12. In addition, Kyoto resulted in the acceptance of three instruments designed to facilitate reductions: joint implementation, the clean development mechanism, and international emission trading. The first two instruments allow countries to take into account the reductions realized by projects in which they invest, including reforestation (forests act as sinks which can absorb carbon

dioxide). Emission trading allows countries that exceed reduction requirements to sell their unneeded emission units to others.

The need to reduce greenhouse emissions presents a serious challenge
to the viability of industrial economies, and many have had difficulty
implementing the commitments made in Kyoto. The United States (which
had been intransigent at Rio in 1992) has yet to ratify the final agreement,
arguing the southern countries must make firmer commitments before
northern countries do so. In the Canadian case, the federalist political
system has presented a huge obstacle. A "national consensus" position
negotiated between the Canadian provinces and the federal government
was announced in November 1997 (to reduce greenhouse gases to 1990
levels by 2010), but the national delegation to Kyoto committed to a
stronger position (perhaps to demonstrate that Canada was willing to
exceed the American commitment). By 2001, it was clear that Canada had
not yet developed the means to implement this commitment.[4] Provinces
such as Alberta and Ontario simply refuse to go along with what they consider an unrealistic agenda. Canada's continued reliance on high per-capita
emissions, mostly for energy production, further limits any immediate
ability to cut back on emissions.

We are far from the stage at which a global authority can accurately
measure emissions from all the states that might, eventually, form part of
the Kyoto regime. There is no end in sight to the expansion of the world
economy, which remains highly dependent on fossil fuel energy production
and automobile use. The flexibility mechanisms introduced at Kyoto are
often criticized as a way for northern states to export pollution, thereby
avoiding more concrete actions at home. For example, if some states do
not meet their quota in terms of emissions, they can profit by selling their
remaining allotments to states which exceed their own. Similarly, investment opportunities that promote carbon sinks and other joint implementation projects may benefit the investors more than the local economy or the
environment. One Canadian policy expert concludes:

> The negotiations at Kyoto and beyond have not been about the
> integrity of the environment but about the maintenance of the liberal
> economic system. The negotiations have also been about maintaining
> a lifestyle to which we in Canada have grown accustomed and to
> which those in less developed states aspire. Canada's behaviour in the
> area of climate change is not about the articulation of a new vision. It
> is about the legitimization and perpetuation of the dominant dis-
> course. (Smith, 2000:89-100)

Resource Sharing Agreements: The North Atlantic Fisheries Organization and the Turbot Dispute

While it is obvious that Canada must share transboundary resources with the United States, some natural resources are the object of other states' interests as well. This is most noticeable in the case of fisheries and oceans. As a major consumer and exporter of fish, Canada has a vested interest in conserving the fish stocks close to its shores. However, managing fisheries has proven to be a complex problem of the commons (described in Chapter 5). This was evident in the west-coast dispute over Pacific salmon with the United States, but has been a point of even greater contention on the east coast, where several countries fish for various species.

In 1995, a dispute over "straddling stocks" of turbot off the coast of Newfoundland assumed international proportions. Straddling stocks refer to fish which live both in the open seas and within the 200-nautical mile "exclusive economic zone" (EEZ) off the coast (although the EEZ principle is recognized in international law under the 1984 Law of the Sea, Canada had unilaterally declared its own EEZ in the early 1970s). The 1995 case involved the Spanish fishing fleet and an uncharacteristically assertive Canadian Liberal government. The Spanish Basques fished off the coast of Newfoundland as early as 1530 and, by the 1580s, French Basque ships were returning from the area loaded with cod and whale oil. Spain still employs a large fishing fleet in the North Atlantic, where it takes a variety of species to sell in Europe and elsewhere. Because Spain is part of the European Union, the EU often represents Spain abroad in fisheries negotiations.

Turbot (or Greenland Halibut) have appeared in recent years beyond the 200-n. mile limit on the Flemish Cap and nose and tail of the Grand Banks. Spanish and Portuguese fishers have engaged in progressively intensive fishing efforts. The average Spanish turbot catch in the early 1990s was approximately 50,000 tons a year. Newfoundlanders, in contrast, took around 3000 tons in 1994. However, the cod moratorium forced Canadian fishers to look elsewhere, and a large demand for turbot arose that year. The quota determined by the Northwest Atlantic Fisheries Organization (NAFO)[5] was a mere 3400 tons for the European Union (namely, the Spanish and Portuguese), and 16,300 tons for Canada. The EU objected to NAFO quotas, and, consistent with the rules of NAFO, established its own quota, which was much higher than that suggested by NAFO. The Spanish made little effort to hide the fact that they were grossly overfishing off the Grand Banks; it was in fact legal activity. For the Canadian government this came as no surprise; foreign overfishing has long been a hot political issue.

On March 9, 1995, the Canadian Coast Guard fired over the bow of the Spanish trawler *Estai* and seized the vessel for overfishing turbot. Its crew members were held, temporarily, on Canadian soil. The Spanish government sent vessels to protect the remainder of its fleet, but on March 20, Canadian officials cut the nets of another Spanish trawler. Canada, concerned with the depletion of turbot stocks, had imposed a unilateral moratorium and seized the trawler, claiming not only that it was violating the quota rules but that it was using illegal fish nets in the process. Since the vessel was on the high seas, Canada was, in effect, breaking international law, even though the action was directed against a state with a reputation for questionable foreign fishing practices.

Canada's seizure of the Spanish trawler led to international tension, since Canada's international legal jurisdiction stops after the 200-nautical mile limit imposed by the EEZ provision of the law of the sea. Before 1977, Canada had a 12-mile limit; it was expanded that year, and non-Canadian trawlers, at one point the largest consumers of cod, withdrew. However, foreign vessels, often associated with European nations but flying the flags of Central American countries, continued to take cod and other fish immediately beyond the limit on the Grand Banks. Thus, the fishery dilemma quickly became a foreign policy problem. Spain argued that its right to freedom on the high seas had been violated. Canada argued it was necessary, given the greater concern for conserving fish stocks. The *Estai* was accused of using undersized nets (which take under-age fish), of keeping a false hold to conceal illegal catches, and of misreporting its activity (in a theatrical display Canada towed the seized nets up the Hudson River to UN Headquarters). Spain sent military vessels to escort its remaining ships, but no further violence ensued. Instead, an agreement was hammered out with the EU, which (perhaps surprisingly) had steadfastly supported Spain throughout the episode. The eventual agreement negotiated through the United Nations, in the retrospective way international law enables, roughly justified Canada's initial unilateralism.

In retrospect, this bold move by Canada can be explained by a number of factors. The federal government repeatedly had declared its willingness to block non-NAFO members from sending trawlers onto the Grand Banks off Newfoundland. The 1994 Amendment of the Canadian Coastal Fisheries Protection Act unilaterally extended Canadian jurisdiction to deal with pirate vessels fishing in adjacent international waters.[6] Brian Tobin, the Oceans and Fisheries minister at the time, was fully prepared to make a significant impact with the issue. He was subsequently elected premier of Newfoundland. Pressure had been mounting for some time for the federal government to do something about overfishing, especially in the wake of the moratorium on cod fishing, which had put tens of thousands of Newfoundlanders out of work.

Although Canada was criticized in some quarters for breaking international law, in the end things seem to have worked out for the better. After an agreement that went into effect on January 1, 1996, the total allowable catch was dropped to 20,000 tons (from 27,000); Canada was to take 15 per cent of it (3000 tons), and the European Union 55 per cent (11,000 tons). This represented an absolute loss of 45 per cent for Canada, hardly a victory in the quantitative sense. However, stricter observation procedures were implemented, reducing the chances of improper overfishing techniques being employed in the area, and the incident added pressure to the diplomatic agenda of the evolving law of the sea, which at the time was struggling to add the management of straddling stocks to the international oceans regime.

The straddling stocks dispute is only one example of the importance to Canada of ocean resources. Canada has the largest coastline in the world, and almost one-quarter of Canada's population lives in coastal areas. The total value of output from the oceans sector was $18.9-billion in 1996 (http://www.ncr.dfo.ca). However, Canada has been reluctant to ratify the major international treaty concerning the oceans, UNCLOS, and has yet to ratify the 1995 Agreement on Straddling Fish Stocks and Highly Migratory Fish Stocks, described above. Canada shares this reluctance with the United States, which has traditionally rejected UNCLOS for being too interventionist (it would force states to share in the gains from deep seabed mining, for example). Domestically, Canada passed the Oceans Act in 1997 and has developed a strategy for oceans management, establishing Marine Protected Areas and ecosystem health and environmental quality guidelines and standards. Canada signed the UN Global Program of Action for the Protection of the Marine Environment from Land-based Activities in 1995. This is a non-binding agreement to reduce and control contamination of the marine environment by coordinating all levels of government activity. However, despite repeated promises to do so, the federal government has yet to ratify the central piece of international oceans law, UNCLOS.

Forestry

Canada is steward to 10 per cent of the world's forests, and is the world's largest exporter of forest products. It is difficult to overestimate the impact of deforestation on many states, such as Haiti and the Philippines, where people rely on wood for fuel. Fears of large-scale deforestation in Asian states such as Malaysia and Indonesia and the burning of the Amazon rainforest in Brazil have turned forestry issues into global concerns.

However, the concern with the biodiverse rainforests of central America and Africa, which prompted a flurry of international activity in the late 1980s and early 1990s, has not led to a similar intergovernmental attention in northern states with temperate boreal forests.

This comes as no surprise, given the politically volatile nature of the debate over old-growth forest clear-cutting in Canada. Forests are viewed as important economic resources over which most states jealously protect their sovereign rights. There have been embryonic efforts to establish a global forestry accord to give some semblance of equality between the need for enhanced protection of southern rainforests and northern forests, but these have not yet produced a viable regime. At the UNCED in 1992, delegates arrived at what Linda Reif refers to as a "nonbinding, and substantively incoherent, Statement of Principles on Forests" (1995). In 1995 the Intergovernmental Panel of Forests was created by the UN Commission on Sustainable Development; it continued in 1997 as the Intergovernmental Forum on Forests (IFF). Canada and Malaysia were both involved in setting up this forum, which should be seen "not as an intergovernmental negotiating forum but as a confidence-building process" (Humphreys, 1996:137).

But the main global treaty covering forestry remains the International Tropical Timber Agreement (1994), ratified by Canada in 1996. This agreement does not include temperate zone forestry, but rather seeks to promote an effective framework for cooperation and consultation between countries that produce and countries that consume tropical timber. The agreement is seen by some as a prelude to a wider conservationist treaty, but also as an effort to justify current rates of exploitation. Meanwhile, the Canadian Forest Service of Natural Resources Canada is also involved in international affairs, mainly as a way to promote the progressively sustainable development of the Canadian industry. The Canadian Model Forest Program is heralded as "an international success story" (www.nrcan.gc.ca/cfs). Ten model forests now exist in Canada (there are two in Mexico and one in Russia). As in the case of climate change, however, federal initiatives on forestry issues have to meet with the approval of, and obtain voluntary implementation by, the provincial governments.

Closely related to deforestation is desertification, which can be seen as a resource-issue because it is essentially about the destruction of arable land. Although this is not a major issue in Canada, it is in the United States, China, many African states, and elsewhere. Canada ratified the UN Convention to Combat Desertification in Countries Experiencing Serious Drought and/or Desertification, Particularly in Africa, signed originally in 1994, in December 1995. Canada is an affected country (in the prairies), but is largely recognized as a "donor country" to the Convention. CIDA is the lead agency for Canada's contribution. While there is little doubt that soil erosion, due to drought and commercial exploitation, is affecting many African and Asian states (and the American midwest), there remains debate over whether desertification is a natural process (for example, the expansion of the Sahara desert), or whether it is feasible to focus efforts on human-induced change.

Wildlife Conservation: The Convention on International Trade in Endangered Species

Canada's wildlife is world renowned. But Canada has an obligation to do what it can for endangered species elsewhere as well. One of the first international agreements dealing with wildlife issues emerged from a meeting in 1965 between five "polar bear states": Canada, Greenland (Denmark), Norway, the former Soviet Union, and the United States. Because there is a real possibility these majestic animals may become extinct, the five agreed to preserve polar bears by reducing hunting pressure, and to exchange related information about the bears. A formal International Agreement on the Conservation of Polar Bears and Their Habitat was signed in Oslo, Norway, in November 1973. Canada also has signed conventions such as the International Plant Protection Convention, the International Convention for the Protection of New Varieties of Plants, the North American Agreement for Plant Protection, the International Tropical Timber Agreement (see above), the Agreement Between Canada and the United States on the Conservation of the Porcupine Caribou Herd, and the important Convention on Wetlands of International Importance, Especially as Waterfowl Habitat, commonly known as the Ramsar Convention. The International Union for the Conservation of Nature (IUCN, or World Conservation Union) remains an important forum for international cooperation; its Species Survival Commission produces the Red List, which catalogues the world's most endangered species and is widely considered an authoritative source. In addition, Canadian zoos are involved in extensive efforts, based on international cooperative management, to save highly endangered species ex situ (see Wiese and Hutchins, 1994).

One of the greatest threats to endangered wildlife is the highly lucrative trade in their parts. The Convention on International Trade in Endangered Species (CITES), largely an American initiative, was adopted in 1973 in Washington, D.C., and entered into force in 1975. There are currently more than 140 party states to this convention. Its main forum for decision-making is a Conference of the Parties (COP), which meets once every two to three years. These meetings are high-profile events, generating widespread media coverage and the attention of hundreds of non-governmental organizations (NGOS). However, media coverage is usually limited to debates over the more popular species. The real of work of CITES takes place on many other levels, including that of national governments, regional organizations, and global conservation networks. In addition to elephants and whales, for example, there are some 15 species of tropical timber listed in CITES, and hundreds of endangered flowers and birds. Many popular, and many more obscure species found in Canada are listed in the CITES appendices. The polar bear, river otter, and burrowing owl are examples of Canadian species on Appendix II, as are the lynx, bobcat, and cougar. The black bear is an example of a Canadian species listed for "look alike" reasons, a controversial category that requires export permits (the majority of which have been obtained by American hunters returning trophies to the US). Recent regulatory proposals would eliminate the need for these permits. The walrus is on Appendix III.

As a signatory to CITES, Canada has an obligation not only to curtail the export of endangered species, but to confiscate attempted imports as well. In principle, CITES administration is centred in the Canadian Wildlife Service (CWS) of Environment Canada, with head offices in Hull. Although the CWS plays an important role, particularly in attending the Conferences of the Parties (COPS) and deciding on Canadian voting patterns, other agencies are involved in implementation at home, including many federal departments which deal with CITES issues, such as Fisheries and Oceans Canada, Agriculture Canada, External Affairs and International Trade, the RCMP, and Revenue Canada, Customs and Excise, and the Canadian Food Inspection Agency. The Canadian Museum of Nature also provides an advisory role. Generally, Parks Canada monitors wildlife trafficking in national parks. Provincial natural resources ministries monitor wildlife in their provincial parks and issue hunting and export permits (with the exception of Alberta, which relies on the federal government). Both federal and provincial agencies conduct spot-checks or routine inspections of wildlife businesses, conduct investigations, and undertake intelligence gathering. However, there is little overall coordination of activity, and resources suffer from chronic underfunding. Canada's lack of domestic endangered species legislation, despite several false starts in this area, lessens its credibility abroad on related issues.

Saving endangered wildlife outside of Canada has been the main focus of CITES activity at the COPS. Several high-profile NGOS have used whales and panda bears as symbols of their efforts, and the oft-celebrated campaign to ban international trade in ivory has been a constant CITES issue. A ban was implemented in 1989, although it has been partially lifted to allow some southern African states to sell stockpiled ivory to Japan. This was a highly controversial development, reflecting on the one hand the high status accorded to elephants by the NGO community, and on the other the legitimate claims to developmental rewards for conservation practices (see Stoett, 1997). The most recent COP continued to reflect divisions on the theme of wildlife utilization, as whaling states were defeated in their efforts to delist several species of whales, and diverging states agreed basically to maintain the status quo on elephants. However, all these regulations are inconsequential without an effective compliance mechanism in place for the regime itself. Import and export restrictions are often violated and are subject to official corruption; not all signatories are in clear compliance, and it remains difficult to monitor them; and the regime remains hostage to threats of withdrawal made routinely by several African and Asian states that dislike current conditions.

The Convention on Biological Diversity

Beyond the CITES focus on individual species, there has emerged a broader concern with habitat preservation and conservation of biodiversity itself. Several international arrangements, such as the Global Environment Facility, have a specific mandate to reduce biodiversity loss (Fairman, 1996). The United Nations Environment Programme (UNEP) is involved in a number of areas, including a partnership with the IUCN. Another bilateral/multilateral instrument involving both governments and non-governmental organizations is "debt-for-forest" swaps (Jakobeit, 1996), though Canada has had limited involvement in these so far. Other mechanisms are taking shape, such as agreements between northern pharmaceutical companies and southern governments to conserve rainforest for the purpose of "bioprospecting" (Mulligan and Stoett, 2000), but are driven mainly by American, European, and Japanese concerns.

At the Rio Summit in 1992, Canada was one of the first states to sign the Convention on Biological Diversity (CBD). Various proponents worked toward the Convention. The destruction of tropical rainforests prompted the international community, especially NGOs, to seek a unifying legal framework to protect biodiversity. At the same time, the influential pharmaceutical industry acquired a renewed interest in the potential benefits that could be derived from the exploitation of biodiversity as biotechniques improved. The executive director of the UNEP, Mostafa Tolba, was active in pushing for a convention. The 1987 Brundtland report also called for a biodiversity convention. One hundred and fifty-six states signed the Convention at Rio which entered into force 18 months later, on December

29, 1993, after ratification by 30 countries. Canada was fifth to sign and rat-ified the Convention within six months. By the end of 1999, there were 176 parties to the Convention. Significantly, the United States did not sign the Convention in 1992, but the Clinton Administration signed on in 1993 (however, the American Senate has yet to ratify the agreement).

The CDB has three basic objectives:

1. the conservation of biological diversity, including all plant and animal species as well as their genes and the ecosystems to which they belong. In situ conservation is favoured, notably through the creation of national parks and protected areas;
2. the sustainable use of the components of biodiversity through programs aiming at both economic development and the protection of the bio-logical resources on which it is based;
3. the fair and equitable sharing of the benefits derived from the use of genetic resources. This goal invites developed countries to devise ways of compensating the biologically-rich developing countries for the com-mercial use of their genetic resources. These compensations can be financial, technological, commercial, or scientific.

Canada's principal pledge following the signing of the Convention was to expand its protected areas by 12 per cent. During the Convention negotia-tions, Canada, together with Sweden and Peru, introduced the concept of equitable sharing of benefits linked to the exploitation of genetic material, recognizing that biological resources have cultural significance for indige-nous persons. These concerns were later embodied in Article 8(j). Another substantial Canadian contribution to the Convention is the location of the secretariat in Montreal. In 1999, Canada changed its position in the nego-tiations toward a biosafety protocol and took the lead of the Miami Group that stood in opposition to much of the rest of the world by defending the interests of the seed industry. An agreement was reached in 2000.

It is still too early to judge the success of the CBD. Few expect it to stop the rapid loss of biodiversity related to population growth and environ-mental alteration. The matter is complicated by concern over genetically modified organisms (the Biosafety Protocol deals with this issue), intel-lectual property rights, and resource-sharing arrangements. In the Canadian case, as usual, it will be up to provinces to fully implement the Convention, and this creates further problems. However, the fact that such a convention exists is heartening. It serves as a public expression of concern and a statement that the interests of commerce must not super-sede those of nature.

Development Assistance

Canada also has contributed to environmental protection abroad through development assistance, both bilateral and multilateral. On the bilateral level, most activity takes place through CIDA, the Canadian International Development Agency. On the multilateral level, many institutions, such as the World Bank and various regional development banks, contribute to funding projects in the southern hemisphere. Although CIDA and the World Bank have adopted various sustainable development initiatives and policies, they are criticized for focusing on large-scale infrastructure projects that benefit donor states as much as anything else. We will return to this very controversial theme in both Chapter 10, in which we discuss women in development, and in Chapter 11, in which we explore the concept of "human security."

It would be unfair to overlook the extent of Canada's participation in sustainable development projects abroad, keeping in mind that some form of Canada's national interest, whether it be the participation of Canadian engineering firms or the purchase of Canadian equipment, is always present. One example is nuclear power. Since the unprecedented nuclear disaster at Chernobyl, there has been increased concern about the safety of Soviet nuclear technology and operations. A nuclear safety account has been set up at the European Bank for Reconstruction and Development, to which Canada has contributed. The Canadian Nuclear Safety Initiative was established in 1992 to enhance the short-term safety of Soviet-designed plants, in particular the RBMK reactors (which, though they use graphite instead of heavy water, are similar enough to the Canadian-produced CANDU reactors to enable Canadian technical expertise). It is clear that the cash-strapped nations of Eastern Europe, and particularly the Commonwealth of Independent States, are in no position to discontinue the use of atomic energy, since they depend on it for rudimentary necessities such as heat and lighting. Nuclear suppliers such as Canada are interested in the possibility of a market for CANDU reactors in Eastern Europe, once the current reactors are discontinued or replaced. Canada recently participated in a controversial sale of CANDU technology to China (Sens and Stoett, 1998:352).

In general, the debate over development assistance follows familiar lines. Critics argue that the federal government puts trade and commerce before other factors, such as sustainable development and human rights. This became apparent when cuts to foreign aid had an impact in the 1990s. Supporters argue that it is imperative that development assistance be in Canada's own economic interest in order to generate the approval of industry and the public, and that environmental concerns are slowly working their way onto the agenda.

CONCLUSION: A LEADER, A LAGGARD, OR BOTH?

Canadians are no strangers to the growing realm of international environmental diplomacy. Two of the first four executive directors of the UNEP were Canadian. Maurice Strong, its founder, organized and chaired the two defining global conferences on the environment in 1972 and in 1992. James McNeill was the secretary of the influential Brundtland Commission in 1987. In addition, Canadian scientists contributed significantly to the development of ozone science, and Canada played an important role in the adoption of the Montreal Protocol. The International Joint Commission remains a model of interstate cooperation on shared resource issues.

Given the tendency to marry commercial interests with environmental commitments, however, we might ask whether Canada's environmental diplomacy can really make a significant difference. On the one hand, we would be mistaken to assume ecological matters are a priority in Ottawa; they will continue to play second fiddle to the competitiveness agenda that trade-related issues encourage. On the other hand, Canada's participation in the regimes outlined above is vital, since it lends credibility to the process, and Canada has significant resources to contribute. Ultimately, we cannot answer the "leader or laggard?" question without a more thorough examination of the overall direction of domestic policy (see Paehlke, 2000). Although Canada's external representation has been strong, Canada does not always live up to its reputation (see Chapter 9).

NOTES

1   In early January 2001, Canada and the United States announced a funding commitment for a five-year IJC study of water levels and flows in Lake Ontario and the international section of the St. Lawrence River.

2   Governments have recently (December 2000) arrived at an international agreement to control for POP production and distribution. The negotiations took place at the UNEP headquarters in Nairobi, and were chaired by Canadian John Buccini. Most of the 12 chemicals under discussion were subject to an immediate ban, but a partial "health exemption" was granted for DDT use, since it is still one of the most effective means of combatting malaria. *UNEP News Release 00/138.*

3   The main concerns related to ozone-layer loss are the impact of increased ultraviolet radiation on human and other immune systems, on the world's food supplies, and on aquatic ecosystems (see Litfin, 1994:105).

4   The federal government has established Issue Tables/Working Groups to provide expert advice in several key areas of implementation, as well as the National Climate Change Secretariat (including both federal and provincial representatives), which reports to the deputy ministers of Natural Resources Canada and Environment Canada.

5   NAFAO was established by the *Convention on Future Multilateral Cooperation in the Northwest Atlantic Fisheries*, signed in Ottawa, 24 October 1978. Its headquarters are in Dartmouth, Nova Scotia. Current members of NAFO include Bulgaria, Canada, Cuba, Denmark (for the Faeroe Islands and Greenland), the EU, Estonia, France, Iceland, Norway, Japan, Korea, Latvia, Lithuania, Poland, Romania, Spain, Russia, the United Kingdom, and the United States.

6   This was meant especially to deal with flag-of-convenience countries, which were even listed, as follows: Belize, Cayman Islands, Honduras, Panama, Saint-Vincent and the Grenadines, and Sierra Leone.

NINE
CANADA'S SUSTAINABLE DEVELOPMENT STRATEGIES

> Sustainable development presents a new paradigm for decision making in all sectors of society and at all levels from the global to the local. It challenges existing decision making practices insofar as it demands both the integration of economic, environmental, and social considerations; and attention to the long run consequences for future generations of present-day decisions and policies. (Bell, 2000:1)

INTRODUCTION

Sustainable development is an important concept in environmental policy-making. Policy-makers in Canada were quick to adopt the language and rhetoric of sustainable development. However, the relevance of sustainable development as a "new paradigm for decision-making" and its potential to challenge "existing decision-making practices" are thwarted by a diminishing supply of the resources required to translate policies into action. This chapter examines the challenges to the implementation of sustainable development policies as well as the opportunities that these policies offer to Canadians and to Canada's international activities. On August 31, 2000, the *Globe and Mail* featured an article on the front page titled "We as a Species Can Do Better," which provided a summary of the consequences of human actions on the environment and the likely impacts of global warming. The report predicted a loss of 46 per cent of the life-sustaining habitats in Canada within the next 100 years as a result of human-caused global warming and climate change. This report echoes concerns for the state of Canada's environment raised in Chapter 2 of this book. The report also addresses the causes of environmental decay in Canada, pointing to the high rate of energy consumption and waste production. Based on Canada's international commitments to the environment and sustainable development, Canada appears to be committed to addressing environment and development concerns.

Canada's commitments to sustainable development have been articulated at the national, provincial, and local levels. However, cuts to spending on the environment impede progress on sustainable development activities. Figures available in Environment Canada's *Estimates* demonstrate how funding for environment in Canada has continued in a downward trend since the early 1990s. Thus, sustainable development policies are receiving increasing attention in Canada, while environmental spending continues to decline. The lack of financial support and resources for environmental programs challenges Canada's ability to move from intentions to performance.

This chapter begins by reviewing Canadian policy commitments and sustainable development strategies (SDSS), taking a critical, analytical perspective on the Canadian SDSS and green planning, drawing on the important criticisms raised by a number of round tables and interest groups as well as by the Commissioner on Environment and Sustainable Development (CESD). In keeping with Canada's commitment to the United Nations Conference on Environment and Development, Canada has developed National Sustainable Development Strategies that are updated and presented annually to the United Nations Commission on Sustainable Development. However, "translating words into concrete policy and action will test the mettle of most countries, and Canada is no exception" (Sadler, 1996:23). Despite the many challenges that face Canadian policy-makers and community members, the governments in Canada have made important progress in the preparation of policy commitments. Nevertheless, the governments of Canada have a long way to go to make these policy commitments a reality.

DEFINITIONS AND ORIGINS OF SUSTAINABLE DEVELOPMENT

The term "sustainable development" was popularized by the work of the World Commission on Environment and Development (WCED) in the mid-1980s, but its origins date back to the eighteenth and nineteenth centuries when foresters in Europe used the word "sustainable" to voice their concern for clear-cutting methods of logging. Since the forests were not regenerating adequately, the foresters wanted to ensure that trees were planted to replace the ones logged. Canada's earliest documented commitment to sustainability planning was the designation of Canada's first national park, Banff, in 1885. Over time, a number of actors have struggled to increase attention to the preservation of nature as a moral and ethical imperative.

Conservationists also have fought for conservation of nature to ensure the continued supply of natural resources for ongoing human consumption. A series of additional activities have paved the way for our current understanding of sustainable development, including the setting up of the Canadian Commission of Conservation 1909. During the early to mid-1900s, environmental concerns were submerged as a result of the Great Depression, World War II, and the post-war boom. Environmental interests re-emerged in the 1960s when activists and protesters began to express concern about the generation and use of nuclear power and increased awareness of air and water pollution. These protests and awareness-raising efforts placed environmental matters centre stage and called on governments to be accountable for environmental problems in Canada. In 1970, Canada established the International Development Research Centre, and in 1972, Canada participated in the Stockholm Conference on Human Environment, headed by Canadian Maurice Strong.

Environmental concerns gained international attention during the Brundtland Commission. The Commission brought more than a conservation or environmental preservation perspective to the table. In addition, the Commission was concerned with merging environmental sustainability with social and economic development, recognizing the nature of inequality and its relationship to resource availability. Norwegian Prime Minister Gro Harlem Brundtland chaired the Brundtland Commission. The Secretary General of the Commission was Canadian Jim MacNeill. The Commission played an important role in shaping the ways in which Canada would develop and address environmental and economic policies. The most immediate result was a decision by the Canadian Council of Resource and Environment Ministers (CCREM) to form a National Task Force on Environment and Economy (Bell, 2000). The Task Force members were drawn from the private sector, business, government, academic, and leading environmental organizations. Their mandate was to foster and promote environmentally sound economic development (Manitoba Government, 1990).

From the Brundtland Commission emerged a document entitled *Our Common Future* in 1987 in which sustainable development was defined as meeting the needs of the people today without jeopardizing the needs of future generations (WCED, 1987). The term sustainable development implies a long-term view of development and environmental integrity. The World Commission on Environment and Development stressed the necessity for active participation of a variety of actors (i.e., governments, NGOs, and community members) to ensure sustainable development, and paid specific attention to the need for economically viable solutions and for the management of natural resources in environmentally sound ways.

Sustainable development, an increasingly popular concept, offers a framework for the integration of environmental policies and development strategies. The increasing importance attached to environmental sustainability and social and economic development, as noted by the Brundtland Commission, solidified the term sustainable development as a guiding principle.

In 1992, during the United Nations Conference on Environment and Development (UNCED), sustainable development was brought into another forum of international planning and policy process. The UNCED, or Earth Summit as it was commonly called, offered a venue for heads of states, representatives from UN agencies, and non-governmental organizations (NGOs) to discuss and debate the challenges of sustainable development. Following the Earth Summit, the United Nations Commission for Sustainable Development (CSD) was created in December 1992. The purpose of the Commission was to ensure effective follow-up of UNCED and to monitor and report on implementation of the Earth Summit agreements. The CSD has 53 members and operates as a functional commission of the United Nations Economic and Social Council. Each year, the CSD holds a meeting to address progress in meeting the agreements of *Agenda 21*, one of the documents that emerged out of the 1992 United Nations Conference on Environment and Development. More than 50 ministers and over 1000 NGOs participated in the Commission's work. As central to its mandate, the Commission ensures that sustainable development issues are visible and addressed within the UN system (CSD, 1999).

Multisectoral agencies or round tables are recent, but important, additions to the sustainable development policy-making process in Canada. For example the International Institute for Sustainable Development (IISD) was established in 1990 and the National Round Table on the Environment and the Economy (NRTEE) was legislated as an act of Parliament in 1994. In addition, Canada's governmental, non-governmental, and private-sector contributions and participation in various international conferences are examples of Canada's commitment to sustainable development policy-making. There are now numerous agencies, organizations, governments, and communities which design policies aimed at addressing sustainable development. However, sustainable development is not without its critics. Disagreements over the meaning of the term continue, and the term is criticized for having a veneer of environmental respectability while promoting continued unsustainable economic growth. Nevertheless, the concept has become a central feature of Canadian environmental policy planning: "In Canada, the concept of sustainable development has been integrated into federal legislation and into the amendments to the Auditor General Act, which established the

Commissioner of the Environment and Sustainable Development" (Environment Canada, 2000c).

THE POLICY PROCESS

Similarly, there is a division in the policy community over the nature and types of environmental problems that governments should be addressing (Hessing and Howlett, 1997). The policy community is composed of those who have some knowledge or expertise in the area concerned, including state policy-makers (administrative, political, and judicial), members of non-governmental organizations (NGOs) concerned with the subject, members of the media who report on the subject, academics who follow or research the area, businesses, labour unions, formal interest groups or professional organizations, and members of the general public who take an interest in the subject (Hessing and Howlett, 1997). The list of policy community members is often long and may appear inclusive. However, certain groups remain excluded from the policy process or are under-represented in the policy process: "Women and First Nations, for example, have vested interests in environmental policy but continue to be underrepresented in existing processes" (Hessing and Howlett, 1997:251). (We explore the limited representation of women and indigenous groups in environmental policy-making in Chapter 10.) Public policy is central to the decision-making process, affecting people and organizations at all levels.

Throughout Canada's history, resource and environmental policy have become interventionist and extensive in nature: "Governments have shifted from espousing the unfettered exploitation of resources to a more active, if evolving, conception of environmental stewardship. These changes occurred slowly as the resource sector developed and, in the modern period, as existing Canadian resource and environmental policies were challenged by environmental activists and other emerging stakeholders" (Hessing and Howlett, 1997:9). Canada's environmental policy process has been shaped by the country's unique history and has changed as the country has shifted from a staples economy, dependent on resource extraction, to a more diversified economy. The result of this shift to a diverse economy has been that old interests have been replaced by new ones. New actors and interest groups have entered the policy-making process and have altered the policy process (Hessing and Howlett, 1997). As sustainable development has gained popularity within Canada and internationally, it has also become a major feature of the policy-making process, reflected in Canada's governmental activities and various strategies adopted at the international, federal, provincial, and community levels.

A HISTORY OF SUSTAINABLE DEVELOPMENT STRATEGIES (SDS) IN CANADA

The introduction of the federal Green Plan in Canada in the early 1990s marked the beginning of sustainable development policy-making. On December 11, 1990, "the Progressive Conservative government committed $3 billion in new funding to the Green Plan, an initiative that was billed as a comprehensive national strategy and action plan for sustainable development ... the federal government itself declared the Green Plan to be an expression of the popular will" (Morrison, 1997:55). The Green Plan "highlighted sustainable development and global environmental security as two of Canada's major priorities" (Kyba and Dwivedi, 1998). The Green Plan's origins can be traced to events leading up to and following the Brundtland Commission and its influential report, *Our Common Future* (WCED, 1987). As Morrison says, "It was also motivated by a series of political missteps that had damaged the environmental reputation of the ruling Progressive Conservative Party. Within the government, the development of the Green Plan was led by Environment Canada through an internal brainstorming approach and reflected the ideological orientation of what had been a relatively small, science-oriented department" (Morrison, 1997:56). The goals of the Green Plan included ensuring clean air, water, and land; promoting the sustainable use of renewable resources; protecting natural spaces and wildlife species; preserving Arctic ecosystems; acting on international agreements on air pollution; promoting environmentally responsible decision-making; promoting stewardship in federal government operations; and minimizing the impact of environmental emergencies. An additional goal of the Green Plan was to achieve a balance or "win-win" solution to environment and economic development trade-offs. More specifically, the Green Plan aimed at maintaining economic growth while ensuring sound environmental management.

The change in government meant the end of the Green Plan by 1995. The Green Plan's demise was attributed to a failure to consult with environmental NGOs and to the plan's inability to devise a "comprehensive government-wide approach to environment-economy integration, let alone a national policy for sustainable development" (Sadler, 1996:49). The Green Plan relied too heavily on Environment Canada to carry out its mandate, without integrating green planning into other federal departments. However, various other activities were initiated to keep environmental issues central to government policy planning. For example, the Canadian Environmental Assessment Act was revised, commitments to the implementation of *Agenda 21* were made, a program to promote environmental awareness received $10-million per year, and a Commission of the

Environment and Sustainable Development was established to operate out of the Auditor General's office (Morrison, 1997). These events led to the creation of a new focus on sustainable development strategies (SDS). This new focus integrated environmental considerations with national, social, and economic development policy-making. The focus provided a forum or context for dialogues and gave the country a vision based on shared values. Additional goals were identifying issues and priorities, providing policy and research, and building the capacity to implement strategies. The ultimate goal of SDS was to work toward long-term societal transformation.

Each federal department was mandated with the task of producing a sustainable development strategy to be tabled in Parliament by 1997. This brought sustainable development strategies into the practical arenas of policy-making and exposed a number of departments to this important federal approach: "The concept was well known in a few departments that had a connection to environmental issues, but it was totally unfamiliar to most departments" (Bell, 2000:2). Some departments continue to experience difficulties producing their SDSs. The Commissioner on Environment and Sustainable Development has since assessed the 28 strategies, tabled in the House of Commons in 1997 (see below). Since 1997, federal departments have updated their SDSs for introduction to Parliament by December 2000. In order to prepare and revise these strategies, departments sought input from both within and outside government.

NATIONAL SUSTAINABLE DEVELOPMENT STRATEGIES (NSDSs)

The sustainable development strategies introduced in Parliament are part of a broader international and national strategy to address sustainable development called the National Sustainable Development Strategy (NSDS). National sustainable development strategies are frameworks and processes for giving the "highest level of policy force and expression to sustainable development" (Sadler, 1996:47). As such, NSDSs act as guides for sustainable planning, integrating environmental considerations into national social and economic development policy-making. To date, more than 100 countries have developed NSDSs to provide a forum and context for dialogue on sustainability, and to foster visions and values for sustainability. The national strategies facilitate a process whereby major issues and priorities can be identified and addressed. In Canada, the NSDS has been the work primarily of the national government and Environment Canada. However, the strategy has benefited greatly from the inputs of national, provincial, and local round tables (Sadler, 1996:47). In keeping with the commitments made at UNCED, Canada has embarked on a number of initiatives in support of its NSDS. Two of these are the creation of a Commissioner on Environment and Sustainable Development and the facilitation of departmental sustainable development strategies (SDSS). The SDSS enhance the federal government's ability to report to the United Nations Commission on Sustainable Development in its National Sustainable Development Strategy by highlighting what each department is doing to address sustainable development and green planning.

The position of the Commissioner on Environment and Sustainable Development was introduced in December 1995 as part of the Auditor General Act amendments. The first commissioner, Brian Emmett, was appointed in June 1996. In August 2000 the Auditor General of Canada announced the appointment of Johanne Gélinas as the second Commissioner of the Environment and Sustainable Development. She began her duties in September 2000 (Office of the Auditor General, 2000). The responsibilities of the Commissioner include monitoring sustainable development strategies, performing audits and special studies, receiving public petitions, and providing green reports to the House of Commons. The purpose of the SDS is to turn words into concrete actions. The departmental SDS is a systematic process that consists of a number of activities. It begins by identifying what the department does and how it does it. In conducting their SDS, departments seek views from various stakeholders on the priority areas to be addressed. The SDS consists of goals, objectives, and benchmarks for measuring progress and translates these goals into concrete actions through the development of action plans. The final component of the SDS is a detailed explanation of how the department will measure and report on its performance (Office of the Auditor General, 2000). The following is a summary of Environment Canada's SDS.

ENVIRONMENT CANADA'S SDS

Environment Canada (EC) tabled its first SDS in April 1997. This policy document contained four broad strategic directions: to strengthen EC's ability to meet SD goals; to be a more effective advocate of sustainable development; to give Canadians the tools they need to make sound decisions in a changing environment; and to set a good example in the greening of government operations. These commitments "have been incorporated into the department's ongoing planning process" (Environment Canada, 2000c). Environment Canada's primary responsibilities include "the protection and conservation of Canada's environment and the delivery of weather and environmental predictions." Science, community engagement, and Environment Canada's work on issues such as climate change, endangered species, contaminated sites, toxics, and ecosystems are driven primarily by these weather and environmental predictions, and by its environmental protection and conservation mandate (Environment Canada, 2000c). Environment Canada's mission statement is "to make sustainable development a reality in Canada by helping Canadians live and prosper in an environment that needs to be respected, protected and conserved" (Environment Canada, 2000c). The document goes on to note that Environment Canada believes "that if Canada's environmental heritage is to be sustained for the benefit of present and future generations, support for sustainable development must be built across government and throughout Canada" (Environment Canada, 2000c). Environment Canada bears the greatest responsibility for sustainable development since it is mandated to ensure that other departments have the knowledge and information necessary to develop their own sustainable development strategies.

Other departments such as the Department of Foreign Affairs and International Trade (DFAIT) also tabled their SDS in Parliament in 1997. In DFAIT's SDS, four sustainable development goals were highlighted, corresponding to its strategic objectives. These objectives include promoting economic growth and prosperity, building peace and security, fostering Canadian values and culture, and implementing green operations. DFAIT recognizes that Canada is "a nation dependent upon exports, deriving in 1996 close to 40 per cent of our Gross Domestic Product (GDP) from the sale of goods and services outside Canada. We are also a nation dependent on the sustainable use of natural resources as it equates to the long-term viability of Canadian communities and the livelihoods supported by forestry, fishing, mining and agriculture" (DFAIT, 2000a).

AN ASSESSMENT OF THE SDSs

In reviewing departmental sustainable strategies, a number of weaknesses and challenges were noted. The first weakness was that almost all the departments did not establish clear and measurable targets to ensure that goals and action plans would be reached. A second major weakness was the focus on past achievements rather than future plans (Office of the Auditor General, 1999). Furthermore, the departments failed to systematically identify priorities, define management expectations, assign accountability results, identify training needs in more junior positions, and perform self-assessments to facilitate departmental and program improvements (Office of the Auditor General, 1999). The challenges faced by departments include the remaining gaps between intentions and actions, poor interdepartmental cooperation in research, incomplete monitoring networks, unfulfilled commitments, lack of evaluation of pesticides against new health and environmental standards, and a gap between demands of departments and availability of resources (Office of the Auditor General, 1999). In addition, departments were divided on key issues and disagreed on the risk of toxic substances; federal/provincial relations are weak; the federal government does not have enough information to enter into agreements with other governments; the federal government does not analyse documents to determine their potential for failure and the capacity of provinces to carry out the activity; and there is no ongoing analysis of the impact of agreements. While Canada has made substantial contributions to the Arctic program and to the actions needed to protect the Arctic, environmental performance could be improved by strengthening basic management practices. Overall, the federal government is only beginning to translate strategies into actions, and there is a clear need for government staff to have proper training to facilitate the translation of policies into action (Office of the Auditor General, 1999). Brian Emmett, the Commissioner on Environment and Sustainable Development at the time, articulated these challenges.

A number of working groups were formed to reflect on the environment and sustainable development issues facing Canada and Canadians. These working groups make recommendations to the federal government. The following section highlights the work of the National Round Table on the Environment and Economy, the Provincial and Local Round Tables, and the Projet de Société and their important contributions to the sustainable development policy process.

ROUND TABLES ON THE ENVIRONMENT AND THE ECONOMY (NRTEE)

Canada's National Round Table on Environment and Economy (NRTEE) "was one of the first bodies set up at a national level to research and respond to sustainable development issues" (NRTEE, 2000). At the provincial level, round tables were also set up to address sustainable development, environment, and economic concerns. The NRTEE developed a number of activities to address sustainable development including the Sustainable Development Indicators (SDI) initiative. The SDI is designed to generate a national set of sustainable development indicators to be used universally in Canada. One of the motivations for this initiative was the potential to integrate environmental and social considerations into economic decision-making by governments, business, and civil society. The SDI will be used also to determine the nature and extent to which sustainability is being achieved in Canada. The NRTEE examines how decisions are made to protect human health from harmful substances found in the environment. The NRTEE relies on federal funding for 95 per cent of its funding. The other 5 per cent of funding is met by the private sector. The future of the NRTEE is dependent on the federal commitment to keep this initiative alive.

Round tables on the environment and the economy formerly existed at the provincial level. However, funding cutbacks and lack of government support have resulted in the cessation of funding to most of the provincial round tables. The British Columbia Round Table on the Environment and the Economy (BCRTEE) began its work in the early 1990s. In 1992, the round table "released an assessment of the state of sustainability in British Columbia, concluding 'that, in many cases, present patterns of human activity and trends in expectations are not sustainable'" (BCRTEE, 1992:15 as quoted by Sadler, 1996:55). Despite the progress made by the BCRTEE and its important work, the round table was closed in 1993. The work of this round table has been incorporated into a separate initiative called the Commission on Resources and the Environment (CORE). CORE developed a strategy for land use planning and resource and environmental management. A land use charter that defines principles of sustainability and consensus decision-making was also created by CORE (Sadler, 1996).

The Manitoba Round Table — one of the last fully active and operational provincial round tables — reports to the Premier's office. The work of the round table is supported by the Sustainable Development Co-ordination Unit, which coordinates and assists the committees of the round table, and ensures that the suggestions of the round table are brought to the attention of relevant government departments. *Manitoba's Sustainable Development Strategy*, designed by the Manitoba Round Table on Environment and Economy, was written in a spirit of cooperation and partnership between the Manitoba Round Table on Environment and Economy and the Manitoba government. These two bodies have initiated a dialogue on the environment and economy, which is grounded in the belief that "Sustainable Development is a grass-roots concept. It depends on the active involvement and participation of all citizens to find solutions to problems, identify opportunities and mould the type of society that meets our needs and those of future generations" (Manitoba Government, 1990). The vision of environmentally sound and sustainable economic growth for Manitoba was governed by 10 principles, including integration of environmental and economic decisions, stewardship, shared responsibility, prevention, conservation, recycling, enhancement, rehabilitation and reclamation, scientific and technological innovation, and global responsibility. In order to achieve these principles, the round table devised six fundamental guidelines indicating how the vision for Manitoba will be achieved, pointing to efficient use of resources, public participation, understanding and respect, access to adequate information, integrated decision-making and planning, and substitution.

New Brunswick's SDS included two documents entitled *Towards Sustainable Development in New Brunswick: A Plan for Action* and *Sustainable Development in New Brunswick: Because we want to stay.* These documents are the product of a two-and-a-half year process involving the New Brunswick public, members of 13 sectoral groups and the Premier's Round Table on the Environment and Economy. The sectoral groups, made up of stakeholders who volunteered their time, represent all aspects of environment and economy: energy, forestry, mining, agriculture, fisheries and aquaculture, natural areas, wildlife, rural and urban development, transportation, water/air/land, commerce/service/manufacturing, recreation and tourism, and education/information. There were five specific principles which guided the round table's approach. These principles included promoting development that ensures maintenance of essential ecological processes, biological diversity, and renewable resources at sustainable levels. In order to do this, the government of New Brunswick highlighted the need to limit pollution and the use of renewable resources. The second principle was to ensure that the decision-making process integrated economic and environmental factors. The round table noted that it is important to recognize the inextricable link between economic sustainability and the state of the environment. Short-term economic goals should not take precedence over long-term economic and environmental concerns. Third, the province called for economic and environmental sustainability to be demonstrated for all major development projects and to be geared to the prevention of environmental damage in all development projects. The province identified a need for well-managed non-renewable resources to contribute to the economic and environmental sustainability of future generations. Another principle highlighted the need for public financial support to ensure development based on renewable resources rather than development based on exhaustible, non-renewable resources. The final principle stressed the need for pricing mechanisms to reflect the full cost of the resources used. These would allow for the non-renewability of a resource to be factored into the cost and for the attribution of real economic value to such resources.

In summary, the work of the round tables has emphasized the importance of community involvement in decision-making, protection of the environment, innovation in research and development to prevent environmental damage, and the need to address non-renewable energy shortages while at the same time ensuring economic growth. Although most of the provincial-level round tables are now closed, a number of local-level round tables continue to develop sustainable development strategies and to devise green plans at the community level. These community-level initiatives can be found at the municipal government level, local round tables, the Canadian Healthy Communities Network, and sustainable city initiatives. As Sadler says, "In Manitoba alone, there are fifty-two local round tables, approximately 40 per cent of which have completed sustainability vision statements or strategies" (Sadler, 1996:56). One of the notable differences between the local networks and the national level activities is the extent to which words get put into action at the local level. The level of action witnessed at the community level can perhaps be understood as a reflection of the immediacy of environmental problems in a number of communities. In Atlantic Canada, for example, local sustainability requires immediate action to address the economic, ecological, political, cultural, and social changes taking place as a result of the collapsed east-coast fisheries. In order to facilitate strategies for community resilience and foster self-reliance, the Sustainable Communities Network of Nova Scotia has been working with these communities to create new opportunities for sustainable livelihoods in the region (Sadler, 1996). The round tables have suffered as a result of the cutbacks in funding for environmental programs. Nevertheless, the round tables have demonstrated a means for enhancing the participation of under-represented groups in the environmental decision-making processes.

CANADIAN COUNCILS OF MINISTERS ON THE ENVIRONMENT (CCME)

Another important body set up to address environmental issues and sustainable development is the Canadian Council of Ministers on the Environment (ccme). The ccme is an interjurisdictional body that promotes cooperation on issues such as waste management, air pollution, and toxic chemicals. This body strives also for continuity in environmental standards across the provinces and territories. The ccme, however, only provides suggestions and proposals. The decision to cooperate is made by each jurisdiction individually. The ccme consists of 14 ministers representing the federal, provincial, and territorial governments. These 14 ministers meet twice a year "to discuss national environmental priorities and determine work to be carried out under the auspices of ccme. A Steering Committee, the Environmental Planning and Protection Committee, made up of senior staff of each jurisdiction, provide on-going advice to the Council of Ministers and co-ordinate specific ccme projects assigned to intergovernmental task groups. In this way, member governments can respond quickly to emerging issues, set national environmental strategies and develop long-term plans" (CCME, 2000). (The CCME and its roles are discussed in depth in Chapter 3.)

PROJET DE SOCIÉTÉ

The Projet de Société is an initiative of the International Institute for Sustainable Development (IISD) which began in the fall of 1992 as a forum for business, government, and civil society groups to discuss sustainable development issues and Canada's commitment to *Agenda 21*. The Projet ended in 1996, but out of this process a number of important documents emerged and a variety of perspectives were advanced. Two important documents that emerged from this group were *Canada and Agenda 21*, an electronic publication consisting of numerous Canadian responses to *Agenda 21* by representatives of all sectors of Canadian society, and a *Guide to Sustainability*. The Projet provided a detailed summary of Canadian policies and positions with respect to Earth Summit objectives, what Canadians are doing, or are planning to do, in respect to the objectives highlighted in *Agenda 21*. In an important chapter by François Bregha, the author offers an analysis of some of the challenges facing the Government of Canada in *Integrating Environment and Development in Decision-Making*, Chapter 8 of *Agenda 21*. Bregha notes that "decisions are made through a process that separates socio-economic and environmental factors. This is true in government, business, or in cases of individuals making decisions. It is necessary to understand the links between environment and development in order to make development choices that will be economically efficient, socially responsible, and environmentally sound" (Projet de société, 1995a). The chapter on integrating environment and development in decision-making, like the other chapters in this document, highlights the positions and commitments made by various groups represented at UNCED, including government, business and industry, non-governmental organizations, and indigenous groups. The Canadian National Statement at UNCED, prepared by then Minister of the Environment, Jean Charest, stated that UNCED "has brought two separate public policy tracks irrevocably together" (Charest as quoted in Projet de société, 1995a). However, other Canadian groups such as the Global Forum prepared statements and alternative strategies.

The International Non-Governmental Organisation Forum (Global Forum) was held concurrent to the UNCED. The Global Forum brought together representatives from more than 3000 NGOs around the world to discuss matters related to environment and development. Out of the Global Forum came an additional set of documents, including the NGO Earth

Charter and 38 Alternative NGO Treaties. *The Rio Framework Treaty on NGO Global Decision-Making* summarized NGO commitments, including strengthening existing networks and global alliances; working towards the recognition of all NGOs; securing NGOs' participation in decision-making processes at all levels; enhancing and promoting participatory democracy; and seeking the empowerment of all oppressed peoples, especially those who are socially and ecologically marginalized (Projet de société, 1995a). A second alternative forum that took place about the same time as UNCED and the Global Forum was the International Conference on Territory, Environment and Development (the Kari-Oca Conference). The Kari-Oca Conference hosted 650 indigenous representatives and resulted in an additional supplementary document called the *Indigenous Peoples Earth Charter.* This Charter stated that indigenous people are "victims of development and that in many cases they have been exterminated in the name of development programs. As such, indigenous peoples insist that they must consent to all projects in their territories, and that they must be involved, fully and entirely, in any decision-making processes. Failure to do so should be considered a crime" (as cited in Projet de société, 1995a).

The Projet de société developed a series of sustainable development principles that include the following:

» all deliberations must be informed by respect for nature, including the rights of other species and future generations;
» all persons should be able to participate in transitions to sustainability;
» the process should be based on anticipation and prevention;
» issues related to sustainability should be neither won nor lost, but resolved;
» informed decision making must consider the full cost of actions;
» the process should take into account social, interregional, and intergenerational equity; and
» the process should be a dynamic learning one. (Projet de société, 1995b)

These principles point to some of the opportunities and constraints within Canada's sustainable development policy and planning process.

OPPORTUNITIES AND CONSTRAINTS OF THE SDS

The sustainable development approach offers Canadians and others an opportunity to integrate economic strategies, environmental integrity, and social equality. The sustainable development policy approach — and the strategies that have arisen as a result of it — have been integrative, forward-looking, cross-sectoral processes for linking together and balancing environmental, social, and economic policy objectives. The strategies point to the important roles various actors play in the decision-making process, and the need for additional information and research to form objectives. Sustainable development approaches are frequently credited with their ability to provide long-term visions for societies and ways to move beyond short-term solutions. Emphasis has been placed on local strategies, community networks, and widespread decision-making. Increased decision-making power at the community level has the potential to empower communities to find their own solutions and to make use of local knowledge.

Overall, the SDS exercise has accomplished several important objectives. It has increased awareness of the concept and meaning of sustainability in Ottawa, particularly within the departments that have not traditionally addressed environmental, social, and economic development concerns: "Now literally every federal department has had to come to terms with this discourse, and try [sic] to interpret and adapt it to its own operations" (Bell, 2000:9). Public servants working in these departments have benefited from the exercise, gaining familiarity with the concept of sustainable development and becoming committed to the sustainability agenda: "With continued leadership and constant nagging, sustainable development strategies and reporting may indeed transform the federal government" (Bell, 2000:9). However, with these advances and opportunities also come a number of constraints.

One of the most central constraints to the SDS is the elusive nature of the concept and disagreements over the definition of the term. Many departmental SDS s view sustainable development primarily as an environmental issue, and few strategies have been able to integrate the multiple social, economic, and environmental dimensions of sustainability. The strategies also lack clear goals, objectives, and action plans. Furthermore, the various agencies working on sustainable development in Canada (i.e., the federal departments, the Projet de société, the CCME, and the NRTEE) do not collaborate sufficiently on research and policy activities.

THE COMMISSIONER'S REPORT

In order to design sustainable development policy, the federal and provincial governments require scientific information to demonstrate the links between sustainability and environmental integrity. This science-based information is more likely to convince policy-makers of the urgency of environmentally sound policy-making. Brian Emmett, the first commissioner of environment and sustainable development, stated that Canada has done little to control greenhouse gases. The potential impact of

Canada's slow response to greenhouse gas emissions may result in hotter and drier summers and therefore more forest fires, greater insect infestations, and coastal flooding. Lack of scientific information and/or lack of analysis of existing data also resulted in a slow response to the impact of pollution on biological diversity. This means all species are potentially threatened by pollution and loss of habitat (CBC, 1998).

A second major criticism of Canada's sustainable development approaches is the inability of governments in Canada to translate policy commitments into practice. The Commissioner's report noted "that governments in Canada are much better at policy development — planning and making commitments — than they are at policy implementation – monitoring impacts and assessing results" (Bell, 2000:5). In addition, reporting on the lack of action and practices has been weak or non-existent. It is difficult for the departments to monitor those commitments that have been put into practice. Few monitoring schemes were identified by the Commissioner. The result is that few activities or policies that are created are measured. The Commissioner noted that "...by measuring more and by measuring better and more consistently, both between departments and over time, we will contribute to the advancement of a sustainable development agenda" (Emmett as quoted in Bell, 2000:5).

The Commission on Environment and Sustainable Development (CESD) has proved to be a central focus of the sustainable development strategy in Canada. The reports prepared by the Commissioner have highlighted some of the many challenges the governments in Canada currently face if they are to achieve sustainable development and promote environmentally, socially, and economically healthy livelihoods. Despite the pivotal role played by the Commissioner, this work is not enough. The CESD is also faced with a number of challenges. The impact of the Commissioner on Environment and Development "will depend on the extent to which sustainability becomes a core value of all government policy, and ultimately transforms the culture of decision making of the Canadian government. At present the SDS exercise is simply that — a legislated requirement imposed on the bureaucracy, to which all departments have conformed, but without yet transforming their policies and operations to the extent anticipated by the legislation and strived for by the Commissioner" (Bell, 2000:8)

CONCLUSION

In order to address the criticisms raised by the Commissioner on Environment and Sustainable Development, there are specific actions that governments in Canada must take. Of paramount importance is the need for governments in Canada to question the economic primacy of resource management in light of dwindling resources. Why does economic policy continue to dominate the political, social, and economic agendas, in the face of rampant environmental degradation and habitat loss? Answering this question requires changes "in personal attitudes and values that ultimately circumscribe the 'politics of consumption'" (Sadler, 1996:28). Furthermore, there need to be significant changes in public policy and governance; a change in the structure of the economy that supports a market for cheap resources that do not factor in the environmental costs of exploitation; a change in personal attitudes and values that ultimately encompass "the politics of consumption"; and a need to think and act locally and globally. In order to secure a sustainable future, Sadler's three pillars of sustainability need to be reconciled. These pillars include: "(1) living within global biophysical carrying capacity; (2) providing a decent living standard for all people; [and] (3) ensuring a reasonable measure of distributional fairness in access to resources and their economic benefits" (Sadler, 1996:26). These offer some of the practical solutions and idealistic goals of sustainability. However, they do not tackle the fundamental causes of unsustainable development and offer us few avenues for policy direction. What is needed is a deeper understanding of who lacks access and control of resources and why.

The national sustainable development strategy developed by the federal government, as well as the departmental strategies, are important initial steps. The SDSs offer excellent guides for securing a sustainable future in Canada. However, additional commitments to ensuring that multisectoral perspectives and approaches are incorporated into the policy-planning and decision-making processes are crucial. Sustainable development policy planning requires more attention to who makes decisions about resource management, who has access to — and control over — those resources, and how marginalized voices and perspectives can be more fully incorporated into the policy-making process. In order to address these concerns, there is a need for a shift in our understanding of sustainable development as development as usual. As long as sustainable development policies are given economic policy primacy, we will continue to live unsustainably. If we as a species can do better, then we need to begin to identify how these changes can take place and how policy can be translated more expediently into practice.

PART THREE
ETHICS & VALUES

TEN

GENDER, RESOURCES, AND
THE ENVIRONMENT

INTRODUCTION

In Clayoquot Sound on Vancouver Island, British Columbia, women activists protested the clear-cutting of the rainforest. During the protests, many women risked arrest or were arrested, including Sue Fraser, a 71-year-old grandmother. The Clayoquot story gained a great deal of media attention and resulted in the largest civil disobedience action in Canadian history in defence of public land. In Sydney, Nova Scotia, women were at the forefront of the activism to clean up the Sydney tar ponds and to relocate those families who suffered from illnesses believed to be caused by toxic chemicals dumped in the area. As one woman recalled after coming home from work and finding men in space suits about 180 metres away, "I was starting to think I was underdressed. The only thing between them and us was a new ten foot high fence" (McKenzie as quoted by the Sierra Club of Canada, 1998).

Around the world, women have been involved in a number of environmental projects as key environmental activists. Approximately 80 per cent of environmental activists worldwide are women. These female environmental activists include the much celebrated Chipko women of India who, by hugging trees (the literal translation of Chipko), were able to prevent the trees from being cut down. In the United States, Julia Butterfly Hill gained popularity for her commitment to preserving old-growth forests in California by climbing 60 metres up an ancient redwood where she lived for two years to protest the logging of old-growth forests.

These examples from around the world share a number of common themes. One is the central importance of environmental management and natural resource protection to women. A second is that women have been at the centre of environmental activism. Despite women's concern for the environment, they are over-represented in polluted and/or resource-poor areas and under-represented in environmental policy decision-making. In the past two decades, the Canadian federal government and intergovernmental organizations have attempted to address gender inequality and the environment but have seen them as separate themes, rather than identifying the important connections between them. More recently, national and international policies have drawn attention to gender issues surrounding environmental management and created policy guidelines to ensure that women can participate more fully in environmental management activities in their communities. For example, the federal government has adopted the United Nations Conference on Environment and Development (UNCED) policy document entitled *Agenda 21*, which has an entire chapter devoted to recommendations for gender equitable sustainable development. The *Beijing Platform for Action* that came out of the Fourth World Conference on Women (FWCW) also dedicated a chapter to gender and environment.

Despite these national and international policy resolutions, there is still a long way to go. One of the major criticisms of the national and international policies is the failure of these policies to challenge the status quo (MacDonald, 1996). One can argue that Canadian foreign policy and international channels of policy-making are themselves gendered and reinforce masculinity, thus perpetuating gender inequality and gender bias. The gender bias inherent in international decision-making and policy documents "actually leads to women's disproportionate poverty and experience of environmental degradation" (Kettel, 1996:162). This chapter examines these arguments and some of the key issues surrounding gender inequality, poverty, and environmental management. This discussion is followed by an exploration of recent policy documents that address gender and environmental management concerns and of the important contributions and policy commitments that Canadians and the federal government have made in addressing gender and the environment in national and international policy documents.

The following section summarizes the relationship between environmental degradation and gender inequality by highlighting the major causes of women's disproportionate representation in resource-poor households. The first issue addresses the geographical location of resource-poor and polluted communities and the disproportionate representation of women in these neighbourhoods. The gender-specific roles and responsibilities carried out by women and how they relate to environmental management constitute the second issue covered in this chapter. The third issue draws on examples of the macro-level policies that influence the nature of their activities at the local, community level. The final issue demonstrates the low representation of women in environmental decision-making positions, and therefore women's limited capacity to address the above three issues.

GENDER AND ENVIRONMENTAL ISSUES

Women's Disproportionate Representation among the Resource-Poor

> For me, home and environment and health are all closely intertwined. I am appalled by the toxic condition of the homes and neighbour-hoods in which we live our lives and raise our children and by the circumstances that make this the status quo. Yet, I am inspired by the stories of the women who make it their mission to confront the power structures threatening their families. (Susan McIntosh, 1994)

Environmental degradation has a disproportionate impact on women, particularly poor women, who are more likely to live in environmentally degraded communities and neighbourhoods in Canada and elsewhere in the world. For example, "[t]he poorest 20 per cent of people in the world live in ecologically vulnerable or fragile settings ... land degradation is widespread, with entire regions threatened by the spreading impact of deforestation, desertification, coastal and interior flooding, soil degradation, and loss of biodiversity" (Kettel, 1996:164). Poverty is linked with exposure to environmental contamination and degradation. Women and their families living in resource-poor, low-income neighbourhoods are faced with the environmental threats of toxic chemicals, lack of proper sanitation facilities, and pollution. Nesmith and Wright (1995) found that toxic waste facilities were disproportionately located within poorer, racial, or ethnic minority neighbourhoods. Furthermore, resource-poor women are more likely to find affordable housing in neighbourhoods and regions that are environmentally marginal, degraded, or polluted. There tends to be a cyclical effect whereby increased poverty resulting from reduced material resources perpetuates environmental degradation (Kettel, 1996).

The increasing stress of poverty and environmental degradation has meant that resource-poor households frequently resort to unsustainable environmental activities (Mehra, 1993) which perpetuate environmental degradation. Women in particular experience the impact of environmental degradation since they have to walk long distances to gain access to the resources they need. Additional problems experienced by resource-poor women include slum-like housing conditions, inadequate shelter, lack of water and waste disposal facilities, overcrowding, inadequate transportation systems, hazardous public spaces, pollution, and lack of open air, trees, and parks. For many resource-poor women and their families, poverty and environmental degradation around their homes and communities cause environmental illness and health problems. Environmental degradation and lack of access to — and control of — resources cause poverty in both rural and urban environments. Also, poverty exacerbates natural resource depletion since poor communities resort to environmentally unsustainable practices to produce food for their families and to meet daily needs. Health research studies demonstrate the link between environmental degradation, pollution, and human health. Studies conducted with Canadian women in the Arctic have found traces of toxic chemicals in the women's breast milk. In many cases, these levels of toxic chemicals were deemed unsafe.

At the federal level, the Canadian Department of Health has undertaken four studies to investigate the link between the neighbourhoods in which women live, their roles, and their exposure to environmental risks. One of the studies examines the health of women and children in farm families. A second considers the relationship between exposure to environmental risks (such as pesticides) and reproductive outcomes (e.g., miscarriages and birth defects). A third study examines the impact of high-risk geographic areas (such as toxic dumpsites) on birth outcomes. A fourth study analyses the specific environmental risks to women's reproductive health (Environment Canada, 1994). More information is needed to demonstrate the link between environmental risks and human health in order to guide policy-making. However, many of the environmental impacts noted above point to the risk women and their children face from exposure to environmental pollution. Many of the environmental risks that women experience are a result of women's socially defined gender roles.

Roles, Responsibilities, and the Gender Division of Labour

The nature of women's socialized roles suggests that women are primarily responsible for the provision of goods and services to meet the immediate needs of the family. In less developed areas in both the north and south, these needs include ensuring that food is available (i.e., subsistence agriculture), that this food is cooked (i.e., collecting firewood to make the fire), and that there is water (i.e., collecting water) available for washing, cooking, and preparation of food. Women are more likely than men to bear the burden of environmental degradation in resource-poor communities due to women's socially ascribed roles as providers for the family (Dankelman and Davidson, 1988; Kettel, 1996). Micro-level analyses of gender relations in natural resource management provide gender- and sex-disaggregated data which reveal women's and men's socialized roles and responsibilities in environmental management, the impact of environmental degradation on women and men, and the effects of external environmental projects and economic policies on community members. A number of authors have documented women's roles and activities in natural resource management (Davidson, 1993; Dankelman and Davidson, 1988; Elliot, 1994, Harcourt, 1994). These authors demonstrate the integral role women play in managing resources for family and community use.

Women are under-represented in the primary sector in which resource extraction takes place. However, women's roles in resource use and management are significant. Women's environmental work involves converting natural resources such as fish, food crops, and timber into products which are consumed at the community and household level (Hessing and Howlett, 1997). Logging, however, "is a bastion of male work" (Langer and Bate, 1994). In the case of Clayoquot Sound, British Columbia, the debate became one of jobs versus the environment. Those protesting to save the old-growth forests were accused of preventing hard-working Canadian men from making a living. The logging companies produced posters that "show a solid bunch of working fellows, chainsaws in hand, gathered around a giant, newly felled tree. The caption above declares 'Don't Let Your Love of the Wilderness Blind You to the Needs of Your Fellow Man'" (Langer and Bate, 1994:82). The posters argued that jobs and environmental preservation are at odds. However, Langer and Bate argue that this is not true, and furthermore that this division of jobs and nature is a gendered fallacy. Tofino, the small town outside of Clayoquot Sound, is home to many women who depend on the tourism industry for employment. These women have built small enterprises (such as bed and breakfasts, bakeries, and cafés) that cater to the tourists who come to enjoy the wilderness and the old-growth forests of Clayoquot Sound. Gender roles, as socially defined sets of responsibilities, determine the kinds of work women do, and therefore the sorts of risks they face in the work they are doing.

The Impact of Macro-level Policies on Women

Case studies documenting the impact of macro-economic policies, such as structural adjustment programs (SAPs), for example, highlight the challenge women farmers face when they are forced to produce more cash crops on increasingly degraded land. Increased cash crop production is necessary to secure the cash income to pay for the rising costs of goods and services around the world (see Elson, 1991; Lele, 1991; Meena, 1995 for examples from Africa). Macro-economic policies form the basis of global restructuring and have negatively impacted women in all countries, including

Canada. Women who formerly relied on the natural environment to survive are facing increasing difficulty since they now have fewer opportunities to earn an income as their resources dwindle (Sachs, 1996). For many women, these macro-level policies have resulted in greater poverty. Furthermore, women rarely own as much of the natural environment as men. Private companies and the government increasingly are buying up land, and thus land is increasingly owned by male owners, absentee landlords, and transnational corporations. Women may have access to the land, which allows them to grow food. However, women lack control over how the land is used, what crops are grown, and who will benefit from the crops produced.

The impact of limited control over decision-making in land use is a reduced capacity for women to make decisions about their natural environments. Moreover, women are less able to contribute to sustainable development, basic food production, and environmental conservation (Kettel, 1996). These factors have culminated in — and reflect — the masculinization of wealth and monopoly that some men hold on power, land, resources, and decision-making (Kettel, 1996). It is difficult for women to influence change and to make decisions that affect their lives since they lack representation on environmental planning and decision-making bodies at the local, national, and international levels.

Representation of Women in Decision-making Positions

In Canada, the representation of women in decision-making positions has traditionally been poor. A few women (such as Kim Campbell, Flora Macdonald, and Barbara MacDougall) have had short-lived responsibilities in national decision-making positions (Keeble and Smith, 1999). Women have also been denied equitable access to the leadership of trade unions and political parties across the continents. Thus, women are "grossly under-represented in public decision-making" at the international and the national political level (Kettel, 1996:177).

The representation of women in decision-making positions tends to be low in all institutions and organizations. Women are under-represented in UN decision-making, government positions, NGO decision-making positions, universities, and in certain areas of specialization. Women's poor representation in decision-making bodies is not limited to environmental planning. Women are un- or under-represented in decision-making positions in numerous decision-making bodies. For example, of the United Nations member states, only 3.8 per cent were headed by women at the end of 1990 (Kettel, 1996). At the United Nations Conference on Environment and Development (UNCED) in 1992, only 15 per cent of the official delegates and advisors were women (Kettel, 1996). Furthermore, of the heads of state represented at UNCED, only 3 out of 118 were women (Kettel, 1996). The poor representation of women in decision-making positions in environmental forums is surprising since the majority of environmental activists are women. Women are activists in environmental movements but are "rarely leaders of national or international environmental NGOs, including those based in the northern countries, in spite of the current visibility of some very well-known women environmentalists" (Kneipp, 1994:49 in Kettel, 1996:177) such as Elizabeth May.

Representation of Women in Resource Management Careers

In Canada, the representation of women in resource management careers is substantially poorer than the representation of men (Nesmith and Wright, 1995). Furthermore, less than 16 per cent of the workforce, including clerical positions, in traditional resource management fields (forestry, fisheries, mining, trapping) is composed of women (Nesmith and Wright, 1995). In British Columbia, women comprise approximately 90 per cent of the clerical and supervisory clerical jobs. But the representation of women in key decision-making positions (such as professional, semi-professional, and technical positions) is less than 11 per cent (Nesmith and Wright, 1995:85). The authors identify some of the barriers to women's participation in decision-making positions and representation in these positions, including isolation, men's lack of awareness of changing roles and values, sexual harassment, maternity leave, and a lack of qualified female applicants (Nesmith and Wright, 1995). Women therefore have fewer opportunities than men to effect environmental change through decision-making and participation in industrial decision-making and national legislative processes (Kettel, 1996).

Women's poor representation in decision-making positions can also be extended to the universities. Nesmith and Wright (1995) identify a division between different environmental programs and summarize women's representation in these programs. They note that the more scientific and specialized environmental science programs such as forestry have fewer female academics than men. Multidisciplinary environmental programs (i.e., environmental studies) which often include social, political, and economic analyses of environmental problems tend to have a higher representation of female academics and a higher percentage of female students. The authors suggest that overall there are few academics to act as role models for female students. The representation of female students declines significantly at the doctoral level, where less than one quarter (22 per cent) of all forestry students are women (Nesmith and Wright, 1995).

The representation of women in environmental activist groups, non-governmental organizations (NGOs), and non-profit agencies tends to be high. Women are more heavily represented in membership and leadership of voluntary organizations, particularly grass-roots and community-based organizations that tend to be less hierarchical (Nesmith and Wright, 1995). In a study conducted between 1997 and 1998 on gender representation in environmental organizations in Malawi, the findings pointed to poor representation of women in decision-making positions (Tiessen, 1999). Canadian international NGOs operating in Malawi also had few female representatives among their staff. Women held few senior-level positions. The majority of female staff were in support staff roles and were not involved in policy-making processes.

The poor representation of women in decision-making positions in environmental organizations, national governments, and international bodies is an extension of women's lack of decision-making power at the household and community level. At the community level, women lack opportunities to influence the use and management of the natural resources around them. Women are excluded from decision-making forums pertaining to their homes and neighbourhoods. In northern Canada, "women's exclusion from the environmental decisions that affect their lives is particularly clear with regard to the production, management, and distribution of environmental contaminants in northern communities" (Kettel, 1996:171). All of these studies point to the poor representation of women in decision-making positions and the barriers to their participation. Unless women are able to influence policy and practice, they will not be able develop policies and strategies to effect change.

FEMINIST PERSPECTIVES ON GENDER RELATIONS IN ENVIRONMENTAL MANAGEMENT

Gender, as a core concept in feminist literature, has been used to describe the social and cultural roles that are attributed to males and females. These roles tend to be classified as masculine or feminine and are most often learned through the process of socialization. Gender issues are those issues that arise from the investigation of power relations between men and women, and inequality between the social hierarchy of masculine and feminine. Gender issues can be understood by conducting a gender analysis. Gender analysis, as a conceptual framework, gained popularity in the 1970s when feminists began to distinguish between masculine and feminine socially constructed roles and the status and power accorded to each term. This distinction rejected the biological determinism previously attached to male and female roles in society. The rejection of biological determinism meant that women are disadvantaged not because they are biologically predisposed to care for the family, but because women's roles in the private sector as mothers, and bearers of children are socially undervalued. Kabeer extended the argument of socially defined roles of masculinity and femininity to account for locally-defined attributes of males and females in specific social categories (Kabeer, 1994). Meena further noted that masculine and feminine roles are not merely attributable to men and women but are "constructed by society" (Meena, 1992:1). These roles are thus reinforced through custom and institutional norms.

Mounting concern for environmental conservation and natural resource management in the second half of the twentieth century has evoked increasing attention to the role of women in environmental management. Consequently, a body of literature emerged in the 1970s and 1980s called ecofeminism. Ecofeminism pointed to women as the key actors in environmental movements, promoting women as "privileged environmental managers" who possess specific skills and knowledge in environmental care (Braidotti et al., 1994:88), calling on women to save the environment, and urging them to rally to protect the soils and water systems of their lands (Jackson, 1993:1948). Ecofeminism builds on the idea that the earth is a living organism, in which everything is interrelated and an integral part of the system. The concept of ecofeminism emerged from the notion of Mother Earth and supports an ethic of caring and nurturing. The term ecofeminism was first used by Francoise D'Eaubonne who in 1974 "called upon women to lead an ecological revolution to save the planet." This revolution was expected to bring about new relations not only between men and women but also between humans and nature (Merchant, 1995).

Ecofeminism explores the relationship between the devaluing and subordination of the environment and the devaluing and subordination of women. Ecofeminist literature emphasizes the domination of women and nature as interrelated, having "historically emerged together from a common world view, giving women a special interest in ending the domination of nature and, by implication, their own subordination" (Agarwal, 1997:36). Ecofeminism gained popularity in the 1980s as a way to explain dichotomous divisions and the ways in which these divisions represent hierarchy and discrimination, particularly how women and nature are subordinated to men and culture. Ecofeminism represents an important feature of Canadian perspectives on gender and the environment. As a body of literature and a theoretical construct, the concept has a lot to offer to those interested in understanding the exploitation of nature and women as a result of capitalist expansion and natural resource degradation. However, the literature on ecofeminism has faced a number of important criticisms which point to the limitations of this theoretical construct.

Some of the main critiques of ecofeminism include its lack of attention to power relations between women. Ecofeminism uses women as an essentialist category rather than employing the concept of gender to identify strategic constraints among women and men in a community. Ecofeminism, relying more on anecdotal evidence than strong argument, finds connections between women and the environment, which assumes a harmony of interests between women which enables them to mobilize and unite their voices. However, women, as a group, do not experience environmental degradation in a uniform manner. Environmental relations of particular women depend upon a class-gender system. Inequalities among women at the household level such as seniority, division of labour, access to and control of resources, and decision-making power indicate power relations within the household and the community, thus negating the possibility of defining women as a homogeneous, united group (Jackson, 1993:1948). Ecofeminist literature conceptualizes women as closer to nature than their male counterparts because of their biology (Agarwal, 1997:36; Jackson, 1993). Yet women act as environmental agents in both positive and negative ways. Some women engage in benign environmental activities at certain times and in environmentally destructive ways at other times. Thus, women have no inherent affinity to nature. Their relationship with natural resources is socially constructed and varies between groups of women and within individual women throughout their lives (Jackson, 1993; Rathgeber, 1995:215).

Despite these criticisms, ecofeminism remains an important approach to the study of gender, natural resources, and the environment. "A more critical ecofeminist position argues that women's roles are limited by the larger context of class and gender inequality. The dual subordination of women and nature reflects the combined power exerted by patriarchy and capitalism" (Hessing and Howlett, 1997). Furthermore, ecofeminism has offered important philosophical notions that have formed the basis for international conferences and policies on gender and environment. One example of an international conference that drew on ecofeminist contributions was Planeta Fêmea. This conference was part of the Global Forum, the NGO conference that ran parallel to the 1992 Earth Summit. Planeta Fêmea "put forward the political dimensions needed for a new partnership ethic of earthcare" (Merchant, 1995:209). Two major policy documents emerged from Planeta Fêmea. The first, *The Global Action for Women towards Sustainable and Equitable Development*, was included as Chapter 24 in the United Nation's Conference on Environment and Development final document, entitled *Agenda 21*. The second was the women's *Code of Environmental Ethics and Accountability*. This document highlighted the importance of balance between humans and non-humans and an end to the domination of nature. Other priority areas highlighted in this policy document included the need for the fulfilment of basic needs to take precedence over profit, sound and sustainable environmental management, and shared responsibilities and accountability for environmental care and clean-up.

CANADA'S POLICIES AND COMMITMENTS AT THE INTERNATIONAL AND NATIONAL LEVELS

The government of Canada has been involved in a number of international initiatives to promote gender equality and environmental management. For example, the Department of Foreign Affairs and International Trade (DFAIT) provided financial and policy support for the participation of Canadian indigenous women at a biodiversity convention working group meeting and at the Madrid Workshop on UN Biodiversity Convention/Traditional Knowledge. Canada's commitment to promoting sustainable development in circumpolar countries is further evidenced by Canada's commitment to ensure that Canadian indigenous women were represented at the Northern Lives Conference in 1997. One of Canada's six priorities for Overseas Development Assistance (ODA) is "to strengthen the full participation of women as equal partners in the sustainable development of their societies by supporting initiatives within and among developing countries to increase women's participation in decision-making processes, improve women's income levels and economic conditions, and improve women's access to basic health" (CIDA, 1999). The Canadian International Development Agency (CIDA) is involved in a number of projects worldwide which are geared to women and sustainable development projects. For example, in India, a women's organization is reclaiming unproductive land and engaging in sustainable agriculture and development. Other examples of Canada's international support for women include contributions made through CIDA's support for a UNIFEM project in Mali. This project trained women and provided them with credit in order to establish a waste-disposal business in Bamako, the capital of Mali. Reports on this project point to the high degree of success it has achieved. The project now offers garbage removal services to 18,000 residents (Status of Women Canada, 1999).

International research institutions addressing environmental issues have also demonstrated their commitment to investigating issues of gender equity. For example, the International Development Research Centre

(IDRC) is a Canadian research centre committed to studying the "differential impact that change will have on the lives of men and women. To ensure that all IDRC projects promote sustainable and equitable development, the Gender and Sustainable Development unit supports gender mainstreaming and analysis in all the Centre's programming" (IDRC, 1999).

The context in which gender and environment are being addressed at the international level is primarily within sustainable development initiatives. Canada has sought representation in many international forums to discuss and devise policies on the environment and sustainable development. In fact, Canada has taken a leading role in many of these debates, and a number of Canadians have held pivotal posts in the organization and implementation of international environmental conferences. For example, Maurice Strong was the Secretary General for the United Nations Conference on Environment and Development (UNCED), also known as the Rio Conference. The government of Canada is also a signatory to the UNCED document *Agenda 21*, as well as the conventions coming out of this conference (*the Convention on Biological Diversity* and the *Convention to Combat Desertification*).

As a signatory to *Agenda 21*, Canada has expressed its commitment to gender equality as expressed in Chapter 24 of this document. This chapter is dedicated to "global action for women towards sustainable and equitable development" (UNIFEM, 1999). The objective is to increase the proportion of women decision-makers, planners, managers, and extension workers in the field of environment and development (24.2b). The chapter highlights the specific activities and recommendations for governments to adopt in order to achieve gender equality in environmental projects. Of particular interest is the commitment stated in Agenda 21 section 24.3(f), "...to support and strengthen equal employment opportunities and equitable remuneration for women in formal and informal sectors with adequate economic, political, and social support systems and services..." (24.3f). The objectives of women's involvement are reiterated in section 24.7 of this document, which states that women should be fully involved in decision-making and implementation of sustainable development activities (UNIFEM, 1999).

The attention paid to women and gender issues in *Agenda 21* is a result of "a preceding series of local, national, regional and international meetings of women's groups, such as the *Global Assembly of Women and Environment: Partners in Life and the World Women's Congress for a Healthy Planet* (WEDO, 1992). At this meeting, women from around the world were able to reach consensus on what successful sustainable development would be and to put that consensus forward to the politicians at Rio (MacDonald, 1996). However, there is an inherent lack of political will among politicians to implement these conference recommendations: "This lack of will is central to political stability, to the resistance of political systems to change in the status quo" (MacDonald, 1996:191). There is need for a more decentralized political system in which the politicians live in the environment in which they make decisions and therefore also experience the consequences of their decisions.

A second example of an international commitment to address gender and sustainable development can be found in the UNDP's programs. UNDP's programs "support a broad range of activities on gender equality and the advancement of women" (UNDP, 1999). Some of the programs include the mainstreaming of gender analysis into all programs, and the implementation of the *Beijing Platform for Action* and the *Convention on the Elimination of All Forms of Discrimination Against Women* (CEDAW) (UNDP, 1999). Canada is a signatory country to the CEDAW and also to the Fourth World Conference on Women (FWCW) *Beijing Platform for Action*. The *Platform for Action* specifically addresses environmental issues in Section K. Prior to taking part in the FWCW in 1995, Canadian representatives met on a number of occasions in various forums to discuss the federal government's position, plan, and strategy for gender equality. These activities and meetings culminated in *Canada's National Action Plan for the FWCW*.

Canada's National Action Plan for the FWCW

In a 1994 conference entitled *Women and Sustainable Development: Canadian Perspectives Conference*, a group of participants met in Vancouver to develop a set of policy recommendations to be considered at the FWCW. These policy recommendations highlighted nine areas: recognition of women farmers' work, environmental legislation, strategy of social dialogue, women in transportation, valuing rural regions, strategies for including the perspectives of indigenous women in the consultation and decision-making process, women's quality of life in urban settings, valuing childcare, and women's education and international aid (Sustainable Development Research Institute, 1994).

This meeting paid special attention to Canada's external affairs and called attention to a number of CIDA-funded activities to ensure that women were able to review Canadian foreign policy to determine if it is ecologically sound. The meeting also encouraged the representation of women in all areas of employment and in all areas of the economy. In rethinking the *Beijing Platform's* proposed 12 critical areas of concern, the participants came up with additional recommendations such as an end to non-sustainable consumption patterns. The workshop participants also recognized the role of globalization of trade in perpetuating inequality and promoting resource scarcity. This group further called for a policy on food security to ensure the development of sustainable agricultural practices. The participants highlighted the need to buy locally grown food, promote seed and species diversity, follow sound farming practices, and expand community-level activities.

The workshop brought together women from a range of backgrounds to challenge concepts and ideas in an effort to promote sustainable livelihoods and sustainable communities (the term "sustainable development" was rejected). Many women attending this workshop (nearly half) felt that "sustainability" as defined by the World Conference on Environment and Development (WCED)/*Brundtland Commission* was too vague and did not address difference and the status quo (MacDonald, 1996).

Canada made a federal commitment, presented at the 1995 FWCW, to offer more than 3000 federal activities to promote women's equality. This commitment was based on the objectives identified as critical areas of concern in the *Beijing Platform for Action*. In Canada's National Action Plan for the FWCW, entitled *Setting the Stage for the Next Century: The Federal Plan for Gender Equality*, a delegation from Status of Women Canada (SWC) discussed Canada's position on gender equality in a number of areas. These areas were represented in this document as a set of eight objectives, including implementation of gender-based analysis throughout federal departments and agencies; improving women's economic autonomy and well-being; improving women's physical and psychological well-being; reducing violence in society (particularly violence against women and children); promoting gender equality in all aspects of Canada's cultural life; incorporating women's perspectives in governance; promoting and supporting global gender equality; and advancing gender equality for employees of federal departments and agencies.

Although the *Beijing Platform for Action* identifies women and environment as one of the 12 critical areas of concern, Canada does not. Instead, only brief mention of gender and environment is made in this plan under the objective to improve "women's physical and psychological well-being" and in global gender equality. As a result, the Canadian federal government has made limited progress in addressing gender inequality and the environment. Furthermore, the federal government has made only minimal commitments to addressing gender issues nationally.

Canada's commitment to gender equality is integrated into Canadian legislation, policies, and programs, and is subject to the *Canadian Charter of Rights and Freedoms*. "Canada's promotion of gender equality is based on a belief that equal rights for women are an essential component of progress on human rights and democratic development; and that sustainable and

equitable development will only be achieved if women are able to participate as equal decision-makers in and beneficiaries of that development"
(swc, 2000). Canada's commitments to gender equality can be found in a
number of policy documents. Under the *Canadian Charter of Rights and
Freedoms*, Canada is committed to ensuring "equality before and under law
and equal protection and benefit of law" (*Canadian Charter of Rights and
Freedoms*). Specifically, the Charter states that "[e]very individual is equal
before and under the law and has the right to the equal protection and
equal benefit of the law without discrimination and, in particular, without
discrimination based on race, national or ethnic origin, colour, religion,
sex, age or mental or physical disability" (*Canadian Charter of Rights and
Freedoms*). The government of Canada further promotes affirmative action
since it "does not preclude any law, program or activity that has as its
object the amelioration of conditions of disadvantaged individuals or
groups including those that are disadvantaged because of race, national or
ethnic origin, colour, religion, sex, age or mental or physical disability"
(*Canadian Charter of Rights and Freedoms*).

The Status of Women Canada (swc) was established as a federal government agency to promote "gender equality, and the full participation of
women in the economic, social, cultural and political life of the country.
swc focuses its work in three areas: improving women's economic
autonomy and well-being, eliminating systemic violence against women
and children, and advancing women's human rights" (swc, 2000). The
major role of the swc is to design public policy that promotes equality.
This is done through gender-based analyses and advocacy on gender issues
within the federal government. swc works in collaboration with other
countries, international organizations, as well as the private sector.

The swc promotes research to enhance public policy and has funded
four research projects that meet the criterion by calling for proposals on
factoring diversity into policy analysis and development. One of the funds
was awarded to a study entitled *If Gender Mattered: A Case Study of Inuit
Women, Land Claims and the Voisey's Bay Nickel Project*. This report highlighted the need for federal government to do additional work on environmental policies and land claims. The report noted that policies and
negotiation processes "promote and support self-reliance and equality of
Inuit and other Aboriginal women within their own societies and the
larger Canadian society" (Archibald and Crnkovich, 1999). The purpose
of this report was to illustrate the important link between gender issues,
land claims, and environmental assessment policies, since the policies and
processes of the Voisey's Bay nickel mining project greatly influence the
lives of Inuit women in Labrador. The report highlighted a number of
recommendations to guide future policies and initiatives, including

involving aboriginal women's organizations in discussions, ensuring aboriginal women are able to participate as equals in these discussions, guaranteeing adequate resources and time to research the needs of aboriginal
women, and providing funding for aboriginal women's organizations
affected by a particular land claims agreement or environmental assessment to do research on the issues at hand.

CONCLUSION: WOMEN ENVIRONMENTALISTS SPEAK OUT

Involving women in environmental planning can provide opportunities for
women's needs and interests to be expressed. Women need to be seen and
heard as environmental actors who are knowledgeable and informed of the
environmental risks and opportunities they face. Numerous women's
groups and individual women have articulated their environmental concerns. For example, the Indigenous Women's Environmental Network is
an organization made up of aboriginal women in Saskatchewan who are
concerned about environmental issues and the impact that megaprojects
have on indigenous people. This group has been working for several years
to raise awareness about the impact of uranium mining, clear-cutting, and
the damming of river systems. The Indigenous Women's Environmental
Network is also concerned with the impact these environmental problems
will have on the survival of aboriginal people in Saskatchewan
(Environmental Connections for Canada, Canadian First Nations, 2000).
Another group of environmental activists, called the Environment Group,
is a group of women within the Older Women's Network (OWN). The
Environment Group began in 1989. The women in this group believe "that
environmentalism must determine economics and politics rather than the
reverse, and the environmentalists have the uphill task of persuading
politicians to understand this, and to act in accordance with it" (Phillips,
1994). Sarah, a young environmental activist, became concerned with clear-
cutting in the Walbran Valley on Vancouver Island: "After driving for
hours ... through clearcuts, to come upon this enchanted ancient rainforest
was a very emotional experience" (Sarah as quoted by Benson, 1994). To
draw attention to the need for environmental protection of the Walbran,
Sarah held a 47-day fast. She later chained herself to the bottom of a logging truck in order to prevent the clearing of forest for a logging road
(Benson, 1994).

In response to the numerous concerns raised by environmental activists,
the federal government of Canada has devised national and international
commitments to achieve gender equality in environmental management
and sustainable development. There is now "an abundance of policies to

improve the status of women relative to that of men and promote equality of participation" (MacDonald, 1996:183). The policies highlight strategies to incorporate women more fully into the environmental policy-making process. The entry of women into policy-making structures has led to the introduction of new ideas that challenge how we think about natural resources and the environment. Yet the day-to-day reality of women faced with environmental risks and poverty is frequently obscured in these policy documents. In addition to factoring in the day-to-day reality of women, a number of additional changes are needed to incorporate women more fully into the environmental policy process, including the need for equal participation of men and women in environmental and sustainable development decision-making.

Specific indicators are needed to determine how well Canada is doing in improving the status of women and providing opportunities for women to enter decision-making positions. Attention must be paid to the location of women in environmentally degraded and polluted areas, and solutions must be devised to address the link between poverty, women's lack of economic opportunities, and the environmental risks of living in polluted communities. The impact of environmental risks on women's health needs further research, and more information is needed to understand the nature of women's roles and responsibilities that increase their risks. Macro-economic policies that contribute to women's limited and declining access to and control over resources (such as land, water, and forests) must be challenged. Gender equality policies that "have been ineffective against the inertia of the political status quo" (MacDonald, 1996:183) must offer strategic approaches to effect change. Addressing these concerns will assist women and men in finding solutions to environmental problems and enhance prospects for implementing gender-sensitive sustainable development policies. More research is also needed to uncover how broader institutional norms and practices perpetuate gender inequality at all levels.

ELEVEN

SUSTAINABLE DEVELOPMENT, HUMAN SECURITY, AND CIVIL SOCIETY

... we have never faced a security challenge as great and pervasive as that we face today through our excessive impact on the earth's environment and life systems. (Maurice Strong, 1992)

INTRODUCTION

This section on values would be incomplete without a closer examination of three key concepts which have emerged in the transnational context of ecopolitics introduced in Chapter 5 and which resurfaced in the preceding two chapters as well: sustainable development, human security, and civil society. Although traditional international relations have been largely fixated on the security of the nation, or the state, in recent years we have seen a shift in official focus towards the security of the individual. This applies to Canadians and non-Canadians alike, but the very term "human security" is not without controversy, since many reject the implications it carries. At the same time, the gradual rise to significance of the concept of sustainable development has shaped many governmental policies, both domestic and foreign, yet remains as contestable.

If we assume that values are part of the puzzle shaping policies, and that values come not only from technocratic policy managers and bureaucratic elites, then we must also consider the impact of possible changes in prevalent assumptions and societal prescriptions. For decades, environmentalists have called for a "paradigm shift" in the way we relate to the environment and one another. Although some, such as Murray Bookchin (1995), have called for a radical reordering of society, most have demanded a new focus that views long-term sustainability as the most important element in designing management strategies, supported by the adoption of specific approaches, such as the precautionary principle.[1] Furthermore, environmentalists have complained often about the lack of political willingness to sacrifice individual state autonomy to pursue such strategies on the international level. Are we reaching an age when environmental awareness and the recognition of the fundamental human right to environmental security are changing the broad outlook of political and corporate leaders?

In short, we do not subscribe to an optimistic answer to this question. Although one can certainly identify much rhetoric leading this way, it is less clear — as many of the preceding chapters have suggested — that significant concrete change is occurring. Nonetheless, Canadians are talking in terms that only a decade ago were confined to the language of peace activists and ecological crusaders. Indeed, one might argue that, if real change is to occur, it will stem not from government regulations, international organizations, or large corporations, but from committed individuals, some of them organized in groups but many not, operationalizing their own definitions of sustainable development and human security. And, although most of this book has focused on governmental policy, we have also emphasized the important role played by non-state actors in the pursuit of both human security and sustainable development in what has come to be termed, somewhat problematically, "civil society." This is another concept we discuss in this chapter, before moving on to a more explicit treatment of spiritual and ethical environmentalism in Chapter 12.

SUSTAINABLE DEVELOPMENT

Ultimately, most practitioners of environmental policy claim they are trying to pursue a path toward *sustainable development*. Since this term is almost omnipresent in the literature and government proclamations today, we should at least discuss it here, reminding the reader that we have dealt at some length with the term in Chapter 9. The Bruntland Commission report, *Our Common Future*, was released in 1987.[2] It helped pave the way toward the important United Nations Conference on Environment and Development (UNCED). The Commission defined sustainable development as "development that meets the needs of the present without compromising the ability of future generations to meet their own needs" (WCED, 1987:43). This is an imprecise statement that asks more questions than it answers. Whose needs are being met? What are the limitations imposed by technology — or by our awareness of the possible harmful effects of technology — when we go about meeting these needs? Will future generations perceive needs as we do presently? A great deal of controversy has surfaced regarding the true meaning, if indeed a universal one can be found, of this term.[3]

Nonetheless, sustainable development survives as the reigning platitude upon which public declarations by government, environmentalists, and even business leaders base their promises and calls for future action. At the very least, a conception of environmentally sustainable development recognizes the interconnectedness of scientific, technological, social, cultural, and economic dimensions. This concept perhaps can engender the necessary interconnection and coordination between various government sectors, particularly those concerned with fulfilling basic needs, alleviating poverty, and conserving the natural resource base; and it gives new-found urgency to the task of coordinating the activities of different governments engaged in the same struggle. It also entails looking at the economics of development in a manner different from the modern, growth-based paradigm, though some have suggested the WCED does little to move us away from this, but merely suggests that we need to share the benefits of this growth.

In his first report to the Government of Canada, the official Commissioner of the Environment and Sustainable Development noted three facets of sustainable development, emphasized earlier in the federal Government's *Guide to Green Government*. These include:

» a *quality of life dimension* that recognizes the role a sound natural environment plays in maintaining Canadian's lifestyle, but also recognizes the importance of the economy to Canadians;

» integrated decision-making, which means involving environmental considerations when pursuing economic objectives; and

» a commitment to equity, involving "the fair distribution of the costs and benefits of development between the rich and the poor, between generations, and among nations." (Canada, CESD, 1997:6)

A close examination of the above statement reveals a very demanding agenda indeed. Point one merely reiterates the importance of economic and trade policy vis-à-vis the environment, though it does suggest that a "sound natural environment" plays a role in maintaining the Canadian quality of life. Point two, however, implies that the first theme is meaningless unless there is an institutionalization of environmental concern; that decision-making become more "integrated" implies that it become more open, accessible, and perhaps accountable. Finally, point three raises the question, troubling to the political right, of equality, and not just between the "rich and the poor" (although it is rather unclear how the benefits of development are to be distributed to the poor), but between "generations, and among nations." The latter inclusion — non-Canadians, by definition — raises questions related to foreign policy and development aid; the former is trade-oriented, the latter has been declining for years.

Critics argue it is not relevant how we break down and access the Canadian government's rhetorical commitments. To many, the term sustainable development means nothing more than "business as usual," and the third point, with its redistributive connotations, was never a serious promise in the first place. Critics point to the proliferation of the use of the term *sustainable development* (SD) among industrial lobbyists and strategists; the international community's wide use of the term in various proclamations which fail to force states to actually change policies; and its adoption by multilateral lending institutions, such as the World Bank, that have chequered histories in the areas of environmental impact assessment. Indeed, some critics argue that the term is self-contradictory. Can "development," as we have come to know it, which is based primarily on overtaking nature, using it, and reconstructing it to serve our ends (this is the *utilitarian* perspective on nature) really be sustainable in the long term? Sharachchandra Lele argues that sustainable development "is being packaged as the inevitable outcome of objective scientific analysis, virtually an historical necessity, that does not contradict the deep-rooted normative notion of development as economic growth. In other words, SD is an attempt to have one's cake and eat it too" (1991:619). There is also a tendency to view the term as purposively misleading, lulling citizens into the false belief that things are being done to benefit the environment in the long-term although, in fact, little is taking place. In short, critics view the term as an erroneous label at best, and a purposefully misleading one at worst.

If we think seriously about the implications of SD, it is a fairly demanding concept. It demands restraint from current activities many value as the producers of wealth, and for the sake largely not of Canadians or others today, but for future generations whom we will never know personally. This may be seen as a great sacrifice in a consumer culture, especially among those without children (or plans to have them). As Edith Brown Weiss argues, it also entails that we accept the concept of group rights, as opposed to individual rights: "Intergenerational planetary rights [are] group rights ... in the sense that individuals hold these rights as groups in relation to other generations — past, present and future" (1993:344). The problem is that there is no universal perception of what the needs of these groups will be; or even, for that matter, what type of environmental problems they will face even if we do little to damage the current ecosystems which sustain us. Beyond this there are many fundamental disagreements about what types of activities merit condemnation or approval.

This controversy can be seen most vividly in discussions and official debates over the question of species extinction. The Convention on International Trade in Endangered Species (CITES), mentioned in Chapter 8, is best viewed as a virtual battleground between participants with contrasting ideological perspectives. On one side were *preservationists*, who hold that nature and wildlife should be preserved in as "pristine" a condition as possible, and that the widespread utilization of (usually select) species should be abandoned in favour of a new environmental ethic. *Conservationists*, however, have no problem with utilization, provided it is not excessive and does not threaten the future of the species (which would make future utilization impossible). These are the two ideal types of the debate.

Most people fall somewhere between the two, favouring some species over others. Polar and panda bears, whales, elephants, gorillas: these "charismatic megavertebrates" tend to stand out as worthy of complete protection, while concern is less concentrated for snail darts, mussels, and the thousands of plant species facing extinction. Although not all these species are found in Canada, Canadians have been very active in lobbying for their protection. The elephant issue has been one of the most controversial, because the mammal has become an icon for preservationists. But there is another reason why the African elephant, in particular, has become such an important issue. International treaties are generally based on the prior principle that states are not to be asked to surrender a considerable amount of their sovereignty, or the ability of state leaders to pursue the policies they wish inside their borders, including what they export to and import from the outside world. A ban on trade, it is argued, curtails this right, demanding that states who might disagree comply voluntarily. Without this compliance, the regime means little more than a congruence of interests. The question is, when push comes to shove, for how long will state leaders be willing to play along? Will they reach a breaking point at which they will trade regardless of the CITES conference? Would the threat of sanctions prevent this? Would the legitimacy of the institution survive the challenge? Beyond the ideological issue that has permeated its personality, CITES is not unlike other international institutions: it is inherently weak, and its legitimacy is both crucial and on permanent probation.

In 1985, CITES established the Ivory Trade Review Group, coordinated by the CITES Secretariat. That year, a general amnesty on illegal ivory stockpiles, designed to flush the market and reduce future illegal shipments, turned disastrous. Prices soared due to unanticipated demand from the rapidly growing economies of Asia. The Trade Review Group found that the African elephant was, indeed, on the way to extinction. Between 1979 and 1989, the number of elephants in Africa underwent a precipitous decline, from roughly 1.3 million to about 625,000. It has been estimated that some 300,000 were killed between 1986-1989 alone; and as the full-grown bulls, with their massive tusks, were killed off, even more younger elephants were taken to produce the same amount of ivory. This outcome was, without question, largely the result of intense poaching. Ivory was selling for as much as $100 (US) per kilogram by the time the Appendix One listing occurred (a listing in Appendix One curtailed almost all legal trade in any products from the species). Shortly after, the price dropped significantly, and poaching became much less common; indeed, elephants began returning to some areas, such as Northern Kenya, where they had been all but eradicated. Lower ivory prices may have increased the domestic consumption of ivory, but this was apparently small in comparison to the foreign demand. The American market, which previously had imported some 12 per cent of the trade, was closed altogether.

To preservationists, the strategy behind the Appendix One listing of the elephant was simple: it would cut off demand. Poaching would make less sense if trade in resultant products was virtually impossible. Naturally, an underground market would survive, but African states that pursued elephant protection in a vigorous manner would be able to ensure the survival of their elephants. Preservationists hoped that, aside from the symbolic victory the ivory ban represented, demand would eventually wither away. Much the same long-term thinking has gone into the moratorium on commercial whaling. By disrupting the market, we can create a potential space for changing attitudes toward wildlife and the environment in general, generating wider acceptance of a particular interpretation of the meaning of sustainable development itself.

The problem with this approach, of course, is that it is representative of urban western environmentalism. Even within Western states there is no consensus: Although some Canadians accept the idea that elephants, whales, seals, bison, and other mammals should not be killed for commercial activity, many do not, especially in rural areas and on the east coast, where a seal fishery has operated for many years. Aboriginals, in particular, reject the idea that organizations such as the International Whaling Commission should have any right to tell them what sustainable development entails. Although attitudes toward nature have shifted in the West (though the degree to which this has taken place is highly controversial), this does not translate into a universal experience. More people in the United States, Canada, and Europe may be sensitive to the plight of elephants and rhinoceros, but what about the people living in Africa, who coexist with these mammals? Should they be prohibited from trading elephant parts, after rescuing the elephant from near-extinction? It is one thing to wax poetic about elephants belonging to us all as part of our common heritage, part of our spirit of oneness with the cosmos. But that doesn't compensate farmers whose livelihood is squashed by a six-ton *Loxodonta africana*, and it doesn't encourage African governments to pay conservation officers that may have to risk their lives to combat poachers.

Conservationists point out that, whether they are killed for ivory or because there isn't enough living space for them to coexist with agriculturists, elephants will be killed unless they are perceived as valuable. Alternative techniques at population control are welcome and hold some promise, though they take us far from the preservationist stance described above. But the essential point that can't be overlooked is that local communities need to be rewarded for their conservation efforts, not punished for them. Clearly, there was widespread opinion in the affected southern African countries that the latter was the case. Similarly, native Canadians and others reliant on fur trapping and sealing consider groups such as the International Fund for Animal Welfare to be cultural imperialists, imposing their own set of values on others. The case of species conservation gives us some idea of how complex the interplay between values, international politics, and trade can be, and demonstrates the difficulty of achieving a consensus on what, exactly, is meant by terms such as sustainable development.[4]

This being said, it is clear that threats to environmental security, from local pollution to global warming, are the result of a path of development adopted by most societies today that stresses the value of industrialization, the mass production of commodities which are sold at home and abroad, and the use of large-scale energy to power the process. In short, the economy generates wealth and environmental threats at the same time. Any attempt to curb the latter will involve regulatory forces that can, at least partially, influence or manage the economy.

ENVIRONMENTAL SECURITY AND NATIONAL SECURITY

Environmental insecurity is caused by resource scarcity. Homer-Dixon identifies three ways humans cause a scarcity of renewable resources. The combination of these three creates environmental scarcity. The first is decreased quality and quantity of renewable resources at higher rates than they are naturally renewed (supply-induced scarcity). The second is increased population growth or per capita consumption (demand-induced scarcity), and the third, unequal resource access (structural scarcity) (Homer-Dixon, 1994). The impact of resource scarcity can be felt as decreased agricultural production, decreased economic productivity, population displacement, and disrupted institutions and social relations. Given the relationship between conflict and resource scarcity, it is clear that environmental security is an important feature of current social, economic, and political trends.

Kaplan (1994) argues that the environment is the national security issue of the early twenty-first century, pointing to the political and strategic impact of surging populations, spreading disease, deforestation and soil erosion, water depletion, air pollution, and, possibly, rising sea levels which could lead to mass migrations and increasing group conflict. Water, he argues, will be in dangerously short supply in areas such as Saudi Arabia, Central Asia, and the southwestern United States. Wars could erupt over access to fresh water and the damming of rivers. People living in low-lying areas will be forced to move if waters rise. This section of the population accounts for more than one billion people or 20 per cent of the world's population (Kaplan, 1994). The natural environment may be considered one of the causes of violent conflict in the southern hemisphere and elsewhere, and should be examined for its potential to cause conflict in other parts of the world.

Environmental security can be understood in different ways. For example, it can refer to environmental degradation as a source of conflict and thus a threat to the security of the state. Environmental security may also refer to impacts of military activities in preparation for war or in the conduct and aftermath of war, or what is more commonly termed *ecocide*. Environmental security may also challenge how we understand the impact of environmental change on the human environment.

The link between environmental insecurity and conflict is complex. Conflicts may arise from resource scarcity (as Kaplan and Homer-Dixon point out), and conflicts also may cause environmental degradation, leading to resource scarcity. Thus, as Thakur notes, environmental factors are catalysts to war whether or not they directly cause war. Since a country's ability to respond to environmental scarcity depends on its capacity to deal with change and its ability to adapt to environmental problems, environmental security is "embedded in the broader social, political and economic context" (Thakur, 1999:53) of that country. This necessitates a wider understanding of the country's capacity to cope and be flexible. Interstate conflict may also be caused or exacerbated by environmental disruption. Many refugees leave their country of origin as a result of environmental disruption that threatens their existence or seriously affects the quality of their life (Terriff, 1994). Examples of such disruptions include earthquakes, avalanches, floods, and drought. Environmental disruptions may undermine one's ability to make a living and pose risks to one's health and well-being. Conflict-oriented disruptions include problems pertaining to destroyed food crops as a war tactic and the presence of landmines in fields and forests upon which people depend for their livelihoods.

Military activities also contribute to environmental insecurity. Examples of military activities and their impact on the environment include scorched earth policies, dumping of toxic chemicals, oil spills, and cutting off the flow of water to certain areas. Terriff argues that destruction of the environment may be a deliberate act and may become a commonly used strategy in future conflicts (Terriff, 1994). The extent to which military personnel and facilities are allocated to monitor environmental change and protect regions from environmental degradation is expected to increase as natural resources dwindle. Protecting these resources is increasingly being taken up by the military.

Understanding environmental security within the context of human security moves the notion of environmental security from a state-centred perspective to the environmental security of humans. Forging a new understanding of environmental security through a human security lens brings people into international discussions and highlights issues and concerns about the safety and environmental security of people, not just territories. The role of the state is still central but the emphasis shifts from protecting the state from environmental insecurities to an emphasis on protecting the citizens from environmental insecurity. The role of the state then becomes geared to ensuring that people have the capacity and opportunities to access resources and to manage or control those resources in a sustainable way. Most importantly, it means that civil society is involved in the decision-making process about how resources are distributed, protected, regenerated, and controlled.

ENVIRONMENTAL SECURITY AS A HUMAN SECURITY CONCERN

One of the most popular of terms emanating from Ottawa today, "human security," is meant to imply a discontinuity with the Cold War era, when national security was the chief concern. Indeed, the construction of the DEW lines, discussed briefly in Chapter 5, was a clear indication of the relative importance both Ottawa and Washington placed on security from attack compared to environmental concerns. Lloyd Axworthy, former Minister of Foreign Affairs, adopted the term "human security" to refer to a foreign policy that emphasizes human rights and factors affecting the quality of life of individuals both at home and abroad. As Tom Keating demonstrates in a recent essay, there is nothing entirely new about a human security agenda in international affairs (2000). What *is* new is the use of the term to describe a foreign policy approach. New issues that were previously kept off the official security agenda include mass migration, transnational crime, disease, overpopulation, underdevelopment, and of course, environmental security.

The shift toward concern with environmental security was the result of several factors: the end of the Cold War, which opened new conceptual vistas; highly publicized disasters, such as the spill of the Exxon Valdez off the coast of Alaska; the realization that resource scarcity would damage even advanced, industrial economies, as Canada learned with the collapse of the eastern fisheries in the early 1990s. These events coincided with a rise in concern about the global nature of ecological issues, moving beyond transborder pollution and resource-sharing questions into the even more complex realm of ozone-layer depletion and global warming. The importance of nonstate actors, both profit-oriented and issue-related, was also increasingly obvious, and represented yet another radical departure from traditional security based on the territorial integrity of a state. For example, multinational corporations (MNCs) fearing the threat of expropriation of their property or "unfair" taxation policies pushed for a Multilateral Agreement on Investment (MAI). NGOs, meanwhile, might define security as protection from arbitrary state arrest or torture, freedom from coerced gender roles, or the avoidance of losing limbs to landmines. The idea of directly linking the environment to security concerns was clearly articulated by Peter Gleick, who identified what he regards as primary environmental threats to security, all relevant to resource studies. Resource acquisitions are strategic goals in themselves, and are often attacked as part of military strategy; resources can be utilized as military tools ("ecosabotage" is gaining currency as a concept, but this category has equally sinister implications for the use of food and water as weapons); and, finally, various disruptions to environmental services, such as water supply, are obvious threats to the well-being of citizens (Gleick, 1991). According to this perspective, it is necessary to view environmental threats within their proper context, as challenges to the national interest, but they can also be seen as threats to a broader conception as well: the interests of humanity itself.

It is not difficult to explain why environmental security is vital. The key to the survival of any species, providing it is not being hunted directly by an overwhelming force, is habitat. Without it, no one can survive (though technological optimists might believe this day will come). During the Cold War, the most direct threat to human habitat in the industrialized states was annihilation by nuclear weapons. Although this threat remains, others, such as global warming, have gained attention. Yet we still see a disregard for environmental security in many areas, perhaps because it is not clearly linked to a sense of identity with habitat itself in the modern era. The need for environmental security, and its correspondence to some image of community, is perhaps much less controversial to the more recently colonized world; in the Canadian case, the Inuit, Cree, and Pacific First Nations all have faced direct threats to their habitat. The threats faced by most

Canadian communities, however, are diffuse in nature, and in many cases are long-term. Nevertheless, it is clear that the flurry of environmental diplomacy in the last two decades, and the close ties between environmental survival and human rights, have at least pushed the environment quite firmly onto the human security agenda.

However, it would be naïve to assume that a shift from a focus on East-West relations has completely changed the foreign policy decision-making environment in Ottawa. The heart of Canadian foreign policy is the promotion of the Canadian economy. This is evident from the Prime Minister's participation in various "Team Canada" excursions designed to solicit business contracts abroad. As Andy Knight points out, the Chretien government has established trade links with China, Vietnam, Myanmar, Thailand, Turkey, Colombia, and other Latin American and Caribbean countries: "This has been done, however, at the expense of global human rights. This being the case, the Liberals have failed to differentiate their foreign policy from that of the Tories" (1997:244). Canada also remains committed to international institutions, such as the International Monetary Fund, which critics charge perpetuate suffering and ecological degradation through their conditional lending policies.

The most recent white paper on foreign policy, *Canada in the World*, makes repeated reference to sustainable development, including a pledge to "ensure that Canadian foreign policy promotes sustainable development globally through the careful and responsible balancing of trade, development and environmental considerations" (36-37).

> The notions of human security and sustainable development are, in my view, closely linked. They are based on the recognition that what happens in our own backyard can have global implications and conversely, that global trends can affect our everyday lives. And they point us ultimately in the same policy directions. (Lloyd Axworthy, DFAIT, 1999a)

The environment, along with basic human needs, women in development, infrastructural services, human rights, democracy and good governance, and private-sector development, remain priorities for development assistance. However, the vast majority of Canadian development projects abroad are in the form of tied aid, which obliges the recipient to spend aid money on Canadian products or expertise. There is also the matter of selective assistance: Beyond emergency aid situations, Ottawa is primarily interested in "developing" the newly emerging markets in southeast Asia and eastern Europe, and in selling CANDU nuclear reactors abroad.

Another controversial facet of the whole human security ideal involves Canadian investment activities abroad. At least three recent events have

brought this to light: Reports suggest that Talisman, Inc., has been sup-
plying the Sudanese government with funds which have been used to carry
out genocide and engage in oil drilling in south Sudan; and two industrial
accidents have occurred with ecological consequences. The more infamous
of the accidents occurred in southern Spain on April 24, 1998, when four
billion litres of toxic waste spilled from a tailings dam at a Canadian-owned
zinc mine. Hundreds of acres of farmland were stained by the sudden flood,
and the company involved, Toronto's Boliden Limited, refused to accept
full responsibility. The other accident occurred when a truck carrying
sodium cyanide up the Tienshin mountain range crashed in Kyrgyzstan.
Again, it was a Canadian-owned gold mining firm, Cameco, that was running the mine and, again, refused to pay compensation to those affected
(there is some dispute as to the extent of damages in question in both
cases). The cyanide fell into the Barskan River, which supplies a local town
with drinking water and eventually runs into Lake Issyk-kal. These cases
tarnish Canada's reputation abroad and challenge the idea that Ottawa is
serious about making Canadian-owned firms behave themselves abroad.

CIVIL SOCIETY

Many argue that if governments and international organizations have a
difficult time implementing polices that support human and environmental security, people will take matters into their own hands and take
actions designed to resist environmental injustice and the spread of globalization. The concept of civil society has a long tradition of interpretation
by many philosophers and political scientists (see Van Rooy, 1998). The
term has become popular today, suggesting that governments and multinational corporations are just part of the story of ecopolitics: groups representing citizens, in Canada and abroad, also play an important role (recall
our discussion of NGOs in Chapter 4). Involving "civil society" in the
broader human security agenda is vital, since individuals and small groups,
taken as a whole, can be an impressive political force.

Indeed, Canada has taken measures to support civil society movements:
CIDA "civil society programming" includes a variety of programs aimed at
strengthening the impact of civil society institutions, such as the National
Council on the Role of Filipino Women; "grandir ensemble" les enfants de
la rue in Haiti; microcredit programs for women in Togo; community
health projects in Bolivia; and other initiatives. There are efforts also to
help foreign NGOs implement sustainable development programs at the
local level, though these NGOs are often closely linked with Western
fundraising operations.

On a critical note, however, there is a discernable tendency to equate NGO activity with civil society, irrespective of the rich philosophical tradition of the latter term. This is problematic not only because it reduces civil society, with all of its complicated and often contradictory impulses and imperatives, to a singular form of representation. It also frees NGOs from much critical evaluation, since they are frequently assumed to be progressive organizations operating independently from the profit motive and out of the grip of the state/capital nexus. Indeed, the vital and progressive work of such actors could be threatened by attaching their role (or place) in world politics to such a vague, even confusing, term. Rather than connoting a truly transformative phenomenon, the term may be decried by opposing forces as merely a decorative mantle adopted by the self-righteous (see Stoett and Teitelbaum, 2000). Critics argue that large-scale NGOs have adapted many of the techniques employed by their enemies in the environmental policy field (see for example Chartier and Deleage, 1998; and Law, 1997). It is also argued that the NGOs' use of the term "civil society," and the attendant assumption that they actually represent such a conceptual political space, opens them to criticisms that they are self-aggrandizing. Yet, as the protests in Quebec City in April 2001 demonstrated, the term has considerable emotive appeal.

International campaigns may attract newspaper headlines, but the objects of the campaigns have every right to question the role of NGOs in the process. Narmada, according to William Fisher, the editor of an excellent collection of essays on the controversial dam construction in India, "became a symbol for the struggle for local autonomy against forced displacement associated with state-directed and internationally funded development" (1995:7). Indeed, NGOs are by necessity often quick to move on to other projects once they have achieved their immediate goals, and this raises problems as well: "… large-scale economic development projects have a unity of identity and a structure of control that makes them ready focal points for local and transnational mobilization to a much greater extent than more incremental or diffuse sources of equally profound and disruptive changes…. The actual consequences of a court victory, a policy change, or cancellation of a project are not necessarily experienced in the same way by the local populace as by more distant NGOs, who can declare the battle over and move on" (Kingsbury, 1999:367-68).

Furthermore, the implication that NGOs hold legitimate claim to the space of political representation is in itself problematic. NGOs engage in activism in a particular sector of concern, although some do combine varied interests with coalition formation. But to argue, as some Western NGOs do, that they represent the voice of those affected by environmental degradation in the southern hemisphere, raises accusations of voice appropriation, hardly what most activists would want to incur.[5] In many cases, such as in Bangladesh, analysts have argued that development NGOS acquire goals that are tightly intertwined with those of the state (White, 1999; Edwards and Hulme, 1996). Funding distribution and competing priorities between NGOS can lead to what one analyst, evaluating their impact in Guatemala's Maya Biosphere Reserve, calls the "Balkanization of the landscape" (see Sundberg, 1998). Of course, it would be mistaken to assume that international financial institutions or, for that matter, United Nations agencies, have any right to claim legitimate representation either. In fact, despite the best of intentions of thousands of their employees, they are constrained by the needs of dominant economic states in what they do and how far they may go in conceptualizing concrete political change.

Whether or not one accepts the centrality of NGOS in the process, there is little doubt that civil society remains an important, if contested, concept in both ecopolitics and local-global relations. It is impossible to conceive of the pursuit of human security without the input of citizens and non-state representatives, whether they belong to labour unions, local conservation organizations, or are the voices of people working in the informal economies of developing states. We need to keep this in mind, because the state — be it Canadian or any other — is not enough. In fact, we need to go one step further here to stress the importance of individual responsibility in the process as well.

CONCLUSION

Environmental protection can take many forms. Individuals make count-less decisions over the course of their lives, and when taken in the aggregate, these decisions have a great impact on environmental health. It is clear also that, as time passes and more and more people become aware of the importance of their actions, they take adaptive measures. For example, recycling programs are a success in some regions of Canada precisely because people have decided to use them, sorting their garbage and refraining from disposing of newspapers and other easily recyclable products. We must keep this individual responsibility in mind when discussing sustainable development and challenge ourselves further to find new solutions beyond recycling. This effort quite likely will involve a new set of values concerning consumer behaviour and the reduction of consumer goods. Furthermore, leaders of the private sector make decisions that influence the level of pollution released into the atmosphere and into rivers and other "sinks"; these decisions are often prompted by governmental regulations, but they may also be taken at the level of individual initiative. In short, it is important to realize that individual responsibility is vital both to sustainable development and to the pursuit of human security.

We claim no sociological insight in this text, and do not even attempt the difficult question of what makes people think the way they do. Certainly, political institutions such as the ones described in this book have an influence, as do other organizations related to people's cultural and religious beliefs. The normative context for decision-making is hard to quantify, and as our discussion on gender issues suggests, even activists disagree about the proper source of people's perspectives. We do, however, outline some of the dominant value systems and their influence on determining environmental ethics in Chapter 12.

NOTES

1 The precautionary principle has been enshrined in many of the international conventions discussed in Chapter 8. It suggests that development projects or large-scale industrial processes should not take place if we are unsure of the outcome.

2 The less formal name, Bruntland Commission, reflected the Chair of the WCED, and the Prime Minister of Norway, Gro Harlem Bruntland.

3 In an important book (written by an economist, in itself an exception) Raymond Mikesell offers a more precise definition: "the maintenance of the natural resource base, including the waste absorptive capacity of the environment, for the use of future generations so that their opportunities to maintain or advance their well being are undiminished" (1992:6). See also the work of Herman Daly (1996).

4 For a more detailed discussion of the CITES/elephants debate, see Stoett, 1997.

5 There are other problems with using the concept of *civil society* in such a self-celebratory manner. One of the contradistinctions it assumes is that, although states are rigidly hierarchical structures (and they certainly are), NGOs are not. Anyone who has worked in an NGO knows this is nonsense, not just within the organizations themselves but, even, among them.

TWELVE

ENVIRONMENTAL VALUES
AND ETHICS

INTRODUCTION

Ecology, a term derived from the Greek work "oikos," meaning "home" or "household," is concerned with the totality of relationships between living organisms and their living (biotic) and non-living (abiotic) surroundings. The word "home" is meant to convey the notion that all components of nature are integral to its functioning, just as the various activities of people in the home are integral to the functioning of the household as a whole. In essence, ecology deals with the interconnections and the balance of nature. However, the term "ecology" has been used by natural scientists to denote a sub-discipline of zoology which examines the totality of relationships between organisms and their environment; humans, not considered organisms, are excluded from such a study. Thus, human beings are viewed by disciplinary ecologists as being "outside nature"; consequently the concept of nature in science carries no ethical value, since various organisms and animals are regarded as morally neutral as molecules, atoms, or objects falling from space. Such a concept of nature places human beings in a position of dominance over nature, and makes it acceptable morally to exploit nature for the "benefit" of humans.

The roots of such a view of nature go back to the times of Bacon and Descartes, which brought into our psyche the amoral view of nature. The scientific image of nature, as developed in the past, meant that nature was purposeless, except to be used by human beings as they saw fit. Any reasoning which placed intrinsic value within nature was considered unthinkable, arbitrary, or false. But when humanity began to realize the significance of environmental crises, particularly after World War II, questions were raised as to whether the prevailing concept of nature was appropriate, and whether we were making a fundamental error in placing our blind faith in science and technology (see, for example, Dwivedi, 1981).

PERSPECTIVES ON HUMAN-NATURE RELATIONS

Humans are a species, albeit the ecologically dominant one in the ecosystem we inhabit. Although we have the same needs as all other species, such as heat, light, water, and food, humans alone possess those attributes that give us dominance over other living species, and thus we are able to compete more successfully than other living creatures. Furthermore, humans have been able to manipulate natural forces in the ecosystem with an intensity unsurpassed by any other living being. This manipulation has given rise to the breakdown of the natural self-protective and self-perpetuating mechanisms that are built into nature, a situation made worse by our belief that we have the right to use the natural environment for our own designs and ends, without consideration for the consequences of our actions to the system. In the Western world, at least, this view has dominated our thinking with respect to the environment and has provided a justification for our actions toward nature and the ecosystem.

The subjugation of nature, along with an emphasis on the use of technology and machines, became the credo of the industrial revolution and the motto of modern humanity, boosted by many scientific discoveries and technological advances. By the 1960s, when journeying to the moon became a reality, it seemed our hegemony over nature and the universe was complete. Many in the West thought there was nothing that science and technology could not solve or achieve. Pollution (but not "environmental crisis") was seen, at least until the late 1960s, as a necessary side-effect of progress which could be prevented and controlled, just as dreaded diseases such as smallpox and the plague had been. It was only in the 1970s that the effects of our activity on the biosphere became obvious, and questions such as the following were raised: Do we have a right to continuously exploit nature in the name of economic development and material progress? Were the belief in our superiority over nature and the myth that we are endowed with an abundance of natural resources the causes of many environmental problems and natural disasters? What are the factors that have influenced our view of nature?

FACTORS INFLUENCING OUR VIEW OF NATURE

Our attitudes toward nature, and how we treat it, depend largely upon certain values, norms, and beliefs which we acquired over the past centuries. These factors can be grouped into four major divisions:

1. A desire to dominate and control nature
2. Acquisitive materialism

3. A blind faith in science and technology
4. An unconstrained growth ethic in a limited world

Much of the blame for fostering such attitudes toward nature lies with these values and attitudes, as well as with institutions (such as laws, regulatory mechanisms, political process, market forces, scientific and professional bodies, and political ideologies) that reinforce such ethics and values. One of the paradoxes of the environmental protection movement is that it seeks solutions to problems from the same institutions which are a part of the problem. For example, we look to scientists and engineers to develop better technologies, thereby increasing our dependence on the "technological fix." We look to lawyers who have favoured the pro-development lobby, cleverly manipulating legal mechanisms and judicial procedures in favour of industrial and business interests. We look to politicians for comprehensive, long-term legislative mechanisms, "knowing full well that the short-term, reactive perspective of the political process impairs their view of the problem" (Emond, 1985:99). We look to economists for better economic plans, not realizing that most are proponents of the philosophy of "acquisitive materialism." Then we blame others for the mess we are in. Each group, be they scientists, engineers, economists, lawyers, business leaders, or others, has come out with its own paradigm of environmental issues and solutions. But the sum total of all the parts does not constitute a complete whole.

There is no doubt that much good has come from the determined and vigorous pursuit of such values by our scientists, technicians, engineers, economists, lawyers, industrialists, and entrepreneurs. In the industrial countries of the OECD people enjoy material benefits not even dreamed of by their ancestors two generations ago. Furthermore, great strides have been made in eradicating disease, and the quality of health care is at an all-time high. The more the West secures a better quality of life for its citizens, the more emulative the policies put in place by the leaders of the Third World. But the same values and attitudes which gave rise to these material benefits and progress also have led to a situation in which the exploitation of nature is taken for granted; the continuation of these pursuits has resulted, and may again result, in dire consequences for humankind, reaching even beyond our planet. Many of these consequences have been documented in the stories of dying lakes, Minimata disease, and cancer deaths.

How, then, can we who inhabit this planet preserve, protect, and sustain the environment while maintaining the benefits thus accrued? How can we lay a foundation for an appropriate relationship with nature? Such a foundation, to be an effective, workable, and comprehensive paradigm, must be based on a holistic approach to the comprehension, study, research, and solution of environmental problems. Such an approach must be built on a paradigm which includes at least the following main components:

» our values and beliefs, which are based on our religions and cultures
» our scientific and technological capabilities, and limits to such innovations
» the pursuit of happiness and material progress
» our governing institutions, legal mechanisms, political processes, and ideologies which condition our socio-economic and cultural behaviour.

Thus, the paradigm for our understanding of environmental behaviour, and thereby the theory of ecology, must be multidisciplinary, multidimensional, and holistic in approach. Consequently, the "reductionist" approach (the opposite of synthesis) which many scientific disciplines use so effectively to advance knowledge in their own jurisdictions cannot be applied to the case of ecology or environmental sciences. As Lynton K. Caldwell so aptly described the problem, "To insist that true science is advanced only by a particular methodology is to unduly narrow the range of the knowledge. Excessive disciplinary conservatism can retard the advancement of knowledge" (1983:250).

We should not assume that basic sciences are not the key to our understanding of environmental problems. On the contrary, our comprehension will not be complete without the foundation stones of the physical and biological sciences; however, the issue is not one of either/or. Basic sciences, as well as other disciplines, are required to fill in the missing links. Thus, a theory of ecology should include all kinds of human knowledge necessary to cover the variety of factors which influence the continuation and further deterioration of our precious environment. We can no longer afford to accept the conventional "protectionist" policy of keeping the study of environmental issues purely a "lab-oriented" discipline. We need to integrate and expand our horizon rather than let it be dominated by a "reductionist" approach and increasing specialization. The suggested integrated approach should not be dismissed as an indeterminate, and hence hard to quantify, method of understanding our relationship with nature, or worse as "overemphasizing the social-cultural" components. The case was ably presented in a MAB (UNESCO) report on human-environment interactions:

> For, we should not pursue our competitive interests in the name of science; rather we should design "a formal structure that will give equal voice not only to different disciplinary approaches to a particular problem, but also to non-scientific approaches among people whose interests are involved." The task of the scientist is, after all, to increase

information and understanding. Policy decisions belong to the political process, which should be informed by science. If scientific research is organized as democratically as we firmly believe the political process should be organized, we would be able finally to see ecological processes in three dimensions: physical, biological and socio-cultural. (UNESCO, 1983:38)

To the above three dimensions, one more must be added — the spiritual/religious. Thus the theory of ecology should include four dimensions: physical, biological, social/cultural, and spiritual.

The Physical and Biological Dimensions

In order to appreciate the physical and biological dimensions of the ecological process, it is desirable to discuss the concept of ecology.

The concept of ecology was introduced in 1868 by a German biologist, Ernst Haechal, in his "Natural History of Creation" (Leiss, 1979:21), as a name for a sub-discipline of zoology that would investigate the totality of relationships between the animal species and the inorganic and organic environments. The prefix "eco" is derived from the Greek word "oikos," meaning "house" or "surroundings." "Logos" refers to "one who speaks in a certain way," or "one who treats of a certain subject." Thus, ecology literally means the relationships between living and non-living organisms, including humans with their surroundings (the environment).

Since Haechal's time, the field of ecology has been broadened to embrace other living organisms, and our relationship with our physical and living environment. The word ecology has also come to be used by various disciplines in different ways and to convey different meanings. John Maddox in his "Doomsday Syndrome" points out that ecology is more of "an attitude of mind" rather than a scientific discipline; Paul Sheppard states that ecology is neither a science nor a study, but the relationship of organisms with their environment. Consequently, in dealing with the relationship of these elements, ecology acts as a way of seeing and thinking across boundaries between them. Others have described ecology as a basic division of biology, specifically concerned with the principles that are fundamentally common to all life (Sheppard, 1971). William Ophuls, quoting from Webster's "Third New International," described ecology from three perspectives:

1. Ecology is a branch of science concerned with the interrelationships of organisms and their environment. This refers to the work of the profes-

sional ecologist (a scientist) who is engaged in the laboratory in trying to understand the laws governing the interactions of organisms with their living and non-living environment.

2. Ecology is the totality or patterns of relations between organisms and their environment. Here, ecology is used in general terms referring to a particular community of living and non-living things. Plants and animals living in the forest, for instance, make up a forest community.

3. Ecology studies the relationship between the human community and its environment. In this case, ecology is referred to as human ecology which is the name given when one person or human kind becomes the central focus. (Ophuls, 1973:3-5)

Since the field of ecology cuts across various natural science disciplines, one discipline cannot cover all the implications inherent in the concept. Furthermore, because of its integrating and synthetic nature, ecology should be regarded more as an approach to a study rather than a study or science in itself. Thus, the essential concept and usually the unit of study in any approach to the study of the interrelationship of living organisms and their environment is the ecological system or ecosystem. The word ecosystem, coined by A.G. Taylor in 1935, comes from two words: "eco" in ecology, and system. Ecosystem refers to the community of living and non-living environments functioning and interacting together as an ecological system. Hence, the ecosystem is formed from two components: one organic — the community of living organisms, including humans, and the other both inorganic and organic — the habitat which supports the community.

From a structural point of view, the ecosystem can be said to be composed of four main components:

1. The organic and inorganic materials — the abiotic environment which includes sunlight, air, and the soil.

2. Autotrophic organisms — grass and other green plants (producers) capable of manufacturing organic from inorganic materials.

3. Heterotrophic organisms — e.g., field mice, snakes, the ants, earthworms in the soil (consumers) who get their energy and nutrients by eating plants and other animals.

4. Saprophytes (decomposers) — which degrade organic materials into organic compounds (feed on dead plants and animals) and break down their complex organic compounds. (Odum, 1963:7)

A good example of this process of a life foodchain in the ecosystem is a dead tree which falls to the ground. The fallen tree creates a shelter, home, and food supply for other living organisms, mice, snails, worms, beetles, snakes, birds, and, possibly, humans. As the dead tree crumbles into humus, seemingly disappearing into oblivion, its life-giving elements return to the earth that gave it birth. In this way, its cycle of life is ready to begin again.

From the foregoing analysis, a fundamental principle stands out. A common thread of interdependence runs through all constituent parts of the ecosystem — humans as well as other organisms — an indication that nothing (including humans) stands alone in an ecosystem. In other words, no species in the ecosystem lives in isolation from other species; nor can they live apart from their physical and biological environment (although migration, hibernation, or dormancy are adaptive mechanisms that help organisms avoid intolerable environmental stresses).

As mentioned earlier, humanity is the dominant species in the ecosystem which we inhabit. Although we are affected by the same environmental conditions such as heat, light, water, and food and the activities of other organisms, we possess two attributes which place us over and above other living species. First, we can compete more successfully than other living organisms for the essentials of life. Secondly, we can exert a greater influence on the habitat in which we live and hence on other associated living components.

These attributes have contributed to our ability to manipulate natural forces in the ecosystem with an intensity that goes far beyond those attainable by any other living being. This intrusion of humans into the ecosystem gives rise to the breakdown of natural mechanisms built into nature (i.e., the ecosystem) for self-protection and self-renewal. The situation is aggravated further by our view that we can manipulate, command, or conquer the natural environment according to our own design and ends without consideration for the consequences to the system, as long as our own species is not overly harmed. In shaping such an attitude toward nature and the ecosystem, our greatest allies have been science and technology.

The Dimension of Science and Technology

Francis Bacon asserted that it was a duty of humans to regain our rights over nature, assigned to us in the beginning by God, and to secure dominion over nature. His writings exerted a profound influence on the belief that the power of science and technology can improve the human condition. In his utopian work, *New Atlantis* (published in 1624), he described a science-oriented community on an imaginary island where science and technology were pursued not so much as ends in themselves but to subdue and improve nature to meet human demands. He would not permit nature to be left on its own because of his firm belief that "the secrets of nature betray themselves more readily when tormented by art than when left to their own course" (see his *Novum Organum*). Bacon was the first to stress the need for experimental science instead of purely intellectual philosophical discussions of natural phenomena. Bacon's dream was a science-based technology whereby applied scientists would replace craftsmen. In the spirit of the "Idea of Progress" — a philosophy which later became popular in the eighteenth century in the West — Bacon was convinced that, through science, humans could extend their power over the universe. Consequently, Bacon advocated the restoration to humanity of our original dominion over nature, and such restoration was to come through science.

Two major developments took place as a result of Bacon's new science-based technological scheme. First, his teachings led to the formation of the Royal Society, whose fellows (members) set out to investigate not only new patents but followed a specified program of practical applications of science, such as the search for an engine to drain mines which led to the discovery of a practical steam engine (Forbes, 1968:20). In addition, Bacon influenced others who expanded his theme. First to take the lead was Descartes, who agreed with Bacon's objectives but rejected his religious approach — "that God has created all things for man" on the grounds that "an infinitude of things exist or did exist which have never been of any use of man." Instead, Descartes's emphasis was on the scientist-technologist approach, making free use of nature which was created to serve humanity. Another scientist, Isaac Newton, also taking direction from Bacon, placed all of nature under the laws of mathematics, and developed a "mechanical view of nature which dealt exclusively with material in motion since this was the only thing that could be measured through the application of mathematics." In keeping with the image of a machine, the Newtonian model was essentially atomistic and reductionistic in its outlook and appraisal of both humans and the universe. It promised a world that could best be comprehended in terms of so many particles of matter in motion. "The new science promised the transformation of man himself into the measurable and manipulative parts of the great machine ... Man was expelled from the centre of the stage — from the active part in the drama — to a seat in the audience and the passive role of spectator." The full meaning of this tableau was that humans had disappeared as *subject* and reappeared in the world as *object*.

> Thus nature gets credit for what in truth should be reserved for ourselves; the rose for its scent, the nightingale for its song, and the sun for its radiance. The poets are entirely mistaken. They should address their lyrics to themselves ... Nature is a dull affair, soundless, scent-

less, colourless, merely the hurrying of material, endlessly, meaning-
lessly. (Whitehead, 1925:56)

The dualism inherent in the Western world-view (that is, separating
human beings from nature and placing them above nature) found further
expression in the mechanistic paradigm with its separation of facts and
values. However, with the advent of Baconian, Galilean, and Newtonian
science from the seventeenth century onward, came the radical view that
the world of nature was to be regarded as being essentially value-free,
devoid of intrinsic worth, to be used by humans as they saw fit. Thus,
beginning in the seventeenth century, empiricism, together with the separation of facts and values, became the intellectual orthodoxy in the development of modernity. The new scientific attitude, particularly from the 18th
century onward, was "to deprive nature of its carefully guarded secrets, to
leave it no longer in the dark to be marvelled at as an incomprehensible
mystery but to bring it under the light of reason and to analyze it with all its
fundamental forces." Caroline Merchant contends that the development of
modernity went hand in hand with the de-animization and hence the
"objectification" of nature (Merchant, 1995). As a consequence, nature came
to be regarded no longer as a "thou" but as an "it" — to be exploited by
humans for their use. This view was sometimes taken to its absurd end
when colonizers conquering new lands considered inhabitants ("natives") as
dumb animals to be "subdued." Thus, subjugation of nature, along with a
primary emphasis on the use of machines, became the credo of the industrial revolution and the motto of modern humanity, aided by scientific discoveries and technological advances. By the middle of the twentieth
century, when the horrors of World War II were fading, and our journey to
the moon was to become a reality — an epitome of scientific and technological prowess — humanity's hegemony over nature and the universe was
complete and unquestioned. It was thought by many in the West that there
was no problem science and technology could not solve. Hence, pollution
was seen, at least until the early 1960s, as a side-effect of progress, which
could be prevented in the same manner as dreaded diseases such as the
plague and smallpox. It was only in the 1970s that the impact of human
activities which threatened the biosphere came to be properly appreciated,
thereby raising the possibility that the separation of humans from nature,
and facts from values, could endanger our existence if we continued to
believe in the myth of a "superabundance" of natural resources, and in the
idea of perpetual progress at the cost of continuous exploitation of nature
and the domination of the universe. Such beliefs, values, and attitudes,
which gave rise to the present state of environmental crisis, based on our

cultural and religious heritage, became an important and integral part of our understanding of the environment.

The Cultural and Religious Dimension

Our present social ethic places emphasis on nature or the environment as serving humankind and contributing to the progress of human beings. Human beings in the West have traditionally dominated and used the environment for their own goals and prosperity. No doubt this ethic has contributed greatly to our material advancement and improved quality of life, but it has also encouraged acquisitive materialism. Furthermore, one of the major problems associated with our present social ethic is that nature's overall importance has been ignored because of our view that nature is there for us to exploit. Is it not ironic that, although we stress interpersonal relationships, our relationship to nature is dismissed cursorily? That Western culture dominates the world is an understatement. There is no part of the world not influenced by it. The countervailing forces of other cultures and religions have been ineffective against pervasive Western influence. At the same time, the West has demonstrated high awareness of environmental problems. Scientists and professionals in the West have documented and projected trends for environmental destruction, although the information is incomplete since not all destruction is readily apparent. Nevertheless, "as the twentieth century passes, mankind … has achieved such a degree of dominance throughout the world that this assault on the environment is fraught with unknown consequences" (Morse, 1975:11). Forms of destruction with wide-reaching environmental consequences include the deterioration and loss of resources needed for agriculture, water pollution, the deforestation of tropical forests, declining air quality, the risk of radioactive contamination, and wildlife extinction.

CAN RELIGION PROVIDE AN ANSWER?

World religions can provide a foundation for moral guidelines towards environmental preservation and conservation. Environmental ethics were propounded in the past but generally have been disregarded until now even by some Oriental religions which exhorted non-injury to other living-beings. These beliefs can be integrated into a new universal concept based on the partnership-cum-stewardship ethic, which stands for holding of the land (including its trees, rivers, mountains, and minerals) in trust for God and for the general benefit of humankind. If we believe we are the trustees of the universe, we are authorized to use natural resources, but hold no divine power of control over nature and its elements. Hence, from the perspective of many world religions, abuse and exploitation of nature for immediate gain is unjust, immoral, and unethical. In the ancient past, Hindus and Buddhists were careful to observe such moral tenets. In their culture, not only common people but even rulers and kings followed ethical guidelines and tried to create an example for others. However, the twentieth century and its materialistic orientation have affected the cultures of countries such as India, Sri Lanka, Thailand, and Japan which have witnessed the wanton exploitation of the environment by their own people despite strictures and injunctions inherent in their religions and cultures. Thus, no culture and no part of the world is immune from the exploitation of nature, and in the process we are destroying ourselves and our progeny. What can be done?

It has been demonstrated, even in those countries of the West where secularism and religious toleration is practised, that religion can be both a powerful partner and a sobering aid in defusing explosive issues and can enhance positive attitudes toward other issues. Religion can evoke awareness of that dimension of the human personality which is not affected by scientific or technological reasoning. In creating the appropriate awareness, religion helps us to realize that there are limits to our control over the animate and inanimate world, and that our arrogance and manipulative power over nature can backfire. Religion tells us that a person's life cannot be measured by material possessions, and that the ends of life go beyond consumption. Thus, religion provides at least three fundamental strengths for human beings surrounded by a technological society. First, it defends the individual's existence against the depersonalizing tendencies of the techno-industrial process. Secondly, it forces people to recognize human fallibility, thus combining realism with idealism, helping us to be more cautious of our errors which have resulted in catastrophic consequences in the past. Thirdly, when technology gives us power to destroy ourselves, it is religion which provides restraint, humility, and liberation from self-centredness. Thus, religion can be a source of individual as well as social transformation.

Two major trends can be discerned in studying the influence of six major religions of the world on people's attitudes and beliefs with respect to nature. Three Oriental religions (Hinduism, Buddhism, and Taoism) emphasize the sanctity and sacredness of all God's creations, thereby defining people as a part of the nature without special rights. Three other religions (Judaism, Christianity, and Islam) impel humanity's desire to dominate and use nature for its purposes. Zoroastrianism perhaps provides a bridge between these two trends in religious thinking. However, one finds contrary practices and emerging thoughts in both Oriental and Occidental religions. Demands are now made in the West to protect nature and preserve it for future generations, and in the Orient instances of wanton destruction of the environment are on the rise. Thomas Derr deftly makes this point:

> ... if ecological disaster is a particularly Christian habit, how can one explain the disasters non-Christian cultures have visited upon their environments? Primitive cultures, Oriental cultures, classical cultures — all show examples of human domination over nature which have led to ecological catastrophe. Overgrazing, deforestation and similar errors of sufficient magnitude to destroy civilizations have been committed by Egyptians, Assyrians, Romans, North Africans, Persians, Indians, Aztecs, and even Buddhists who are foolishly supposed by some Western admirers to be immune from this sort of thing. (Derr, 1975:43)

Obviously, modern humans, irrespective of their cultural background and religious beliefs, have found a rationalization to disrupt, exploit, and destroy the environment. Consequently, what we need is a strategy, a theory of ecology with an appropriate philosophy of life, a theoretical foundation to protect our common heritage and the universe (Dwivedi, 1997a).

World religions, each in their own way, offer a unique set of moral values and rules to guide humanity's relationship with the environment. Many religions, compared to secular laws and institutions, provide sanctions and offer stiffer penalties (although after death) for those who abuse the environment. Although the traditional religions have been unable to protect the environment from human greed and exploitative tendencies aided and abetted by technology, these religions *in their own right* can be helpful. A synthesis emerging from them could become a foundation for preventing further degradation and thus become our salvation from the environmental crisis.

THE GREENING OF WORLD RELIGIONS

The World Commission on Environment and Development, reporting in 1987, realized at the beginning of its task that a look across cultural, economic, and historical barriers was essential and that there was a need to appreciate different perspectives and influences which affect our understanding of the forces of nature. Thus, the Commission concluded it was desirable to build a common framework and action plan to communicate across the divides of world cultures, religions, and regions. Therefore, after identifying sources of environmental stresses and interlocking crises, it recommended endeavours for managing the commons and for making efforts to secure peace, environmental quality, and sustainable development. The Commission conceded that "Our cultural and spiritual heritages can reinforce our economic interests and survival imperatives" (WCED, 1987:1). However, the Commission left it to individuals and nations to develop such ethical principles. We take the view that world religions can be one of the key sources for developing such principles for environmental protection.

Three Mainstays

To repeat, each religion and culture provides at least three fundamental mainstays to help human beings cope in a technological society. First, it defends the individual's existence against the depersonalizing effects of the techno-industrial process. Secondly, it forces us to recognize human fallibility, combining realism with idealism, and helps the individual to be more cautious of the errors that have resulted in the catastrophes of the past. Thirdly, while technology gives the individual the physical power to destroy, religion gives us moral strength to grow and provides restraint, humility, and liberation from self-centredness. Directly or indirectly, religion can be a powerful source for environmental protection and conservation. We know that modern peoples, irrespective of their cultural backgrounds or religious beliefs, have been able to justify the disruption, exploitation, and destruction of the environment. Thus, we require a framework, an action plan perhaps, in the form of a code of conduct which includes the powerful influence of religions, and draws from various religious and cultural traditions. Any framework relating to environmental conservation and sustainable development that ignores the role of morality and ethics in shaping our attitudes towards nature will remain unbalanced.

An appreciation and understanding of Canada's spiritual dimension is important in addressing complex issues such as the importance of spirituality in a secular world, the search for spirituality, the relationship between church and state, addressing moral issues in a secular world without religion as a guide, and the Judeo-Christian foundation of Western culture and social life.

Each religion and culture has something to offer to the promotion of conservation and environmental protection. From each, injunctions or exhortations can be brought forth to form a code for environmentally sound and sustainable development. No religion says that we have the right to destroy our habitat and creation; no religion sanctions environmental destruction. On the contrary, penalties and admonitions are provided for those who do so. This is amply demonstrated in the views of the nine religions which are followed by the majority of people in the world: Zoroastrianism, Judaism, Christianity, Islam, Hinduism, Buddhism, Jainism, Sikhism, and Baha'i (Dwivedi, 1994:31-78). Other religions hold a similar view about respect for nature and for God's creation.

Zoroastrianism

Zoroastrianism is one of the oldest religions on earth. It was founded by Zarathustra, who lived around 1400-1200 BCE.

> For Zarathustra, the creation of the world was an act of sublime goodness by a sublimely good and omniscient God, Mazda Ahura, and the means by which He would ultimately defeat the Evil One at the end of the world when the living would be raised from the dead. Humanity was created and placed on earth to assist in this defeat — if we choose to do so. Our role in the battle is to live fruitfully upon the earth preserving life, the creation of God, against death and destruction which was introduced by the Evil One. (New Road, 1991:1)

One of the great strengths of the Zoroastrian faith is that it emphasizes caring for the physical world more than the spiritual world. It is through an awareness of the physical world that a Zoroastrian seeks spiritual salvation. Since humanity is the purposeful creation of Mazda Ahura, the wise Lord, the task for human beings is to promote and maintain an equilibrium between the seen and unseen worlds. Therefore, in Zoroastrian theology, the physical and spiritual worlds complement each other. Such dualism, in its proper context, is a crucial theme for an ecologist who seeks a balance that involves the promotion and conservation of the world. This balance is fostered by the Good Spirit, whereas a lack of ecological concern results in the destruction of our habitat and is clearly the work of evil.

The Zoroastrian use of the elements of nature is evident in the disposal of human remains in a Tower of Silence. This traditional Zoroastrian method of disposal of the dead is cheap, hygienic, and above all, ecologically sound. A limited amount of space is used by way of the "tower," and no natural resources are wasted or polluted when this disposal method is used. The body is exposed to the sky and sun. The pollution of the earth, the desecration of fire, or the sullying of waters are not compatible with the beliefs and practices of the faith.

One of the important duties of a Zoroastrian is to look after the seven creations of the skies, waters, earth, plants, cattle, humans, and fire. Purity and cleanliness are forms of caring for these creations, for "whosoever has learned the care of all these seven, acts and pleases well, his soul never comes into the possession of Ahriman and the demons" (West, 1880:373). Thus, caring for the creations is basic ecology for Zoroastrians, and nothing impure should contaminate the seven creations. Zoroastrians have special short prayers which are recited to maintain the purity of every creation: "I invoke the holy world made by Mazda Ahura, I invoke the earth made by Ahura, the water made by Mazda and the holy trees. I invoke the sea, I invoke the beautiful heaven (sky), I invoke the endless and sovereign light" (Darmesteter, 1880:214). This is ecology in the form of spiritual reverence for the seven creations.

For over 3000 years, Zoroastrians have been nature-conscious in their thoughts, words, and deeds. This reverence for the seven creations through prayer and worship is central to the belief of Zoroastrians.

Judaism

There is an ethical theme in Judaism that lays a foundation of caring and consideration for other life forms. For example, there are injunctions that call for mercy (*rahmanut*), humility (*anivat*) and caring (*gemilut hasidim*). While these injunctions apply to human beings, in "Biblical times, it seems that these characteristics also applied to our relationships with other animals, and with the land. The Talmud asks, `Why was man created on the last day? So that, when pride takes hold of him, he can be told: God created gnat before you'" (Wyman, 1991:11). Jews were warned, as stated in *Kohelet Rabbah*: "Do not corrupt or destroy My world; for if you do, there will be no one to set it right after you" (7:13). The ultimate proprietor of the world is God alone. In the words of the Talmud, "God acquired possession of the world and apportioned it to humanity, but God always remains the master of the world" (*Rosh Ha-Shanah* 31a).

In the Talmud it is written (Shabbat 151b) that heaven rewards the person who has concern and compassion for the rest of creation. In Genesis (2:19), Adam named all of God's creatures, and swore to live in harmony with those whom he had named. Thus, at the very beginning of time, man and woman accepted responsibility for all of creation before God (Hertzberg, 1986). Furthermore, the festivals of the Jewish religion call upon the faithful to stand before God in awe at His majesty, and trembling before His judgments. The festivals joyfully celebrate the cycle of the seasons of nature. The rabbis insisted that "He who has denied himself any one of the rightful joys of the world is a sinner" (Baba Kama 9lb). The highest form of obedience to God's commandments is to perform them not in mere acceptance, but in the nature of union with Him. The very rightness of the world is affirmed in such a joyous encounter between humans and God. The encounter of God and humanity in nature is thus conceived in Judaism as a seamless web, with humanity as the leader and custodian of the natural world.

While it may be said that under Jewish tradition, the world was created essentially for human benefit, Jewish concern for the environment, as stated by Rabbi Troster, is "fundamentally utilitarian: human beings must preserve, protect and not squander the environment, in striving to attain the goal of creating the Kingdom of God upon earth. Nature is precious as a creation of God; it is not sacred in and of itself" (Troster, 1991:17).

Christianity

There is a common thread of thought found in both the Old Testament and the New Testament concerning the concept of nature and the rules governing our responsibility to nature (Veeraraj, 1989). In the case of Christianity, although certain verses from Genesis (1:26 and 1:28) have been interpreted as giving humanity dominion over nature, there are places where the responsibility of human beings has been clearly defined. For example, Genesis (2:15) says: "And the Lord God took the man and put him into the Garden of Eden to dress it and keep it." The word "dress" has been interpreted as the duty of humans to manage, and the word "keep" has been interpreted as the second duty, to protect from harm. Furthermore, the scripture clearly establishes God as the sole owner of the natural world, while humanity is actively responsible for the care of the world: "The earth is the Lord's, and everything in it, the world, and all who live in it" (Psalm 24:1), and "Every animal in the forest is mine, and the cattle on a thousand hills" (Psalm 50:10). Furthermore, we are advised that we have no rightful ownership over the land "because the land is mine, and you are but aliens and my tenants."

The New Testament provides instructions on stewardship and the consequences of not carrying out the stewardship role in accordance with scriptural teachings. The key instruction is that people must be faithful to use and put to work that which God has entrusted to them and act as His steward "... as servants of Christ and stewards of the mysteries of God. Moreover it is required of stewards that they be found trustworthy" (1 Corinthians 4.1 and 2). But this is done with the sole purpose of honouring God and glorifying His gift of creation (1 Corinthians 6:20). People are accountable for their stewardship role in Christianity. Thus, the Christian religious tradition prescribes a good working and harmonious relationship between humanity and nature.

One of the first assumptions of the Bible is that God is the creator of the whole universe, and that all the world is God's creation. Its continuity and preservation are completely dependent upon God's mercy. Similarly, human beings, who are part of God's creation, are dependent upon Him for their lives and survival. In this respect, the Bible does not make a distinction between the two categories of "the world of nature" and "the world of human beings." Creation unites both humanity and the world of nature; furthermore, it brings in the divine as an integral part of this system. Interpreted in this manner, creation is a viable, ongoing cosmic community — a community made up of God, humanity, and the rest of world. The doctrine of creation teaches us that the whole of creation is a sacred gift because God creates, sustains, and preserves all things, both animate and inanimate. In this regard, humanity does not differ from the rest of God's creation.

The Bible also confirms that the purpose of creation is to proclaim God's glory because it is His handiwork (Psalm 19:1). Divine life is actively manifested in and through the created world. As such, the earth is not to be considered a lifeless entity or a means to some higher end. To an extent, a triadic harmonious relationship is considered to exist: between the divine and humanity, among human beings themselves, and between human beings and nature. Thus, any failure to maintain this harmony may alienate humanity from its creator and also from nature. Because, as the Lord said, "I am the Alpha and the Omega, the first and the last, the beginning and the end" (Revelation: 22:13). Consequently, every part of the creation has His divine hand in it; no human being has an absolute right to destroy it. Perhaps it is this view which impelled St. Francis of Assisi to be respectful of all creatures, and call them his brothers and sisters. In his personal relationship with all creatures, St. Francis recognized his duty to reciprocate divine love with love and praise, not only in the name of creatures, but also through them. It is from this perspective that Father Lanfranco Serrini, Minister General, OFM, Rome, said: "All human effort in the world must therefore lead to a mutual enrichment of man and creatures" (Serrini, 1986).

Islam

In Islam, the Holy *Qur'an* and the divinely-inspired word of Prophet Muhammad establish the foundation of and the rules for the conservation of nature (Mekouar, 1984; Rafiq and Ajmal, 1989). The Qur'anic message is one of unity, harmony, balance, and order. The *Qur'an* stresses that nature's laws must be observed, and that limits should not be exceeded. Humanity was created in the universe so that we could become a manifestation of divine attributes, and should serve as a mirror to reflect the beautiful image of God. The *Qur'an* says:

> Surely, your Lord is Allah, who created the heavens and the earth in six periods ... His is the creation and its regulations ... (*Qur'an* 7:54) ... And there is not a thing, but we have unbounded stores there of and we send it in regulated quantities (*Qur'an* 15:21). We have created everything in due measure. (*Qur'an* 54:49)

Thus, everyone has to observe the balance, and acknowledge that certain limits must not be exceeded. In other words, humanity has only a guardianship role (the role of vice-regent) in God's heaven and earth, and not a position of outright ownership; and this guardianship brings with it certain obligations. Because no other creatures were able to perform the task of guardianship, God entrusted humans with the duty of vice-regent, a duty so onerous and burdensome that no other creature would accept it: "Lo! We offered the trust unto the heavens and the earth and the hills, but they shrank from bearing it and were afraid of it, and man assumed it" (*Surah* 33:72). That is why, according to the Islamic view of the ideal environment, alteration of God's creation is not permissible. The *Qur'an*, in a suggestive and meaningful verse (Qur'an 47:15), says:

> A picture of the Garden which is promised to those who are safeguarded (against evil). Therein are rivers of water unpolluted and rivers of milk whose flavour changeth not, and rivers of wine, delicious to the drinkers, and rivers of clear run honey. Therein for them are all kinds of fruits with protection from their Evolver, Nourisher and Sustainer.

Punishment for disrupting the delicate balance of nature is given in the *Qur'an* and in the sayings of the Prophet. The basic essence of punishment is accountability before God after death. Iqtidar Zaidi quotes from the Holy *Qur'an* to substantiate this point concerning humanity's interaction with the environment:

> Unto Allah (belongeth) whatsoever is in the heavens and whatsoever
> is in the earth, and whether ye make known what is in your minds or
> hide it, Allah will bring you to account for it. He will forgive whom
> He will and He will punish whom He will. Allah is able to do all
> things. (Zaidi, 1981:41)

The Islamic ethic holds that humanity does have a choice in our interaction with nature. People have been given the intellect and the ability to
reason to decide what is just and unjust, what is right and what is wrong.
Accordingly, to do good and act justly is to mirror God's desire on earth,
while to do wrong and to be unjust is to mirror Satan's desire on earth.
People should realize that their stay on earth is temporary. They all shall
have to face the day of judgment. If they choose to pollute the environment and do harm to living creatures for earthly comforts, the believers in
the Holy *Qur'an* will face a terrible end: a hell from which there will be no
escape, as well as the denial of a place in heaven in the life hereafter.

In Islamic environmental ethics, the "vice-regent" is one who exercises
delegated power on behalf of a greater authority. It is instructive to look at
what the *Qur'an* has to say about how and why humanity was created:

> Behold, your Lord said to the angels: "I will create a vice-regent on
> Earth." They said: "Will You place there one who will make mischief
> there shed blood, while we celebrate Your praises and glorify Your
> Holy Name?" He said, "I know what you do not know." And He
> taught Adam the nature of all things: then He placed before the
> Angels and said: "Tell Me the nature of these if you are right." They
> said: "Glory to You of Knowledge. We have none, except what You
> have taught us." (*Surah* 2:30-32)

Finally, in the eyes of Islam, the riches of the earth are a common heritage. All may benefit from them, make them productive, and use them for
their well-being and improvement. Therefore, our quest for progress and
development must not be detrimental to the environment; instead, it
should ensure conservation (Rafiq and Ajmal, 1989:135). The *Qur'an* is clear
on this point: "And commit not disorders on the earth after it hath been
well ordered" (7:56). Any disorder leading to pollution, deterioration, or
harmful alteration to the environment is considered in Islam as *Fasad*; it is
the duty of all Muslims to respect the God-created environment.

Both in the *Qur'an* and in the Shariah, the legal codes of Islam, the
rights of the natural world are strongly expressed and the abuse of them by
humanity is condemned. The *Qur'an* says: "He set on the Earth, firmly

rooted, mountains rising above it, and blessed the Earth and provided sustenance for all, according to their needs."

Regarding conservation of the environment, it is believed that all the individual components of the environment were created by God, and that all living things were created with different functions that were carefully measured and meticulously balanced by the Almighty Creator. Although the various components of the natural environment serve humanity as one of their functions, this does not imply that human use is the sole reason for their creation. In this respect, the central concept is *tawheed* (the unity of God); Allah is Unity, and His Unity is reflected in the unity of mankind and nature. Furthermore, His trustees have been made responsible for maintaining the unity of His creation, the integrity of earth, including its flora, fauna, wildlife, and the natural environment. Thus, the environment is not in the service of the present generation alone. Rather, it is the gift of God to all ages — past, present, and future. This message can be found in *Surah* 2:29: "He it is Who created for you all that is in the earth." The word "you" as used here refers to all persons, with no limit as to time or place. Thus, any disorder leading to pollution or deterioration of the environment is considered *Fasad* in Islam.

Hindu Religion

In the Hindu religion, one finds a most challenging perspective being offered on the subject of respect for nature and environmental conservation: the principle of the sanctity of all life on this planet and elsewhere is clearly ingrained in this religion. Only the supreme God has absolute sovereignty over all creatures, including humanity's life and death: human beings have been given no absolute dominion over our own lives or over non-human life. Consequently, people cannot act as viceroys of God over the earth, nor can they assign degrees of relative worth to other species. The sacredness of God's creation demands that no damage be inflicted on other species without adequate justification. Therefore, all lives, human and non-human, are of equal value, and have the same right to existence.

According to Hindu scriptures, people must not demand or take dominion over other creatures (Dwivedi, 1997b). They are forbidden from exploiting nature; instead, they are advised to seek peace and live in harmony with nature. The Hindu religion demands veneration, respect, and obedience to maintain and protect the natural harmonious unity of God and nature. This is demonstrated by a series of divine incarnations, as enunciated by Dr. Karan Singh in the Assisi Declaration:

The evolution of life on this planet is symbolized by a series of divine incarnations beginning with fish, moving through amphibious forms and mammals, and then on into human incarnations. This view clearly holds that man did not spring fully formed to dominate the lesser life forms, but rather evolved out of these forms itself, and is therefore integrally linked to the whole of creation. (Singh, 1986)

All the Hindu scriptures attest to the belief that the creation, maintenance, and annihilation of the cosmos is completely up to the Supreme Will. In the *Gita*, Lord Krishna says to Arjuna: "Of all that is material and all that is spiritual in this world, know for certain that I am both its origin and dissolution. And is under Me. By My will it is manifested again and again and by My will, it is annihilated at the end" (*Gita*, 9:8). Furthermore, the Lord says: "I am the origin, the end, existence, and the maintainer (of all)" (*Gita*, 9:17-18). Thus, for Hindus, God and *Prakriti* (nature) are one and the same.

The Hindu belief in the cycle of birth and rebirth, wherein a person may come back as an animal or a bird, means not only that Hindus give other species respect, but also reverence. This provides a solid foundation for the doctrine of *ahimsa* — non-violence (or non-injury) toward animals and human beings alike. Hindus have a deep faith in the doctrine of non-violence. It should be noted that the doctrine of *Ahimsa* presupposes the doctrines of *Karma* and rebirth (*punarjanma*) (Dwivedi, 1995). The soul continues to take birth in different life forms such as birds, fish, animals, and humans. Based on this belief, there is a profound opposition in the Hindu religion (as well as in Buddhist and Jain religions) to the institutionalized killing of animals, birds, and fish for human consumption. Almost all the Hindu scriptures place emphasis on the notion that God's grace can be received by not killing his creatures or harming his creation: "God, Kesava, is pleased with a person who does not harm or destroy other non-speaking creatures or animals" (*Vishnupurana* 3.8.15). The pain a human being causes other living beings to suffer will eventually be suffered by that person, either in this life or in a later rebirth. It is through the transmigration of the soul that a link is provided between the lowliest forms of life and human beings.

Many trees and plants were worshipped during the time of Rig Veda because they symbolized the various attributes of God. Later, during the Puranic period, a popular belief emerged that each tree had its own deity; thus people offered water and circled trees with sacred threads. These rituals gave protection to trees and plants. Through such exhortations and various writings, the Hindu religion provided moral guidelines for environmental preservation and conservation. From the perspective of Hindu culture, the abuse and exploitation of nature for selfish gain is considered unjust and sacrilegious.

Buddhism

The very core of Buddhist religion revolves around an attitude of compassion, respect, tolerance, and *ahimsa* (non-injury) toward every human being as well as toward all other creatures who share this planet (Tripathi and Bhante, 1989). This is exemplified in a Metta-Suttam prayer:

> As the mother protects her child even at the risk of her own life, so there should be mutual protection and goodwill which is limitless among all beings. Let limitless goodwill prevail in the whole world — bove, below, all around, untarnished with any feeling of disharmony and discord. (Kassap, 1959)

Buddha also set down rules forbidding pollution of water in rivers, ponds, and wells. Buddha says in *Sutta-Nipata*:

> Know ye the grasses and the trees ... Then know ye the worms, and the different sorts of ants ... Know ye also the four-footed animals small and great ... the serpents ... the fish which range in the water ... The birds that are borne along on wings and move through the air ... (Kabilsingh, 1987:14)

Monks are forbidden to cut down trees; all of them know the story of the monk who cut a tree's main branch. The spirit of that tree complained to Buddha that by cutting down the branch, the monk has cut off his child's arms. The monk was appropriately punished. As the above verse from *Sutta-Nipata* illustrates, animals are not to be harmed by Buddhists. While humans are higher beings, they are still a part of nature. Their disregard or abuse of the laws of nature could result in disasters.

Buddhists regard survival of all species as an undeniable right because as co-inhabitants of this planet, other species have the same right of survival that human beings enjoy. Whatever people do, their *karma* will follow them; because there is always a co-relationship between cause and effect. Consequently, any human endeavour which is undertaken through ignorance or capriciousness brings suffering and misery. But a positive attitude causes happiness and peace. Buddhism is a religion of love, understanding, and compassion, and is committed to the ideal of non-violence. As such, it attaches great importance to the conservation and protection of the environment. Universal compassion, non-violence, love, and service to others are attributes of Buddhism which are needed *now* in order to protect the environment and save our common future.

In Buddhism, the rivers, forests, grass, mountains, and night are highly respected and regarded as bliss bestowers. Buddhist thinkers have always had great respect for the sun, moon, and other planets. They have recognized grasses, creepers, and herbs as bestowers of bliss and objects of adoration. In Metta-Sutta a prayer is offered in the following words:

> Let there be mutual protection and limitless goodwill among all beings. Let limitless goodwill prevail in the whole world — above, below, all round, untarnished with any feeling of disharmony and discord. (Kassap, 1959)

The teachings of Buddhism have concentrated on the theory of Karma, which relates to the concept of "cause and effect." They demonstrate that unmindful neglect of these principles of right living may lead to chaos, and to environmental crisis if people are not careful. By following the theory of Karma and believing that all life forms are interconnected, people may be able to avoid cruelty to other living creatures, to control their exploitative tendencies towards nature.

This message — that all life is interconnected and requires caring — lays the foundation for the Buddhist ethics of nature. The Dalai Lama expressed this clearly in the following way:

> Have you ever wondered what a beautiful place this world would be if everyone would treat all animals and life in the same manner? And realize the fact that, whether it is more complex groups like human beings, or simpler groups such as animals, the feeling of pain and appreciation of happiness is common. All want to live and do not wish to die. As a Buddhist, I believe in the interdependence of all things, the interrelationship among the whole spectrum of plant and animal life, including the elements of nature which express themselves as mountains, valleys, rivers, sky, and sunshine. (Palmer and Bisset, 1985)

Jainism

Jainism places emphasis on the cultural principle that one should refrain from easily avoidable acts which are harmful to oneself or to others (Amar, 1989). Violence grows out of passion. Therefore it is the one who has passion who causes self-injury. Whether injury is then caused to other living beings or not is immaterial. Desisting from injury is accomplished by control of speech, control of thought, regulation of movement, care in taking and placing things, and examining food and drink. This is a vow taken by Jainis; and it can be transgressed by binding, beating, mutilating limbs, overburdening, and withholding food and drink from both human beings and animals.

Ahimsa, which is the fundamental trait of the Jain way of life, is a term that is clearly allied with realism, common sense, and personal worth and responsibility. It touches the deepest and noblest aspects of human nature: The term relates to the universal law which says that like produces like, order comes of order, and peace can be achieved only through peace. It maintains that in all situations the ends and the means are one and the same, and that truth, honesty, and compassion must be the foundation of any truly civilized community (Amar, 1989:210). As enunciated by Amrit Chandra Acharya in *Purus Artha Siddhi Upaya*:

> One should never think of hunting, victory, defeat, battle, adultery, theft etc., because they only lead to sin. *Sinful advice should never be given to persons living upon art, trade, writing, agriculture, arts and crafts, service and industry.* One should not without reason dig ground, uproot trees, trample lawns, sprinkle water etc., nor pluck leaves, fruit and flower. One should be careful not to give instruments of *himsa* (violence), such as knife, poison, fire, plough, sword, bowl, etc. One may not listen to, accept, or teach such bad stories as increase attachment etc., and are full of absurdities. Renounce gambling from a distance. It is the first of all evils, the destroyer of contentment, the home of deceit, and abode of theft and falsehood. (Acharya, 1933)

For the Jainis, environmental harmony through spirituality ought to be followed by all. This can be done by adhering to three precepts: the right belief, the right knowledge, and the right conduct. It also means believing in *Ahimsa*, which is the basic foundation of the Jain way of life. *Ahimsa* relates to the deepest and noblest aspect of human nature. It is a part of that universal law which states that order comes from order in the same way as harm generates destruction, and peace flows only through peace. It also means that all things (living and non-living) are destined for the same end; therefore one should not feel superior to others. Hence, all should be benevolent towards all living beings (including all organisms), compassionate for the weak, tolerant of the insolent, and joyful at the sight of the virtuous. This is the Jain way of bringing environmental harmony.

Sikhism

Guru Nanak, the founder of the Sikh religion, assigned divine attributes to nature. According to Sikhism, people should have respect for God's creation and know the eternal truth regarding their place in the universe (Jolly, 1989). God has not granted any special or absolute power to humans to control and dominate nature. On the contrary, the human race is an integral part of nature and is linked to the rest of creation by indissoluble bonds.

God Himself is the source of the birth, sustenance, and eventual destruction of all living organisms. It is He who created the universe through His divine will and with His word. The *Guru Granth Sahib* says: "From the Divine Command occurs the creation and the dissolution of the universe" (Adi Guru Granth Sahib, 1987). The basis of creation was divine will, and the universe was produced by His *Hukum* (command). However, it should be noted that God is submerged in creation, as stated in the *Adi Guru Granth Sahib* (p. 19):

> From Primal truth emanated air
> From air emanated water
> From water emanated three worlds
> And Himself he merged with the creation.

The principal tenets of the *Guru Granth Sahib* proclaim the glory of God in nature and the environment. Sikhs believe that the universe was created by an almighty God. He Himself is the creator and the master of all forms in the universe, and He is responsible for all modes of nature and all elements in the world. As their creator, the natural beauty found in all living things, whether animals, birds or fish, belongs to Him, and He alone is their master, without His *Hukum*, nothing exists, changes, or develops. A balance between all elements in nature is necessary for the continuation of the universe. Any disruption of the balance brings distress and disaster. Thus, for Sikhs, divinity is in nature. Furthermore, Sikhism teaches that the natural environment and the survival of all life forms are closely linked in the rhythm of nature. The history of the Gurus contains many stories of their love and special relationship with the natural environment — with animals, birds, vegetation, earth, rivers, mountains, and the sky.

Baha'i Perspective on Nature and the Environment

In the Baha'i faith, nature is seen as following scientific laws that are themselves the expression of a divine reality. Baha'u'llah said: "Nature is God's Will and is its expression in and through the contingent world" (Baha'u'llah). It is further explained:

> This nature is subjected to an absolute organization, to determined laws, to a complete order and to a finished design, from which it will never depart to such a degree, indeed, that if you look carefully and with keen sight, from the smallest invisible atom up to such large bodies of the world of existence as the globe of the sun or the other great stars and luminous spheres, whether you regard their arrangement, their composition, their form or their movement, you will find that all are in the highest degree of organization and are under one law from which they will never depart. (Abdu'l-Baha)

In the Baha'i faith nature refers to those inherent properties and necessary relations derived from the realities of things. The realities of things are both utterly diverse and yet intimately connected one with the other (Abdu'l-Baha, 1955:223).

Humanity has a special place in the natural world. The human body is like an animal's and therefore subject to nature's laws. But humans are endowed with a second reality, the rational or intellectual reality, and the intellectual reality of humankind predominates over nature (Abdu'l-Baha, 1945). Of course, God has given humanity wonderful powers to guide, control, and overcome nature.

> Yet there is a third reality in man, the spiritual reality.... That celestial reality ... delivers man from the material world. Its power causes man to escape from nature's world. Escaping, he will find an illuminating reality, transcending the limited reality of man and causing him to attain to the infinitude of God, abstracting him from the world of superstitions and imaginations, and submerging him in the sea of rays of the Sun of Reality. (Abdu'l-Baha, 1945:51)

For the Baha'i, while nature is not an end in itself to be worshipped and adored, creation does reflect the qualities and attributes of God:

> When ... thou dost contemplate the innermost essence of all things, and the individuality of each, thou wilt behold the signs of thy Lord's mercy in every created thing, and see the spreading rays of His Names and

Attributes throughout all the realm of being.... Then wilt thou observe that the universe is a scroll that discloseth His hidden secrets, which are preserved in the well-guarded Tablet. And not an atom of all the atoms in existence, not a creature from amongst the creatures but speaketh His praise and telleth of His attributes and names, revealeth the glory of His might and guideth to His oneness and His mercy. (Abdu'l-Baha)

Respect for the natural world and moderation in the use of its resources are also reflected in the Baha'i prohibition against cruelty to animals and warnings about hunting to excess. Thus, Baha'i people approach nature with an awareness of the interrelatedness of themselves and the natural world, and with an awareness of the importance of all the world's resources for the civilization they are building. Indeed, their leaders set the example for this philosophy, showing the spiritual and aesthetic values of wilderness, the countryside, and the diversity of natural life.

Summary

In the above section, an exploration has been provided of how different religious traditions treat the environment. In addition, there are other cultural traditions, legacies, and folklores that have been influential in shaping the behaviour of individuals toward the environment. For example, the aboriginal, tribal, or native people living in Asia, Africa, Australia, and the Americas have a rich cultural tradition which entreats them to protect their natural legacy rather than misuse or mistreat it. Among several such worldwide spiritual traditions, we have concentrated on the Canadian perspective.

Canadian Aboriginal Spiritual Tradition

One of the more visible examples, relevant to Canadian perspectives, is from the aboriginal people of the Americas. To these people, human beings and others (such as animals, birds, plants, rivers, mountains) are created by the Great Spirit. They are all natural manifestations to be honoured and revered, and in doing so, no harm will come to their tribe from any source. For example, among the Netsilik Inuits, the Ojibway, the Cree, and other tribes of the northwest coast of North America, a common world view demands respect for seals, caribou, bears, salmon, herring, and whales; it is assumed that these life forms have powerful souls that require respect and reverence. Thus, humans and animals are in a reciprocal relationship. Taken to the extreme, this notion means that even a hunter may receive his "due share" (which means a hunter killing only that number of animals or fish that is absolutely essential for his and his family's well-being and not for pleasure or gamesmanship) because the animals "may give themselves to be killed" (Chawla, 1991).

Although the aboriginal people of North America lived in environments quite different from one another, there was a complementary unity among them with respect to their attitudes toward the many forms and forces of the natural world. Their rites and ceremonies were expressed in terms of denoting respect and care for nature, since for them, earth, rocks, water, and wind were very much alive (Erodoes, 1996). Furthermore, for these aboriginals, natural objects (including stones, plants, and animals) were not merely material objects (as understood in the European civilization) but were alive with spirit residing in every one of them. In the Sioux spiritual tradition, the earth is mother, the sky is father. All things have souls, and they die, but their souls are reincarnated again (Jenness, 1935). For them and for other North American aboriginals, the natural world was seen as inspirited because the natural world could be "felt, perceived, deliberated, and responded voluntarily as persons" (Callicott, 1982:310). Even hunting was based on a kind of social relationship between men and animals. This anthropomorphic view of the animate and inanimate world is interpreted as superstition by those who are preoccupied with a scientific world-view. Nevertheless, the Amerindians treated nature with awe and concern in ways that did not exploit the environment indiscriminately. This perspective is illustrated by the following quotation:

> At the conclusion of the pipe ceremony among the Lakota the participants all exclaim: "We are all related." Acknowledged here is not only the relatedness of the immediate participating group; there is also an affirmation of the mysterious interrelatedness of all that is. The rites of the pipe make specific mention of the fact that each of the infinite number of grains of tobacco placed in the bowl of the pipe represents ritually, or really *is*, some specific form or possibility of creation. The act of smoking then is a rite of communion. Through the agency of man's breath the apparent multiplicity and separateness of phenomena (the tobacco) is absorbed within an ultimate unity (the fire). (Brown, 1976:32)

Perhaps it would not be out of place to include an example from the Australian aboriginals who believe that their ancestral beings journeyed across the land, and in the process created mountains, valleys, waterfalls, outcrops, and other features of the environment. Thus, the landscape is sacred to these aboriginals; its destruction is seen as a sin. In their stories, the aboriginals of Australia talk about the idea of Dreaming, which means leading a life in harmony and at peace with nature (Palmer, 1988). For these aboriginals, anyone who drastically alters the landscape disturbs the sacred site of their ancestors, and this disturbance could bring about unspeakably dire consequences. Recently, they declared one of the uranium sites a sacred place and are trying to protect the site because they fear that disturbing such places may bring great suffering to them. The sense of interrelatedness between humans and the natural world is the key to understanding the reverence for nature that has been a central tradition in many cultures. The American Indians saw the manifestation of the Great Spirit in rocks, trees, and animals, as well as in people; and that concept of interrelatedness implied that people should behave as worthy relatives of the entire universe. Behaving otherwise meant not obeying the dictates of the Great Spirit.

ENVIRONMENTAL STEWARDSHIP

The term "stewardship," originating in the Judeo-Christian tradition, means different things to different people. In Western culture, the concept has biblical roots. For example, in the Hebrew Bible, the image of a steward has been used to identify a person who is a manager of the king's household, and is accountable to the king for the proper management and care of people and objects. During the Roman Empire, the term steward (*oikonomos*) was used to denote an overseer, generally a slave who was in a position of authority over other slaves. It also mentioned in the New Testament:

> And the Lord said, Who then is that faithful and wise steward, whom *his* lord shall make ruler over his household ... Blessed *is* that servant, whom his lord when he cometh shall find so doing ... For unto whomsoever much is given, of him shall be much required ... (Luke 12:42, 43, 48)

According to the above verse, human beings have been appointed stewards of God's creation ("household"); when the final day of judgment comes, individuals will be judged according to whether they behaved responsibly towards the creation, because the authority to manage creation implies a responsibility to manage with care. It is a relationship of trust. From this image of stewardship, one infers the responsibility of humans toward nature. Creation (or nature) is the sacred trust for which humans were made responsible. The metaphor of the steward, while originating in Hebrew and Christian scriptures, was not used by their theologians in the context of the environment or nature until the late 1960s. Although some authors found the concept of stewardship "somewhat shallow, anthropocentric ... with roots in hierarchy, patriarchy and slavery" (Beavis, 1994), in the 1970s, Rene Dubos, John Macquarrie, and Hugh Montefiore used it as a part of Christian environmental ethics (Macquarrie, 1974). The term environmental stewardship has influenced the broader environmental community of planners, policy-makers, lawyers, ethicists, and theologians, although the strength of its influence has yet to be assessed.

World religions and indigenous spiritual traditions can provide a framework for changing our attitudes. World religions teach us that the land, rivers, mountains, minerals, oceans, and other species should be held in trust for God, but may be used for the general welfare of humanity. Religions tell us that people should consider themselves only as trustees of the world. Of course, as trustees, they are authorized by God to use natural resources, but they have no *divine power of control over nature and elements*. Moreover, from the perspective of many religions, the abuse and exploitation of nature for immediate gain is unjust and unethical.

Religions can be meaningful in a techno-nuclear age only if they address the eternal truth of our place in the universe. Without the fusion of spirituality with technology, humanity will continue to be torn between science, which promises heaven on earth, and religion, which promises heaven after death. Both spirituality and technology have to face the challenge of working together for the environment. Thus, the values of caring and respect for nature which are taught by various religions can be our guide to managing environmental problems. It is only by bringing religious, cultural, traditional, and secular domains together that we can wage a good fight to defend the environment; furthermore, only by enlisting the assistance of all societal forces (including world religions and other spiritual traditions) can we work together for sustainable development, and only then can we have a secure common future. In the appendix to this chapter we include a proposed "code of conduct," written by O.P. Dwivedi, as an example of how these diverse elements might be drawn together.

Religion and culture can evoke an awareness of that dimension of the human personality which is not involved in scientific or technological reasoning. Religion can help humanity to realize that there are limits to our dominance and control over the animate and inanimate world, and that our arrogant manipulation of nature can backfire. Religion recognizes that our lives cannot be measured by material possessions alone, and that the ends of life go beyond conspicuous consumption. These values are not easily incorporated into official governmental policy or the work of international organizations. But it is essential that we, as students of ecology and political science, take them into consideration in our own lives and in our political decision-making. In the appendix, we include a possible "code of conduct" for environmental protection that takes these factors into account.

APPENDIX
A PROPOSED CODE OF CONDUCT AND GUIDING PRINCIPLES FOR ENVIRONMENTAL PROTECTION

The role of a code is to provide not only inner incentives so that individuals may act in a way which is conducive to their self-preservation, but also external motivations in the form of laws, rules, and regulations so that individuals, groups, industries, and governments are impelled to care for the well-being of the environment. Such "inner incentives" become necessary when external inducements, either in the form of governmental directives, laws, or regulations, are either unenforceable or unworkable. This code also acts as an adaptive instrument to strengthen our obligation towards nature, which is seen as the provider and sustainer of our life support system. Below, we present such a code, developed by O.P. Dwivedi (adapted from Dwivedi, 1992).

The following are the basic principles which ought to govern the proposed Code:

a. Human beings have an obligation for the stewardship of the earth and the planetary system.

b. Nations should aim for sustainable development which is ecologically sound.

c. We must recognize that there is an interdependence between all species on earth, and that the obliteration of any one species may have disastrous consequences for all others.

d. Individuals, corporations, and business concerns, and various groups in society must accept responsibility as trustees and guardians of the environment for both present and future generations. We must be accountable environmentally for our individual as well as our collective actions which endanger the environment.

e. We must acknowledge our responsibility, individually and collectively, of educating our fellow beings about environmental protection and conservation.

These five principles are supplemented by the following tenets which are aimed at securing the future for forthcoming generations:

A. Future generations have a right to an unmanipulated human genetic inheritance — that is, a genetic inheritance which is not altered artificially by the present generation of humans.

B. Future generations have a right to the same richness of biogenetic variety in plant and animal world which is available at present.

C. Future generations have a right to healthy air, an intact ozone layer, clean water, fertile soil, and a vigorous forest cover.

D. Future generations have a right to substantial reserves of non-renewable energy resources and relevant raw materials.

E. Future generations have a right to a "cultural inheritance," created and bequeathed by earlier generations, which must not be so altered by the present generation that the future generations cannot enjoy that inheritance.

These basic principles and tenets are the foundation on which the main features of the proposed code have been formulated. The following ten main features are listed:

1. A respect for nature and all its constituent parts;
2. The right of all life on earth to perpetuate itself;
3. The duty of each society to act as the environment's keeper;
4. The need for society to encourage restraint and caution in the use of natural resources, and to control human greed and exploitative tendencies;
5. A recognition of the societal obligation to hold natural resources in trust for the appropriate use not only of the present generation but also of future generations;
6. A commitment to the moral obligation of all individuals to protect and conserve the environment;
7. The duty to protect and preserve endangered species;
8. The education of all people concerning their responsibility for maintaining ecological balance, biological diversity, and environmental sustainability;
9. A determination to secure the right of the public to participate in environmental decision-making, to receive information, and to be consulted by governmental bodies;
10. A commitment to enhance the flow of information to the public concerning the state of environmental quality, including the possible dangers arising from industrial and developmental projects.

THIRTEEN
CONCLUSION:
TOWARD SUSTAINABLE INDIVIDUAL
AND GOVERNMENTAL RESPONSIBILITY

At this point, we offer a brief summary of the contents of this book. The first chapter introduced the two fields of environmental and political science, and argued that the two meet in the exciting subfield of ecopolitics. We also outlined some of the main concerns we would deal with in subsequent chapters, and the structure of the book. In Part One of the text, we were chiefly concerned with providing a rough guideline for understanding the natural, administrative, and political context in which environmental policy decisions are made. This necessitated a quick overview of the state of the Canadian environment, which we found to be troubled in many important areas, including water and air quality, the fisheries, biodiversity reduction, and waste management. Canada also contributes to global warming and other transnational problems which in turn adversely affect wildlife and habitat in Canada. Although Canada retains a better environmental image than most states, including the industrial behemoth to the south, there certainly are no grounds for complacency.

The next chapter moved us away from environmental science and toward public policy and administration as a field of inquiry. After a brief description of the Canadian political system, we detailed the evolution of the principal federal institution, Environment Canada (EC). EC has gone through many phases, reflecting broader changes in Canadian society and the environment. Chapter 4 discussed the main political actors related to environmental policy, including political parties, First Nations groups, the business lobby, environmental interest groups, and the media. Although all these actors have interests related to environmental policy, it is clear that some are more powerful than others, and that some are more focused on ecological matters than others. The final chapter in this section introduced the transnational context, including the current state of globalization and the rise of environmental concerns as matters of national security. We situated Canada in international affairs, paying special attention to the often determining role of this country's proximity to the United States, and Canada's connection to other Arctic states, before discussing the complexities of international environmental diplomacy.

Section Two, Regulation and Management, offered a panoramic view of actual law, policy, and administration in Canada in the late 1990s and early 2000s. A chapter on laws and regulation preceded a lengthier discussion of environmental impact assessment and risk management, complete with case studies of toxic chemicals and hazardous wastes. In both chapters we saw the complexity of the bureaucratic maze that a federal system such as Canada's presents, as well as the roles of both provincial governments and non-governmental actors in the process of establishing policy and regulations. Chapter 8, designed to advance our understanding of the factors introduced in Chapter 5, detailed some of Canada's many international commitments, at the continental, regional, and global levels. While there is no shortage of commitments, the difficulties of implementation suggest that Canada might be described as a laggard, rather than a leader, in environmental policies at home and abroad. Finally, we closed this section with an evaluation of Canada's success in implementing the goals of sustainable development as put forth by the government itself, aided by the critical evaluation of the Auditor General's office. We concluded that there is still a long way to go, and an ongoing need to keep environmental issues on the public agenda, lest they be ignored in favour of more immediate political goals.

The first two sections were largely devoted to description and analysis. Section Three, by contrast, was the most normative in the book. Here we attempted to articulate some of the values and ethical concerns raised in ecopolitical discourse. A chapter on gender and resources pointed to the special concerns raised by ecofeminists and others, including the effort to incorporate sustainable development practices with foreign assistance programs. Chapter 11 dealt with the foreign policy plank of "human security" and offered a broad discussion of environmental security, examining some of the gaps between government rhetoric, actual policy, and the controversial concept of civil society. Finally, Chapter 12 summarized some of the more popular spiritual views on the relationship between humanity and ecology. We have argued that, given Canada's cosmopolitan society, it is necessary to cover a broad range of viewpoints, and that this diversity can be a strength in a democratic society, especially if certain points of convergence, such as the need to protect the environment, can be found. The chapter also offered a potential "environmental code of conduct," as an appendix, to guide citizens and policy-makers concerned with the imperatives of sustainable development.

This volume has covered a wide array of topics, from environmental impact assessment to ecofeminism to the Great Lakes Water Quality Agreement. Many institutions have been discussed, including various levels of Canadian government, relevant non-governmental organizations (in the private sector and the non-profit sector), and international organizations formed to promote cooperation on common problems in the context of a competitive global economy. We have tried to present a mix designed to prepare readers for the important environmental policy questions Canadians will face in the present century, beginning with the political and administrative context, moving into actual policies and regulatory mechanisms, and then finishing with a conceptual discussion of the ideas and ethical values that accompany context and policy.

This makes for quite a bit of material, yet we have presented but a small part of the broad field that is Canadian environmental policy today. We are aware of the errors of omission here: In particular, more attention could have been paid to the provincial level, where many key policy, funding, and enforcement decisions are made. Indeed, many of the constructive environmental programs, such as blue-box recycling, have been implemented at the *municipal* level, and decisions made by local school boards, native band councils, and others have a substantial aggregate effect not only on issues such as waste disposal, but also on the values that are passed on to new generations of Canadian children. Similarly, decisions made in the private sector may be instrumental in slowing down or speeding up the process of ecological deterioration. However, we have not been able to present an overview of the many industries which impact on the environment through their daily activities.

Nevertheless, we feel we have remained true to the book's original intent: to provide an overview of the policy questions government officials, operating in a globalized world economy, must deal with if we are to survive into the twenty-second century. On a national basis, the federal government is still the most influential player in this scenario, although lobby and interest groups have enhanced their abilities to persuade public opinion and pressure governments in recent years. This includes not only the powerful economic elite and industrial associations, but the NGOs as well. These groups have wide international as well as national connections which can be used to great effect. The ideas discussed in section three of the text, from gender to human security to spiritual commitment, are promulgated by NGOs and others dedicated to the environmentalist cause. Nevertheless, the federal government remains the source of the most widely disseminated ecological information and, if committed, retains the ability to increase funding and pass national legislation to make the path to sustainable development a more feasible prospect.

As Robert Paehlke and others have suggested, however, this is not as simple as it sounds, because the federal government sits between two strong forces: decentralizationist forces within Canada (especially the chorus of calls for more provincial autonomy), and the forces of globalization reaching from the outside. Paehlke refers to this condition as being "caught between centrifugal and centripetal forces, between globalization and decentralization" (2000:173). One force encourages Canada to increase its extractive activity, to focus on trade instead of development in its foreign policy, and to accept more foreign investment than ever before, while making international commitments to stem global fears of planetary collapse. The other force, manifested through initiatives such as the Harmonization Accord, lessens the ability of Ottawa to pass strong and meaningful national legislation and to implement the international commitments that have been made. In the face of severe cutbacks in environmental protection funding — consistent with a political philosophy favouring a privatization agenda and fiscal prudence — provinces such as Alberta and Ontario are in effect harming Canada's international reputation as an environmental policy leader. Indeed, the image of Canada as a laggard is becoming stronger as time passes and little is done to coordinate an effective response to the commitments at Kyoto, or to pass endangered species legislation, or to follow through with water quality promises.

However, there is another side to these twin processes as well. In terms of globalization, increased interaction among states and through international regimes affords states the opportunity to forge mutually beneficial bonds based on common principles. If those principles reflect a growing awareness that we are continuing to slide toward a point of limited recovery, anything is possible. Globalization has led to the massive protests which have erupted in the late 1990s and early 2000s as people clamour for increased control over the seemingly omnipotent forces of trade liberalization and foreign investment. There is room for those concerned with the ecological impact of globalization on Canada and elsewhere to express their fears and to seek an even broader audience, both in opposition to and, in some cases, in cooperation with international institutions. This can be done in the context of typical protest politics, using political parties to articulate this opposition, or it can be done in a technologically advanced setting, using the Internet and other communication systems to coordinate public displays of disaffection, or to openly discuss the pursuit of alternative lifestyle basics (such as the Code of Conduct offered in the previous chapter).

Although many environmentalists view decentralization as an immediate problem, it might also be seen as a window of opportunity. Provincial governments are no more costly to pressure than the federal government, and there are limits to the public's tolerance of environmental negligence.

All the provincial governments have mixed records, depending on whom you ask, but those which have made ignoring environmental concerns a matter of routine may pay the price at the electoral booth in the near future. Many NGOs and local conservation groups who lack sufficient resources to campaign nationally can have an impact on smaller units of government. It is an axiom of politics that people become most engaged when an issue affects them personally. For example, the contaminated water tragedy in Walkerton, Ontario, in the summer of 2000, sparked a lively debate about water quality and regulation. Because of the dictates of the Canadian Constitution, this is an issue only the provincial government can deal with effectively.

But whether it is a transnational or a backyard campaign, one thing remains certain: If people do not commit themselves to the cause of conservation, and if they are not willing to make noise about it, nothing will be done. The natural beauty of Canada, so long its definitive possession, is under threat from a wide variety of sources, some from outside the country. It is the responsibility of all Canadian citizens to consider what contribution they, both as individuals and as members of larger groups, can make to reverse these trends.

At the same time, it must be remembered that individuals and groups can do little unless their governments have the courage and foresight to enact and enforce environmental legislation despite the determined opposition of those who continue to regard nature as a resource to be exploited for personal and corporate profit. Governments have an obligation to devise policies in the public interest and must be held accountable for their actions or negligence. The Canadian public and Canadian governments need not and should not be adversaries in this process. We recognize that "good government" is often the art of balancing many competing interests for the benefit of all. However, as has been demonstrated in this book, Canadian governments have not always lived up to their responsibilities or to their rhetoric in the area of environmental policy, both at home and abroad. Accordingly, it is imperative that Canadian environmentalists do everything they can to ensure that environmental concerns remain high on their governments' lists of priorities.

REFERENCES

Abdu'l-Baha. 1945. *Foundations of World Unity*. Wilmette: Baha'i Publishing Trust.

Abdu'l-Baha. 1955. "Tablet to Dr. Forel" in *The Baha'i Revelation*. London: Baha'i Publishing Trust.

Abdu'l-Baha. 1969. *Paris Talks: Addresses Given by Abdu'l-Baha in Paris in 1911-1912*. London: Baha'i Publishing Trust.

Abdu'l-Baha. 1986. *Some Answered Questions*. Wilmette: Baha'i Publishing Trust.

Acharya, A.C. 1933. "Purushartha Siddhi Upaya verses 141-146, quoted by Acharya Gopi Lal Amar" in A.G.L. Amar, 1989. "Jainism and Environmental Harmony." In O.P. Dwivedi (ed.) *World Religions and the Environment*. New Delhi: Gitanjali Publishing. 208-81.

Adi Sri Guru Granth Sahib Ji. 1987. *Sudhai Sri Damdami Bir Katak Sudi Duj Sambat 1765 Bikrami*, trans. Gurbachan Singh Talib. Patiala: Punjabi University.

Agarwal, B. 1997. "Environmental Action, Gender Equity and Women's Partici-pation." *Development and Change* 28: 439-64.

Allison, J.E. 1999. "Fortuitous Conse-quence: the Domestic Politics of the 1991 Canada-United States Agreement on Air Quality." *Policy Studies Journal* 27(2): 347-59.

Almond, G., and G. Powell. 1996. *Comparative Politics Today: A World View*. New York: HarperCollins.

Amar, A.G.L. 1989. "Jainism and Environmental Harmony." In O.P. Dwivedi (ed.) *World Religions and the Environment*. New Delhi: Gitanjali Publishing. 208-81.

Archer, K., *et al.* 1995. *Parameters of Power: Canada's Political Institutions*. Toronto: Nelson Canada.

Archibald, L., and M. Crnkovich. 1999. "If Gender Mattered: A Case Study of Inuit Women, Land Claims and the Voisey's Bay Nickel Project," *Status of Women Canada*, November. Online. Internet. http://www.swc-cfc.gc.ca

Arctic Council. 1998. *Report of the Senior Arctic Officials to the Arctic Council*. Iqaluit: Arctic Council. Online. Internet. www.arctic-council.usgs.gov/98rep.html

Aucoin, P. 1979. "Portfolio Structures and Policy Coordination." In G.B. Doern and P. Aucoin (eds.) *Public Policy in Canada: Organization, Process and Management*. Toronto: MacMillan.

Axworthy, L. 1997. *Canada and Human Security: The Need for Leadership*. Online. Internet. http://www.dfait-maeci.gc.ca/foreignp/sechume.html

Axworthy, L., and S. Taylor. 1998. "A Ban For All Seasons: The Landmines Convention and Its Implications for Canadian Diplomacy." *International Journal*, Spring LIII(2): 189-203.

Baha'u'llah. 1986. *Tablets of Baha'u'llah.* Wilmette: Baha'i Publishing Trust.

Beavis, M.A. 1994. *Environmental Stewardship: History Theory and Practice Workshop Proceedings.* Winnipeg: Institute of Urban Studies, University of Winnipeg.

Bell, D.V.J. 2000. "Canada's Commissioner of the Environment and Sustainable Development: A Case Study," York Centre for Applied Sustainability. Online. Internet. http://iisd.ca/measure/scipol/case2.doc

Benson, H. 1994. "'Ecofemmes': Young Women Activists." *Canadian Woman Studies* 13(3):100-02.

Bergerson, H.O., M. Norderhaug, and G. Parmann. 1995. *Green Globe Yearbook, 1995.* New York: Oxford University Press.

Bloom, E.T. 1999. "Establishment of the Arctic Council." *The American Journal of International Law* 93(3): 712-22.

Bookchin, M. 1995. *The Philosophy of Social Ecology: Essays on Dialectical Naturalism.* Montreal: Black Rose.

Braidotti, R., E. Charkiewicz, S. Hausler, and S. Wieringa. 1994. *Women, the Environment and Sustainable Development.* London: Zed Books.

British Columbia, Government of. 1996. *Environmental Management Act.* RSBC. Chapters 118-19.

British Columbia, Government of. 1996. *Ministry of Environment Act.* RSBC. Chapter 299.

British Columbia, Government of. 1996. *Waste Management Act.* RSBC. Chapter 482.

Brown, J.E. 1976. "The Roots of Renewal." In W.H. Capps (ed.) *Seeing with a Native Eye.* New York: Harper Forum Books.

Brown, M.P. 1986. "Environment Canada and the Pursuit of Administrative Decentralization." *Canadian Public Administration* 29(2): 218-36.

Brown, P. 1992. "Target or Participant? The Hatching of Environmental Industry Policy." In R. Boardman (ed.) *Canadian Environmental Policy: Ecosystems, Politics, Process.* Toronto: Oxford University Press.

Caldwell, L.K. 1983. "Environmental Studies: Discipline or Metadiscipline." *The Environmental Professional* 5: n/a.

Caldwell, L.K. 1996. *International Environmental Policy: From the Twentieth to the Twenty-First Century.* Third Edition. Durham: Duke University Press.

Callicott, J.B. 1982. "Traditional American Indian and West European Attitudes Towards Nature: An Overview." *Environmental Ethics* 4(4): 293-18.

Callow. P. (ed). 1998. *Handbook of Environmental Risk Assessment and Management.* London: Blackwell Science.

Canada, Government of. 1985a. *The Fisheries Act.* R.S.C. Chapter F-14.

Canada, Government of. 1985b. *Canadian Environmental Protection Act.* Fourth supplement. Chapter 16, Section 113.

Canada, Government of. 1985c. *Department of the Environment Act.* R.S.C. Chapter E-10.

Canada, Government of. 1985d. *Pest Control Products Act.* R.S.C. Chapter P-9.

Canada, Government of. 1992. *Canadian Environmental Assessment Act.* R.S.C. Chapter 37.

Canada, Government of. 1995. *Canadian Delegation Report*. A Climate Change First Conference of Parties. Ottawa.

Canada, Government of. 1996. *Report of Canada to the United Nations Commission on Sustainable Development*. Fourth Session of the Commission April 18-May 3. Ottawa.

Canada, Government of. 1997. Commissioner of the Environment and Sustainable Development. *Report*. Ottawa.

Canada, Government of. 1997a. *CEPA: Strengthening Environmental Protection in Canada: A Guide to the New Legislation*.

Canada, Government of. 1998. *Report of Canada to the United Nations Commission on Sustainable Development*, Fourth Session of the Commission April 18-May 3, Ottawa-Hull.

Canada, Government of. 1999. *Canadian Environmental Protection Act*. S.C. Chapter 33.

Canada-United States Air Quality Agreement: Progress Report. 1992. March Canadian Broadcasting Corporation (CBC). 1998. "Ottawa weak in key environment areas: commissioner." Online. Internet. http://cbc.ca/cgi-bin/templates/view.cgi?/news/1998/05/26/emmett980526b

Canadian Council of Ministers on the Environment (CCME). 1996. A Fresh Look at Economic Instruments Final Report. Pembina Institute for Appropriate Development with Apogee Research International LTD. November.

Canadian Council of Ministers on the Environment (CCME). 2000. "About CCME." Online. Internet. http://www.ccme.ca/1e_about/1e.html

Canadian Environmental Law Association (CELA). 2000. Online. Internet. www.cela.ca

Canadian Environmental Network. 1993. *The Green List: A Guide to Environmental Organization in Canada*. Second edition. Ottawa: Canadian Environmental Network.

Canadian Institute for Environmental Law and Policy. 1999. *Hazardous Water and Toxic Substances*. Online. Internet. www.web.net/~cielp/hazwaste.htm

Canadian International Development Agency (CIDA). 1999. "Program Priorities." Online. Internet. http://www.acdi-cida.gc.ca

Carson, R. 1962. *Silent Spring*. New York: Random House.

Castrilli, J.F. 1985. "Hazardous Wastes Law in Canada: At the Skull and Crossroads." *How to Fight for What's Left of the Environment*. Toronto: CELRF.

Cataldo, E. 1992. "Acid Rain Policy in the United States: An Exploration of Canadian Influence." *The Social Science Journal* 29(4): 395-409.

Chamberlin, A., and L. Legault. 1997. "International Joint Commission Looks to the 21st Century." *Focus on IJC Activities* 22(3): 3-5.

Chang, E., D. Macdonald, and J. Wolfson. 1998. "Who Killed CIPSI?" *Alternatives Journal* 24(2): 20-25.

Chartier, D., and J. Deleage. 1998. "The International Environmental NGOs: from the Revolutionary Alternative to the Pragmatism of Reform." *Environmental Politics* 7(3): 26-41.

Chawla, S. 1991. "Linguistic and Philosophical Roots of our Ecological Crisis." *Environmental Ethics* 13(3): 257-58.

Chiotti, Q. 1998. "An Assessment of the Regional Impacts and Opportunities from Climate Change in Canada." *The Canadian Geographer* 42(2): 380-93.

Christian, W., and C. Campbell. 1990. *Political Parties and Ideologies in Canada.* Third edition. Toronto: McGraw-Hill Ryerson.

Climate Change Secretariat. 2000. Online. Internet. www.climatechange.gc.ca

Commission for Environmental Cooperation (CEC). 1996. *Status of Pollution Prevention in North America.* Montreal: CEC Secretariat.

Commission for Environmental Cooperation (CEC). 1998. *The Sound Management of Chemicals Initiative under the NAAEC: Regional Commitments and Action Plans.* Montreal: CEC Secretariat.

Commission for Environmental Cooperation (CEC). 1999a. *North American Agenda for Action 1999-2000.* Montreal: CEC Secretariat.

Commission for Environmental Cooperation (CEC). 1999b. *Ribbon of Life: An Agenda for Preserving Transboundary Migratory Bird Habitat on the Upper San Pedro River.* Montreal: CEC Secretariat.

Commission for Environmental Cooperation (CEC). 2000. Online. Internet. www.cec.org/programs_projects

Commission on Sustainable Development (CSD). 1999. "About Commission on Sustainable Development." Online. Internet. http://www.un.org/esa/sustdev/csdgen.htm

Committee on the Status of Endangered Wildlife in Canada (COSEWIC). May, 2000. "Canadian Species at Risk." May. Online. Internet. http://cosewic.gc.ca/cosewic/2000_list.pdf

Cooper, A., and J. Fritz. 1992. "Bringing the NGOs in: UNCED and Canada's International Environmental Policy." *International Journal* 47(4): 796-817.

Cox, D. 1988. "Canada's Changing Defence Priorities: Comparing Notes with Other Nordic States." In Karl Möttölä (ed.) *The Arctic Challenge: Nordic and Canadian Approaches to Security and Cooperation in an Emerging International Region.* Boulder: Westview Press. 15-38.

Daly, H. 1996. *Beyond Growth: The Economics of Sustainable Development.* Boston: Beacon.

Dankelman, I., and J. Davidson. 1988. *Women and Environment in the Third World: Alliance for the Future.* London: Earthscan.

Darmesteter, J. (Translation). 1880. *The Vendidad* SBE IV, Chapter XIX. 35: 214. (Quoted by Khojeste Mistry. 1989. In "Ecology — A Zoroashtrian Experience"). In O.P. Dwivedi (ed.) *World Religions and the Environment.* New Delhi: Gitanjali Publishing House. 138-57.

Dauvergne, P. 1997. *Shadows in the Forest: Japan and the Politics of Timber in Southeast Asia.* Cambridge: MIT Press.

Davidson, J. 1993. "Women's Relationship with the Environment." *Focus on Gender.* Oxford: Oxfam 1: 5-10.

Davies, J. 1996. *Comparing Environmental Risks: Tools for Setting Government Priorities.* New York: Resources for the Future.

Department of Fisheries and Oceans Canada. 2000. Online. Internet. www.dfo-mpo.gc.ca

Department of Foreign Affairs and International Trade (DFAIT). 1997. *Agenda 2000: A Sustainable Development Strategy for the DFAIT.* Online. Internet. www.dfait-maeci.gc.ca

Department of Foreign Affairs and International Trade (DFAIT). 1999a. "Human Security: Safety for People in a Changing World." Online. Internet. http://www.dfait-maeci.gc.ca/foreignp/secur-e.html

Department of Foreign Affairs and International Trade (DFAIT). 1999b. "Strategy Launched to Prohibit the Bulk Removal of Canadian Water, Including Water for Export." Online. Internet. February 10. http://www.dfait-maeci.gc.ca/english/news/press_releases/99_press/99_023-e.htm

Department of Foreign Affairs and International Trade (DFAIT). 1999c. *Canada Strives for an International Forest Convention*. Online. Internet. www.dfait-maeci.gc.ca/sustain/EnvironIssu/forest/forest-e.asp

Department of Foreign Affairs and International Trade (DFAIT). 2000a. *Sustainable Development* Online. Internet. www.dfait-maeci.gc.ca/sustain/EnvironIssu/

Department of Foreign Affairs and International Trade (DFAIT). 2000b. "Agenda 2000". Online. Internet. http://www.dfait-maeci.gc.ca

Derr, T.S. 1975. "Religion's Responsibility for the Ecological Crisis." *World View* 28(1).

Deudney, D. 1990. "The Case Against Linking Environmental Degradation and National Security." *Millennium* 19(3): 461-76.

Dewailly, E., A. Nantel, J.P. Weber, and F. Meyer. 1989. "High Levels of PCBs in breast milk of Inuit women from Arctic Quebec." *Bulletin of Environmental Contamination and Toxicology* 43(2): 641-46.

Dobell, R., A. Fenech, and H.A. Smith. 1993. *The Issue of Climate Change in Canada*, Contribution D.1 V.3, to the Project on Social Learning in the Management of Global Environmental Risks. August.

Doern, B., and R. Phidd. 1983. *Canadian Public Policy: Ideas, Structure, Process*. Toronto: Methuen.

Doern, G.B.M., J. Prince, and G. McNaughton. 1982. *Living with Contradictions: Health and Safety Regulations in Ontario*. Ottawa: Carleton University, School of Public Administration.

Duval, J. 1995. "Advertising, Consumption and Environment: an Interview with Jacques Duval." *Ecodecision* 16: 57-59.

Dwivedi, O.P. 1980. *Resources and the Environment: Policy Perspectives for Canada*. Toronto: McClelland and Stewart.

Dwivedi, O.P. 1981. "Man and Nature: A Holistic Approach to a Theory of Ecology." *Environmental Professional* 10: 8-15.

Dwivedi, O.P. 1986. "Political Science and the Environment." *International Social Science Journal* 109: 377-90.

Dwivedi, O.P. 1992. "An Ethical Approach to Environmental Protection: A Code of Conduct and Guiding Principles." *Canadian Public Administration* Autumn 35(3): 363-80.

Dwivedi, O.P. 1994. *Environmental Ethics: Our Dharma to the Environment*. New Delhi: Sanchar Publishing.

Dwivedi, O.P. 1995. "Our Karma and Dharma to the Environment: An Eastern perspective." In M.A. Beavis (ed.) *Environmental Stewardship, History, Theory and Practice: Workshop Proceedings*. Winnipeg: University of Winnipeg. 59-74.

Dwivedi, O.P. 1997a. *India's Environmental Policies, Programmes and Stewardship*. London: Macmillan Press.

Dwivedi, O.P. 1997b. "Vedic Heritage for Environmental Stewardship." *Worldviews: Environment, Culture and Religion* 1: 25-36.

Dwivedi, O.P., and P. Kyba. 1996. "Environmental Policy Formation and Administration." University of Guelph, Guelph, University of Guelph Course Manual.

Edwards, M., and D. Hulme. 1996. "Too Close for Comfort? The Impact of Official Aid on Nongovernmental Organizations." *World Development* 24(6): 961-73.

Ekos. 1998. "Rethinking Government." Online. Internet. www.ec.gc.ca

Elliot, J.A. 1994. *An Introduction to Sustainable Development.* London: Routledge.

Elson, D. 1991. *Male Bias in the Development Process.* Manchester: Manchester University Press.

Emmett B. 1999. House of Commons Debates. 25 May 1999.

Emond, D.P. 1985. "Environmental Law and Policy: A Retrospective Examination of the Canadian Experience." In I. Bernier and A. Lajoie (eds.) *Consumer Protection, Environmental Law and Corporate Power.* Royal Commission on Economic Union and Development Prospects for Canada. Toronto: University of Toronto.

Environics. 1999. "The Environics Environmental Monitor." Online. Internet.www.ec.gc.ca/prog99/view-e.html

Environment Canada. 1971. *Annual Report 1971-1972.* Ottawa: Information Canada.

Environment Canada. 1971. *Its Organization and Objectives.* Ottawa: Information Canada.

Environment Canada. 1982. *Its Evolving Mission.* Ottawa.

Environment Canada. 1982. *Department Strategic Plan.* Ottawa.

Environment Canada. 1989. *Annual Report 1987-1988.* Ottawa: Supply and Services.

Environment Canada. 1990, 1995, 1998. *Mission Statements.* Ottawa.

Environment Canada. 1993. "Environmental Implications of the Automobile." *State of the Environment Fact Sheet Series,* No. 93-1. Online. Internet. http://www.ec.gc.ca

Environment Canada. 1994. "Protecting and Promoting Human Health: Health Care in Canada." Online. Internet. http://www.ec.gc.ca

Environment Canada. 1995a. "Caring for Canada's Biodiversity: Canada's First National Report to the Conference of the Parties to the Convention on Biological Diversity." Online. Internet. http://www.bco.ec.gc.ca

Environment Canada. 1995b. "A Guide to Green Planning." Online. Internet. http://www.ec.gc.ca

Environment Canada. 1996a. *Chlorinated Substances Action Plan: Progress Report.* Hull.

Environment Canada. 1996b. "Energy Consumption." National Indicator Series, State of the Environment Bulletin 96(3). Online. Internet. http://www3.ec.gc.ca

Environment Canada. 1997a. *International to Action on Climate Change: The Road to Kyoto.* Online. Internet. http://www.ec.gc.ca/climate/fact/action.html

Environment Canada. 1997b. "The State of Canada's Environment 1996." Online. Internet. http://www1.ec.gc.ca/~soer/default.htm

Environment Canada. 1997c. "Sustaining Canada's Forests: Forest Biodiversity." National Environmental Indicator Series. *State of the Environment Bulletin* 97(1) Summer. Online. Internet. http://199.212.18.79/~ind/English/For_Bio/default.cfm

Environment Canada. 1997d. "Towards a National Acid Rain Strategy." October. Online. Internet. http://www.ec.gc.ca/special/ar_strat_e.html

Environment Canada. 1998a. "Canada Country Study." Online. Internet. http://www.ec.gc.ca/climate/ccs/ccs_e.htm

Environment Canada. 1998b. *Enforcing Canada's Pollution Laws: The Public Interest Must Come First!* Ottawa: Environment Canada.

Environment Canada. 1998c. *Progress in Pollution Prevention, 1996–97.* www.ec.gc.ca/agenda21/eneng1.html

Environment Canada. 1999a. "The Importance of Nature to Canadians: Survey Highlights." Online. Internet. http://www.ec.gc.ca/nature/summary.html

Environment Canada. 1999b. "Canada's Oceans: Experiences and Practices." Online. Internet. http://www.ec.gc.ca/agenda21/99/canocean.html

Environment Canada. 1999c. "Urban Air Quality." National Environmental Indicator Series. *State of the Environment Bulletin* 99(1). Online. Internet. http://www3.ec.gc.ca/~ind/English/Urb_Air/Bulletin/ua_iss_e.cfm

Environment Canada. 1999d. "Smog Fact Sheet." Online. Internet. http://www1.tor.ec.gc.ca/cd/factsheets/smog/index_e.cfm

Environment Canada. 1999e. "Stratospheric Ozone Depletion." National Environmental Indicator Series. *State of the Environment Bulletin* 9(2). Online. Internet. http://www3.ec.gc.ca/~ind/English/Ozone/Bulletin/st_iss_e.cfm

Environment Canada. 1999f. "Acid Rain Fact Sheet." Online. Internet. http://www1.tor.ec.gc.ca/cd/factsheets/acidrain/index_e.cfm

Environment Canada. 1999g. "Ozone Depletion and CFCs." March 9. Online. Internet. http://www.ec.gc.ca/ecoaction/gtips/ozone_e.htm

Environment Canada. 2000a. "Canadian consumption of energy (1961–97)." December 1997. Online. Internet. www3.ec.gc.ca/ind/English/energy/Tables/ectb01_e.cfm

Environment Canada. 2000b. "Hazardous Waste Management in Canada." July. Online. Internet. http://www.ec.gc.ca/press/000727_f_e.htm

Environment Canada. 2000c. "Sustainable Development Information System." Online. Internet. http://www.sdinfo.gc.ca

Environmental Connections for Canada Canadian First Nations. 2000. Online. Internet. http://www.bluecrow.com/members/guardian/firstnat.html

Epstein, S. 1979. *The Politics of Cancer.* New York: Random House.

Erdoes, R. 1996. *Lone Deer: Seeker of Visions.* New York: Simon & Schuster.

Estrin, D., and J. Swaigen. 1978. *Environment on Trial.* Toronto: CELRF.

European Environment Agency. 1999. *Environment in the European Union at the Turn of the Century.* Copenhagen: EEA.

Falk, R. 1995. *On Humane Governance: Toward A New Global Politics.* University Park, PA: Penn State University Press.

Farbridge, K., and P. Cameron. 1998. "PIRG Power: Public Interest Research Groups in Canada Celebrate 25 Years of Student Activism." *Alternatives* 24(3): 22-27.

Federal Statistical Office Germany. 2000. "Daily Water Consumption per capita decreased since 1991." Online. Internet. http://www.statistik-bund.de/presse/englisch/pm/p0344155.htm

Feshbach, M., and A. Friendly. 1992. *Ecocide in the USSR*. New York: Basic Books.

Fikkan, A., G. Osherenko, and A. Arikainen. 1993. "Polar Bears: The Importance of Simplicity." In O.R. Young and G. Osherenko (eds.) *Polar Politics: Creating International Environmental Regimes*. Ithaca: Cornell University Press 1-21.

Filyk, G., and R. Cote. 1992. "Pressures from Inside: Advisory Groups and the Environmental Policy Community." In R. Boardman (ed.) Canadian Environmental Policy: Ecosystems, Politics, Process. Toronto: Oxford University Press. 60-81.

Finlayson, A. 1985. "An Enduring Menace." *Macleans*. April 15.

Fisher, W. 1995. "Development and Resistance in the Narmada Valley." In W. Fisher, (ed.) *Toward Sustainable Development? Struggling Over India's Narmada River*. London: M.E. Sharpe. 3-26.

Fleming, T. 1997. *The Environment and Canadian Society*. Toronto: ITP Nelson.

Fletcher, F., and L. Stahlbrand. 1992. "Mirror or Participant? The News Media and Environmental Policy." In R. Boardman (ed.) *Canadian Environmental Policy: Ecosystems, Politics, Process*. Toronto: Oxford University Press. 179-99.

Forbes, R. 1968. *The Conquest of Nature, Technology and Its Consequences*. New York: Frederick A. Praeger.

Franks, C.C.S. 1987. *The Parliament of Canada*. Toronto: University of Toronto Press.

Gallon, G. 1997. *The Gallon Letter*. Canadian Institute for Business and the Environment. May 7.

Gizewski, P. 1993-94. "Military Activity and Environmental Security: The Case of Radioactivity in the Arctic." *Northern Perspectives* 21(4). Online. Internet. http://www.carc.org/pubs/v21no4/military.htm

Gleick, P. 1991. "Environment and Security: The Clear Connections." *Bulletin of the Atomic Scientists* 47(3): 16-21.

Glode, M., and B. Glode. 1993. "Transboundary Pollution: Acid Rain and United States-Canadian Relations." *Environmental Affairs* 20(1): 1-35.

Government of Canada. 1988a. *Canadian Environmental Protection Act*.

Government of Canada. 1988b. *Environmental Assessment in Canada*.

Government of Canada. 1990a. *The Green Plan in Brief*.

Government of Canada. 1990b. *Canada's Green Plan*.

Government of Canada. 1991. *The State of Canada's Environment*.

Government of Canada. 1994. *Estimates — 1994-95, Part III Expenditure Plan, Environment Canada*.

Government of Canada. 1996. *State of the Environment*.

Government of Canada. 1997. *Canada's Seconds National Report on Climate Change: Actions to Meet Commitments Under the UNFCCC*.

Government of Canada. 1998a. *International Environmental Agreements*.

Government of Canada. 1998b. *Response to the 8th Report of the Standing Committee on the Environment and Sustainable Development*. Online. Internet. www.fin.gc.ca/resp/

Government of Canada. 1999a. *Review of the Canadian Environmental Assessment Act*.

Government of Canada. 1999b. *Canada's Oceans: Experiences and Practices.* Sustainable Development in Canada Series. Monograph No. 7. Ottawa: Government of Canada.

Green, M. 1976. *Pesticides: Boon or Bane?* Denver: WEF.

Griffiths, F. 1997. "Environment and Security in Arctic Waters: A Canadian Perspective." INSROP Working Paper no. 83.

Halucha, P. 1998. "Climate Change Policies and the Pursuit of National Interests." In F.O. Hampson, *et al.* (eds.) *Canada Among Nations 1998: Leadership and Dialogue.* Ottawa: Norman Patterson.

Hampson, F. Osler, and M.A. Malot. 1998. *Canada Among Nations 1998: Leadership and Dialogue.* Ottawa: Norman Patterson. 285-304.

Hampson, F. Osler, and D.F. Oliver. 1998. "A Pundit Diplomacy: A Critical Assessment of the Axworthy Doctrine." *International Journal* Summer LIII(3): 379-406.

Harcourt, W. 1994. *Feminist Perspectives on Sustainable Development.* London: Zed Books.

Harrison, K. 1996. *Passing the Buck: Federalism and Canadian Environmental Policy.* Vancouver: UBC Press.

Harrison, K., and G. Hoberg. 1991. "Setting the Environmental Agenda in Canada and the United States: The Cases of Dioxin and Radon." *Canadian Journal of Political Science* 14(1): 3-28.

Heady, F. 1996. *Public Administration: A Comparative Perspective.* Fifth Edition. New York: Marcel Dekker.

Hertig, M. 1991. *The Betrayal of Canada.* Toronto: Stoddart.

Hertzberg, Rabbi A. 1986. "The Jewish Declaration of Nature." From the Assisi Declarations made in Assisi, Italy, 29 September. Geneva: WWF.

Hessing, M., and M. Howlett. 1997. *Canadian Natural Resource and Environmental Policy.* Vancouver: UBC Press.

Higgins, P.T. 1973. "Canada's Strategies for Water Pollution Control." From the Advance Seminar on Water Pollution in Buenos Aires, Argentina.

Hoberg, G. 1991. "Sleeping with an Elephant: The American Influence on Canadian Environmental Regulation." *Journal of Public Policy* 11(1): 107-31.

Hocking, B. 1996. "The Woods and the Trees: Catalytic Diplomacy and Canada's Trials as a 'Forestry super-power.'" *Environmental Politics* 5(3): 448-75.

Holmes, J.W. 1981. "The IJC and Canada-United States Relations." In R. Spencer, J. Kirton, and K.R. Nossal (eds.) *The International Joint Commission Seventy Years On.* Toronto: Centre for International Studies, University of Toronto 3(7).

Homer-Dixon, T.F. 1991. "Environmental Change and Human Security." *Behind the Headlines* Spring 48(3): 5-40.

Homer-Dixon, T.F. 1993. "Global Environmental Change and International Security." In D. Dewitt, D. Haglund, and J. Kirton (eds.) *Building A New Global Order: Emerging Trends in International Security.* Toronto: Oxford University Press.

Homer-Dixon, T.F. 1994. "Environmental Scarcities and Violent Conflict: Evidence from Cases." *International Security* 19(2).

Hornung, R. 1998. "The Voluntary Challenge Program Will Not Work." *Policy Options* 19(4): 10-13.

Howlett, M. 1997. "Sustainable Development: Environmental Policy." In A. Johnson and A. Stritch (eds.) *Canadian Public Policy: Globalisation and Political Parties.* Toronto: Copp Clark. 99-121.

Huebert, R. 1998. "New Directions in Circumpolar Cooperation: Canada, the Arctic Environmental Strategy, and the Arctic Council." *Canadian Foreign Policy* 5(2): 37-57.

Huebert, R. 1999. "Canadian Arctic Security Issues." *International Journal* 54(2): 203-29.

Humphreys, D. 1996. *Forest Politics: The Evolution of International Cooperation.* London: Earthscan.

Intergovernmental Panel on Climate Change. 1995. "IPCC Second Assessment — Climate Change 1995." *A Report of the Intergovernmental Panel on Climate Change.* Geneva: IPCC.

International Development Research Centre (IDRC). 1999. "Gender and Sustainable Development Unit." Online. Internet. http://www.idrc.ca/institution/eprogram.html

International Institute for Sustainable Development (IISD). 1997. *Earth Negotiations Bulletin* 12(76). 13 December. Online. Internet. http://www.iisd.ca/linkages/download/asc/enb1276e.txt

International Institute for Sustainable Development (IISD). 1998. *Earth Negotiations Bulletin* 12(97). 16 November.

International Institute for Sustainable Development (IISD). 1999. "Public Policy." Online. Internet. http://iisd.ca/policy.htm

International Joint Commission (IJC). 1970. *Report on Pollution of Lake Erie, Lake Ontario, and the International Section of the St. Lawrence River.* Ottawa: IJC.

International Joint Commission (IJC). 1999. As quoted in the *Kitchener-Waterloo Record.* September 24.

International Joint Commission (IJC). 2000. Online. Internet. ww.ijc.org/about/how.html

Jabbra, J., and O.P. Dwivedi. 1998. *Governmental Response to Environmental Challenges in Global Perspective.* Amsterdam: ISO Press.

Jackson, C. 1993. "Doing What Comes Naturally? Women and Environment in Development." *World Bank* 21(12): 1947-1963.

Jackson, J., and P. Weiler. 1982. *Chemical Nightmare.* Toronto: CIELP.

Jakobeit, C. 1996. "Nonstate Actors Leading the Way: Debt-for-Nature Swaps." In R. Keohane and M. Levy (eds.) *Institutions for Environmental Aid: Pitfalls and promise.* Cambridge: MIT Press. 127-65.

Janigan, M. 1985. *Macleans.* April 19.

Jasnoff. S. 1999. *Environmental Values.* London: Whitehorse Press.

Jeffery, M.I., and O.P. Dwivedi. 1988. "The Environmental Assessment Board of Ontario." *The Environmental Professional* 10: 257-65.

Jenness, D. 1935. *The Ojibwa Indians of Parry Island: Their Social and Religious Life,* Ottawa: Canadian Department of Mines. Series No. 17.

Jockel, J. 1990. *Canadian-American Public Policy: Canada-U.S. Relations in the Bush Era.* Orono: University of Maine Press.

Johnson, P.M., and A. Beaulieu. 1996. *The Environment and NAFTA: Understanding and Implementing the New Continental Law.* Washington, DC: Island Press.

Jolly, S. 1989. "Sikhism and the Environment." In O. P. Dwivedi (ed.) *World Religion and the Environment.* New Delhi: Gitanjali Publishing. 282-95.

Kabeer, N. 1994. *Reversed Realities: Gender Hierarchies in Development Thought.* London: Verso.

Kabilsingh, C. 1987. "How Buddhism Can Help Protect Nature." In S. Davies (ed.) *Tree of Life.* Geneva: WWF.

Kassap, B.J. 1959. *Metta-sutta.* Patna: Bihar State Pali Publications Board Volume 8.

Keating, T. 2000. "The Promise and Pitfalls of Human Security." Paper presented at the Canadian Political Science Association Annual Meeting, Quebec City, July.

Keeble, E., and H.A. Smith. 1999. *(Re)Defining Traditions: Gender and Canadian Foreign Policy.* Halifax: Fernwood Publishing.

Kernaghan, K., and D. Siegel. 1995. *Public Administration in Canada: A Text.* Third Edition. Toronto: Nelson.

Kettel, B. 1996. "Putting Women and the Environment First: Poverty Alleviation and Sustainable Development." In A. Dale and J.B. Robinson (eds.) *Achieving Sustainable Development.* Vancouver: UBC Press. 160-82.

Kingsbury, B. 1999. "The Applicability of the International Legal Concept of 'Indigenous Peoples' in Asia." In J. Bauer and D. Bell (eds.) *The East Asian Challenge for Human Rights.* Cambridge: Cambridge University Press. 336-77.

Knight, A. 1997. "Foreign Policy: Coping with a Post-Cold War Environment." In A. Johnson and A. Stritch (eds.) *Canadian Public Policy: Globalisation and Political Parties.* Toronto: Copp Clark. 213-50.

Knox, P. 1997. "The World Confronts Global Warming: Canada Limps into Kyoto Arena." *Globe and Mail.* Nov. 20. Online. Internet. http://www.theglobe-andmail-con/docs/news/19971128/UWARMN.html

Kyba, J.P., and O.P. Dwivedi. 1998. "Environmental Challenges: The Canadian Response." In J.G. Jabbra and O.P. Dwivedi (eds.) *Governmental Response to Environmental Challenges in Global Perspective.* Amsterdam: IOS Press.

Laferriere, E., and P. Stoett. 1999. *International Relations Theory and Ecological Thought: Towards a Synthesis.* London: Routledge.

Langer, V., and J. Bate. 1994. "Women Out Front in Clayoquot Sound." *Canadian Woman Studies* 13(3): 81-83.

Law, P. 1997. "Misunderstanding the Past, Misleading the Present." *Ecos: a Review of Conservation* 18(3-4): 9-15.

Law Reform Commission, Canada. 1985. *Crimes Against the Environment.* Working Paper 44. Ottawa: Law Reform Commission.

Leiss, W. 1979. *Ecology Versus Politics in Canada.* Toronto: University of Toronto Press.

Lele, S. 1991. "Sustainable Development: A Critical Review." *World Development* 19(6): 607-21.

Lele, U. 1991. "Women, Structural Adjustment and Transformation: Some Lessons and Questions from the African Experience." In Gladwin (ed.) *Structural Adjustment and African Women Farmers.* Gainesville: University of Florida Press.

Litfin, K. 1994. *Ozone Discourses: Science and Politics in Global Environmental Cooperation.* New York: Columbia University Press.

Litfin, Karen T. 2000. "Advocacy Coalitions along the Domestic-Foreign Frontier: Globalizaton and Canadian Climate Change Policy." *Policy Studies Journal* 28(1): 236-52.

Lyon, V. 1992. "Green Politics: Political Parties, Elections, and Environmental Policy." In R. Boardman (ed.) *Canadian Environmental Policy: Ecosystems, Politics, Process.* Toronto: Oxford University Press. 126-43.

MacDonald, D. 1993. *The Politics of Pollution.* Toronto: CELA.

Macdonald, D., and H.A. Smith. 1999. "Promises Made, Promises Broken: Questioning Canada's Commitments to Climate Change." *International Journal*, Winter: 107-24.

MacDonald, M. 1996. "Promises, Promises: Canadian Campaign Rhetoric, *Agenda 21*, and the Status of Women." In A. Dale and J. B. Robinson (eds.) *Achieving Sustainable Development.* Vancouver: UBC Press. 182-204.

Macquarrie, J. 1974. "Creation and the Environment." In D. and E. Spring (eds.) *Ecology and Religion and History.* New York: Harper Torch Books.

Manitoba Government. 1990. *Sustainable Development: Towards A Sustainable Development Strategy for Manitobans.* Manitoba Round Table on Environment and Economy.

Martin, C.B., and P.C. Kupa. 1977. "The Rationale, Methodology and Administration Used in Ontario to Determine Ambient Air Objectives and Emission Standards." Paper presented at the Annual Meeting of the Air Pollution Control Association. Toronto, June 19-24.

McBean, G., and H. Hengeveld. 1998. "The Science of Climate Change." *Policy Options* 19(4): 3-6.

McIlroy, A. 1998. "Green Just Not Ottawa's Colour." *The Globe and Mail.* May 27. A3.

McIntosh, S. 1994. "On the Homefront: In Defence of the Health of Our Families." *Canadian Woman Studies* 13(3): 89-93.

Mearsheimer, J. 1990. "Why We Will Soon Miss the Cold War." *The Atlantic Monthly.* August 266(2).

Meena, R. 1992. "Gender Research/Studies in Southern Africa: An Overview." Gender in Southern Africa: Conceptual and Theoretical Issues. Harare: Sapes Books.

Meena, R. 1995. "Women and Sustainable Development." *Voices from Africa* 5(June): n/a.

Mehra, R. 1993. "Gender in Community Development and Resource Management". In G. Young, V. Samarasinghe, and K. Kusterer (eds.) *Women at the Centre: Development Issues and Practices for the 1990s.* West Hartford: Kumarian Press 145-61.

Mekouar, M.A. 1984. "The Islamic Ethic." *IUCN Bulletin* July 15(7): 75-76.

Merchant, C. 1995. "Gaia: Ecofeminism and the Earth." *Earthcare: Women and the Environment.* New York: Routledge.

Mikesell, R. 1992. *Economic Development and the Environment: A Comparison of Sustainable Development with Conventional Development Economics.* London: Mansell.

Mitchell, A. 2000a. "The Northwest Passage Thawed." *Globe and Mail.* Feb. 5. A9.

Mitchell, A. 2000b. "'We as a species can do better': Update on global warming predicts dire consequences for Canada." Online. Internet. http://www.solutions.ca/eat/dobetter_e.htm

Mitchell, B. 1980. "The Provincial Domain in Environmental Management and Resource Development." In O.P. Dwivedi (ed.) *Resources and the Environment.* Toronto: McClelland and Stewart.

Moon, P. 1997. "Remedying the Ills of the DEW Line." *Globe and Mail.* March 28. A8.

Moore, E. 2000. "Food Safety, Labelling, and the Role of Science: Regulating Genetically-Engineered Food Crops in Canada and the United States." Paper presented to the ECPR Joint Sessions Workshop on the Politics of Food. Copenhagen, April 14-19.

Morrison, P. 1997. "Canada's Green Plan: An Expression of the Popular Will?" In A. Frizzell and J.H. Pammett (eds.) *Shades of Green: Environmental Attitudes in Canada and Around the World.* Ottawa: Carleton University Press.

Morse, N.H. 1975. "An Environmental Ethic: Its Formulation and Implications." *Canadian Environmental Advisory Council Report Number 2.*

Mulligan, S., and P. Stoett. 2000. "A Global Bioprospecting Regime: Partnership or Piracy?" *International Journal* LV(2): 224-46.

Mulrennan, M. 1998. *A Casebook of Environmental Issues in Canada.* New York: John Wiley and Sons.

Munton, D. 1980. "Great Lakes Water Quality." In O.P. Dwivedi (ed.) *Resources and the Environment.* Toronto: McClelland and Stewart. 153-78.

Munton, D., and G. Castle. 1992. "The Continental Dimension: Canada and the United States." In R. Boardman (ed.) *Canadian Environmental Policy: Ecosystems, Politics, Process.* Toronto: Oxford University Press. 203-23.

NAAEC. 1993. *North American Agreement on Environmental Cooperation.*

NAFTA. 1992. *North American Free Trade Agreement, Canadian Environmental Review: Executive Summary.* Ottawa: Government of Canada.

NAWMP. 1998. *Expanding the Vision: 1998 Update.* Hull: Canadian Wildlife Service.

National Round Table on the Environment and the Economy (NRTEE). 2000. "Liveable Cities for All." Online. Internet. Review 2000 Newsletter of the NRTEE. Summer. http://www. nrtee-trnee.ca/eng/newsletter

Natural Resources Canada. 1997. "The Sustainable Management of Forests." Online. http://www.ec.gc.ca/agenda21/ 97/mono1.htm#s2

Nesmith, C., and P. Wright. 1995. "Gender, Resources and Environmental Management." In B. Mitchell (ed.) *Resource and Environmental Management in Canada: Addressing Conflict and Uncertainty.* Second Edition. Toronto: Oxford University Press. 80-89.

Neufeld, M. 1999. "Democratization in/ of Canadian Foreign Policy: Critical Reflections." *Studies in Political Economy* Spring 58: 97-119.

New Road. 1991. Bulletin Number 18. March-April.

Nova Scotia. 1994-95. *Environment Act.* SNS. Chapter 1.

Nova Scotia. 1989. *Water Act.* RSNS. Chapter 500.

Oberthur, S. 1996. "The Second Conference of Parties." *Environmental Policy and Law* 26(5): 195-201.

Oberthur, S., and H. Ott. 1995. "The First Conference of Parties." *Environmental Policy and Law* 25(4/5): 144-56.

Odum, E.P. 1963. *Ecology.* New York: Holt, Rinehart and Winston.

Office of the Auditor General. 1999. "1999 Report of the Commissioner of the Environment and Sustainable Development." Online. Internet. http://www. oag-bvg.gc.ca/domino/reports.nsf/html/ c9menu_e.html

Office of the Auditor General. 2000. "The Commissioner's Mandate." Online. Internet. http://www.oag-bvg.gc.ca/domino/cesd_cedd.nsf/html/99mand_e.html

O'Hara, J. 1981. *Macleans*. June 22.

O'Malley, M., and A. Mulholland. 2000. "Canada's Waters." CBC News. Online. Internet. http://cbc.ca/news/indepth/water/

Ontario, Government of. 1970a. *Regulation 15* as amended by O. Reg. 873/74.

Ontario, Government of. 1970b. *The Ontario Water Resources Act*. RSO 1970. Chapter 332.

Ontario, Government of. 1973. March 20. *Debates*.

Ontario, Government of. 1978. *A Citizen's Guide to Environmental Assessment*.

Ontario, Government of. 1981. *Consolidated Hearings Act*. Chapter 361.

Ontario, Government of. 1990. *The Environmental Protection Act*. R.S.O. Chapter E-19.

Ontario, Government of. 1990. *Environmental Assessment Act*. R.S.O. Chapter E.18.

Ontario, Government of. 1990. *Ontario Water Resources Act*. R.S.O. Chapter O.40.

Ontario, Government of. 1990. *Pesticides Act*. R.S.O. Chapter P.11.

Ontario, Government of. 1993. *Bill 26 — An Act Respecting Environmental Rights in Ontario*.

Ontario, Ministry of Environment. 1978. *Water Management Goals, Policies, Objectives and Implementation Procedures*.

Ophuls, W. 1973. *Ecology and the Politics of Scarcity*. San Francisco: W.H. Freeman and Company.

Organisation for Economic Co-operation and Development (OECD). 1999. *Trade Measures in Multilateral Environmental Agreements*. Paris: OECD.

Osherenko, G., and O. R. Young. 1993. "The Formation of International Regimes: Hypotheses and Cases." *Polar Politics: Creating International Environmental Regimes*. Ithaca: Cornell University Press. 96-151.

Ott, H. E. 1998a. "The Kyoto Protocol to the United Nations Framework Convention on Climate Change — Finished and Unfinished Business." Wuppertal Institute. Online. Internet. February. http://www.wupperinst.org/wi/Projects_e/Kyoto/Kyoto_Protokoll.html

Ott, H.E. 1998b. "The Kyoto Protocol: Unfinished Business." *Environment* July/August 40(6): n/a.

Paehlke, R. 2000. "Environmentalism in One Country: Canadian Environmental Policy in an Era of Globalization." *Policy Studies Journal* 281: 160-75.

Paehlke, R., and D. Torgerson. 1990. *Managing Leviathan: Environmental Politics and the Administrative State*. Peterborough: Broadview Press.

Palmer, M. 1988. *Genesis or Nemesis: Belief, Meaning and Ecology*. London: Dryad Press.

Palmer, M., and E. Bisset. 1985. *Worlds of Difference*. Glasgow: Blackie.

Phillips, R. 1994. "Environment Group: Older Women's Network." *Canadian Woman Studies* 13(3): 98-99.

Pirages, D. 1978. *The New Context for International Relations: Global Ecopolitics*. North Scituate, MA: Duxbury Press.

POLLARA. 1999. Online. Internet. www.ec.gc.ca/prog99/view-e.html

Projet de société. 1995a. "Canada and Agenda 21." Winnipeg: IISD. Online. Internet. http://iisd.ca/worldsd/canada/projet/co8.htm

Projet de société. 1995b. "Canadian Choices for Transitions to Sustainability." Ottawa: Final draft. May. Chapter 1. Online. Internet. http://iisd.ca/worldsd/canada/projet

Pross, P. 1986. *Group Politics and Public Policy.* Toronto: Oxford University Press.

Quebec, Government of. 1994a. *Environment Quality Act.* S.Q. Chapter 17.

Quebec, Government of. 1994b. *Ministry of the Environment Act.* S.Q., Chapter 17.

Quebec, Government of. 1997. *Pesticides Act.* S.Q., Chapter P-9.3.

Rafiq, M., and M. Ajmal. 1989. "Islam and the Present Ecological Crisis." In O.P. Dwivedi (ed.) *World Religions and the Environment.* New Delhi: Gitanjali Publishing. 119-37.

Rathgeber, E.M. 1995. "Integrating Gender into Environmental Education in Africa." *Canadian Journal of Development Studies* Special Issue: 89-103.

Reif, L. 1998. "Environmental Policy: The Rio Summit Five Years Later." In F. Osler Hampson and M. Appel Malot (eds.) *Canada Among Nations 1998: Leadership and Dialogue.* Carleton: Norman Patterson. 267-84.

Renner, M. 1996. *Fighting for Survival: Environmental Decline, Social Conflict, and the New Age of Insecurity.* New York: W.W. Norton.

Revised Statutes of Canada. 1970. *Pest Control Products Act.*

Revised Statutes of Ontario. 1982. *Pesticides Act.*

Roberge, I. 2000. "The Natural Environment and the Canadian News Media." Paper prepared for Peter Stoett. Department of Political Science, Concordia University.

Roberts, Hon. J. 1982. Speech at the University of Guelph. September 22.

Robinson, J., *et al.* 1993. *Canadian Options for Greenhouse Emissions Reduction.* Ottawa: Canadian Global Change Program.

Ronneberg, E. 1998. "Sinks and the Clean Development Mechanism." Online. Internet. Linkages Journal 3(4): 26 October. http/www.iisd.ca/linkage/journal/ronneberg.html

Ross, R., and K. Trachte. 1990. *Global Capitalism: The New Leviathan.* Albany: State University of New York Press.

Rugman, A., J. Kirton, and J. Soloway. 1999. *Environmental Regulations and Corporate Strategy: A NAFTA Perspective.* Oxford: Oxford University Press.

Sachs, C. 1996. *Gendered Fields: Rural Women, Agriculture, and Environment.* Boulder: Westview Press.

Sadler, B. 1996. "Sustainability Strategies and Green Planning: Recent Canadian and International Experience." In A. Dale and J. B. Robinson (eds.) *Achieving Sustainable Development.* Vancouver: UBC Press. 23-70.

Schofer, E. 1999. "Science Associations in the International Sphere, 1875-1990: The Rationalization of Science and the Scientization of Society." In J. Boli and G. Thomas (eds.) *Constructing World Culture.* Stanford: Stanford University Press. 249-66.

Science Council of Canada. 1977. *Poisons and Policies Report #28.*

Sens, A., and P. Stoett. 1998. *Global Politics: Origins, Currents, Directions.* Toronto: ITP Nelson.

Serrini, Father L. 1986. "The Christian Declaration of Nature." *The Assisi Declarations: Declarations on Religion and Nature Made in Assisi, Italy.* Geneva: WWF.

Sheppard, P. 1971. "Ecology and Man — A Viewpoint." *It's Not Too Late.* California: Glencoe Press. 190-210.

Shiva, V. 1993. "Homeless in the Global Village." In M. Mies and V. Shiva. *Ecofeminism.* London: Zed Books.

Sierra Club of Canada. 1998. "Interview with Juanita McKenzie — Frederick Street Group Interview." July 10. Online. Internet. http://www.sierraclub.ca/stp/stp-factsheet.html

Singh, Dr. K. 1986. "The Hindu Declaration on Nature." In the *Assisi Declarations on Religion and Nature made at Assisi, Italy.* 29 September. Geneva: WWF.

Smith, H.A. 1998a. *Canadian Federalism and International Environmental Policy Making: The Case of Climate Change.* Institute of Intergovermental Relations Working Paper 1998 (5). Kingston: Queen's University.

Smith, H.A. 1998b. "A Stopped Cold." *Alternatives* Fall 24(4): 10-16.

Smith, R.L. 1972. *The Ecology of Man — An Ecosystem Approach.* New York: Harper and Row Publishers.

Smith, Z. 1995. *The Environmental Policy Paradox.* Englewood Cliffs, NJ: Prentice Hall.

Status of Women Canada (SWC). 1999. "Beijing +5 Women: 2000: Gender Equality, Development and Peace for the 21st Century." Online. Internet. http://www.swc-cfc.gc.ca

Status of Women Canada (SWC). 2000. "Women and Human Rights." Online. Internet. http://www.swc-cfc.gc.ca/direct.html

Stoett, P. 1997. "To Trade or Not to Trade? The African Elephant and the Convention on International Trade in Endangered Species." *International Journal* LII(4): 567-75.

Stoett, P. 1999. *Human and Global Security: An Exploration of Terms.* Toronto: University of Toronto Press.

Stoett, P. 2000. "Mission Diplomacy Or Arctic Haze? Canada and Circumpolar Cooperation." In A. Cooper and G. Hayes (eds.) *Worthwhile Initiatives? Canadian Mission-Oriented Diplomacy.* Toronto: Irwin. 90-102.

Stoett, P., and P. Teitelbaum. 2000. "The Hague Appeal for Peace Conference: Reflections on 'civil society' and NGOs." *International Journal* Winter 55(1): 35-44.

Strong, M. 1992. "Beyond Rio: A New Role for Canada." O.D. Skelton Memorial Lecture. Vancouver, November 10.

Sundberg, J. 1998. "NGO Landscapes in the Maya Biosphere Reserve, Guatemala." *Geographical Review* 88(3): n/a.

Sustainable Development Research Institute (SDRI). 1994. *"Women and Sustainable Development: Canadian Perspectives Conference."* Online. Internet. http://www.sdri.ubc.ca/

Switzer, J. 1997. *Green Backlash: The History and Politics of Environmental Opposition in the U.S.* Boulder: Lynne Rienner.

Terriff, T. 1994. "The Linkages Between Environmental Degradation and Security." Conference Paper Presented at the Tenth Annual Political Studies Students' Conference: Security and Survival, January 27-29, Centre for Defence and Security Studies Occasional Paper #24.

Thakur, R. 1999. "The United Nations and Human Security." *Canadian Foreign Policy* Fall 7(1): 51-60.

Therien, J.P. 1991. "Les Organisations non gouvernementales et la politique canadienne d'aide au développement." *Canadian Public Policy* 17(1): 37-51.

Thompson, A . 2000. "Canadian Foreign Policy and Straddling Fish Stocks: Sustainability in an Independent World." *Policy Studies Journal* 28(1): 219-35.

Tickner, J.A. 1992. *Gender and International Relations: Feminist Perspectives on Achieving Global Security.* New York: Columbia University Press.

Tiessen, R. 1999. "Navigating Gendered Terrain: Gender Inequality and Environmental Nongovernmental Organisations (ENGOS) in Malawi." Ph.D. Thesis. Guelph: University of Guelph. August.

Tripathi, S.S., and A. Bhante. 1989. "Buddhism and the Ecological Crisis." In O.P. Dwivedi (ed.) *World Religions and the Environment.* New Delhi: Gitanjali Publishing. 187-207.

Troster, Rabbi L. 1991. "Created in the Image of God: Humanity and Divinity in an Age of Environmentalism." *Conservative Judaism* XLIV(1).

UNESCO. 1983. "Man and the Biosphere, Task Force on Methods and Concepts for Studying Man-Environment Interactions." Final Report. MAB Report Series Number 55. Paris, 13-16 June.

UNIFEM. 1999. "Agenda 21 — An Easy Reference to the Specific Recommendations on Women." Online. Internet. gopher://gopher.undp.org:70/oo/unifem/public/agenda21/agenda3

United Nations Development Programme (UNDP). 1999. "Gender in Development." Online. Internet. http://www.undp.org/gender/

Valiante, M. 1999. "Evaluating Ontario's Environmental Assessment Reforms." *Journal of Environmental Law and Practice.* 2: n/a.

Vanderzwaag, D., and L. Duncan. 1992. "Canada and Environmental Protection: Confident Political Faces, Uncertain Legal Hands." In R. Boardman (ed.) *Canadian Environmental Policy: Ecosystems, Politics, Process.* Toronto: Oxford University Press. 3-23.

Van Rooy, A. 1999. "Civil Society as Idea: an Analytical Hatstand?" In A. Van Rooy (ed.) *Civil Society and the Aid Industry: the Politics and Promise.* London: Earthscan. 6-29.

Veeraraj, Rev. A. 1989. "Christianity and the Environment." In O.P. Dwivedi (ed.) *World Religions and the Environment.* New Delhi: Gitanjali Publishing. 36-118.

Wallace, I., and R. Shields. 1997. "Contested Terrains: Social Space and the Canadian Environment." In W. Clement (ed.) *Understanding Canada: Building on the New Canadian Political Economy.* Montreal & Kingston: McGill-Queen's University Press. 386-408.

Walt, S. 1991. "The Renaissance of Security Studies." *International Studies Quarterly* 35(2): 217-39.

Weiss, E.B. 1993. "Intergenerational Equity: Toward an International Legal Framework." In N. Choucri (ed.) *Global Accord: Environmental Challenges and International Responses* Cambridge: MIT Press. 333-54.

Wells, D. 1996. *Environmental Policy: A Global Perspective for the Twenty-First Century.* Upper Saddle River, NJ: Prentice Hall.

West, E.W. (Translation). 1880. *The Pahlavi Texts* Part I. SBE Volume V. Chapter XV. Quoted by Khojeste Mistry. 1989. "Ecology — A Zoroashtrian Experience." In O.P. Dwivedi (ed.) *World Religions and the Environment*. New Delhi: Gitanjali Publishing House. 138-57.

White, S. 1999. "NGOs, Civil Society, and the State in Bangladesh: The Politics of Representing the Poor." *Development and Change* 30: 307-26.

Whitehead, A.N. 1925. *Science and the Modern World*. New York: Simon and Schuster.

Wiese, R., and M. Hutchins. 1994. *Species Survival Plans: Strategies for Wildlife Conservation*. American Zoo and Aquarium Association.

Wilson, J. 1992. "Green Lobbies: Pressure groups and Environmental Policy." In R. Boardman (ed.) *Canadian Environmental Policy: Ecosystems, Politics, Process*. Toronto: Oxford University Press. 109-25.

Women's Environment and Development Organization (WEDO). 1992. "Global Assembly of Women and Environment: Parners in Life and the World Women's Congress for a Healthy Planet." Online. Internet. http://www.wedo.org/

World Commission on Environment and Development (WCED). 1987. *Our Common Future*. New York: Oxford University Press.

World Meterological Organization. 1996. "Statement on the Occasion of the Second Session of the Conference of the Parties of the UN Framework Convention on Climate Change." G.O.P. Obasi, Secretary General of the WMO. Online. Internet. http://www.wmo.ch/web/Press/sgspeech.html.

Wyman, M. 1991. "Derekh Eretz: A Personal Exploration." *Conservative Judaism* XLIV(1).

Young, O. 1996. *The Arctic Council: Making a New Era in International Relations*. New York: Twentieth Century Fund.

Young, O.R. 1998. *Creating Regimes: Arctic Accords and International Governance*. Ithaca: Cornell University Press.

Zaidi, I. 1981. "On the Ethics of Man's Interaction with the Environment: An Islamic Approach." *Environmental Ethics* 3(1): 35-47.

INDEX